PROGRAMMING EXPERT SYSTEMS IN OPS5

An Introduction to Rule-Based Programming

PROGRAMMING EXPERT SYSTEMS IN OPS5

An Introduction to Rule-Based Programming

Lee Brownston **Robert Farrell** **Elaine Kant**
CARNEGIE-MELLON UNIVERSITY

Nancy Martin
WANG INSTITUTE OF GRADUATE STUDIES

ADDISON-WESLEY PUBLISHING COMPANY, INC.
Reading, Massachusetts • Menlo Park, California
Don Mills, Ontario • Wokingham, England • Amsterdam
Sydney • Singapore • Tokyo • Mexico City • Bogotá
Santiago • San Juan

This book is in the Addison-Wesley Series in Artificial Intelligence

Library of Congress Cataloging in Publication Data
Main entry under title:

Programming expert systems in OPS5.

Bibliography: p.
Includes index.
1. Expert systems (Computer science) 2. Programming (Electronic computers) 3. OPS5 (Computer system) I. Brownston, Lee. II. Title: Programming expert systems in OPS5. III. Title: Rule-based programming.
QA76.9.E96P76 1985 001.64′2 84-21653
ISBN 0-201-10647-7

BCDEFGHIJ-HA-898765

The Addison-Wesley Series in Artificial Intelligence

Brownston, Farrell, Kant and Martin: *Programming Expert Systems in OPS5: An Introduction to Rule-Based Programming.* (1985)

Buchanan and Shortliffe (eds.): *Rule-Based Expert Systems: The MYCIN Experiments of the Stanford Heuristic Programming Project.* (1984)

Charniak and McDermott: *Introduction to Artificial Intelligence.* (1985)

Clancey and Shortliffe (eds.): *Readings in Medical Artificial Intelligence: The First Decade.* (1984)

Pearl: *Heuristics: Intelligent Search Strategies for Computer Problem Solving.* (1984)

Sager: *Natural Language Information Processing: A Computer Grammar of English and Its Applications.* (1981)

Wilensky: *Planning and Understanding: A Computational Approach to Human Reasoning.* (1983)

Winograd: *Language as a Cognitive Process Vol. I: Syntax.* (1983)

Winston: *Artificial Intelligence,* Second Edition. (1984)

Winston and Horn: *LISP.* (1981)

Preface

This book presents practical techniques for programming expert systems in the rule-based language OPS5.[1] It is primarily a programming-language textbook, with some examination of rule-based programming in general, and is written for experienced programmers in industry and universities. OPS5 is the most widely used language in the family of languages specifically designed to simplify rule-based programming, namely production systems. Production-system programming was developed by artificial intelligence researchers and is one of several techniques whose potential for solving difficult industrial problems is attracting increased interest. The other techniques also have many practical applications, but they are worthy of entire books of their own, and we do not attempt to treat them here.

The purpose of this book is to provide an explanation of production-system languages and programming styles. It offers experienced programmers the basic problem-solving and programming techniques necessary to create and modify programs in OPS5. The book contains numerous examples and includes exercises with selected answers, making it suitable for both classroom and independent study. The first part of the book is a tutorial; it teaches the OPS5 language along with effective programming techniques and follows the development of a small, self-contained OPS5 program from problem definition to testing. The remainder of the book takes a broader view; it considers the nature of production-system architectures and compares OPS5 with other tools for programming expert systems. Readers of this book should emerge with a working knowledge of OPS5, an understanding of the principles of production-system programming and production-system architecture, and an appreciation of desirable features not always included in production-system languages and their run-time support

[1] The name OPS5 stands for **O**fficial **P**roduction **S**ystem, Version **5**, for historical reasons; the "official" should be taken with a grain of salt.

systems. They will gain an understanding of the problem-solving techniques for creating an expert system using a production-system language as well as a knowledge of currently available production-system programming languages and their sources.

We assume that readers of this text will have mastered the following basic computer-science skills and concepts: search techniques (depth-first/breadth-first); recursion; data structures (stacks, queues, trees, linked lists); Boolean algebra; the ability to read first-order logic sentences; programming-language concepts (scoping, control structures, data representations including records and pointers); and the use of interpreters and compilers. Many excellent books are available for prerequisite knowledge. Among them are two that cover all the necessary information and more:

- Niklaus Wirth, *Algorithms + Data Structures = Programs*; Prentice-Hall, 1976.
- Elaine Rich, *Artificial Intelligence*; McGraw-Hill, 1984.

Programming Expert Systems in OPS5 is organized into three parts. Part I is an introduction to the production-system model of computation and gives a brief overview of production-system languages, interpreters, run-time support systems, and programming environments. It also gives a description of the types of problems amenable to production-system programming and the advantages and disadvantages of the production-system approach.

Part II of the book is an introduction to programming practice in OPS5. It explores the methodologies and techniques for writing OPS5 application programs to solve real-world problems. The discussion emphasizes problem-solving techniques that have proven useful in constructing large OPS5 programs, and the goal is to show how to make effective use of the characteristic features of the OPS5 language. Chapter 2 introduces the basics of that language and its run-time support environment. Chapter 3 includes a step-by-step description of how to design and test a small OPS5 program. After studying these chapters the reader should be able to read, run, and modify a simple existing OPS5 program and should have some idea about how to tackle writing one.

The design and optimization of larger OPS5 programs takes up the remainder of Part II. These chapters become increasingly technical and may require more than one reading. Chapter 4 describes the organization and control of knowledge in OPS5 programs. Chapter 5 explores the representation of complex structured objects and gives programming techniques for more advanced concepts and interfacing with other programming languages. Chapter 6 tells how to improve the efficiency of OPS5 programs. After completing Part II, the reader should be able to construct medium-sized production-system programs in OPS5. Although the principles generalize to larger production-system programs, we recommend that an individual gain significant experience with small-to-medium programs before attempting a large one.

While Part II offers the reader a comprehensive introduction to OPS5, it cannot serve as a substitute for an OPS5 user's manual either in organization or in completeness. This text is organized as a tutorial, not a reference manual. It includes additional material rarely found in users' manuals, but some of the more technical points may be harder to locate or less formally defined. Furthermore, a number of the details of the language and the programming and run-time environment vary depending on the implementation. Thus this book is a supplement to, not a replacement for, the manual that comes with the particular OPS5 system being used.

Part III examines the architecture of rule-based systems and contains some additional examples of programming techniques. Chapter 7 defines and compares the architectures of several production-system models. Special features that can be added to production-system models for a variety of applications are discussed in Chapter 8; these include explanation, knowledge acquisition, and learning. Finally, Chapter 9 gives a short description of production-system languages that are readily available for the building of expert systems and for cognitive modeling. Logic programming tools are briefly introduced, as are hybrid programming tools for expert systems. After completing Part III the reader should be able to identify production-system models appropriate to a particular application based on the architecture and special features provided. The experienced programmer will be able to define modifications and extensions to existing production-system languages to provide features of interest.

ACKNOWLEDGMENTS

Because *Programming Expert Systems in OPS5* is a team effort, we have elected to list our names alphabetically as coauthors. There is no other significance attached to the ordering.

Many people have helped us write this book. Without Charles L. Forgy, there would be no OPS5 to write about. He has supplied us with much additional written material and comments on the manuscript, and he has been consistently and generously helpful as well. Mike Rychener, too, has supplied considerable written material and made numerous suggestions. Carl Werowinski helped with an earlier draft of Chapter 3 and commented on an earlier version of the book. John McDermott read and commented on a precursor to this book.

The sections describing the other expert-system languages and features have benefited greatly from the assistance of people who know those topics well. For contributions to, or readings of, these sections, as well as for their helpful general comments, we thank Liz Allen, David Barstow, Dan Bobrow, William Clancey, Lee Erman, Jill Fain, Robert Frederking, Pat Langley, Robert Nado, Paul Rosenbloom, Vijay Saraswat, Peter Shell, Mark Stefik, and Salvatore J. Stolfo.

Wilson Harvey and David McKeown kindly provided examples of rules for the airport scene analysis program, discussed the changes they had made that increased the efficiency of the rules, and reviewed the efficiency chapter.

Proofreading and helpful suggestions were also provided by numerous colleagues and friends: Frank Boyle, Cynthia Hibbard, Deepak Kulkarni, David Marshall, Brian Milnes, Duvvuru Sriram, and David Steier.

Some of this material has been used in teaching classes about OPS5 programming at the Wang Institute of Graduate Studies, at Carnegie-Mellon University, at Sandia National Laboratory, at the Westinghouse Electric Corporation, and for the Internal Revenue Service via Smart Systems Technology. We thank all our students for their feedback.

L. S. B.
R. G. F.
E. K.
N. M.

Contents

PART ONE

INTRODUCTION

1

Computing with Production Systems

Over the past decade, artificial intelligence (AI) researchers have made considerable progress toward solving the related problems of how to represent knowledge and how to use this knowledge in computer programs. The goals of AI research include building computer systems that exhibit expertise in areas of interest to people and learning more about human cognition itself. In pursuing these goals, researchers have developed several different models of knowledge representation and use — new models of computation. Among the serendipitous results for system analysts and programmers are new programming techniques and related programming languages. The popular terms used for these language types are *production-system programming*, with OPS5 and EXPERT as specific languages; *logic programming*, with PROLOG and DUCK as specific languages; *object-oriented programming*, with SMALLTALK and FLAVORS as specific languages; and *hybrid-language programming*, combining several techniques such as the use of rules and the use of objects, with KEE and LOOPS as specific examples.

This book discusses one of the most widely used models of knowledge representation and application, the ***production-system model.*** It also introduces specific languages for implementing production-system models. A particular language, OPS5, and techniques for writing programs in this language, are explored in detail. The production-system model has been used successfully to solve a wide variety of problems such as medical diagnosis [Buchanan, Shortliffe 84] and the automatic configuration of computers [McDermott 80]. Production-system concepts are also used by cognitive scientists to model human memory and problem solving [Anderson 83]. Not all of these application programs have been written in the same production-system language; a variety of production-system programming languages are available, and the model can actually be implemented — although perhaps with difficulty — in any modern programming language.

Many of the application systems created with the production-system model are of a class known as ***expert systems*** or ***knowledge-based systems.*** The term *expert system* is used in AI to refer to a computer program that is able to perform within a specific and limited ***task domain*** (a field or application area) at the level of a human expert in that domain. It should be noted that sometimes the expert performance of the system is more of a goal than a reality. It has been the experience of AI researchers that an expert system has a large component of domain-specific knowledge embedded in its programs. When that knowledge is represented in an identifiable, separate part of the system rather than being dispersed throughout it, the implementation is referred to as a knowledge-based system.

Production systems in general, and the OPS5 language in particular, will be treated here neither as a psychological model of the mind nor as a theoretical formalism for representing knowledge, but rather as a variety of programming language — that is, as a tool for solving problems, expressing solutions, and instructing a computer to apply those solutions. Our primary emphasis is on the techniques that are useful in writing expert systems, since the problems encountered are easily grasped and of great current interest.

In this text, we will not compare the production-system model with other AI models,[1] nor will we make any attempt to justify the use of the model or its component parts. What we will do is relate the production-system model to the more familiar concepts of procedural programming and algorithmic problem solving, and discuss appropriate uses of the production-system model along with its advantages and disadvantages.

1.1 WHAT ARE PRODUCTION SYSTEMS?

Production-system computations are different in style from computations performed with programs written in either procedural languages (such as FORTRAN), applicative languages (such as LISP), or object-oriented languages (such as SMALLTALK). One of the main differences is the production system's use of data-sensitive unordered rules rather than sequenced instructions as the basic unit of computation. A production system is appropriate when the knowledge

[1] For an overview of knowledge representation models, see *The Handbook of Artificial Intelligence* [Barr, Feigenbaum 81] or a basic AI text such as *Artificial Intelligence* [Rich 83]. Note that while production systems are often referred to as rule-based systems, the term *rule-based* actually has a slightly broader definition. For example, logic programming is also a type of rule-based programming. For a summary of the relationship of production systems to similar systems variously referred to as rule-based systems, transformation systems, knowledge-based systems, pattern-directed inference systems, and blackboard systems see [Waterman, Hayes-Roth 78].

to be programmed naturally occurs in rule form, when a program's control is extremely complex, or when a program is expected to be significantly modified over a long period of time.

1.1.1 THE ARCHITECTURE OF PRODUCTION SYSTEMS

The production-system model of computation has the same three major components as the familiar procedural model of computation, but its components differ in details. One component of both models is the *program*, which expresses the computation to be performed; another is the *executer*, which performs the computation. Both models also have *data*, which describe the particulars of the problem to be solved and store intermediate results.

A program in the procedural model is an ordered sequence of basic units called *instructions*. The executer carries out the instructions in the order they are given, transferring out of sequence only when explicitly so commanded by the program instructions. In contrast, a production-system program consists of an unordered collection of basic units, called ***productions, production rules,*** or simply ***rules.***

Figure 1.1 illustrates three rules expressed in English that describe how to treat a customer who has not paid a bill recently. Customers are put in a billing category depending on their payment history. Long-term customers and those with good payment records are given priority treatment, but customers who do not have long-standing familiarity and who have a bad payment history are given normal treatment.

Rule 1: Category:good

```
IF   customer's billing category is not set
 and customer has a good payment history
THEN set the customer's billing category to priority
```

Rule 2: Category:bad

```
IF   customer's billing category is not set
 and customer has a bad payment history
THEN set the customer's billing category to normal
```

Rule 3: Category:bad-but-long-term

```
IF   customer's billing category is not set
 and customer has a bad payment history
 and customer has been a customer over 10 years
THEN set the customer's billing category to priority
```

FIGURE 1.1 Sample Rule Set

The basic architecture of a production-system model of computation is shown in Fig. 1.2. The details of a variety of architectures are discussed in Chapter 7.

As Fig. 1.2 shows, the production-system architecture typically includes three major components:

1. A data store, called ***data memory*** or ***working memory,*** serves as a global database of symbols representing facts and assertions about the problem. The data are instances of ***objects,*** which may represent either physical objects or facts related to the domain of application or conceptual objects (such as goals) related to the problem-solving strategy.
2. A set of rules constitutes the program. Each rule has a ***condition*** part, usually indicated by the keyword "IF" in an English description, which describes the data configuration for which the rule is appropriate. A rule also has an ***action*** part, indicated by the keyword "THEN" in an English description, which gives instructions for changing the data configuration. However, in some systems the rules can be applied in the reverse direction (see Section 1.1.6). The set of rules is stored in ***production memory,*** which is also called ***rule memory.***

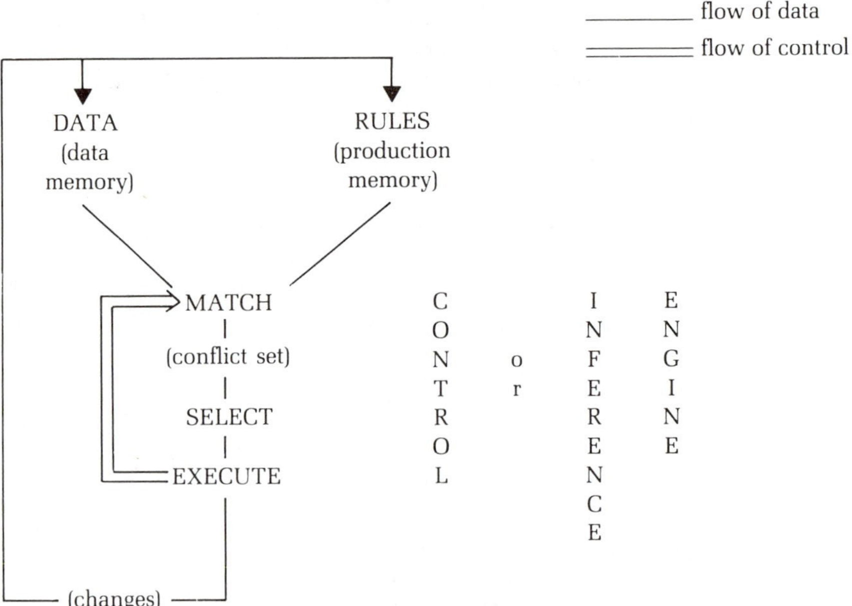

FIGURE 1.2 Architecture of a Production-System Model

3. An ***inference engine*** is needed to ***execute*** the rules. Executing rules is also referred to as ***firing*** rules, by analogy with the firing of neurons. The inference engine is the executer; it must determine which rules are relevant to a given data memory configuration and choose one to apply. This selection or control strategy is often called ***conflict resolution.*** In a few systems, all relevant rules are applied.

The inference engine can be described as a finite-state machine with a cycle consisting of three action states: *match-rules, select-rules,* and *execute-rules.* In the first state, match-rules, the machine finds all of the rules that are satisfied by the current contents of data memory according to the comparison algorithms built into the inference engine. The match may involve the condition part, the action part, or both parts of the rule. The rule matchings that are found are all potential candidates for execution. They are collectively referred to as the ***conflict set.*** The same rule can appear in the conflict set several times if it is satisfied by different sets of data items. The machine then passes along the conflict set to the second state, select-rules. The state select-rules applies some selection strategy (determined by the specific production-system model) to determine which rules will actually be executed. The machine then transfers to the third state, execute-rules, and executes the rules selected. Following this execution, the machine cycles back to the first state and is ready to start over again. Since the rules usually change data memory, a different set of rules will match after the actions performed during rule firing. This control mechanism is referred to as the ***recognize-act cycle.*** The part of the inference engine that can execute the rules by interpreting the conditions and actions of the rules is called the ***rule interpreter.*** Although the term *interpreter* sometimes is used loosely to refer to the entire inference engine rather than to the rule interpreter as defined here, we avoid this usage.

In a rule-based system, control is based on frequent reevaluation of the data states, not on any static control structure of the program. Thus we say that computation in a production-system model is ***data-driven*** rather than instruction-driven. In keeping with this philosophy, the rules can communicate with one another only by way of the data. There is no explicit transfer of control between rules as there is in the procedural model. The rule names are only a documentation aid for the convenience of the programmer; they cannot be referenced by other rules in any sort of subroutine call. Unlike instructions, rules are not executed sequentially, and it is not always possible to determine through inspection of a set of rules which rule will be executed first or which rule could cause the program to terminate. In Fig. 1.1, the conditions of `Rule 2: Category:bad` will match any data configuration matched by the conditions of `Rule 3: Category:bad-but-long-term`.

If the rules were executed sequentially, the special case expressed by `Rule 3` would never have a chance to be executed. Although in this case the problem could be solved by reordering the rules, in a more complex set of rules there would not be one ordering that would always be correct.

In contrast to a procedural computation, in which knowledge about the problem domain is mixed in with instructions about the flow of control, the production-system model allows a more complete separation of the knowledge (in the rules) from the control (provided by the executer). In practice, however, this separation is difficult to achieve in certain production-system models. A consequence of this separation is that the executer in the production-system model is a more complex object than the executer in the procedural model. Furthermore, the executer is necessary to the execution of the production-system program. With a procedural language such as FORTRAN, on the other hand, a set of instructions may be compiled into an object-language program that can be executed without further need for the compiler. While a production-system program may be compiled to create an efficient representation for the rules in the production-system program, the program, even if compiled, can execute only in an environment that includes a complex language executer — the inference engine.

The term ***production-system language*** is used to refer to a production-system programming language, which necessarily includes the model of com-

Program or Computation Description

- A computation description is an ordered list of instructions written in a language with well-defined syntax and semantics.
- The list has a specified beginning.
- The language includes a *stop* instruction or punctuation whose meaning is to cease execution.

The Executer . . .

- can understand perfectly the language in which the computation to be performed is expressed;
- is able to perform all instructions that can be expressed in the language;
- begins execution with the instruction distinguished as the first instruction;
- will perform the instructions sequentially, beginning with the first instruction, unless the instructions specifically indicate a transfer;
- ceases execution upon encountering the *stop* symbol or other ending implied by the punctuation.

FIGURE 1.3 The Procedural Model of Computation

putation embedded in the inference engine for that language. We use the term ***production-system program*** to refer to a specific set of rules written in some production-system language. The term ***production system*** is used ambiguously in most discussions of production-system models. In this text, we use the term in two senses: first, to refer to a specific production-system program and all of the run-time support that the underlying production-system model provides; and second, to refer to a particular variant of the production-system model, usually a particular language. The use should be clear from the context.

Figure 1.3 summarizes the characteristics of a procedural computation. A contrasting summary of the characteristics of computation in the production-system model is given in Fig. 1.4.

1.2.2 A SMALL EXAMPLE

To illustrate the production-system model of computation, we continue the example of Fig. 1.1 describing how to treat a customer who has not paid a bill recently. This example uses simplified versions of the action states with English descriptions of data memory. Suppose data memory contains facts about one object — a customer:

```
Terry is a customer
   whose payment record is bad
   who has been a customer 22 years
   whose billing category is not set
```

With this data memory we will now step through the match/select/execute cycle with the rules in Fig. 1.1 and the action states as specified in Fig. 1.5.

Here is the sequence of steps that our sample data cause:

1. Match-rules creates a match with the data memory element, customer Terry, and `Rule 2: Category:bad`. This match is put in the conflict set.
2. Match-rules creates a match with the data memory element, customer Terry, and `Rule 3: Category:bad-but-long-term`. This match is put in the conflict set.
3. Select-rules selects the match of `Rule 3: Category:bad-but-long-term` and customer Terry, based on the greater number of conditions, or ***specificity,*** of this match. There were two conditions matched for `Rule 2: Category:bad`, and customer Terry:
   a) "Customer's billing category is not set" matches "whose billing category is not set."

Program or Computation Description

- A computation description is a declaration section and an unordered set of rules written in a language with well-defined syntax and semantics.
- The declaration section defines the object classes and the properties of the object classes that can be referenced in the rules. In some models, the range of values of the properties is also defined.
- Each rule in the set of rules, or *production memory*, is composed of two parts: the *condition* part and the *action* part.

The Executer . . .

- can understand perfectly the language in which the computation to be performed is expressed;
- establishes and maintains *data memory*, a global database of symbols representing facts and assertions resulting from execution of the program;
- has a *match-rules* action state that consists of comparison and matching algorithms to compare the rules with the *data memory*, resulting in a *conflict set* of rule matches;
- has a *select-rules* action state that consists of selection algorithms, called *conflict resolution strategies* for choosing rules from the *conflict set*;
- has an *execute-rules* action state, or *rule interpreter*, that consists of algorithms for executing or interpreting the rules;
- operates cyclically over the action states until the *match-rules* state results in an empty conflict set;
- has read-only access to *data memory* in *match-rules* and *select-rules* action states;
- has write access to *data memory* in *execute-rules* action state.

FIGURE 1.4 The Production-System Model of Computation

Match-rules	creates a match, and puts it in the conflict set, when all conditions specified in a rule are met by an element in data memory. It ignores information in data memory not mentioned in the conditions of the rule.
Select-rules	chooses the element of the conflict set for which the match contained the greatest number of conditions, breaking ties randomly.
Execute-rules	modifies data memory by making the changes indicated in the action part of the rule selected.

FIGURE 1.5 Sample Executer Algorithms

   b) "Customer has a bad payment history" matches "whose payment record is bad."

   Three conditions matched for `Rule 3: Category:bad-but-long-term` and customer Terry:

   a) "Customer's billing category is not set" matches "whose billing category is not set."
   b) "Customer has a bad payment history" matches "whose payment record is bad."
   c) "Customer has been a customer over 10 years" matches "who has been a customer 22 years."

4. Execute-rules modifies customer Terry's billing category, leaving data memory in the state:

```
Terry is a customer
   whose payment record is bad
   who has been a customer 22 years
   whose billing category is set to priority
```

5. Match-rules can find no matches, so the conflict set is empty and execution stops.

1.1.3 DATA MEMORY

Data memory stores the current state of knowledge during the problem-solving process by holding symbols that represent facts about the domain world and the problem solver's strategies and goals. The rules act upon these data to update the knowledge about the task being performed. Most data memories are *global* stores; they hold knowledge that is accessible to the entire system. In some systems all data elements are in a single memory; in others there may be separate memories — for example, one for facts and one for goals.

The items in data memory are referred to as ***elements,*** and the representation of elements varies from simple strings to complex structured objects. The format of data in data memory varies substantially among production-system languages. The contents of data memory can be represented as a list, as a set of tuples, as a set of named property lists, or as a collection of recursively defined records. The representation of data in OPS5 is discussed in Section 2.2. Representations for other languages are discussed in Section 7.1.

The elements in data memory may be created, modified, or removed for a variety of reasons. Creation of data memory elements that represent facts usually follows a major inference, while modification augments or corrects existing knowledge slightly. Causes for removing facts include purposeful forgetting (if a fact is too old to be of interest), garbage collection (if a fact was the result of intermediate computation), and subsumption (another fact contains all the information that the current fact does, so the original fact is now superfluous). Similarly, goals are typically created when the system has identified something new toward which to work, while modification of a goal often means that some original assumption was wrong or needed to be elaborated. Reasons for goal removal include unprofitable search (a goal is found to be unlikely to produce a solution), purposeful forgetting (planning too far ahead may be dangerous or not highly productive, so unpursued old goals may be deliberately forgotten), garbage collection (information about previous goals may not be needed), and subsumption (another goal may already include a solution to the current goal).

The state of data memory is the main control over the execution of the production-system program. Control also depends, of course, on the problem-solving strategy embodied in the inference engine. For instance, which portion of a production-system program is available for execution at any particular time is determined by the contents of data memory because only those rules that match the data in memory are executable; the inference engine determines which rule is actually fired. Control also resides in the state of data memory because it is the only communication between the rules of a production-system program; there is no mechanism for passing data from one rule to another directly, as one would do with parameters in a procedure call.

A variety of attributes of data memory elements are useful in determining which of the rule matches are most relevant and should be selected for firing. Most production systems record the ***recency*** with which elements were either added to memory or last modified; the assumption is that more recent items are more relevant. Other data memory attributes available in some production systems include the ***certainty*** or ***confidence*** with which facts are believed, the ***activation*** of concepts (the degree to which they are the focus of attention), and, for goal elements, additional information such as solution methods, goal state, and subgoals. These attributes are discussed in more detail in Section 7.1.3.

Some production systems have complex run-time support systems that structure data memory to facilitate retrieval and matching. The size of data memory, and thus the need for such complex support systems, varies widely with the application domain. Such a structuring mechanism for OPS5 is discussed in Section 6.1.

1.1.4 RULES

The terminology for rules in a production-system language is similar to that for rules in a formal grammar. The ***left-hand side (LHS)*** of the rule is the condition part, also termed the ***antecedent*** or ***situation.*** The ***right-hand side (RHS)*** is the action part of the rule, also termed the ***consequent.***

The left-hand side of a rule is usually a Boolean combination of *clauses.* The types of Boolean operators vary with the production-system language. Many languages allow only the operators *and* and *not.* A clause (sometimes referred to as a *predicate*) specifies a restriction on the value of some particular property or attribute of some object that can be represented in data memory. This object may be a domain object, such as the payment record of a customer in our earlier example, or a problem-solving object, such as a goal.

The right-hand side or action part of the rule is generally a list of modifications to be made to data memory when the rule fires. These actions usually add, modify, or delete elements in data memory, but they may also perform such external operations as writing a message to, or reading data from, an input/output device.

The power allowed in condition and action parts of rules varies widely among production-system languages. Some languages allow only exact matches of data to constants on the right-hand side, while others allow complex pattern matching including the use of variables. A few languages allow the right-hand side to add or modify rules as well as data memory elements. Some older languages allow elements only to be added, never deleted, from data memory. Most production-system languages have some mechanism for allowing arbitrary functions in a standard programming language as actions. This feature is similar to an unrestricted *goto* in a procedural language in that it is extremely powerful when properly used and extremely dangerous when misused. Section 7.2 compares the capabilities of a variety of production-system languages.

Rules in a production-system program can be applied in either direction. The direction used corresponds to the type of reasoning strategy employed by the inference engine. In ***forward chaining,*** the condition (left-hand side) specifies combinations of facts that will be matched against data memory. The matching of the condition is not allowed to have any side effects or in any way change the state of data memory. In effect, the condition part of the rule serves as read-only access to data memory. This is usually termed ***bottom-up*** processing. When rules are used in a ***backward-chaining*** fashion by using the right-hand side for matching, there is an initial goal to be solved and rules that can achieve that goal are sought during the match process. If the rule conditions are not immediately true, the conditions may be used to establish new subgoals. This is usually termed ***top-down*** processing. Forward and backward chaining are discussed in greater depth in Section 1.1.6.

At any given time, production memory may or may not contain all rules that are part of a production-system program. In some systems (OPS5 is one), all rules are continuously active and sensitive to the contents of data memory.

In other systems, rules can be grouped into rule sets or packets and loaded into and removed from production memory as a group.

1.1.5 MATCHING RULES AGAINST DATA

The term ***match*** has been used without proper definition in such phrases as "the condition part matches data memory." There are many different types of matches that must be accommodated in a production-system language. The simplest type is a match to an exact pattern of literals. That is, a pattern in a clause in the left-hand side of a rule is identical to an element of data memory. More generally, the pattern in the left-hand side allows some aspects of the data memory elements to be ignored if not specifically mentioned, allows alternatives to be specified, or tests the truth of predicates on — or tests relationships between — elements of data memory that match the pattern.

The use of variables is another source of flexibility in matching. Variables allow a portion of the pattern to remain unspecified but be referenced for additional testing. During a match, the variable portion of the condition is ***bound*** (replaced by a constant from data memory), and that binding is used consistently throughout the rule in both the condition and action parts. A complete, consistent set of bindings for a rule is called an ***instantiation.***

An example of the utility of variables is that if information on several customers exists in data memory, there must be a way to keep facts about one customer from triggering an action that changes the billing category of another. Consider the rule:

Rule 1: Category:good

```
IF   customer's billing category is not set
 and customer has a good payment history
THEN set the customer's billing category to priority
```

If bindings for the first clause are chosen so that the clause becomes "if Terry's billing category is not set," then we would want the constant "Terry" to be bound to "the customer" throughout the rule. The instantiated rule would read:

```
IF   Terry's billing category is not set
 and Terry has a good payment history
THEN set Terry's billing category to priority
```

This instantiated rule may not have a complete match with elements of data memory. It may be that Terry's billing category is not set, causing the first clause to match, but Terry's payment history is not set, causing the second clause to fail to match. If the instantiated condition does not find data memory elements to match each clause, the rule has not found an exact match. However, a different instantiation (based on a different customer) may lead to a match.

In complex situations it may be unrealistic to expect a rule to match exactly, and it would be preferable to have a selection mechanism that worked from ***partial matches*** (in which some but not all conditions are completely satisfied by data memory elements). For such situations a way of comparing the quality of the partial matches is needed. However, good techniques for performing partial matches and comparisons have not yet been developed, so most production systems do not allow partial matching.

Often there will be more than one instantiation of a rule that leads to a match. When this happens, the selection mechanism of the inference engine must decide between the competing instantiations. The inference engine has components that perform instantiation, matching, and selection efficiently and effectively.

1.1.6 PROBLEM-SOLVING STRATEGY AND THE INFERENCE ENGINE

A variety of problem-solving paradigms can be built into the inference engine for a production-system model. Most inference engines select a single rule instantiation to execute on each recognize-act cycle. Some, however, apply the instantiations in parallel. Another strategy eventually executes all instantiations that apply, but works with one rule at a time in a depth-first manner. These alternatives are discussed in Section 7.3. In this section, we consider two problem-solving paradigms that are particularly relevant to production systems: forward chaining and backward chaining.

We define the direction of chaining in terms of the ***problem space*** model. Problem solving can be conceived as a search in a problem space to find a path between an initial situation and a goal situation. The starting point for the search may be either the initial or the final situation; which direction is preferable depends on characteristics of the problem.[2]

Forward-chaining (or *bottom-up*) systems progress from the given information to a goal. Starting from what is initially known, the current state of knowledge is used to make a chain of inferences until either a goal is reached, a solution is shown to be unattainable, or the search is terminated after exceeding some cutoff in use of resources. In a forward-chaining architecture, the contents of data memory represent what is currently known. The inference engine matches the left-hand sides of rules against data memory, and executes the right-hand

[2] For a thorough exposition of the concept of the problem space, see any recent textbook in artificial intelligence, such as [Nilsson 80] or [Rich 83].

sides of the rules to update the knowledge base by making changes to data memory.

By contrast, backward-chaining (or *top-down*) systems work in the opposite direction. Starting from the overall goal, they break down goals into simpler subgoals until the result is a collection of goals, each of which is either immediately attainable or, at worst, as simple as possible. The right-hand sides of the rules represent unattained goals, with the left-hand sides specifying a conjunction or disjunction of subgoals. In a backward-chaining architecture, the inference engine matches the right-hand sides of rules against the currently unattained goals, expanding goal nodes in a tree of goals (using an and/or tree) until either the leaf goals are directly attainable from the given information or there are no more rules indicating how a given goal can be broken down into simpler subgoals. The solutions to the directly achievable goals are then merged in appropriate ways to construct an overall solution.

Pure forward-chaining systems are most appropriate when there are many equally acceptable goal states and a single initial state. The rules employ heuristic information to guide the search from the initial state to one of the goal states. This heuristic information can also include any amount of control, so the rules in forward-chaining production systems carry both domain knowledge and control information. In this way, forward-chaining production systems can achieve a great deal of flexibility and efficiency at the expense of pure representation of domain knowledge.

Backward-chaining systems, by contrast, are most appropriate for tasks such as diagnosis, in which there is a single goal state (such as the correct diagnosis) and so much potentially relevant initial information that it would be difficult to enter it all at once in the hope that it will prove to be relevant. There is usually a great deal of control knowledge built into the inference engine. The duties of the inference engine may include the following: (1) recognizing immediately-achievable goals; (2) expanding goals that are not immediately achievable into simpler subgoals; (3) taking the necessary action to achieve primitive goals (for example, by querying the user or executing known procedures); (4) backing up the solutions of subgoals to yield solutions of their parent goal; and (5) maintaining a goal tree to permit explanation of the decision-making process. Given the large amount of control that must be built into the inference engine, it is not surprising that backward-chaining production systems suffer diminished flexibility; however, the isolation of control knowledge makes the rules easier to understand and explain.

The best diagnostic programs permit the use of a mixed initiative that combines backward and forward chaining. For example, they allow the user to volunteer data (forward chaining) along with a more usual mode of asking questions based on analyzing which hypotheses ought to be pursued (backward chaining or goal-driven behavior).

The distinction between forward and backward chaining is not absolute; many production systems contain both types of reasoning and, by extension, a system with either architecture can be programmed to emulate the other one. For instance, although OPS5 has a forward-chaining architecture, the example in Chapter 3 uses backward chaining, and Section 4.4 solves the same problem using both forward and backward chaining. One approach to emulating backward chaining involves writing several sets of rules. A first set implements the backward-chaining architecture and can be thought of as maintaining the goal tree. Another set of rules incorporates domain knowledge by matching expandable goals on the left-hand side, and performing right-hand-side actions that create the new subgoals and graft them onto the existing goal tree. A third set of rules recognizes and solves achievable goals. It is more awkward to make a backward-chaining production system look like a forward-chaining one, but control can be exercised by defining facts and goals to have the necessary properties.

If the architecture of the production system supports a problem-solving strategy involving built-in attributes such as recency or certainty, the firing of a rule must include updating the values of the built-in attributes. For example, the certainty of facts concluded in a rule action must be automatically updated based on the certainty of the facts matched in the condition.

1.1.7 INTERPRETERS AND COMPILERS

The inference engine of a production system includes a rule interpreter. The rule interpreter is the portion of the system that understands the syntax of the production-system language and the meanings of the action functions allowed on the right-hand side of a rule.

In some production-system models, a rule compiler transforms the individual rules into a more efficient form and also creates efficient accessing mechanisms for recognizing the rules that may be applicable at a particular stage of processing. When this is done, the run-time support needed from the inference engine is different from that needed when the program (rule set) is not compiled. Some production systems have the ability to run a program either compiled or not.

In today's software-engineering community more and more compilers for traditional languages have the ability to give useful static analysis information such as cross-reference tables and warnings about uninitialized variables. At the present time, most production-system compilers do not have options that give similar static analysis information concerning the production-system program.[3]

1.1.8 PROGRAMMING ENVIRONMENT

Few production-system languages have special intelligent environments for creating and modifying production systems.[4] More typically, the framework for the production system is created using a regular text editor. Then the program is expanded and modified within the environment in which the production-system model is programmed. Most often, this is a LISP environment with the standard LISP debugging facilities.

However, some additional debugging aids are often provided by the production-system environment. These allow the programmer to initialize data memory before execution or modify it during execution, to run the inference engine for a designated number of cycles in either a forward or backward direction, to halt the inference engine after specific productions fire, to add or delete productions from the program, to restore the system to an earlier execution state, to print the contents of data memory or production memory, to print the current conflict set, to print all the matches (partial and complete) for a particular rule, to modify the control strategy, or to trace the rule firings and additions and deletions from data memory performed by the inference engine.

The next section discusses several run-time support features that are not generally available and that might be considered debugging tools.

1.1.9 RUN-TIME SUPPORT SYSTEMS

The user of a production system directs the execution of a particular program, and of debugging and other run-time support systems, from the executive, or top level of the system. This top level allows the user to load files containing a new production memory or data memory, to compile productions, alter the contents of the data memory, begin the execution of a production set, examine the state of execution, perform debugging and tracing functions, and modify the production memory.

Some production-system models have special systems for explanation, knowledge acquisition, and learning. A well-developed run-time support system

[3] The EXPERT system [Weiss, Kulikowski 84] has features for analyzing rules after they have been debugged, and some research has been done on analysis facilities for MYCIN [Buchanan, Shortliffe 84].

[4] EMYCIN and KAS do have special editors.

would include features such as the ability to trace and explain the system's use of rules during a particular run, an interactive mechanism for reviewing and correcting the system's conclusions, the ability to produce automatically an explanation of how the system reached its results at the end of a run, and a verification mechanism that compares the system's results with stored results. However, such support systems are still poorly understood and not widely provided.

Since the behavior of a production-system program is data dependent and data driven, an explanation system that on request can tell the user which rules fired and why is useful for understanding conclusions reached by a production-system program and for verifying the correctness of the program. Such a system should be able to tell the user why certain information is being requested, the justification for the conclusions reached, and what the system is attempting to do at any point of time. An explanation system is useful for the production-system programmer as well as for the person using a production system in problem solving. Section 8.2 discusses explanation facilities in more detail.

A production system may be unable to solve a problem because there are no rules that are applicable in a reached data state; there may be no rules for getting from a present state to one that would allow a solution to the problem. In this case, a knowledge-acquisition system could help the production-system programmer find errors of omission and commission in a rule set and attempt to correct those errors. A rule fired erroneously could be changed, for example, and the system reset to an earlier stage to see if the changed rule still fired. A knowledge-acquisition system could control the mechanics of making such changes. Section 8.1 discusses knowledge acquisition in more detail.

Another way to add knowledge to a system is to generate new rules or modify old rules automatically. This is often termed *learning*. Systems can be instrumented to create new orderings for rules and to find generalizations or important specializations of rules. Several rules can be composed to form one rule, or one rule decomposed into several. The range of possibilities and the systems exhibiting these possibilities for learning are discussed in Section 8.3.

1.2 WHEN SHOULD A PRODUCTION SYSTEM BE USED?

While both production systems and conventional programming languages can be used to implement almost any application, their different characteristics imply that suitability depends on the problem. In this section, we discuss the types of problems and activities for which production-system models are particularly appropriate. These include requirements analysis, rule-based expert systems for analysis problems (such as classification) and for synthesis problems, and very complex programs for which the flow of control is not known in advance.

Production systems were developed to provide a formalism for representing problem-solving knowledge in a uniquely appropriate way [Post 43], [Anderson 83], [Newell 73], [Newell, Simon 72]. Individual rules are sometimes claimed to correspond to the units of human problem-solving knowledge, and the sequence of rule firings to correspond to the process of human thought. Evaluating these claims is beyond the scope of this book, but considering them leads to an appreciation of one of the most important features of production systems: they represent knowledge explicitly in chunks (that is, rules) that seem to be just the right size for capturing the steps that people employ when they attack nontrivial problems. The importance of this feature for requirements analysis and for expert systems can hardly be exaggerated.

1.2.1 REQUIREMENTS-ANALYSIS TASK

Production-system models are excellent for carrying out a requirements analysis and a specification study for any ill-defined or difficult-to-express problem domain. Because of their modularity, rules appear to be the most natural representation for knowledge in systems that are in constant flux. The amount of knowledge needed to capture the capabilities of human experts or the functionality of any complex system is, predictably, quite large. Furthermore, since this knowledge is rarely available in structured form, it often takes months of intense interaction with expert informants to extract enough knowledge to build a reasonable prototype system. Even after this interaction, the prototype is subject to continual revision as its performance is compared to that of the human experts or to an ideal behavior. The term ***knowledge engineering*** has been coined to describe the process of extracting human expertise and representing it in a form suitable for machine manipulation.

Requirements analysis and prototyping is often carried out by a team consisting of a ***knowledge engineer*** (a term used by some to refer to a person able to build expert systems) and a ***domain expert*** — an expert in the field for which the program is being designed. The knowledge engineer or systems analyst writes a program in the production-system language, based on information from the domain expert. Since a production-system program is an executable specification, it is an expressive medium for capturing the analysis as it is performed. The domain expert who works with the knowledge engineer can observe the behavior of the program and receive constant and rapid feedback about the information being transmitted.

The production-system model allows the knowledge engineer to concentrate on the essential problem-solving strategies of the domain expert, rather than on complex data structures or control strategies. Because of the relatively independent nature of the rules and the reduced amount of control information, a production-system specification does not prematurely determine the partitioning, control, and data structure of the ultimate solution. The semi-independent nature of the rules in a production-system program also allows an analyst to concentrate on one portion of the system at a time and to explore various possibilities in parallel. This focus of attention on solution strategies often leads to the discovery of algorithms and problem solutions missed by more conventional techniques.

Rapidly recording and testing information as it is discovered is also made feasible by the production-system model. The knowledge engineer can ferret out important pieces of information about a problem and then immediately express the new object or rule information in an executable form. Because a production-system language is an executable specification language, this essential activity of requirements analysis can be performed incrementally. It is simpler to identify objects, properties, values and value restrictions, operations on the objects, and relationships among objects because the analyst can test the facts, relationships, and rules for correctness and completeness as they are developed.

In rare cases the production-system program resulting from the requirements analysis may be used directly as a production version of the system; more commonly it serves as a prototype. Since the main function of the initial production-system program is to help the analyst understand the problem, it should be expected that the first program(s) will be rewritten. For instance, new structurings for the basic concepts or a clearer organization of the rules will probably be developed as understanding grows, and increasing concern with efficiency may be required as the prototype gets larger.

If the production-system program is efficient and general enough for the final purpose, it may be used directly; otherwise it must be recoded. Once the problem is understood from the prototype, it may be reducible to algorithms more efficiently processed with a procedural programming language than with a production-system language.

1.2.2 RULE-BASED EXPERT SYSTEMS

Expert systems are programs written to solve problems in ways that human experts would solve them. Although this description could easily apply to game-playing programs, the term *expert system* is usually reserved for a system that performs tasks for which the stakes are quite high: typically the domains are medical, industrial, and military. The degree of proficiency required of these programs corresponds to years of specialized training on the part of the human experts. The function of expert systems is to serve as consultants, designers, monitors, problem-solvers, and tutors. Among the domains for which expert systems have been written with varying degrees of success are chemical structure elucidation, mineral exploration, medical diagnosis, electronic troubleshooting, configuring minicomputers, designing genetic experiments, and military tactical situation assessment [Buchanan, Duda 83].

Historically, the term expert systems has been reserved for artificial intelligence programs that represent domain knowledge explicitly, but this is not the only approach to writing programs to arrive at expert judgments. For many important problems, such as diagnosing a disease on the basis of a constellation of symptoms and laboratory results, the decision may be based on statistical reasoning: using tables of conditional probabilities, the maximum likelihood syndrome(s) can be determined using Bayesian methods. Statistical decision-making programs differ from artificial intelligence programs in two important ways, even if they arrive at exactly the same conclusions.

First, statistical programs seldom explain their results other than through a display of marginal probabilities. Their knowledge is so terse that it is useful only for making inferences, not for explaining them. On the other hand, knowledge-based systems represent decision-making steps explicitly and represent knowledge in a form that corresponds to the way the enquirer conceives the problem. Thus they can be made to display their sequences of inferences, which may help the user evaluate the quality of the advice and perhaps even learn from the program.

Second, to improve the performance of a statistical program, one would have to revise the probability tables on the basis of more extensive or more representative sampling; revising a knowledge-based expert system, however, is more a process of education in which the system is taught to recognize and discriminate new patterns or to respond to familiar patterns in more appropriate ways. Strictly speaking, programs that are currently called expert systems should be qualified with the term "knowledge-based."

A major reason for writing rule-based expert systems is that human experts usually find it intuitively appealing to express their domain knowledge in terms of situation-action pairs (not that they find it easy; it's just that rules seem to be most natural). Rules are a relatively uniform way to represent knowledge without complex programming constructs. Some production-system languages have sufficiently restricted languages that a knowledge-acquisition system can be added. In this case highly motivated domain experts can sometimes extend and debug knowledge bases without being trained as programmers.

Because expert systems are built incrementally as the experts' knowledge accrues in piecemeal fashion, and because they are refined throughout the life of these programs, the knowledge must be encoded in a readily extensible and modifiable form. For the same reasons that production systems are appropriate tools for requirement analysis, then, they are quite suitable for debriefing experts.

The methods and tools that can be used in building expert systems are discussed and compared in several books [Hayes-Roth, Waterman, Lenat 83; Buchanan, Shortliffe 84; Weiss, Kulikowski 84]. It is beyond the scope of this text to discuss the unique problems and methods of knowledge engineering, but the nature of the tools used, such as production system languages, will heavily influence the design, coding, testing, and maintenance of an expert system.

Analysis Problems

Rule-based systems are especially easy to write for analysis problems that serve a variety of purposes. Such problems are usually solved by backward-chaining systems, since most of them have a fairly easily defined goal and analysts rarely know in advance what characteristics of a large initial situation are relevant. While we will not attempt to survey the entire set of possible analysis problems or even all expert systems that have been built, we can indicate those problems for which production-system solutions have been developed and described in the literature. Some are simply experimental programs, while others are in everyday use.

In the area of data interpretation, existing production-system programs identify mineral deposits [Duda, Gaschnig, Hart 79] and interpret laboratory instrument data or oil exploration data [Weiss, Kulikowski 84]. Another analysis task is monitoring, and here there have been experimental programs that monitor medical patients [Buchanan, Shortliffe 84] and power plants [Fox, Lowenfeld, Kleinosky 83]. A further subtype of analysis problems is classification problems, which include situation assessment, troubleshooting, fault isolation, and diagnosis. For example, programmers made a series of attempts to write chemical spill assessment programs in different languages [Hayes-Roth, Waterman, Lenat 83]. There are some experimental systems for finding faults in computer hardware [Ennis 82], and a program for locating cable problems in telephone networks is in everyday use [Vesolder et. al 83]. Diagnosing medical diseases has been a popular area for research in production-system programs [Buchanan, Shortliffe 84; Weiss, Kulikowski 84]. Other diagnosis and treatment recommendation systems include one for drilling fluids [Kahn, McDermott 84].

The properties of classification problems make a production-system language ideal for expressing them. Classification problems are special cases of loosely coupled problems that are decomposable into relatively independent subproblems or behaviors. Additions or modifications to such systems can be localized to a subset of rules, usually without requiring an analysis of the complete rule system. The production-system language allows easy refinement or generalization of a class by changing only a few rules. If the decisions leading to the classifications were embedded in complex code, additions and modifications would be more difficult to make.

Many production-system programs are in use in the medical domain, where a production-system language is particularly appropriate for solving classification problems with some added subtlety. Medical problems are classification problems in the sense that identifying a disease is classifying a set of symptoms. When the solution to a classification problem such as a disease is expressed as a set of rules, the conditions leading to a particular classification are easily retrieved; thus possible symptoms can be easily identified and verified. The subtleties that make production-system languages particularly appropriate often involve the confidence with which assertions are held. By combining certainty factors as rules are fired, the classifications determined (possible causes of illness, or possible therapy treatments) are also tagged with a certainty. The use of certainty factors is discussed in Section 7.1.3.

Synthesis Problems

Production-system programs have also been written to solve synthesis problems such as design and planning. In everyday use are programs that configure computers and select computer components given an order and customer characteristics [McDermott 83], and programs are being developed to configure elevators [Marcus, McDermott, Wang 84] and lay out VLSI circuits [Kim, McDermott, Siewiorek 84]. Planning programs schedule jobs and make production schedules for manufacturing processes [McDermott 83] and suggest the steps for experiments in molecular genetics [Martin et. al 77]. Small test programs have been written that suggest fault repairs and automatically write programs from high-level specifications [Kant, Barstow 84]. If enough heuristic knowledge is available, a forward-chaining system can be used for synthesis. The design goals can be inspected or ordered by priority and decisions gradually accumulated.

1.2.3 PRODUCTION SYSTEMS AS COGNITIVE MODELS

Production systems have been embraced by some [Anderson 76], [Anderson 83], [Newell, Simon 72] as an appropriate computational model for human cognition. Psychological models that employ rules as units of action bridge the gap between the traditional behavioristic stimulus-response models and the information-processing models of cognitive psychology. Production systems generalize behaviorist approaches: rules resemble stimulus-response pairs in which the left-hand side can represent a stimulus of arbitrary complexity and the right-hand side can represent a response sequence. At the same time, rules are attractive to cognitive psychologists since left-hand-side patterns allow symbol processing, in which the symbols stand for memories, goals, plans, expectations, and so on. Furthermore, treating rules as units of behavior facilitates an analysis of performance in terms of reaction time — for example, in a memory-scanning task [Newell 73] or in terms of practice effects [Rosenbloom 83].

Traditionally, production systems have been proposed as models of human problem solving, although they have been applied also to the studies of perception, decision making, emotions, and language. One of the most exciting areas of cognitive-modeling research involving production systems is in machine learning (see Section 8.3). By treating the rule as the unit of knowledge, systems can be programmed to learn by generating new rules or adjusting rules already in their knowledge base.

Production systems have also been used to build tutoring systems. A good tutoring system of course requires an understanding of human cognition and learning strategies. Tutoring systems have been implemented in production systems for teaching medicine [Clancey 82], and programming languages [Anderson, Farrell, Sauers 84].

1.2.4 GENERALLY SUITABLE PROBLEM DOMAINS

The power of production systems is most evident when they are applied to large, ill-structured problems for which it is difficult to provide detailed functional specifications. This power is usually hidden when production systems are used to solve well-defined problems, including many of the examples used in this book. Indeed, the simpler the problem, the more awkward and wasteful production systems appear. But the substantial overhead for simple problems is more than compensated by the purchase gained over large, unwieldy problems.

When the problem-solving environment is complex (that is, when there are many independent states in the domain and variations are large and important), and when responses to it must be diverse and based on attention to many factors, then a production system is an appropriate model of computation. As a consequence of the limited and indirect interactions between rules, production-system models are well suited to solving loosely coupled problems that are decomposable into relatively independent subproblems or behaviors. When there is no fixed or apparent order in which the subproblems or behaviors must be solved, a procedural program requires a complex control structure to handle the switching to the appropriate code. In a production system, a subset of the rules appropriate to the subproblem or the behavior will be triggered when that subproblem becomes the focus of attention of the system. This happens through special clauses in the rule conditions that match when data memory contains data targeting the subproblem for concern.

Production-system models are well suited also to applications where the response to the environment is important. Because of their data-directed, recognition-driven mode of problem solving, forward-chaining production-system programs are superior to most conventional programs; they are interruptable and can shift attention quickly. This responsiveness to new inputs allows a production-system program to react to the data presented by the user in an apparently intelligent fashion. The new inputs immediately become part of the data memory state that drives the selection and firing of actions.

Often the human knowledge that is brought to bear on a problem consists of a loosely organized collection of rules of thumb and procedures applicable to special cases (for example, opening strategies in chess). Such knowledge can be captured in production-system languages but is not implemented easily in conventional languages. The possible sequences in which operations should be applied for all acceptable sets of data are not described easily by a structured decomposition; such a decomposition has too many interdependencies. Because human problem solving and learning involves much special-case reasoning and reactivity to complex environments, production-system models are among the useful tools for modeling human problem solving.

1.2.5 UNSUITABLE PROBLEM TYPES

When efficient and provably correct algorithms or even close approximation algorithms exist for a task, using a production-system model is probably not the best approach. Tasks are better implemented in the procedural model when they are highly sequential, require complex but precise flow of control, or have a relatively rigid data format for which essentially the same actions are performed (perhaps repeatedly) for all data. Similarly, problems involving numerical approximation or calculation (linear programming, partial differential equation solvers, Monte Carlo techniques) are not well suited to the production-system model. In general, if the problem and the solution to the problem are *well structured* or *highly structured*, it is unlikely that the best computer representation to the problem will be a production-system program.

The size and nature of the search space affect the decision of whether or not to use a production-system model. For some large problems, such as finding the shortest path for a delivery truck from one depot to another, there are efficient approximation algorithms; but for many other types of problems none are known. If the search space is large, or the criteria for decision at each point are not uniform, a production-system solution may be appropriate. (In chess, for example, the criteria for choosing a move at the beginning of a game are quite different from those at the end.)

1.2.6 HYBRID TASKS

Many realistic tasks are hybrids: they may be primarily data-driven but contain sizable chunks for which strong sequencing is necessary; they may be primarily well-defined algorithmic tasks with subproblems that are primarily data-driven. Consider, for example, building cost-estimation models to help manage software construction. The initial decision-making effort is data-driven and highly unstructured, but underlying the decision making is the need for sophisticated statistical tools, curve fitting routines, report generation capabilities, and database management.

Hybrid tasks call for hybrid implementations. Some parts of design can be handled efficiently by empirical knowledge such as that in rules, while other simulations or analyses are more efficiently implemented in standard procedural languages. For example, the portion of a cost-estimation system seen by the user may be built with a production-system program, but the underlying support systems may be the most efficient procedural packages available. Design problems, for example in engineering, are also well suited to hybrid implementations.

Some languages allow user-defined actions written in other languages; this may hide some of the sequencing required by the task. A well-designed hybrid application program would use such functions only for large, clearly specified subtasks. Ideally, one should be able to mix both procedural and rule-based types of computation in a single language. To varying extents, OPS83, DUCK, ROSIE, EXPERT, LOOPS, and YAPS allow such a mixture. These languages are described in Chapter 9. It is reasonable to expect that future production-system languages will allow even more flexibility in communicating with other languages so that an appropriate language can be used for each task.

1.2.7 ADVANTAGES AND DISADVANTAGES OF PRODUCTION-SYSTEM LANGUAGES

The characteristics of limited interactions between rules and restricted format lead to both advantages and disadvantages in using production-system languages to implement complex systems. The advantages described below are ideals, not absolutes, but they do tend to hold truer for production-system languages than for procedural languages. In any language, however, an advantage is realized only if the language is used with a programming methodology appropriate to the language itself.

Here is a summary of some potential *advantages* of the production system as a model of computation:

Expressibility	Rules easily express basic symbol-processing acts.
Simplicity of control	A consequence of the restricted format is that all facts are stored in a similar form and only a simple inference engine is needed. With the more restricted-format production systems, such as those that use backward chaining, control does not have to be explicitly specified and there is no hidden processing.
Reactivity	A consequence of the separation of knowledge and control is that production systems can cope with unanticipated situations. Unplanned but useful interactions result from applying knowledge when it is appropriate rather than calling on it in predetermined sequences.
Modularity	A consequence of limited interaction between rules and the simplicity of control is that rules tend to be modular. This facilitates reactivity in the system and explanation and modification of rules.
Modifiability	Because knowledge is stored in separate, nearly independent units, rules can be added with very few side effects. This facilitates incremental growth of the system (and somewhat graceful degradation when few specific relevant rules are found).
Explainability	Another consequence of the separation of knowledge and control and restricted formats is that rules are relatively easy to explain, since each specifies one well-understood packet of knowledge. Ease of explanation also depends on the primitive nature of actions.
Machine readability	Restricted format leads to machine-readable rules. This makes possible limited amounts of

	automated modification and explanation, consistency checking, and learning.
Learning	With a standard format, rules can be treated as data and programs can understand and manipulate their own representations, making possible both self-awareness and learning. However, there are tradeoffs between standardization of formats and flexibility in what can be represented.
Parallelism	Pieces of the systems often can execute independently, thus making the efficiencies of parallel computation possible.

It should be noted that few production-system models have implemented run-time support features to allow easy access to all the cited advantages.

Some *disadvantages* of the production system as a model of computation follow:

Difficulties in expressibility	If a system has a highly restricted format, then knowledge cannot always be represented in as unstructured a manner as the production-system model requires. Also, the limitations on the Boolean operators allowed in the rule conditions may force the creation of multiple rules with similar conditions.
Obscure control	A consequence of limited communication between rules, of the separation of control and knowledge, and of having a simple inference engine is that some control patterns such as sequences and complex loops are hard to specify. It is difficult to express and connect concepts in structures larger than simple rules, even if the concepts are essentially simple.
Undesirable interactions among rules	Despite putative independence of rules, problems can result from unexpected interactions among rules. The interactions are a consequence of limited communication and separation of control and knowledge.
Non-transparent behavior	The restricted interactions and primitive nature of rule actions plus the difficulty of localizing control make it virtually impossible to understand and predict the behavior of pro-

	duction systems that use complex conflict-resolution strategies or that introduce complex control into the rules. This also makes explanation and modification difficult.
Difficult debugging	Partly as a result of non-transparent behavior and partly due to the undeveloped programming environments for some production systems, the debugging features for production-system languages are often minimal.
Slowness	Most production systems run from one to two orders of magnitude slower than procedural programs because the matcher has to reevaluate the whole situation to find applicable rules on each cycle. In Chapter 6, we see how some production systems avoid these inefficiencies.

1.3 EXERCISES

1-1 Let the rules be defined as in Fig. 1.1 and let match-rules, select-rules, and execute-rules action states have the actions defined in Fig. 1.5. Let data memory contain:

```
Terry is a customer
   whose payment record is bad
   who has been a customer 22 years
   whose billing category is not set

Jess is a customer
   whose payment record is good
   who has been a customer 9 years
   whose billing category is not set

Robin is a customer
   whose payment record is bad
   who has been a customer 10 years
   whose billing category is not set
```

a) What are the matches found by match-rules?
b) Which rule would be selected by select-rules? Why?
c) Continue through the cycles, showing data memory after each execution of execute-rules, until the conflict set is empty.

1-2 Change the select-rules and execute-rules action states to the following:

Select-rules	selects *all* rules in the conflict set.
Execute-rules	fires the selected rules in the reverse of the order they appear in the program. If a rule has duplicate matches, the rule is fired once for each match, in random order.

Simulate the match-rules/select-rules/execute-rules cycle with these action states on the data memory given for Exercise 1-1. For each cycle, show the rules matched, the order of firing and the state of data memory after the cycle.

PART TWO

PROGRAMMING PRACTICE IN OPS5

2

The OPS5 Programming Language

OPS5, a production-system language, is a member of the family of languages based on the production-system model. This chapter introduces the OPS5 programming language and environment, starting with simple examples to introduce the basic language constructs. Although with simple examples it is difficult to show the true power of production-system programming and the non-sequential nature of program execution, this power should become apparent as the reader progresses through Part Two. Some of the more technical details in this chapter may be skipped on the first reading. A good strategy would be to read this chapter for the basic principles, then go on to the extended example in Chapter 3, which illustrates how the different language and environment features work together, referring back to this chapter to review definitions as needed.

A program in OPS5 consists of a ***declaration section*** that describes the data objects of the program, followed by a ***production section*** that contains the rules. During execution, the data operated on by the program are kept in ***working memory*** and the rules are in ***production memory.*** Working memory is usually initialized *after* the declarations and rules have been loaded. The declaration section contains the definitions of the data object types and of all ***user-defined*** functions that can be referenced in the rules. User-defined functions are external function and procedure calls in another language. Although this capability is available, too great a reliance on external routines indicates either that the programmer is working against the language or that OPS5 may not have been the best choice of an implementation language.

The inference engine in OPS5, consisting of the three algorithms for match-rules, select-rules, and execute-rules, directly supports only forward chaining, with match-rules matching the condition elements against working memory, select-rules choosing one ***dominant*** rule and execute-rules firing the rule by executing the actions of the RHS sequentially. While the inference engine is a forward-chaining engine, backward-chaining problem-solving strategies can be implemented. OPS5 imposes no constraints on the type of application program that can be written. As a result, the programmer must explicitly handle both data representations and flow of control by means of rules. Extensive freedom of choice always implies the risk of being overwhelmed with options; the increased danger of making poor choices is one of the costs of greater flexibility. A discussion of such choices is given in Chapter 4.

We give the reader a taste of a complete OPS5 program in the following small example. The details will be explained later in the chapter. Suppose we want to write a program to maintain a database about people and places. Whenever a new city is mentioned as someone's place of residence we would like to add a new object to represent that city. So, for example, we would like an OPS5 rule that expresses the following:

```
IF   there is a Person who lives in any City <city1>
 and there is no City named <city1> in the database
THEN create a database entry for a City named <city1>
```

To express this rule, we first have to make some declarations about the objects permitted in our system.

```
(literalize City name location state country population)
(literalize Person name father mother age
            street-address city-of-residence)
```

The element *City* will have attributes of *name, location, state, country,* and *population,* while the element *Person* will have attributes of *name, father, mother, age, street-address,* and *city-of-residence.* Now we can express our rule, which we call `make-new-city`, in OPS5 as follows:

```
(p make-new-city
   (Person ↑city-of-residence <city1>)
 - (City ↑name <city1>)
-->
   (make City ↑name <city1>))
```

Suppose working memory contains the following facts:

```
(Person ↑name Rob ↑city-of-residence New Haven)
(Person ↑name Lee ↑city-of-residence Pittsburgh)
(City ↑name Pittsburgh ↑state PA ↑country USA)
```

The first condition of the rule, that there is a *Person* living in some *City,* would match against both Rob and Lee. But since Lee's city of residence, Pittsburgh, already is represented in working memory, the rule as a whole does not match against Lee. However, Rob's city of residence, New Haven, has no working memory element representing it, so the rule `make-new-city` would match. When it fired, it would add a new element to working memory. Working memory would then contain

```
(Person ↑name Rob ↑city-of-residence New Haven)
(Person ↑name Lee ↑city-of-residence Pittsburgh)
(City ↑name Pittsburgh ↑state PA ↑country USA)
(City ↑name New Haven)
```

Other rules in the complete program would obtain information concerning the *state* and *country* for this new *City* of New Haven. The example illustrates the data-driven nature of an OPS5 program. The rule `make-new-city` would be a candidate for selection and execution any time a new city-of-residence value is entered in the database.

2.1 LANGUAGE-DEFINED DATA TYPES

In this section, we describe the language-defined data types of OPS5 and tell how they must be declared. We also give some details of the implementation and the restrictions that the implementation imposes on the declarations and on working memory.

2.1.1 PRIMITIVE DATA TYPES

Two primitive data types, called ***scalar*** types, are used in OPS5: *numbers* and ***symbolic atoms.*** The numeric types available depend on the particular OPS5 implementation you are using. For example, LISP-based systems generally allow both integer and floating-point numbers. The syntax for numbers follows the usual programming language conventions.

Numbers

Here are some examples of integer numbers:

```
+10
  5
 -6.
 33.
```

Here are some examples of floating-point numbers:

```
0.0
3.141592653589793
+.5e-10
3e+5
```

Symbolic Atoms

The definition of a symbolic atom excludes some characters, defining all other character sequences to be symbolic atoms. A symbolic atom is any sequence of characters that is not a number and that your OPS5 implementation will treat as a single unit. Symbolic atoms can be quite long, with some implementations having an upper bound on the length. The FRANZLISP-based system does not do case folding; that is, the symbolic atoms *job* and *Job* are distinct. You should check your implementation to determine if it does case folding. At the time of this writing, the MACLISP and the BLISS implementations do case folding, converting lower-case characters to upper case on input. Sequences including some nonprinting characters, spaces, and certain special symbols such as (,), }, {, ↑ , and . will be treated as a single unit if they are bracketed with a vertical bar (the character |) whenever they are referenced in your program. For example:

Symbolic Atom	Form to Use
`Symbol`	`Symbol`
`name`	`name`
`425 Dartmouth N.E.`	`|425 Dartmouth N.E.|`
`New Haven`	`|New Haven|`
`{strange}`	`|{strange}|`

Which special characters (and symbols containing them) need to be bracketed depends on the implementation. Some programmers prefer to use an underscore, as in `New_Haven`, to create a single atom from multiple words rather than using the vertical bars.

Data Typing

Since OPS5 is not a strongly typed language, there is no mechanism for declaring a variable or an attribute name to be a particular type or to define subtypes of the basic primitive types. As in LISP, type is an attribute of the value, not of the variable. Thus a type mismatch, such as an attempt to perform arithmetic on symbolic operands, can be detected only at runtime. However, as we shall see, it is not an error to apply relational operators to values of different types; the test simply evaluates to false. This design decision reflects the semantics of LISP, in which the original OPS5 system was written. Of course, the lack of type restrictions is not an essential feature of production systems; OPS83, for example, has variables that are even more strongly typed than those in PASCAL.

2.1.2 COMPOUND DATA TYPES

The compound data structure type definable in an OPS5 program is an ***element class.*** An element class declaration is similar to a structure declaration in COBOL or a record declaration in PASCAL. The components of an element class are called ***attributes.*** Since OPS5 is not a strongly typed language, the declarations do not include a type specification for the values of the attributes of the element class. An element class, *C*, is declared as follows:

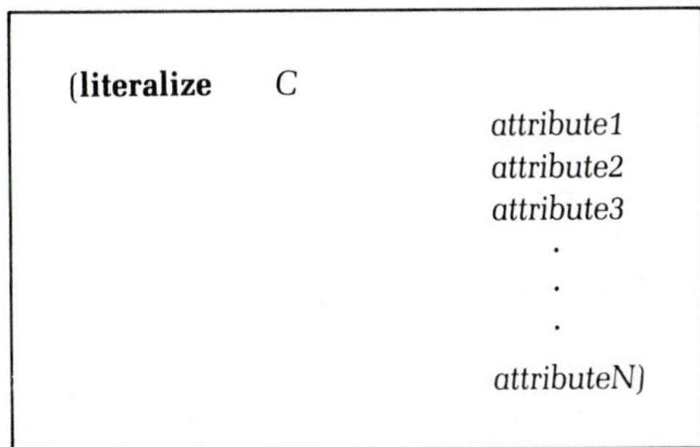

```
(literalize    C
                        attribute1
                        attribute2
                        attribute3
                            .
                            .
                            .
                        attributeN)
```

where *C* is the class name, *attribute1*, . . . , *attributeN* are the attribute names, and **literalize** is an OPS5 command. Element class names and attribute names must be symbolic atoms.

A declaration can have an arbitrary amount of white space — spaces and carriage returns — between items in the declaration. In the first declaration we gave for *Person*, the attributes were all run together on one line, while the following declarations are more spread out and include *comments* describing the intended type of the attributes. Comments begin with a semicolon and continue to the end of the line. A comment may occur within a declaration. The values of attributes must be scalars, either symbolic atoms or numbers, or a vector of scalars. The symbolic atom "nil" is a special value to which all attributes are initialized. When it is used to describe the intended value of an attribute, it means that nothing is known. Examples:

```
(literalize Person          ; Element class representing people
    name                    ; first name of Person
    mother                  ; name attribute of a Person, or nil
    father                  ; name attribute of a Person, or nil
    age                     ; positive integer, or nil
    street-address          ; represents address, or nil
    city-of-residence       ; name attribute of a City, or nil
)
```

```
(literalize City              ; Element class representing cities
    name                      ; name of City
    location                  ; latitude and longitude, or nil
    state                     ; abbreviation, or nil
    country                   ; abbreviation, or nil
    population                ; positive integer, or nil
)
(literalize Request           ; Element class for database queries
    type                      ; type of query
                              ;   e.g., ancestors, descendants
    target                    ; starting point
)                             ;   e.g., name of Person, or nil

(literalize Start)            ; Element class for initialization
```

The element class *Start* has no attributes. We will use it in simple examples to initialize programs. The attribute *name* appears in two different element class declarations, *Person* and *City*. This is acceptable, but is likely to cause confusion and can be a source of bugs. It is recommended only if the two uses have the same general meaning. For each OPS5 implementation there is a limit on how many distinct attribute names can be declared and how many attributes a particular element class may have. These limits and sources of possible confusion are discussed in Section 2.2.

Vector Attributes

Generally, attributes can take only a single scalar value. However, each element class can have at most one attribute, called a ***vector-attribute,*** that can have an arbitrary number of scalar values up to some implementation- and program-determined maximum length (see Section 2.2). A vector attribute must be declared as such. For example, the *location* attribute for the class *City* might contain the latitude and longitude of the city. In this case, the location should be able to contain four values. In keeping with the spirit of a non-typed language, one does not declare limits on the size of the vector, just that an attribute is a vector attribute. This is the general form:

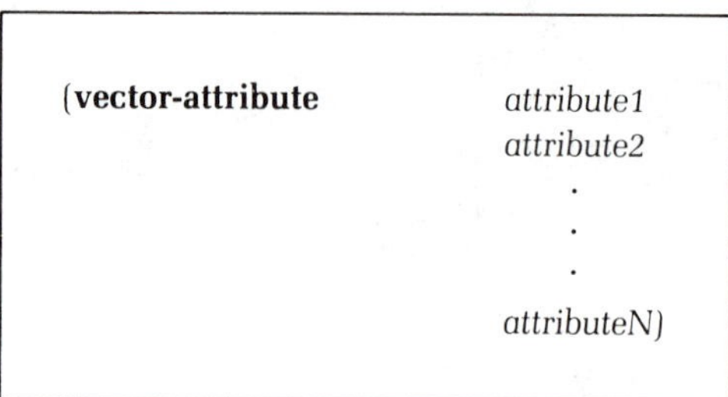
(**vector-attribute** *attribute1*
attribute2
.
.
.
attributeN)

Several vector attributes can be declared in one statement, or they can be declared separately. The vector-attribute declaration can occur anywhere within the initial set of declarations. The following two declaration sets demonstrate various modes of declaring **vector-attributes.** The latter is recommended, as it allows the reader of the program to recognize vector attributes when reading the **literalize** declarations.

```
(literalize City name location state country population)
(vector-attribute location)
(literalize Person name mother father street-address age
                  city-of-residence pocket-contents)
(vector-attribute pocket-contents)
```

or

```
(vector-attribute location pocket-contents)
(literalize City name location state country population)
(literalize Person name mother father street-address age
                  city-of-residence pocket-contents)
```

Some objects are naturally represented with more than one vector-valued attribute. To represent such objects, it is necessary to declare separate elements for each of the desired vectors and link them together through the main object. For example, if we wanted to represent all the items of apparel a *Person* is wearing in addition to the contents of the *Person*'s pockets, we would naturally want a list or vector for each attribute. We can achieve this through the following declarations:

```
(vector-attribute pocket-list apparel-list pocket-names)

(literalize Person       ; Element class representing people
    name                 ; first name of Person
    mother               ; name attribute of a Person, or nil
    father               ; name attribute of a Person, or nil
    age                  ; positive integer, or nil
    street-address       ; represents  address, or nil
    city-of-residence    ; name attribute of a City, or nil
    pocket-names         ; list of name attributes of a Pocket,
                         ;  or nil
    apparel-name         ; name attribute of an Apparel, or nil
)

(literalize Pocket       ; Element class for pocket-contents
    name                 ; uniquely identifies this Pocket
    pocket-list          ; list of pocket items, or nil
)

(literalize Apparel      ; Element class for apparel-items
    name                 ; uniquely identifies this Apparel
    apparel-list         ; list of apparel items, or nil
)
```

Each value of the vector-attribute *pocket-names* will be the same as the value of the *name* attribute for a corresponding *Pocket* element. There might be several pockets with contents to be represented, with the *name* value reflecting a type of pocket. Similarly, the value of the attribute *apparel-name* will be the same as the value of the *name* attribute for the corresponding *Apparel* element. By using the values of the attributes to link the elements in working memory together, it is possible to create more complex structures with the element class data type. Notice that such links are not addresses or pointers in the usual sense. Chapter 5 describes techniques for using vectors to represent arrays and lists. Techniques for representing stacks, queues, and other data structures are also given in Chapter 5.

2.2 WORKING MEMORY

In an OPS5 program, the data are collected and maintained in working memory. Each unit of working memory is an ***attribute-value element,*** also called a ***working memory element.*** The data item is typed by the element class of which it is an instance, and consists of the element-class name followed by pairs of attribute names and values. Not all of the attributes declared for an element class need be assigned a value in the attribute-value element. Any attribute not specifically assigned a value in working memory for a particular instance is given the default value of "nil." In printed representations of the element, a prefix operator, ↑, is used to distinguish attributes from values. A complete definition of the prefix operator is given in Section 2.7.1. Examples of attribute-value elements follow:

```
(Person
    ↑name Thomas-Barry
    ↑mother Nancy
    ↑age 10
    ↑street-address 425 Dartmouth N.E.
    ↑city-of-residence Albuquerque
    ↑apparel-name PlayApparel
    ↑pocket-names JacketPocket)
(Person
    ↑name Nancy ↑mother Helen ↑father Wallace ↑age 44)
```

To represent the elements of a vector attribute, one lists the values in order following the name of the vector attribute:

```
(Pockets
    ↑name JacketPocket
    ↑pocket-list comb hanky quarter frog)
```

```
(Apparel
    ↑name PlayApparel
    ↑apparel-list jacket shirt trousers socks shoes)
```

Working memory elements are created by a **make** command. The following sequence of commands will create five working memory elements:

```
(make Person
    ↑name Thomas-Barry
    ↑mother Nancy
    ↑age 10
    ↑street-address |425 Dartmouth N.E.|
    ↑city-of-residence Albuquerque
    ↑pocket-names JacketPocket
    ↑apparel-name PlayApparel)

(make Pockets
    ↑name Jacket Pocket
    ↑pocket-list comb hanky quarter frog)

(make Apparel
    ↑name PlayApparel
    ↑apparel-list jacket shirt trousers socks shoes)

(make Person
    ↑name Nancy ↑mother Helen ↑father Wallace ↑age 44)

(make City
    ↑name Albuquerque ↑location North 35 West 107
    ↑state NM ↑country USA)
```

The **make** command is discussed in Section 2.3.3. Don't try it out until you read about how to define rules (Section 2.3) since a **make** command must be preceded by both declarations and a rule definition.

Each working memory element is associated with an integer value referred to as a ***time tag***, or ***recency attribute***. This integer value indicates when the element was first entered into working memory or when it was last modified. The larger the time tag, the more recently the element was entered or modified. The time tag is used by the inference engine in conflict resolution. It cannot be modified or accessed by the program directly.

If the example **make** commands were executed in the above order, and working memory were printed with the command `(wm)`, the result would be:

```
1:  (Person ↑name Thomas-Barry ↑mother Nancy ↑age 10
↑street-address 425 Dartmouth N.E. ↑city-of-residence
Albuquerque ↑apparel-name PlayApparel ↑pockets-name
JacketPocket)
```

```
4:  (Person ↑name Nancy ↑mother Helen ↑father Wallace ↑age 44)
2:  (Pockets ↑name JacketPocket ↑pocket-list comb hanky
quarter wallet)
3:  (Apparel ↑name PlayApparel ↑apparel-list jacket shirt
trousers socks shoes)
5:  (City ↑name Albuquerque  ↑state NM ↑country USA
↑location North 35 West 107)
```

Note that working memory is not printed in order of recency. All elements of a particular class are grouped together and printed in order of recency within the class. Attributes with a "nil" value are not printed. Also, the attributes are not printed in the order in which they were declared. The order is dependent on the implementation of the working memory.

The OPS5 implementation imposes restrictions on both the element class declarations and on working memory. The restrictions discussed in this section, based on the FRANZLISP implementation, may be slightly different from those of your particular system. They will serve as a guide to the type of questions you will need to answer before relying on your own system to help you find errors.

Attributes and user-defined functions must be declared before they are referenced in a rule. All declarations must precede the rules. The inference engine determines that the declaration section is complete when it sees the first rule definition (see Section 2.3 for how to define rules). Once at least one rule has been defined, the user can use any of the top level OPS5 commands defining, running, and removing rules from the program and entering and removing elements from working memory. These commands cannot be used before a rule has been entered into production memory. Similarly, declarations cannot be changed after production memory has been initialized with at least one rule definition.

Conceptually, a working memory element is stored as an array with the name of the element as the first entry, and values for the attributes as succeeding entries. OPS5 associates attribute names with indices in the array. Each attribute name is mapped onto an integer between 2 and 127. All the attribute names occurring together as attributes of one element class will have unique integers. However, attribute names not occurring in the same element class may be mapped onto the same integer. It is the integer value, not the attribute name, that is used in the compiled form of the rules. This mapping technique has two consequences. One is that not all attributes of an object are stored contiguously. Which entry of the array stores which value is dependent on the complete set of element-attribute declarations included in the program. The single vector-valued attribute, if one is declared for a particular element, is always stored as the last attribute in the array. It is in this manner that the vector attribute can have a variable number of values. The length of the vector can vary from 1 to 126, depending on the other attributes. The second consequence of the mapping is that, so long as an attribute has been declared for any element class, its appearance in a rule will result in its replacement by the integer value assigned to it. This replacement will occur even if the attribute is used with an element class for which it was not declared.

It is possible for the programmer to retrieve the integer value of the mapping for a particular attribute name, both in the right-hand side of a rule and at the top level, with a function called **litval.** The programmer can also force an ordering of the attributes using the **literal** command to declare the element class. The **literal** declaration should be used only by experienced OPS5 programmers and only when the **literalize** declaration is inadequate — a rare occurrence.

One result of this implementation of working memory elements is that rules and working memory can contain references to element classes (but not attributes) never defined or declared. When a working memory element is created, any symbolic atom appearing as the first value in the attribute-value element will be stored in the first location of the array. No type checking is done to ensure that this symbolic atom was declared as the name of an element class. For example, in Section 2.1.2, a **literalize** declaration was given for an element *Start* with no attributes. Many programmers use element names as initialization devices without bothering to declare them. This is not a recommended practice. The lack of simple type checking for the element classes and their attributes puts a strong obligation on the programmer to define carefully the meanings and intended use of each class and each attribute.

2.3 PRODUCTION MEMORY

Rules, or productions, in OPS5 consist of a unique name, a left-hand side that is a sequence of one or more ***condition elements,*** and a right-hand side that is a sequence of ***actions.*** Each condition element specifies a pattern that is to be matched against working memory; when all condition elements are simultaneously satisfied, a match for the entire left-hand side has been made, and the rule is said to be instantiated. The matching process will be described as we define the syntax of the left-hand side. The actions forming the right-hand side are imperative statements that are executed in sequence when the rule is fired.

Every rule in the production system must be entered into production memory explicitly. A rule can be added either before execution begins, by compiling it in at the top level with the top level command **p** (for production), or it can be added during execution, by calling the action **build** on the right-hand side of a rule. Both the command **p** and the action **build** take as arguments the name of the rule, a sequence of condition elements (the LHS), the atom --> (typed as three adjacent characters), and a sequence of actions (the RHS). For example, in the rule given at the beginning of this chapter:

```
(p make-new-city
   (Person ↑city-of-residence <city1>)
 - (City ↑name <city1>)
-->
   (make City ↑name <city1>))
```

the name of the rule is make-new-city, the LHS consists of the two clauses (Person ↑city-of-residence <city1>) and -(City ↑name <city1>), and the RHS is the single action (make City ↑name <city1>).

2.3.1 CONDITION ELEMENTS

We begin with a simple condition element, ignoring for now the complexity allowed in the syntax of the left-hand side of a rule. A condition element is a specification of restrictions on a working memory element. The condition is said to match a working memory element if all of the restrictions are satisfied by the values of the attributes of the working memory element. The simplest condition element is just the name of an element class:

```
(Person)
```

This condition element will match any working memory element of class *Person*. Each match results in a binding of the condition element to the working memory element matched. In general, if an attribute is not included in the condition element, then no restriction has been placed on the value of that attribute. The condition element that contains only the name of an element class has placed no restrictions on any attributes.

The condition element may specify exact values for some of the attributes by specifying constants as the values of the attributes. The condition element

```
(Person ↑name Thomas-Barry ↑age 10)
```

will match any working memory element of class *Person* with the value "Thomas-Barry" for attribute *name* and value "10" for the attribute *age*. The attributes not mentioned in the condition element may have any value. Thus all the following working memory elements will match the given condition element:

```
(Person ↑name Thomas-Barry ↑age 10
    ↑city-of-residence Albuquerque)
```

```
(Person ↑name Thomas-Barry ↑mother Maria  ↑age 10)
(Person ↑name Thomas-Barry ↑mother Annie
    ↑father Daryll ↑age 10)
```

while

```
(Person ↑name Thomas-Barry  ↑age 16)
```

would not match because the values of *age* differ. In general, scalar values are matched according to the rules:

1. Two symbolic atoms match if the sequences of characters constituting the atoms are identical (that is, if the atoms are literally identical).
2. Two numbers match if their algebraic difference is zero.

As with working memory elements, the prefix operator ↑ is used to interpret symbolic atoms as attribute names. There can be any amount of white space, including none, between the operator and the symbolic atom. This operator is discussed in more detail in Section 2.7.1. Attributes can appear in any order, since the attribute name tells where in the working memory element to look for the value. All symbols following an attribute name are matched against element values until the next attribute operator, the uparrow (↑), is encountered. Thus any prefix of a vector can be matched in OPS5. The condition element

```
(City  ↑location  North 45   ↑country  USA)
```

would match the following:

```
(City ↑name anycity ↑location North 45 ↑country USA)
(City ↑name anothercity ↑location North 45 East 40
    ↑country USA)
```

In a condition element, the attribute name is followed by an ***lhs-value*** expressing the restrictions on the value. If constants were the only possible lhs-values, the programmer would have to know the values of the data beforehand. An lhs-value may also be a variable. A variable used in an lhs-value is indicated by angle brackets — for example, <infantname>, in

```
(Person ↑name <infantname> ↑age 1)
```

This condition element will match every *Person* in working memory whose age is represented as 1. For every match, a binding is created between the variable <infantname> and the value of the *name* attribute of the element matched. We say that a variable is ***bound*** to the value it matches. The condition element

```
(City ↑name Boston ↑location <latitude-hemisphere> <degrees>)
```

will match a working memory element of class *City*, *name* "Boston," and bind the values of the hemisphere and degree for the latitude of the *City* to the variables <latitude-hemisphere> and <degrees>.

Variables have two programming purposes. First, they create a means of communication with the right-hand side of the rule by retrieving values of the attributes of the matched condition element so they can be used by the actions on the right-hand side. Second, they restrict matches by specifying values that must be identical, or related, in different condition elements of a rule. For example, to determine (child, paternal grandfather) pairs in a database containing instances of the *Person* class, the two conditions

```
(Person ↑name <child> ↑father <name1>)
(Person ↑name <name1> ↑father <grandfather>)
```

are related by the variable <name1>. This variable must be paired with the same value when finding matches for the first condition element and the second condition element. Thus the *Person* whose name is <grandfather> is, indeed, the paternal grandfather of the *Person* whose name is <child>. The scope of a variable is a rule; that is, within a single rule all uses of a variable name refer to the same variable, but there is no relationship between variables in different rules. When a specific variable can be bound to the same value for each occurrence in the LHS, we say that a ***consistent match*** or ***consistent binding*** has been found.

More complex forms of matching are also possible. In addition to constants and variables, an *lhs-value* may be a variable or a constant preceded by a *predicate operator*, a *disjunction* of constants or a *conjunction* of lhs-values.

Predicate operator. Predicate operators that may precede only a number, or a variable bound to a number are

```
<  <=  >=  >
```

with their usual algebraic interpretation. Any constant or variable may be preceded by the following predicate operators:

Operator	Meaning
`<>`	not equal to
=	equal to (assumed predicate operator for all constants and variables if none is specified)
`<=>`	of the same type; i.e., `<=> 10` will match any number, `<=> also` will match any symbolic atom, `<=> <v1>` will match any number if `<v1>` is bound to a number or any symbolic atom if `<v1>` is bound to a symbolic atom

Disjunction. A disjunction specifies a set of values, only one of which must match for the lhs-value to match. Disjunctions are denoted with double angle brackets, as in

```
(City ↑name <newengland> ↑state << CT MA ME NH RI VT >>)
```

which matches any *City* in a New England state — i.e., a value for *state* of "CT," "MA," "ME," "NH," "RI," or "VT." Some words of caution are in order on the topic of disjunctions. First of all, spaces must be left between the constants and the angle brackets to avoid confusing the syntax with that for variables. Also, the double angle brackets implicitly state that the symbols contained between them are to be taken literally. Thus we cannot use variables within a disjunction, as in `<< <v1> <v2> >>`, as the symbols `<v1>` and `<v2>` would be matched literally, not matched to the values bound to them.

Conjunction. A conjunction, delimited by curly braces, specifies multiple conditions that must *all* be met for the lhs-value to match. In the condition element

```
(Person ↑name <child> ↑age {> 0  < 5})
```

the restriction on the *age* of the elements that will match is that it be greater than 0 and less than 5. The expressions following the predicate operators are evaluated, not taken literally as in a disjunction. One can also create a variable binding within a conjunction. For example, `(Person ↑name <octogenarian> ↑age {<ageocto> > 80} )` matches working memory elements of class *Person* with an *age* value greater than 80 and binds the *name* of the *Person* to the variable <octogenarian> and the *age* of the *Person* to the variable <ageocto>.

An *lhs-value* may also contain a "take literally" operator, //. This prefix operator can be used to indicate that the symbol following is to be taken literally, not evaluated in the usual manner. Thus // <v1> would match the symbol <v1>, not the value to which the variable <v1> may be bound.

There is an additional restriction on the way variables may be used with predicate operators. The first occurrence of a variable cannot be preceded by any predicate other than = (or equivalently, by no predicate at all). This first occurrence will establish the binding for the variable and thus cannot be a comparative expression.

2.3.2 LEFT-HAND SIDES OF OPS5 RULES

The left-hand side has been defined as a sequence of condition elements. This is not quite true. In this section, we describe how each non-negated condition element may have an ***element variable*** associated with it and how all but the first condition element in the LHS can be negated.

An element variable, denoted like ordinary variables by a symbolic atom surrounded by angle brackets, is a label for the condition element associated with it. When the condition element matches an element of working memory, the element variable is bound to that working memory element. A particular element variable may appear only once in the LHS of a rule. The purpose of the element variable is to communicate with the right-hand side of the rule. The RHS can use the variable to indicate which elements of working memory should be modified or removed. The scope of an element variable is a single rule.

Although an element variable has the same syntax as the variable described previously, it is a different type of object and is interpreted differently by OPS5. An element variable refers to the condition element as a whole, while an ordinary variable can refer only to the value of an attribute. There could be an element variable and an ordinary variable with the same name, but they would be different variables with different interpretations and different values. Using the same symbolic atom for multiple purposes within one rule is confusing to the reader, a potential source of error, and not recommended.

When a condition element is associated with an element variable, curly brackets ({ }) are used to make the association. The element variable may precede or follow the condition element:

```
{(Person ↑name <n1> ↑age {> 0  < 5})     <child>}
```

or

```
{<child> (Person ↑name <n1> ↑age {> 0 < 5})}
```

In both representations the element variable <child> is associated with the condition element `(Person ↑name <n1> ↑age {> 0 < 5})`. The curly brackets used to make the association for element variables are the same symbols used to indicate conjunction.

A condition element may be *negated*. A negated condition element matches exactly in the situation that there is no working memory element that matches the non-negated condition element. A negated condition element therefore does not match any specific working memory element, so trying to assign an element variable to it is meaningless. The syntax is simply to put a minus sign (−) in front of the condition element:

```
- (Person ↑age {> 0 < 5})
```

This condition element will match if there is no element in working memory of class *Person* with a value for the *age* attribute less than 5.

At the beginning of this chapter we presented an example of a rule with a negated condition element. The left-hand side of the rule was given as:

```
    (Person ↑city-of-residence <city1>)
  - (City ↑name <city1>)
```

The first condition element will match any element of class *Person*, binding the *city-of-residence* value to the variable <city1>. The second condition element matches only if there is no element of class *City* with a *name* equal to the value of <city1>. Thus the left-hand side of the rule can be used to find the names of cities that have not yet been entered into the database.

The first condition element of a rule may not be negated in OPS5. Following the first (non-negated) element, there may be any number of negated elements included in any order with any number of non-negated elements. Some implementations have restrictions on the number of condition elements that can be included in a rule.

To summarize, the LHS of a rule consists of a sequence of condition elements and negated condition elements the first of which is not negated. Any elements except the negated ones may have a unique element variable associated with them. Each condition element is a pattern, specifying restrictions on the values of some, possibly none, of the attributes of an element in working memory.

2.3.3 RIGHT-HAND SIDES OF OPS5 RULES

The RHS of an OPS5 rule is composed of a sequence of actions, each of which is a list structure with the name of the action as the first element followed by the arguments to the action. There are twelve predefined *action* types in OPS5. The primitive actions that affect working memory are **make, modify,** and **remove. Make** takes an element class name and a pattern as arguments. **Modify** takes an element designator and a pattern as arguments, while **remove** takes one or more element variables (or working memory time tags at the top level) as arguments. The **write** action is used to output information. The argument for the **write** action is a string of characters to be printed, possibly containing embedded functions to control the spacing of the character string or provide computed values to add to the output string. The **halt** action provides a way of explicitly stopping the firing of rules. Sometimes it is necessary to create a binding of a value to a variable or an element variable in the RHS. This can be done with the **bind** and **cbind** actions, respectively. There are three actions related to the control and source of input and output. The action **openfile** opens files and associates a name with the file, while the action **closefile** closes files that have been previously opened. The action **default** is used to control the source for input and output. The action **build,** defined in Section 5.2.9, creates new rules for production memory during program execution. The action **call,** described in Section 5.2.8, is used to transfer control to special functions written by the user, usually in LISP, although some implementations interface with a variety of languages.

The right-hand side of a rule can also contain *functions* that return values within the actions. For example, the **compute** function allows OPS5 to do arithmetic. The **accept** and **acceptline** functions are used to read input either from files or from the terminal. The function **substr** is used to transfer a sequence of values in a working memory element to a new element under construction. The function **litval,** mentioned earlier, retrieves the integer value of the mapping for a particular attribute name. The function **genatom** creates a new symbolic atom. In the remainder of this section, we shall discuss the most commonly used functions and actions.

Make

The **make** action is the mechanism for creating new elements in working memory. The argument of the action is an *rhs-pattern:* an element class name followed by a sequence of attribute-value pairs. The specification of the attribute is the same as in the LHS of the rule, an uparrow (↑) followed by an attribute name. The second element of the pair, the *rhs-value,* is a constant, a variable that occurred in the LHS of the rule, the operator // followed by a symbol, or an RHS function.

The result of a **make** action is the creation of a new working memory element. In carrying out the action, first a shell of the new element is created with values of "nil" assigned all of the attributes. This is called the ***result element.*** Then the attribute-value pairs are evaluated in the order they occur in the **make** arguments, resulting in the changing of the indicated attributes. If the *rhs-value* is a constant, that constant becomes the value in the new element. If the *rhs-value* is a variable, the value bound to the variable becomes the value in the new element. If the *rhs-value* is the operator // followed by a symbol, then the symbol, taken literally, is the value in the new element. The value for the RHS functions is the value returned by the function, possibly a list of values.

In the introduction to this chapter, the following rule was given as an example:

```
(p make-new-city
   (Person ↑city-of-residence <city1>)
 - (City ↑name <city1>)
-->
   (make City ↑name <city1>))
```

The RHS of this rule is a simple example of the **make** action. The *rhs-pattern* is the name of an element class with one attribute value specified. When the action is executed, an element of class *City* will be added to working memory with "nil" values for all attributes except *name*. The value of *name* will be the value bound to the variable <city1> at the time of execution.

The **make** action can also be used at the top level of OPS5, after at least one rule has been entered into production memory, to create working memory elements. At the top level, the values for the attributes referenced in the **make** action must be symbolic atoms or numbers. No variables or functions may appear at the top level. The following example of the **make** action could be used either at the top level or as an action on the RHS of a rule:

```
(make Person ↑name John ↑father Kai ↑mother Mildred ↑age 48)
(make City ↑name Albuquerque ↑state NM)
```

The **make** actions will create working memory elements of class *Person* and *City* with the attribute values indicated. The attributes not mentioned, such as *city-of-residence*, will have the value "nil." An error message will be given if **make** is used at the top level before any rules are loaded or typed in.

When a rule is compiled, there is no requirement that the attributes referenced in a **make** action have been declared as part of the element class referenced in the action. This feature of OPS5 can occasionally be used to good advantage by the sophisticated OPS5 programmer. However, it can create havoc for the beginner. In creating a new element, the attribute names are evaluated in the order they appeared in the action and the values are stored in the corresponding location of the element. If attributes from other element classes are referenced, it is possible that two attribute names could evaluate to the same integer location and that one value might be overwritten by a succeeding value. Simple errors in the program could cause this to happen. The following partial transcript of a session with OPS5 assumes that the declarations and rules have been processed and production memory has been created. The script, and all others like it, uses the following notational conventions:

1. All user input will be underlined.
2. All commentary on the transcript will begin on a new line, indented with the comment character ";" as the first character in the line.

```
; First, we will use the $litbind function to retrieve
;  the value of the mapping for some of the attributes
;  for Person and City elements.  The function takes one
;  argument, returning the integer value assigned if
;  there is one and the argument otherwise. The
;  function $litbind may be used at the top level
;  or within a user-defined function.
;  Within a rule litval should be used instead.
; The declarations for the element classes
;  appear in Section 2.1.2
```

```
->($litbind 'name)
2
   ; Because implementations differ, your
   ;  version of OPS5 may create a different
   ;  assignment of integers to attribute names.
->($litbind 'mother)
4
->($litbind 'age)
6
->($litbind 'state)
4
->($litbind 'population)
6
   ; Notice that mother and state map to the same integer
   ;  as do age and population.

   ; Now, a common error might be to forget that state is
   ;  not defined for element class Person.  A top level
   ;  make command with this error follows:
->(make Person ↑name Teresa ↑state NC)
   ; Remember that we are assuming that the literalize
   ;  declarations and rules have already been loaded!
nil
   ; The "nil" is the value of the make function - the
   ;  creation of the working memory element is a
   ;  side effect.
   ; Although the attribute state is not defined in the
   ;  element class Person, it is bound to an integer so
   ;  there is no error message.  When working memory is
   ;  printed out, however, OPS5 interprets the numbers of
   ;  all non-nil values in the context of the element
   ;  class.  Since state maps to 4, but 4 is the mapping
   ;  for mother in the Person element class, mother is
   ;  printed as the attribute name.

   ; We use the command wm to print the contents of working
   ;  memory:
->(wm)
1:  (Person    ↑name Teresa    ↑mother NC)nil
   ; As expected, the value of the attribute mother is NC.
   ; In the next example, the error made is in the name of
   ;  the element class.
->(make City ↑name Kam ↑age 17)
nil
   ;
   ; When working memory is printed, the names for element
   ;  class City will be used, and age and population are
   ;  mapped to the same integer:
```

```
->(wm)
1:  (Person    ↑name Teresa    ↑mother NC)nil
2:  (City    ↑name Kam    ↑population 17)nil

    ; The final example shows that if attribute names
    ;  mapping to the same integer are used in one make
    ;  command, the second occurrence will overwrite the
    ;  value assigned by the first.

->(make Person ↑name Thomas-Barry ↑mother Nancy ↑state NM)
nil
->(wm)

1:  (Person    ↑name Teresa    ↑mother NC)nil
2:  (City    ↑name Kam    ↑population 17)nil
3:  (Person    ↑name Thomas-Barry ↑mother NM)nil

    ; Since both state and mother map to the integer 4, the
    ;  execution of the make command first filled the fourth
    ;  slot of the element with the value "Nancy," then
    ;  replaced that value with the value "NM."
```

The use of **make** to initialize working memory is further discussed in Section 2.5.

Remove

The **remove** action is a housekeeping and control action. It removes elements from working memory. Some elements must be removed because they may cause the program to exhibit an inappropriate behavior such as pursuing goals that have already been accomplished. Other elements are removed because they slow down the execution of the program appreciably and are no longer needed. The **remove** action takes as arguments one or more element variables and, upon execution, removes the working memory elements bound to the element variables. If <city1> and <request1> have been bound to working memory elements, then the action

```
(remove <city1> <request1>)
```

will remove those elements from working memory. The **remove** action may also be used at the top level. Since element variables cannot be used at the top level, however, the argument to the **remove** action is a list of time tags of the working memory elements to be removed. Working memory can be completely emptied with the command `(remove *)`.

Suppose working memory contains

```
1:  (Person ↑name Nancy ↑mother Helen ↑father Wallace)
```

```
2:   (Person ↑name Helen ↑mother NancyHelen)
3:   (Person ↑name Teresa ↑father Cleve)
```

and you want to remove the first and third elements. You would use the action

```
(remove 1 3)
```

leaving working memory:

```
2:   (Person ↑name Helen ↑mother NancyHelen)
```

Modify

The action **modify** is used to modify one or more attributes of a particular element of working memory. As an alternative, one could **remove** the element first and then **make** a new element. However, usually only a few of the attribute values are to be changed, and it is inefficient and cumbersome to have to know and explicitly represent all the other attributes and values for the use of the **make** action. The **modify** action, which allows the rule to specify just the attributes to change and the new values for those attributes, is much more convenient. The attributes that are not specified remain unchanged. The **modify** action may not be used at the top level.

The first argument to **modify** is an element variable indicating which element to modify. It is followed by a list of attribute-value pairs. The restrictions on the values are the same as those for the **make** action. The command creates a copy of the working memory element in the result element and modifies those values specified in the argument list. Suppose working memory again contains

```
1:   (Person ↑name Nancy ↑mother Helen ↑father Wallace)
2:   (Person ↑name Helen ↑mother NancyHelen)
3:   (Person ↑name Teresa ↑father Cleve)
```

and new information concerning the city of residence of Teresa has just been obtained in the LHS of a rule. Let <newcity> be the variable bound to the name of Teresa's city and <newname> be the element variable bound to the element Teresa (recency 3) in the LHS of the hypothetical rule. Then the **modify** action would be

```
(modify <newname> ↑city-of-residence <newcity>)
```

Working memory following execution of this action would be

```
1:   (Person ↑name Nancy ↑mother Helen ↑father Wallace)
2:   (Person ↑name Helen ↑mother NancyHelen)
```

```
4:  (Person ↑name Teresa ↑father Cleve
↑city-of-residence Swannanoa)
```

where "Swannanoa" was the value bound to the variable <newcity>.

Write

The action **write** is used to write messages to the terminal or to a file. The output device is the terminal unless the program or user has explicitly changed the default with the I/O control actions, discussed later in this section. Several functions can be used to format the messages being printed. When encountered in the arguments, the function **crlf** causes the **write** to begin a new line. When the function **tabto** is encountered, it causes a tab to the designated column. The argument to **tabto** must be an integer or a variable bound to an integer. If the output has passed the designated column when **tabto** is encountered, a new line is begun with printing starting in the designated column. It is possible to right-justify within a field with the function **rjust,** which takes one integer as argument and right-justifies the value to be printed within a field of width equal to the integer argument. If the value is too large to fit in the specified field, the function is effectively ignored. The arguments to **write** are scalars — numbers and symbolic atoms that evaluate to themselves — variables, and functions. Variables and functions are evaluated as they are encountered in the argument list. As the arguments are evaluated, the values are put into the result element. Many OPS5 implementations automatically insert a space after each value printed.

For example, execution of the action

```
(write (crlf) This is a message (crlf))
```

would print the message starting at the beginning of a new line and finishing at the beginning of the next line. The sequence of actions

```
(write (crlf) This is a message. (crlf))
(write (tabto 10) to all of you (tabto 15) out there)
(write (crlf) WAKE (rjust 19) UP (crlf)))
```

would create the output

```
This is a message.
          to all of you
               out there
WAKE                 UP
```

Notice that the output begins on a new line, the action of the first "(crlf)" in the first **write** action. The output of the second **write** action also begins on a new line, the action of the last "(crlf)" in the first **write** action. The second line of output begins in column 10, the result of the "(tabto 10)" function. Since the string "to all of you" goes past column 15, specified in the function call "(tabto 15)," the output of "out there" continues on the next line in column 15. The final **write** action begins a new line, outputting the string "WAKE" followed by a space (with most implementations). The "(rjust 19)" function right justifies the next value, "UP," in a field 19 characters wide. The final (crlf) leaves the output device at the beginning of a new line.

Bind and Cbind

It is often necessary to store a temporary value computed by the RHS of a rule for use in later actions of that rule. The action **bind** can be used to bind such a value to a variable; **bind** takes one or two arguments. When only one argument is used with **bind,** the argument must be a variable. Upon execution, the action generates a new symbolic atom not already occurring in the program, and binds the variable to the symbolic atom. When two arguments are used, the first argument must be a variable and the second may be an *rhs-value.* Upon execution, the second argument is evaluated and the value in position 1 of the result element is bound to the variable. An example of **bind** is given later in this section.

The action **cbind** is used to bind a working memory element to an element variable. The element bound is the last element added to working memory by **make, modify,** or **call.** The action takes one argument, an element variable.

File Actions

The actions **openfile, closefile,** and **default** are used to open, close, and switch the active file, respectively. The actions vary in the different OPS5 implementations and your system may not behave as described here. The **openfile** action has three arguments, one to specify the symbolic atom by which the rules should refer to the file, one to specify the file to be opened, and one to indicate whether the file is to be used for input or output. The name used to specify the file should be a valid file name for the implementation system. An input use is designated with the atom "in," while an output use is designated with the atom "out." The action causes the operating system to open the designated file as an input or output file and creates an association between the symbolic atom specified and the file. For example,

```
(openfile ruletrace |RuleTrace.ops| out)
```

will open the file named "RuleTrace.ops" for output, allowing the program to reference the file with the symbolic atom "ruletrace." The atom "nil" cannot be used as a file name. It is the specification for the user's terminal.

The **closefile** action takes one or more arguments — each a symbolic atom designating a currently open file. The action causes the operating system to close the files associated with the argument and then removes the associations. To close the file opened with the previous **openfile** command, one would use the action `(closefile ruletrace)`.

The **default** action controls where the **write** action and trace routines print their information and where the **accept** and **acceptline** functions read their information. The first argument should evaluate to "nil" when designating the user's terminal as the default input/output device, and a symbolic atom, associated with a file name, to designate a file for input/output. The second argument to the action indicates which of the three defaults is being set. The argument should evaluate to "trace" for the tracing function default, "write" for the **write** action default, or "accept" for the read default. To default the output of the program to the file opened with the **openfile** example above, one could use the action `(default ruletrace accept)`.

RHS Functions

This section discusses the OPS5 functions **compute, litval,** and **genatom,** and the input functions **accept** and **acceptline.**

Compute. The **compute** function allows OPS5 to do arithmetic. It provides for infix evaluation of + , − , * , // , and \\ (respectively addition, subtraction, multiplication, division, and modulus). Arithmetic operations within the compute function are associated from right to left, with no operator precedence used except that forced by parentheses. For example, the function call `(compute 2 - 1 - 5)` returns the value 6. The following rule computes the approximate age of a father at the birth of a child:

```
(p Father-Age-Birth
   (Person ↑name <childname> ↑father <fathername>
       ↑age <childage>)
   (Person ↑name <fathername> ↑age <fatherage>)
-->
   (write (crlf) <fathername> was approximately
          (compute <fatherage> - <childage>)
          at the birth of <childname>))
```

Without knowledge of the two birth dates and the date on which the ages are given, one can only compute the father's age to within one year.

Genatom. The function **genatom** generates a new symbolic atom. The function takes no arguments. A variation of the **bind** action described above is `(bind <variable>(genatom))`. This action is equivalent to the action `(bind <variable>)`.

Litval. The function **litval** returns the index value assigned to the attribute name argument. Using the example from the discussion of **make,** the function `(litval name)` will evaluate to the integer 2.

Input functions. The behavior of the input functions is dependent on the implementation. This section briefly describes the functions, their arguments, and their results. You should consult your user's manual for details on the functions in your environment. There are two input functions defined for OPS5, **accept** and **acceptline.** If **accept** has no arguments, it takes input from the default input source. If there is an argument, it must evaluate to a symbolic atom associated with an open input file. The function will read either a single scalar or a list. The input is interpreted as a list if the first character is a left parenthesis. The list is terminated by a right parenthesis. If an end-of-file indicator is encountered by **accept,** the value for the function call is the atom "end-of-file." Implementations allowing a list as input often crash with an error message if an end-of-file is encountered in the middle of the list. The function **acceptline** is used to read exactly one line of input. The function reads everything on the line, removing any parentheses, and puts the resulting scalars into the result element. If the first argument to the function evaluates to a symbolic atom associated with an open input file, the input is obtained from the file instead of the default source. Otherwise the first argument is treated as all other arguments and put into the result element when a null line is read or when **acceptline** encounters an end-of-file. A null line is a line with only spaces and tabs. For example, if the command `(openfile ruletr |Ruletrace:ops| in)` is given, then `(acceptline ruletr reading)` will read one line from the file "Ruletrace.ops." If the line is null or an end-of-file is encountered, the result element will contain the atom "reading." Suppose an intervening action has closed the file "ruletrace." Then the function will put both the atom "ruletrace" and the atom "reading" in the result element on a null line or end-of-file.

2.4 THE OPS5 INFERENCE ENGINE

A three-stage process of matching, selecting, and executing rules has been defined as the basis of control in a production-system language. This control mechanism, normally referred to as the recognize-act cycle, is the basis of the OPS5 inference engine. The inference engine cycles over the three states of *match*, *select*, and *execute*. Exiting occurs after the match state, either because of an explicit **halt** or because there are no more rule instantiations in the conflict set. In addition, the user can set an explicit limit on the number of rule firings and can set breakpoints on particular rules (these options are described in Section 2.6). This recognize-act cycle can be summarized as

```
repeat
        perform match
        exit if any of the following are true
            the conflict set is empty
            a halt was performed
            the cycle count has been reached
            a breakpoint has been reached
        perform conflict resolution
        execute the selected rule
end
```

The rules in a program are treated individually with no ordering relationship imposed on the set of rules, nor is the set divided into subsets for the purpose of selective matching. On each cycle, all rules are checked for a match of their LHS with working memory, a process that is further defined in Section 2.4.1. The selection strategy depends on the recency of individual condition elements of an instantiation and the specificity of the LHS of the rule rather than on any ordering of the rules themselves. The selection strategy is described in greater detail in Section 2.4.2. In firing a rule, the ordering of the actions in the right-hand side is important. These actions are executed in the order in which they appear in the selected rule.

2.4.1 MATCHING

The process of matching that was introduced in Section 2.3.1 described the conditions for a match between a particular element of working memory and a condition element, including the requirement of binding variables consistently for all occurrences in the rule. The match algorithm builds an instantiation for every set of elements that match with consistent bindings. An instantiation is an ordered pair whose first item is the name of a rule and whose second item is a list of working memory elements that match the conditions with a consistent set of bindings. The working memory elements in the second item of the pair are listed in the order corresponding to that of the condition elements in the rule. On a given cycle there may be any number of instantiations formed, including none. The conflict set is the set of all such instantiations for all rules on a given cycle. In fact, OPS5 has a very efficient match process, described in Chapter 6, that obviates the necessity of recomputing the match against all of production memory on every cycle.

To summarize the conditions for a match between the LHS of a rule and working memory: Each non-negated condition element matches a working memory element; there are no working memory elements matching negated condition elements; each element variable is bound to the working memory element matched; and each variable can be consistently bound to one value for all occurrences in the LHS.

Most of the computation done in each recognize-act cycle is directed toward finding which patterns are satisfied, what their bindings are, and what rules become applicable because certain patterns are matched successfully. In straightforward implementations of production systems there are many redundancies in the matching process; these redundancies decrease efficiency. Chapter 6 discusses the matching process used in OPS5, explains how it exploits these redundancies, and advises how to write efficient rules. While the order of the condition elements (except sometimes the first) and of the attributes does not affect the correctness of the rules, the order does have efficiency implications, also discussed in Chapter 6.

2.4.2 SELECTION STRATEGY

If the match step produces a conflict set containing more than one rule instantiation, a series of tests collectively constituting conflict resolution is performed to select one instantiation for firing. Each test partially orders the conflict set, and then those instantiations that are *dominated* by others (deemed less important by the conflict-resolution tests) are no longer considered in the current cycle. Thus successive tests reduce the conflict set to a smaller set of dominating instantiations until only a single instantiation remains. The OPS5 programmer has a choice of two conflict resolution strategies, called LEX and MEA, which differ slightly in the series of tests used to choose an instantiation from the conflict set.

LEX

The LEX strategy is the simpler of the two alternatives for conflict resolution. We describe the algorithm using terminology somewhat different from that used in some user manuals. Also, the actual implementation of the algorithm is more efficient than the version we describe here.

The first step in LEX is termed *refraction*, by analogy with the refractory period of neurons. No amount of stimulation can trigger a neuron to generate a second impulse within a few milliseconds of firing. Similarly, refraction in OPS5 means that all instantiations previously selected and fired are deleted from the conflict set. Refraction specifies that the same instantiation cannot fire again. However, if one of the elements of working memory has been modified, it will have a new recency number and the instantiation with the modified element will be different from any previous instantiation and thus will not be removed from the conflict set by refraction.

The second step of the LEX strategy partially orders the instantiations remaining in the conflict set on the basis of the *recency* of the time tags corresponding to the working memory elements that match the condition elements. The time tags corresponding to each instantiation are considered in decreasing order. Conceptually, all instantiations containing the largest value for their maximum recency number are grouped and the others are discarded from the conflict set. If the resulting conflict set contains only one element, then that element is selected. If none of the instantiations of the remaining group has a second condition element, then the algorithm proceeds to step three. Otherwise, all instantiations without a second condition element are discarded from the conflict set and the process is repeated, looking at the second largest recency value for the remaining group. This process continues looking at the third, fourth, and succeedingly next largest recency value until either the set has one instantiation, or all instantiations in the set have the same number of condition elements. This step is almost equivalent to a lexicographic ordering, giving the strategy its name.

The third step, required if no single instantiation dominated the original conflict set after refraction and the comparison of recency values, uses the principle of *specificity*. The inference engine imposes a partial ordering of the instantiations remaining in the conflict set based on the total number of tests in all conditions of a rule. These tests are the relational tests (including equality tests) against constants or variables required to compute the match. Simple variable assignment is not counted as a test. The instantiations requiring the greatest number of tests are the dominating ones and remain.

If one instantiation dominates because it matches all the same working memory elements as the others but has additional condition elements, the intuitive explanation is that it dominates because it is more specific. However, this condition is actually checked as part of the recency calculation. We will therefore say that the principle of *recency specificity* is used to resolve the conflict when one instantiation dominates because it has more elements, and that the principle of *test specificity* is used when one instantiation has more relational tests.

Finally, if all these attempts to find a single dominant instantiation fail, and more than one instantiation remains in the conflict set, the inference engine selects an *arbitrary* instantiation from those remaining in the conflict set.

MEA

The MEA strategy differs from LEX in that it places extra emphasis on the recency of a working memory element that matches the first condition element of the rule. Immediately after the refraction mechanism removes from the conflict set instantiations that have already fired, an additional test is inserted. This test compares instantiations on the basis of the recency of the first condition element. If no single instantiation dominates, the remaining set is passed through the same sequence of orderings as in the LEX strategy. The name MEA has its origins in the term *means-ends analysis,* since this strategy was intended to facilitate the orderly handling of subgoals. If the first condition element of a rule is always a goal element, then the system will never be distracted by a very recent working memory element that is not a goal.

2.4.3 EXAMPLE

This section contains a small example program illustrating the conflict resolution strategies discussed in the previous sections. The problem assumes that a database of information concerning people, using the *Person* element class defined in Section 2.1.2, is in working memory. The task is to query the user for a name in the database and print all of the ancestors of that person. Our solution will assume that there are no *Person* elements with the *name* of "nil" and that the user has initiated the activity by putting a *Start* element in working memory. We will use two rules to solve this problem, one to get the name of a person from the user and one to print out that person's ancestors.

The first rule will ask the user for the name of a person and create an instance of the *Request* element class with *type* "ancestor" and *name* equal to the name typed by the user. The rule is

```
(p FindAncestors::Initialize
   {(Start) <initialize>}
-->
   (remove <initialize>)
   (write (crlf) |Please type the first name of a person|
       (crlf) |whose ancestors you would like to find:|
       (crlf))
   (make Request ↑type ancestor ↑target (accept)))
```

An instantiation of this rule will enter the conflict set whenever there is an element of class *Start* in working memory. If this instantiation is selected, the firing of the rule will cause the output message

```
Please type the first name of a person
whose ancestors you would like to find:
```

to be printed. The **make** action will create a working memory element of class *Request* with the value "ancestor" for *type* attribute. The function **accept** will read a single scalar. If the user does not ever type a space or carriage return or other symbol indicating the end of a scalar, the rule will just wait patiently for more input. The rule does no checking on the value read by the function **accept.** If a number were typed or an end-of-file were encountered, the rule would just go ahead and create the *Request* element with the number or the end-of-file designator.

Now that the search for ancestors is initiated, our strategy will be to find the parents of the target person, print out their names, and initiate requests to find the ancestors of each parent. We assume that there are no loops in the ancestor chain of the sort: "Penelope is the mother of Winston is the father of Jeremy is the mother of Penelope." If there are, the next rule will loop forever over the chain.

The next rule finds and prints the ancestors, matching and firing so long as there are still *Request* elements and matching people. The rule should terminate when there are no longer any matching people to print as ancestors. An English description of the rule follows:

```
IF   there is a Request to find
        the ancestor of <myparent> (not nil)
 and there is a Person whose name is <myparent>
THEN remove the Request
 and print a message that the <mother-name> and <father-name>
        of <myparent> are ancestors through <myparent>
 and create two new Requests to find the ancestors of the
        <mother-name> and the <father-name>
```

In OPS5 the rule is

```
(p PrintAncestors
   {(Request ↑type ancestor
       ↑target {<myparents> <> nil}) <request1>}
   (Person ↑name <myparents> ↑mother <mother-name>
       ↑father <father-name>)
-->
   (remove <request1>)
   (write (crlf) <mother-name> and
                 <father-name> are ancestors
                      via <myparents>)
   (make Request ↑type ancestor ↑target <mother-name>)
   (make Request ↑type ancestor ↑target <father-name>))
```

The first condition element of the rule matches an element of class *Request* whose *type* is "ancestor" and whose *target* is not "nil." The matched element is bound to the element variable <request1>. The *target* attribute of the matched element is bound to the variable <myparents>. The second condition element matches a *Person* whose *name* is the value of <myparents>. The value of the *father* of <myparents> is bound to <father-name> and the value of the *mother* is bound to <mother-name>. It is possible that the values of <father-name> and <mother-name> will be the atom "nil," or the names of people not yet entered into working memory. The RHS has four actions. The first action removes the *Request* element that was bound to <request1>. This will keep working memory from being cluttered with requests. The next action writes out a message that the <father-name> and <mother-name> are ancestors of <myparents>. This action will go right ahead and print out any "nil" values encountered as ancestors. The last two actions create *Request* elements to search for the ancestors of the <father-name> and the <mother-name>. Note that this may generate some requests to search for the ancestors of "nil." The program is guaranteed to terminate so long as there are no loops in the ancestor chain in working memory. As *Request* elements are removed when processed, no single *Request* element can cause the rule to match more than once. Since working memory has a finite number of *Person* elements, eventually all of the remaining *Request* elements will have a *target* of "nil" or a symbolic atom that is not the *name* attribute of any *Person* in working memory. In exactly this case it will be impossible to find a consistent binding for the LHS and `PrintAncestors` will not match.

If the user is not entering *Person* elements between rule firings (Section 2.8 describes how this can be done), all elements of class *Request* will have a greater recency than any element of class *Person*. Since we are assuming that the *names* in the database are unique, each *Request* will be involved in at most one instantiation. Therefore, whether MEA or LEX is used, the search for ancestors will be a depth-first search, starting with the first *target*'s father.

Both MEA and LEX will select the instantiations with the most recent *Request* element in working memory. Since the *father Request* is added to working memory after the *mother Request*, the *father* will be the dominant *Request* element. Thus the search for ancestors will be depth first, exploring *father* branches before *mother* branches. To explore *mother* branches first, interchange the two **make** actions of the rule `PrintAncestors`. Effecting a breadth-first search is more difficult. Each level of the ancestor tree must be explored in a different phase of the process. Section 5.2.3 develops a mechanism for using multiple phases.

If working memory contains the following elements:

```
1:  (Person ↑name Penelope ↑mother Jessica ↑father Jeremy)
2:  (Person ↑name Jessica ↑mother Mary-Elizabeth ↑father Homer)
3:  (Person ↑name Jeremy ↑mother Jenny ↑father Steven)
4:  (Person ↑name Steven ↑mother Loree)
5:  (Person ↑name Loree ↑father Jason)
```

```
6:  (Person ↑name Homer ↑mother Stephanie)
7:  (Start)
```

then the output of the program would be as follows:

```
Please type the first name of a person
whose ancestors you would like to find:
Penelope
Jessica and Jeremy are ancestors via Penelope
Jenny and Steven are ancestors via Jeremy
    ; following father branch
Loree and nil are ancestors via Steven
    ; following father branch
nil and Jason are ancestors via Loree
    ; no father, choose mother
Mary-Elizabeth and Homer are ancestors via Jessica
    ; backtrack to mother
Stephanie and nil are ancestors via Homer
    ; last father branch
```

After finding the parents of Penelope, there would be two instantiations of the rule `PrintAncestors`: one matching Jeremy and one matching Jessica. However, the instantiation matching the *Request* for the ancestors of Jeremy will be selected because it matches the most recent working memory element. Notice in the output sequence that the instantiation matching Jessica does not fire until all other requests with a non-nil name fire. The Jessica instantiation will be in every conflict set until it is finally selected.

The program is very clumsy because it prints out the value "nil" in the place of ancestor names. The next version of the rule solves this problem. The rule `PrintAncestor::Start` will not be modified. The second rule will be replaced with three rules. One rule will find the ancestors, another rule will print out only the non-nil values, and a final rule will stop the program. `FindAncestors` is the driving rule for locating the ancestors. It matches a *Request* element in working memory of *type* "ancestor" and a *Person* element whose *name* is the *target* of the request. The rule establishes two new *Request* elements for the mother and the father of the *target* Person. The rule is

```
(p FindAncestors
   (Request ↑type ancestor ↑target {<name> <> nil})
   (Person ↑name <name> ↑mother <mother-name>
       ↑father <father-name>)
-->
   (make Request  ↑type ancestor  ↑target <mother-name>)
   (make Request ↑type ancestor ↑target <father-name>))
```

The first condition element of this rule restricts the value of *target* to be other than "nil." This is not strictly necessary since the value bound to <name> must also be the value of the *name* attribute of a *Person* element. This value is not supposed to be "nil." The rule does not remove any existing working memory elements, it just creates new ones. Because of refraction, this rule will fire exactly once for each *Request-Person* combination in working memory. Note that the rule may set up requests for "nil" people, just as `PrintAncestors` did. The rule will also generate new requests in a depth-first, father-before-mother fashion.

The rule `FindAncestors::Print` prints the values of the *names* of the *Person* elements found as ancestors. It matches *Request* elements with a non-nil *target*, printing the value. The rule then removes the *Request* element from working memory.

```
(p FindAncestors::Print
   {(Request ↑type ancestor
        ↑target {<name> <> nil}) <request1>}
-->
   (write (crlf) <name> is an ancestor)
   (remove <request1>))
```

Notice that the first condition element of this rule is identical to that of the rule `FindAncestors`. However, the `FindAncestors` rule is more specific because it includes two condition elements in the left-hand side. When both of these rules are matched by working memory, with the same *Request* element bound to the first condition, conflict resolution strategy chooses the more recent rule to fire first (any second element is more recent than no element). Therefore `FindAncestors::Print` will not remove the *Request* element before the *mother* and *father* have been found by `FindAncestors`. The order in which the rules will be selected is not dependent on the conflict resolution strategy selected. So long as there is an instantiation in the conflict set for rule `FindAncestors` with a match to the last *Request* for a non-nil *Person*, it will be chosen based on recency and specificity over other instantiations. The print rule will be triggered only after all of a *Person*'s ancestors have been printed. For either conflict resolution strategy, the output of the previous three rules would be as follows:

```
Please type the first name of a person
whose ancestors you would like to find:
Penelope
Jason is an ancestor
Loree is an ancestor
Steven is an ancestor
Jenny is an ancestor
Jeremy is an ancestor
```

```
Stephanie is an ancestor
Homer is an ancestor
Mary-Elizabeth is an ancestor
Jessica is an ancestor
Penelope is an ancestor
```

When the above program started, working memory was

```
1: (Person ↑mother Jessica ↑name Penelope ↑father Jeremy)
2: (Person ↑mother Mary-Elizabeth ↑name Jessica ↑father Homer)
3: (Person ↑mother Jenny ↑name Jeremy ↑father Steven)
4: (Person ↑mother Loree ↑name Steven)
5: (Person ↑name Loree  ↑father Jason)
6: (Person ↑mother Stephanie ↑name Homer)
7: (Start)
```

and the dominant rule was `PrintAncestors::Start`. This rule produced the output asking for the name of the person and creating a request element to find the ancestors of Penelope. A conflict set containing both of the other rules, `FindAncestors` and `FindAncestors::Print`, resulted. Now the rule `FindAncestors` generates requests depth-first, father-before-mother until the most recent request in working memory is for a *Person* not in the database. There will be four firings of `FindAncestors`, one each for Penelope, Jeremy, Steven, and Loree. Working memory will be as follows:

```
1: (Person ↑mother Jessica ↑name Penelope ↑father Jeremy)
2: (Person ↑mother Mary-Elizabeth ↑name Jessica ↑father Homer)
3: (Person ↑mother Jenny ↑name Jeremy ↑father Steven)
4: (Person ↑mother Loree ↑name Steven)
5: (Person ↑name Loree ↑father Jason)
6: (Person ↑mother Stephanie ↑name Homer)
9: (Request ↑type ancestor ↑target Penelope)
  ;FindAncestors has fired for element 9
10: (Request ↑type ancestor ↑target Jessica)
  ;FindAncestors has not fired for element 10
11: (Request ↑type ancestor ↑target Jeremy)
  ;FindAncestors has fired for element 11
12: (Request ↑type ancestor ↑target Jenny)
  ;FindAncestors doesn't match for element 12
13: (Request ↑type ancestor ↑target Steven)
  ;FindAncestors has fired for element 13
14: (Request ↑type ancestor ↑target Loree)
  ;FindAncestors has fired for element 14
15: (Request ↑type ancestor)
  ;FindAncestors doesn't match for element 15
16: (Request ↑type ancestor)
  ;FindAncestors doesn't match for element 16
17: (Request ↑type ancestor ↑target Jason)
  ;FindAncestors doesn't match for element 17
```

Since there is no *Person* element to match the most recent *Request* element, `FindAncestors::Print` now takes over, printing all of the ancestors generated after working memory element 10. The rule `FindAncestors` does match this element and has not fired. After printing

```
Jason is an ancestor
Loree is an ancestor
Steven is an ancestor
Jenny is an ancestor
Jeremy is an ancestor
```

the conflict set will be as follows:

```
FindAncestors:Print     (2 occurrences)
FindAncestors
(FindAncestors dominates)
```

`FindAncestors` will fire twice more, resulting in working memory:

```
1: (Person ↑mother Jessica ↑name Penelope ↑father Jeremy)
2: (Person ↑mother Mary-Elizabeth ↑name Jessica ↑father Homer)
3: (Person ↑mother Jenny ↑name Jeremy  ↑father Steven)
4: (Person ↑mother Loree ↑name Steven)
5: (Person ↑name Loree ↑father Jason)
6: (Person ↑mother Stephanie ↑name Homer)
9: (Request ↑type ancestor ↑target Penelope)
  ;FindAncestors has fired for element 9
10: (Request ↑type ancestor ↑target Jessica)
  ;FindAncestors has fired for element 10
15: (Request ↑type ancestor)
  ;FindAncestors doesn't match for element 15
16: (Request ↑type ancestor)
  ;FindAncestors doesn't match for element 16
23: (Request ↑type ancestor ↑target Mary-Elizabeth)
  ;FindAncestors doesn't match for element 23
24: (Request ↑type ancestor ↑target Homer)
  ;FindAncestors has fired for element 24
25: (Request ↑type ancestor ↑target Stephanie)
  ;FindAncestors doesn't match for element 25
26: (Request ↑type ancestor)
  ;FindAncestors doesn't match for element 26
```

The only rule to match now is `FindAncestors::Print`. It prints the values of all the non-nil *targets* of all the *Request* elements left in working memory.

The last line of output lists "Penelope" as her own ancestor. To avoid this line of output and to gracefully end the program, we develop one more rule. The final rule, `FindAncestors::Stop`, matches when there is only one working memory element of class *Request* for an "ancestor" with a non-nil *name*. There may be other *Request* elements with "nil" values for the *name*. The rule prints a termination message and stops the processing of the program:

```
(p FindAncestors::Stop
   (Request ↑type ancestor ↑target {<name1> <> nil})
 - (Request ↑type ancestor ↑target {<> <name1> <> nil})
-->
   (write (crlf) No More Ancestors (crlf))
   (halt))
```

This rule will be instantiated when the very first *Request* element is entered into working memory, along with rules `FindAncestors` and `FindAncestors::Print`. `FindAncestors` will be selected. It has one more condition element than `FindAncestors::Print`, and the recency of the second element will win over the negated second element of `FindAncestors::Stop`. Thus, when the rules have finished finding and printing the ancestors, this rule will be selected. It will print the final message that there are no more ancestors and halt execution of the program.

2.5 TECHNIQUES FOR INITIALIZING WORKING MEMORY

Before any rule in an OPS5 program can successfully fire, there must be some element in working memory for the rule to match. Attempting to run a program when working memory is empty will lead to immediate termination with no computations performed. Earlier we stated that a program in the production-system model had no distinguished starting rule. Working memory is initialized by executing a top-level **make** action, either by typing directly to the system or by loading a file. For reasons that depend on the implementation of OPS5, all top-level **make** actions must follow the declarations *and* the compilation of at least one rule into production memory. Although initialization is probably the most common reason for executing **make** actions at the top level, debugging is another reason.

The OPS5 system offers the programmer a number of different options for initializing the contents of working memory: the **make** actions can be typed in by the user, stored in a file that is loaded after the rules, or executed by some combination of both methods. The problem with the first method is that the user must type everything perfectly, with no errors. Therefore it is advantageous to require that the user type only one **make** action. The problem with the second method is that a different file must be loaded for each initial configuration to be tested, and that implies a lot of separate test files for even a small program. The simplest combination technique is to define an element class such as *Start* (see Section 2.1.2) and use a *Start* element to trigger a rule whose right-hand side contains the initializing **make** action. The user only needs to type a `(make Start)` action and then run the program. A detailed transcript demonstrating working memory initialization is given in Section 3.6.3.

2.5.1 INITIALIZING WITH A SINGLE RULE

If the contents of working memory are to be the same each time the production system is run (for example, in some game-playing programs), the easiest way to initialize working memory is to declare a distinguished element. When entered into working memory from the top level, the distinguished element will serve as a trigger for a single rule, which through a series of **make** actions will initialize working memory. A database consisting of *People* and *Cities* as described in this chapter could be initialized using the element class *Start* as a trigger. An element of this class is created at the top level as a signal to the rule `Initialize`.

```
; When an element of class Start enters working memory,
; this rule initializes the People database.
(p Initialize
   {(Start) <initialize>}
-->
   (make Person ↑name Penelope ↑mother Jessica ↑father Jeremy)
   (make Person ↑name Jessica ↑mother Mary-Elizabeth
       ↑father Homer)
   (make Person ↑name Jeremy ↑mother Jenny ↑father Steven)
   (make Person ↑name Steven ↑mother Loree)
   (make Person ↑name Loree ↑father Jason)
   (make Person ↑name Homer ↑mother Stephanie)
   (remove <initialize>))
```

When the user creates one of these elements at the top level with the command `(make Start)`, the rule `Initialize` stocks working memory so that the other rules (not shown here) can subsequently fire.

Two features of this example are worth noting. First, the rule `Initialize` removes the element of class *Start* from working memory. This is not necessary to prevent the rule from firing again (since both conflict-resolution strategies perform refraction), but it is a good practice to have rules clean up their refuse. It just slows down the system to have the rule `Initialize` instantiated on each cycle, only to be discarded from the conflict set because it has already fired. Second, since the element class *Start* has no attributes, it does not need a **literalize** declaration. Nevertheless, it is good practice to declare all element classes for purposes of program documentation.

2.5.2 PARAMETERIZED INITIALIZATION

If the programmer wants to provide a choice of initial working memory configurations, initialization can be parameterized. The user is given a choice of triggering elements, and production memory contains a separate rule for each of the allowable choices. These rules differ in what they place into working memory. The user's choice can consist either of selecting one (or more) of a set of different element classes, or of selecting the values assigned to a single element class. The latter method is used to elaborate on the database example. If we want to test the set of rules developed for finding the ancestor of a person in the database, there are several different initial working memory configurations that should be checked. We define an element class used to direct the testing and then three sample test rules.

```
(literalize Testcase   ; parameterized start element
    type               ; nulldb, singledb, general or other
                       ;  description of type of test case
    name)              ; unique for each testcase
```

The rule `Test::Ancestor:null` only puts the initialize element *Start* in working memory. Since the database is null, two rules should fire: `FindAncestors::Initialize` and `FindAncestors::Stop`. Following the I/O required to obtain the name of a person from the user, the expected program output is simply the message, `"No More Ancestors."` The test rule is this:

```
(p Test::Ancestor:null
   {(Testcase ↑type nulldb ↑name ancestornull) <nulltest>}
-->
   (remove <nulltest>)
   (make Start))
```

The next rule, `Test::Ancestor:Single`, puts a single element in the database with a *Request* element. Again, two rules are expected to fire: `FindAncestors` and `FindAncestors::Stop`. `FindAncestors` will establish *Requests* for the "nil" parents of "Orphan." Since there are no valid *Requests* in addition to the original request for "Orphan," the rule `FindAncestors::Stop` will stop the program. The expected program output is `"No more ancestors."`

```
(p Test::Ancestor:Single
   {(Testcase ↑type singledb ↑name ancestorsingle) <test>}
-->
   (remove <test>)
   (make Person ↑name Orphan)
   (make Request ↑type ancestor ↑target Orphan))
```

The final test rule, `Test::Ancestor:General`, initializes the database with a general case. The rule `FindAncestors` and the rule `FindAncestors::Print` will each fire several times until all of the ancestors are found and printed. Then `FindAncestors::Stop` will fire. The expected program output is

```
   Steven is an ancestor
   Jenny is an ancestor
   Jeremy is an ancestor
   Homer is an ancestor
   Jessica is an ancestor
   No more ancestors
; Rule to initialize database in general case
(p Test::Ancestor:General
   {(Testcase ↑type generaldb ↑name ancestorgeneral) <gentest>}
-->
   (remove <gentest>)
   (make Person ↑name Penelope ↑mother Jessica ↑father Jeremy)
   (make Person ↑name Jessica ↑father Homer)
   (make Person ↑name Jeremy ↑mother Jenny ↑father Steven)
   (make Request ↑type ancestor ↑target Penelope))
```

To initialize working memory, the programmer would enter the command

```
(make Testcase ↑type nulldb ↑name ancestornull)
```

if the test were to be initialized for a null database. If a single-element database were desired, the programmer would enter

```
(make Testcase ↑type singledb ↑name ancestorsingle)
```

The advantage of this approach to initialization is that the user has little to do to initialize working memory, provided that only a few different initial configurations are desired.

2.5.3 INITIALIZING AT THE TOP LEVEL

A flexible approach to initialization in OPS5 is to load working memory directly with a series of top-level **make** actions. To avoid the tedious and error-prone process of typing in each **make** command, the operator need only perform a top-level **load** action, which sends the contents of a specified text file as input stream to the top level of the system. To build up working memory, any number of **load** actions can be performed in any order. Although **load** actions can be nested (that is, a text file that is loaded can itself contain a **load** command), there is usually a severe limit to the number of files that can be opened simultaneously, so one should not get carried away. The exact syntax for loading a file with OPS5 declarations or rules varies depending on the implementation. If you are using a LISP version, be certain to put a single quote before the file name, as in `(load 'makefile)`. Check your user's manual to find the equivalent command for your system.

2.6 PROGRAM TERMINATION

Most of the time, but not always, production system programs are meant to complete a task and then terminate execution. When an OPS5 program terminates normally, it returns control to the top level. There are five ways to effect the transition from the recognize-act cycle to the top level:

1. Use an implementation-specific interrupt character.
2. Fire a rule that has been set to be a breakpoint.
3. Place a bound on the number of cycles in the argument to the **run** command.
4. Fire a rule that performs a right-hand-side **halt** action.
5. Empty the conflict set.

The first three are means of *interactive* termination, and are used mostly during testing and debugging. The latter two, on the other hand, are means of *programmed* control over termination, and as such are part of the application program's design.

2.6.1 EMPTYING THE CONFLICT SET

The preferred way for a production system to terminate itself is by emptying the conflict set: everything that can be done has been done, so the inference engine politely bows out. As the production system carries on its duties, it may consume its data and control elements by deleting them or marking them as inactive; less frequently, it may insert into working memory elements that disable rules that have negated condition elements. Refraction further reduces the conflict set by forbidding the inference engine to repeat itself without being explicitly told to do so. In these ways, the inference engine puts itself out of a job.

Such implicit termination is meant to occur when all goals have been achieved, and therefore is a desirable ending in task-oriented programs. Unfortunately, it sometimes occurs too early: a bug may result in premature termination. An inference engine may stop if rules fail to create needed data or control elements, or create them with the wrong values; if the left-hand sides of rules are incorrectly written so as to be self-contradictory; or if elements that should be removed are allowed to remain and disable rules that have negated condition elements. In debugging, the programmer must compare the final state of working memory with the rule set to determine what went wrong.

The opposite problem can occur; that is, the program may avoid termination and refresh the conflict set with redundant instantiations. Most often, this happens when rules that have previously fired match again with a working memory element that has been altered with a **modify** action.

2.6.2 THE HALT ACTION

Explicit termination with the use of a right-hand-side **halt** action is of limited use. During testing and debugging, the programmer may add **halt** actions to the right-hand sides of critical rules for the purpose, say, of examining working memory or the conflict set after those rules fire. However, it is better to use breakpoints that can be set and removed interactively, without changing the program, using the **pbreak** command. Another use of **halt** is to terminate as soon as the first of many possible solutions to a problem is found, and the programmer sees no point in taking extra effort to prevent the generation of further solutions. Finally, the user may simply want an early out; the **halt** action is sometimes the most graceful way to let the user terminate execution.

2.7 OTHER OPS5 FEATURES

Though highly simplified in its syntax, the subset of OPS5 defined thus far in this chapter is sufficient for most OPS5 application programs. We strongly recommend that the programmer deviate from this subset only after careful consideration. In this section, we'll examine some of the additional features of the language: features designed to allow matching without restricting the condition element to a single element class and without restricting the attributes referenced in the left-hand side to be constants known in advance, and features designed to provide uniform treatment of data via the result element. The syntax definitions given here have ramifications concerning most OPS5 commands and functions, which can have more general arguments than we have previously defined. You should check your OPS5 user's manual to determine the details.

2.7.1 TERMS AND THE ↑ OPERATOR

The OPS5 language actually has a much richer definition of terms than the simplified versions we have described thus far. For example, in Section 2.3.1, all condition elements began with the element class name and were followed by a sequence of attribute-value pairs. In fact, condition elements can be sequences of *lhs-terms*. Similarly, the arguments to many RHS actions can be sequences of *rhs-terms*.

An *lhs-term* may be

- the operator ↑ followed by an attribute name and an *lhs-value*,
- the operator ↑ followed by a number and an *lhs-value*,
- an *lhs-value*.

There can be any amount of white space (blanks and tabs) between the operator ↑ and the operand (attribute name or number).

An *rhs-term* is an *lhs-term* (substituting *rhs-value* for *lhs-value*) with one added possibility: An *rhs-term* can also be the operator ↑ followed by a variable and an *rhs-value*. The operator ↑ is essentially an indexing operator that determines which index to access in the array representation of a working memory element.

2.7.2 LHS-TERMS

To interpret an *lhs-term*, the OPS5 rule compiler determines which fields of a working memory element are to be accessed by each attribute of the condition element. The compiled rule includes the numeric index of the field rather than the original symbolic name. This is why a variable cannot be used as a left-hand-side operand for the ↑ operator — at compilation time there is no value bound to the variable for use in the compiled rule. If the term contains the ↑ operator followed by an attribute name or a number, the numeric index computed is the indicated field of the working memory element. If the term does not contain the ↑ operator and is preceded by a term with numeric index k, then $k + 1$ would be the computed index. If there is no preceding term, the numeric index 1 is used. The behavior of having the index default to 1 greater than the last index referenced is a common source of confusion when uparrows are inadvertently omitted.

With the definitions given in Section 2.3.3, the test `(↑age <=> 10)` is equivalent to `(↑4 <=> 10)`, matching any working memory element whose fourth field has an integer value. The numeric index for the *age* attribute was 4. For elements of class *Person*, the 4 does correspond to the attribute *age*, while for elements of class *City*, the 4 corresponds to the attribute *state*. The condition element

```
(↑location  north 45)
```

consists of two terms, the term "↑location north," and the term "45." The index computed for the first term is the index indicated by the attribute *location*. The term 45 will have the next index associated with it.

A condition element can now be redefined as a left parenthesis followed by some number of *lhs-terms* followed by a right parenthesis.

2.7.3 RHS ACTIONS AND RESULT ELEMENTS

The procedure for determining the proper index for a term in the RHS is similar to that for the LHS except that the index is determined when the RHS action is executed during the firing of the rule. Thus a term can also consist of the ↑ followed by a variable, and the scalar value bound to the variable can be used as the index.

Many RHS actions can take a sequence of *rhs-terms* as an argument, rather than the restricted form of argument defined earlier. The *rhs-values* allowed in the sequence of *rhs-terms* include function calls that may return several scalars. Each of these scalars is evaluated as a term without an ↑ operator and put in successive locations after the last computed index.

The RHS actions use the structure called the *result element*, an element with 127 sequential storage locations, to build up a working memory element. Before an RHS action (except for **modify**) is evaluated, the result element is filled entirely with "nil" values. Then each term in the sequence is evaluated from left to right, filling the result element as indicated by the term. A sequence of *rhs-terms* is the argument to each of the actions **make, openfile, closefile, default,** and **write.** A sequence of *rhs-terms* is the second argument to each of the actions **modify, call,** and **bind** (when used with two arguments).

2.8 USEFUL TOP-LEVEL COMMANDS

The OPS5 top-level commands provide a number of helpful features that add up to a very effective debugging environment. While interacting with the top level of the system, the programmer may examine and manipulate the contents of working memory and production memory (including the set of partial matches of working memory with a specified rule), set breakpoints, step through the recognize-act cycle either forwards or backwards, and examine the current conflict set. It is also possible to monitor the firing of rules and the changes to working memory as they occur. Learning to use these tools effectively will save a great deal of debugging time.

In some implementations, the run-time environment of the implementation language is also available from the top level of OPS5. Since debugging tools are generally implementation dependent, the user's manual should be checked for the specific aids offered in a particular implementation of the language.

2.8.1 THE WATCH COMMAND

With the **watch** command, the OPS5 system can be instructed to write a report of every instantiation that is fired and every change that is made to working memory. The command takes either no argument or one argument, with effects as follows:

(watch)	Write the current watch level (initialized to 1), which remains unchanged.
(watch 0)	Give no report of firings or changes to working memory.
(watch 1)	Report the rule name and the time tags of each working memory element for each instantiation that is fired.
(watch 2)	Report the same information as watch level 1, but in addition report each change to working memory.

2.8.2 THE RUN COMMAND

Executing this command causes rules to be fired. If the **run** command is given a positive integer as argument, the recognize-act cycle will be curtailed, returning control to the top level of the system after no more than the specified number of firings. Of course, the recognize-act cycle may end earlier if the conflict set becomes empty, if a rule is fired that performs a **halt** operation or has a breakpoint set, or if the user types an operating-system dependent control character. During debugging, the programmer can step through the execution with watch level set to 1 or 2 to get a fine-grained view of the program's behavior. By repeatedly typing `(run 1)`, the programmer can step through the execution one firing at a time.

2.8.3 THE BACK COMMAND

The **back** command undoes the effects of up to 32 rule firings, provided there are no external references in the right-hand sides of any of the fired rules. The argument is the number of cycles to back up, which cannot exceed 32. One possible use for this command is to set a breakpoint at a crucial rule, back up one, and then examine the conflict set, the partial matches, and the contents of working memory.

2.8.4 THE WM AND PPWM COMMANDS

Typing the command `(wm)` will result in a listing of the contents of working memory. An optional argument is a sequence of time tags. Those working memory elements that have the specified time tags will be printed; if no time tags are given, the entire contents of working memory will be printed. Thus, the command

```
(wm 54 40)
```

will cause OPS5 to print the working memory element with time tag 54 and the element with time tag 40, if they exist.

The command **ppwm** takes as argument a pattern like a left-hand-side condition element, and prints all working memory elements that match the pattern. The pattern cannot contain variables, predicates (i.e., the relational operators =, >, >=, <, <=, <=>, and <>), the quote operator //, angle brackets (<< >>), or curly braces ({ }). For example, the command

```
(ppwm City ↑state Pennsylvania)
```

will print all working memory elements of class *City* such that the value of its *state* attribute is "Pennsylvania." As with the **wm** command, if a null pattern is given, the entire contents of working memory will be printed.

These commands are essential to debugging. Used in conjunction with other commands such as **cs** and **matches,** they allow the programmer to determine why a rule failed to be instantiated at the right time.

2.8.5 THE PM COMMAND

The user can also give a top-level command to print the text of production memory, namely any rules that are named as arguments to the **pm** command. Any number of rule names may be given. To print the rule `FindAncestors`, give the command `(pm FindAncestors)`.

2.8.6 THE CS COMMAND

To examine the current conflict set, the programmer simply types

```
(cs)
```

and each instantiated rule will be listed, one to a line, followed by the currently dominant instantiation (that is, the one to be fired on the next cycle unless working memory, production memory, or the conflict resolution strategy is changed from the top level). This command does not take any arguments.

2.8.7 THE MATCHES COMMAND

The command **matches** prints the partial matches for rules whose names are given as arguments to the command. For each condition element of the specified rules, the time tags of the matching working memory elements are listed, as well as the intersections of the partial matches. Consider the following example rule:

```
(literalize number
      value                    ; any integer
)

(p example-rule
   (number ↑value {<number-1> > 100})
   (number ↑value {<number-2> <> <number-1>})
   (number ↑value {<number-3> < 50})
-->
   (write (crlf) <number-1> <number-2> <number-3>))
   (make number ↑value 101)   ; given time-tag 1
   (make number ↑value 102)   ; given time-tag 2
   (make number ↑value  11)   ; given time-tag 3
```

As soon as these lines are compiled, the **matches** command will give the following results:

```
->(matches example-rule)
example-rule
 ** matches for (1) **
 2
 1
 ** matches for (2) **
 3
 2
 1
 ** matches for (2 1) **
 3  1
 3  2
 1  2
 2  1
 ** matches for (3)
 3
nil
```

The final intersection, which in this example would be "matches for (3 2 1)," is not included. Using the time tags, the programmer can examine the contents of the working memory elements with the **wm** command.

The information given by the **matches** command can be very helpful in debugging. The programmer can use it to isolate many common bugs, including the following manifestations:

- A given condition element is never matched.
- The intersection of two or more condition elements, each of which is matched, fails to be satisfied.

- A negated condition element is matched.

One type of bug that will *not* be revealed is the failure of an instantiation to dominate in conflict resolution.

2.8.8 THE PBREAK COMMAND

Rules can be set to be breakpoints so that as soon as they fire they return control to the top level. The programmer can then use this opportunity to examine the contents of working memory, the conflict set, and the partial matches. The **pbreak** command takes any number of rule names as arguments. If one of the specified rules is not already set to be a breakpoint, it is set as a breakpoint; if it already is a breakpoint, it reverts to normal status. Giving no arguments to the **pbreak** command will result in a listing of the names of rules that have breakpoints set.

2.8.9 THE MAKE AND REMOVE COMMANDS

Because both the **make** and **remove** actions can be executed as commands at the top level, the programmer can use them during debugging, for instance, to make patches. The top-level **make** command is identical to the right-hand-side action with the exceptions given in Section 2.3.3. The **remove** command must necessarily differ, since working memory elements cannot be bound by matching on the top level: it takes as arguments the time tags of working memory elements that are to be deleted from working memory. The command `(remove *)` deletes everything from working memory.

2.8.10 THE EXCISE COMMAND

The **excise** command deletes rules from production memory. It takes as argument a sequence of production names. Like the **make** and **remove** commands, it can be used to make patches during debugging.

2.9 COMMON ERRORS

In this section, we will discuss some of the common syntactic errors found in OPS5 programs. Which errors are caught by the rule compiler and which are apparent only at run time varies with the implementation, so consult your user's manual. This section is merely a guide to the types of problems you might have. We're using the FRANZLISP implementation for examples. The top-level commands discussed in Section 2.8 are useful in isolating and repairing the problems described here. Remember that not all implementations do case folding (converting lower-case characters to upper case on input), and misspellings can cause many errors that are not obvious from a casual glance at the code. Many error messages received by the user are messages from the implementation language and may be difficult to understand. We demonstrate some of the FRANZLISP error messages in this section.

2.9.1 SYNTAX AND TYPE CHECKING OF DATA

OPS5 is a weakly typed language in which only classes and vector-attributes can be declared. It is not possible to assign types to the values of attributes. However, checks for multiple vector-attribute declarations, multiple definitions of element classes, and illegal names of elements or attributes are performed.

Multiple Vector-Attribute Declarations

While OPS5 does check the declarations to see if more than one vector-attribute is assigned to a given element, the error message does not immediately follow the improper declaration. It is not until the declaration section is terminated with a rule that the rule compiler indicates the error. For example, typing in the declarations

```
(vector-attribute  oldvector)
(vector-attribute  newvector)
(literalize  baddeclaration   oldvector   newvector)
```

at the top level will not result in an immediate error message even though the restriction of one vector-attribute in a declaration is violated. The error message is given the first time a rule using the illegal element class and the two vector attributes is compiled into rule memory.

Multiple Element Class Definitions

Element class definitions are checked to make certain that there are not two definitions with the same class name. In this case, an error message is given immediately. The following declarations give rise to the error message indicated:

```
->(literalize goal Type Status)
nil
->(literalize goal Type Area Status)
nil
?..goal..attempt to redefine classnil
```

The first part of the message is from OPS5. The "nil" is from FRANZLISP.

Illegal Names for Elements and Attributes

Element and attribute names must be symbolic atoms. An attempt to use a number as an element name will cause an error message:

```
->(literalize 3  Name  Date)

Error:  putprop:  Bad first argument:  3
```

Those familiar with FRANZLISP will recognize this error message as a FRANZLISP message. It is often the case that the error messages received are generated from the language in which OPS5 is programmed.

An attempt to use a number as an attribute name will also cause an error message when the declarations are entered; another FRANZLISP error message results:

```
->(literalize trial  3  Name)

?..3..can bind only constant atoms:  Error:  putprop: Bad
      first argument:  3
```

The following typescript illustrates some of the errors just discussed and some of the warnings given earlier in this chapter.

This transcript uses the standard notational conventions:

- All user input will be underlined.
- All commentary on the transcript will begin on a new line, indented with the comment character ";" as the first character in the line.

```
->(literalize Person name  age city-of-residence)
  NIL
->(literalize City name location state country)
  NIL
->(vector-attribute address)
  (ADDRESS)
->(make Person ↑name Janice ↑age 25)

?..name..illegal index after ↑NIL
?..age..illegal index after ↑NIL

        ; Since no rule has been defined, the attribute
        ;  definitions are ignored and the element is inserted
        ;  in working memory as a vector.
->(wm)

1:  (Person Janice 25)

    ; So we define a rule to close the declarations section
```

```
->(p first-rule
     (match anything)
  -->
     (make done))
*NIL

    ;The rule uses the element classes match and done, which
    ; have not been defined, but this is not an OPS5 error.

->(make Person ↑name Mike ↑address Pittsburgh PA)
NIL

    ; Now when we make an object we get no error messages.
    ; If we look in working memory we see that the
    ;  previous elements have been given an interpretation
    ;  retroactively.
    ; It is only luck that the definitions in working memory
    ;  element 1 are correct.  Try this scenario using (make
    ;  Person ↑age 25 ↑name Janice) at the beginning and you
    ;  will see the interpretation is different.
->(wm)

1:  (Person ↑name Janice ↑age  25)
2:  (Person ↑name Mike  ↑city-of-residence Pittsburgh)nil
```

2.9.2 ERRORS IN RULES

The syntax of rules is checked carefully by the compiler when the rule is brought into production memory. However, many errors are not revealed until the rule is executed.

Errors in Rule Names

Rule names are usually not significant in OPS5 programs. However, a few cautions are in order. Obviously, if a rule name is misspelled in a **pm** or **matches** or **excise** command, the desired result will not occur. Less obviously, rules defined with the same name overwrite one another, with only a somewhat obscure message given as a warning:

```
<rulename>
is
excised
nil
```

OPS5 gives a warning rather than an error message to allow the programmer to redefine rules deliberately during debugging.

Errors in Classes and Attributes

Most implementations of OPS5 do not provide error checking for element classes and their attributes when used in the rules.

A rule, like a user at the top level, can create working memory elements of element classes not defined, so long as the attributes referenced have been defined. The only checking that is consistently done in interpreting rules is to ensure that all symbolic atoms used as attribute names have been declared.

A common source of confusion is that an attribute may be used in conditions with element classes for which it was not declared an attribute. This was illustrated in Section 2.3.3. Also, a value for an attribute may be a vector (a sequence of values) even though the attribute was not declared as a vector attribute. If such an assignment is made, the values may unintentionally overwrite other attribute fields.

Leaving out an ↑ has a similar effect. The symbolic atom intended to be an attribute name is interpreted as a value. On the left-hand side of a rule it is then matched against whatever value happens to follow the last index referenced. On the right-hand side of a rule the symbolic atom is inserted in the result element rather than used to determine where to insert the next value.

Since value types cannot be declared, there is obviously no checking to ensure that values used in rules are of an appropriate type. The programmer should add additional rules to do whatever type and range checking is appropriate. An example of this is given in Section 2.10.3.

Errors in Variables

When variables are misspelled, the error can be caught during compilation if a variable used on the right-hand side is never bound (either on the left-hand side or with a right-hand-side **bind** action). But if the variable is to appear in two condition elements and is spelled inconsistently, the rule will be instantiated too many times. Consider the following rule:

```
(p list-data-for-department-managers
   (department ↑name <department> ↑faculty-manager <manager>)
   (person ↑name <manager> ↑office <room> ↑phone <pnum>)
-->
   (write (crlf) The manager of the <department> department
       is <manager> (crlf) office <room> phone <pnum>))
```

The variable name <manager> appears three times. Suppose two of the three spellings are the same, and the third is spelled differently. If the occurrence with the odd spelling is in the right-hand-side action, the error can be caught during compilation. But if the error is in the first or the second condition element, the rule will be instantiated with every possible pairing of departments and managers. Conversely, a spelling error may make two variables identical when they were intended as separate variables.

Similar cautions apply to element variables.

2.10 PROGRAMMING STYLE AND CONVENTIONS

Over the past decade there has been an increasing awareness of the need for proper methodology and discipline in programming. The techniques of software engineering useful for formatting and documenting programs in business and systems programming — decomposition into functionally discrete modules headed by functional descriptions; proper formatting of program text, mnemonic and descriptive variable and procedure names; and concise but helpful commenting — apply equally to production-system programs.

An increasing number of software development organizations have recognized the need for standards and guidelines for all project documentation, and the recognition of programming style and documentation guidelines is universal. However, there are a wide variety of programming styles, and no one standard or guideline will be universally accepted and adhered to. There is evidence that to have a team following *some* guideline consistently and uniformly is more important than *which* guideline is being followed. Such is certainly the case when using a rule-based programming language.

In the remaining sections of this chapter, some general guidelines for good programming style are presented. Some of these precepts are nothing more than common sense, and others are familiar from software engineering or structured programming methodologies. The nature of production systems in general, and of OPS5 in particular, suggests additional ways to increase the readability and maintainability of production-system programs. We have attempted to illustrate these software engineering techniques in the example OPS5 programs and program fragments used in this text.

2.10.1 PROGRAM SEGMENTATION

Rules in a production-system program do not have to be stored in one monolithic file but rather can be loaded from multiple files. Breaking a production system into units can have its advantages. Editing (hence debugging) will take less time with fewer rules in the program segment. Storage units can correspond to functional units organized around the problem-solving strategy of the program. Often there is a particular element class used to distinguish the context in which a rule should apply. The problem presented in Chapter 3 organizes the rules around the *goals* of the planning process. Chapter 5 introduces the notion of a ***context*** as a help in organizing a program. The use of such special element classes to help segment the program has all the advantages that functional decomposition brings. Testing at the unit level involves the testing of one strategy unit. If the unit is stored in a separate file, other rules will not interact during this testing. Testing of larger components and integration testing involves loading several files into production memory. Each file may load its successor, or loading may be tree-structured, with a main file loading a number of subfiles which in turn load other subfiles. However, it is not good to nest loads too deeply, as some systems have restrictions on the number of open files that can be maintained. Unless a very large system is being built, segmentation rarely involves more than a handful of files. As a general guideline, files should be between 5 and 50 rules in length. File names, of course, should be as informative as possible.

2.10.2 ELEMENT CLASS STYLE CONVENTIONS

We recommend that class and attribute names always begin with an alphabetic character and that they do not contain nonprinting characters. A symbolic atom should be used consistently in a program; that is, it should have the same meaning for each use. It is considered good style to declare vector attributes before using them in element class declarations. Some people find it confusing to use the same atom for an attribute name and for an element class name, so you may want to avoid this.

Although there is no mechanism in OPS5 for specifying the type or range for values of attributes, such information should be included as comments in the definition of the object class. *Comments* in most implementations begin with a semicolon (;) and may occur within a declaration or within a rule. Since the complete range of all attributes may not be known when they are first created, the documentation must be modified as knowledge of the domain increases and the program grows.

2.10.3 NAMES

Element classes and attributes, rules, variables, and symbolic constants should have names that are mnemonic and indicate their function in the system. Most production system languages place no meaningful restriction on the length of these names, taking their inspiration from LISP because this is often the implementation language. The payoff in readability is well worth the extra effort expended in typing longer names. Because the scope of variables and element variables is only one rule, there is a tendency to use short non-mnemonic names. We strongly recommend against this practice. Rule names should, whenever possible, reflect groupings of related rules. All rules in the same context should be prefixed by the name of the context, as the ancestor program demonstrated. The separator used may have to vary with the implementation; in some languages, characters such as ":" and "–" are not allowed within identifiers.

It often happens that a group of rules are all special cases of a single parent rule in the rule set. The names of the special-case rules should have as prefixes the name of the parent rule, with the suffix indicating the differential function of the rule. If the parent rule does not actually occur in the rule set, the principle still applies: the prefix should specify what all the rules have in common, as in the following example. This example is a portion of the program designed to input values for a database on people. Ages certainly are positive integer values, and probably are less than 130. An error message should be displayed for any other input and the stage set for triggering the request for input rule.

```
(literalize context         ; A structuring mechanism to be
                            ;  discussed
    goal                    ; The goal of interest here is
                            ;  checking input
)
(literalize input
    token                   ; any symbolic item or number
                            ;  is allowed for input in the
                            ;  general case here we are
                            ;  interested ages represented
                            ;  by numbers between 0 and 130
)

; IF   the inputs are being checked and the input token
;  is greater than 130
; THEN write an error message and remove the input so a
;  new value can be read in
(p check-age-input::bad-value:too-large
   (context ↑goal check-input)
   {(input ↑token {<input-value> > 130}) <input>}
-->
   (write (crlf) The value <input-value> exceeds the
          maximum of 130)
   (remove <input>))

; IF   the inputs are being checked
;  and the input token is less than 0
; THEN write an error message
;  and remove the input so a new value can be read in
```

```
(p check-age-input::bad-value:too-small
   (context ↑goal check-input)
   {(input ↑token {<input-value> <  0}) <input>}
-->
   (write (crlf) The value <input-value> is less than the
          minimum of 0)
   (remove <input>))

; IF   the inputs are being checked and the input token
;  has the symbolic atom type so it cannot be a number,
; THEN write an error message and remove the input so
;  a new value can be read in
(p check-age-input::bad-value:not-a-number
   (context ↑goal check-input)
   {(input ↑token {<input-value> <=> nil}) <input>}
-->
   (write (crlf) The value <input-value> is not a number)
   (remove <input>))
```

Note that in this example there is no parent rule named `check-age-input::bad-value` because the three rules exhaustively cover the set of bad input values.

Here are some other naming conventions that have proven useful:

- To avoid unintentional mismatches, stick to a single case (preferably lower case) for symbolic constants.
- Avoid meaningless enumerations such as <var1>, <var2>, and so on.
- When there is no conflict, name variables after the attributes and classes to which they are bound.
- To distinguish objects of special significance, use lexical conventions such as special characters or case.

It is important that a set of naming conventions be established for a program. Usually a programming group will have its own preferences for conventions. For ease of reading the program, the conventions should be used consistently.

2.10.4 FORMATTING

The following conventions seem appropriate when formatting rules, although these standards are often project-dependent.

- Rules in a given context, as well as other groups of rules that work in concert, should be grouped together with a header comment defining the group and the rules in the group. Such modules should be separated with white space, a row of asterisks, or some other obvious demarcation device.

- All rules should begin along the same vertical line, usually the left margin. All condition elements and right-hand-side actions should be indented the same amount from the left margin and each should start on a separate line.
- Continuations of large condition or action elements should be indented.
- Element variables should be consistently to the right or left of the condition element. The use of element variables should also be consistent.

2.10.5 DOCUMENTATION

Typically, whenever a program is read by someone who's not in the midst of coding it, an enormous amount of time is wasted. Even the original programmer may encounter problems a few months later, when the details of the methods used in coding are no longer easily recalled. The time wasted in analyzing what computation a section of code accomplishes can be minimized by the judicious use of clear and accurate comments. Obvious and redundant comments are worthless, however, and inaccurate ones are just plain harmful.

In production systems, the type declarations, initial working memory, and the rule set should be documented to some degree. Global comments often are necessary to inform the reader of the overall structure of the program, the conditions under which program modules are executed, the role of various program components, and the set of permissible program states.

Although no standard for documentation exists for many production-system languages, the following rules are safe to follow in any application:

- Each rule should be prefaced with an English paraphrase. The comment should also express the reasoning behind the rule's existence. It should indicate the rule's role in the system and should express how the rule is different from other rules having similar form.
- Functionally separate modules, such as sets of rules in a context, should be prefaced by a header giving the name of the context, the function performed, the conditions under which the code is to be executed, and the preconditions and postconditions for execution of the program unit.
- Any type declarations, parameter settings, or initial settings should have some documentation indicating their impact on the production system execution (such as how they organize data or affect conflict resolution).
- An initial working memory configuration should include associated documentation indicating the type of problem being specified and any departure from the standard representation.

A brief header identifying the programmers, giving the date of the most recent revision, and describing the purpose and structure of the program may wait until the program has been largely completed, since this information is often subject to change. If the program is being shipped for use elsewhere, a user's manual and an implementation manual may be necessary. The more detailed the documentation, the fewer the complaints from potential users.

Bear in mind, however, that good documentation and formatting do not substitute for good design and well-chosen names. Rather, the documentation should complement the program by explaining its features, conventions, and goals.

2.11 EXERCISES

2-1 Create lhs-value expressions for the following:

- between −1 and 10
- in the list: NM MA ME NC
- any number or the atom "nil"
- equal to 45

2-2 Extend the definition of the element class *Person* to include attributes of *sex* and *spouse*. How would you modify the definition to allow a determination of marital status?

2-3 Using your extended definition of *Person*, write pairs of condition elements, with variables <thisperson> and <thatperson>, to retrieve the *names* of *Persons* related by the following relationships:

- <thisperson> is the *sibling* of <thatperson>
- <thisperson> is the *sister* of <thatperson>
- <thisperson> is the *maternal grandmother* of <thatperson>
- <thisperson> is the *paternal aunt* of <thatperson>

2-4 Assume a database of working memory elements of class *Person* and class *City*. Write an OPS5 rule to print out the *names* of all *Person* elements who live in New Hampshire.

2-5 Create a test rule(s) for the previous exercise and run the rules.

2-6 Write a rule that will find the oldest *Person* in a database, print the *name* and *age* of the *Person*, and state how many years older than the next-oldest he or she is. That is, if Jedediah is the oldest and is 101, the next-oldest person is 89, your output should be:

```
Jedediah, aged 101,
is approximately 12 years older than anyone else.
```

2-7 Create a test rule(s) for the previous exercise and run the rules.

2-8 Modify the rule `FindAncestors::Initialize` to input both the name of a person and the type of relationship that is to be deduced. The rule should create a *Request* element for the *type* and *target* of the user's input. Call your rule `Find::Initialize`.

2-9 Create a test rule(s) for the previous exercise and run the rules.

2-10 Add a rule to augment your new `Find::Initialize` rule to print a termination message and halt execution if there is a *Request* element of *type* stop.

2-11 Create a test rule(s) for the previous exercise and run the rules.

2-12 Write a sequence of rules that will find all the descendants of a person. Assume that working memory is initialized with a *Request* element for *type* "descendant" and a *Person's name* as *target*.

2-13 Create a test rule(s) for the previous exercise and run the rules.

2-14 Modify the rule `FindAncestors::Stop` to implement the following idea: When a *Request* has been satisfied, print a message like "No More Ancestors," but in place of "Ancestors," put the value of the *type* of the request; remove the excess *Request* elements and reinitialize working memory with a *Start* element. Be careful to check the interactions of your rules with the other rules you have created.

2-15 Create a test rule(s) for the previous exercise and run the rules.

3

An Example in OPS5

This chapter presents the development of an OPS5 program as a solution to a simple problem. A programming methodology for specifying, implementing, and modifying a production-system program is presented and followed. Partial solutions to the problem are generated and rigorously tested before being extended. The presentation also includes a demonstration of how the OPS5 run-time support environment and debugging aids are used to test the partial solutions.

3.1 PROBLEM STATEMENT

The problem to be solved in this chapter is a version of the "Monkey and Bananas Problem," which is described as follows:

In a 10′ × 10′ × 10′ room, there is

- a heavy couch on the floor,
- a light ladder on the floor,
- a bunch of bananas (either suspended from the ceiling or on couch, ladder, or floor),
- one very, very hungry monkey who is incapable of moving heavy objects, and
- the monkey's blanket.

Write a program that will read in a description of the objects and their locations in the room and produce as output a sequence of commands that give the monkey instructions that, if followed, will allow the monkey to grab the bunch of bananas.

An example of possible output, given an initial configuration with the monkey standing on the floor in the room and the bananas suspended from the ceiling, would be as follows:

```
Walk to the ladder
Grab the ladder
Move the ladder to the location directly below the bananas
Drop the ladder
Climb onto the ladder
Grab the bananas
Congratulations!
```

The statement of the problem is obviously underspecified. The programmer or analyst must make many assumptions before beginning to program a solution. Questions that must be answered during the requirements analysis include these: How general or specific should the solution be? For example, should the program mention the bananas and the ladder by name, or should it have abstract objects of which the bananas and ladder are specific instances? What can we assume about the level of detail in commands the monkey can follow? For example, can the monkey find its way from one point in the room to another, moving around or over obstacles, or must the monkey be told a path to follow? How detailed must the representation of the objects and room be? Do we have to deal with concepts such as nearness and details such as size?

3.2 REQUIREMENTS ANALYSIS

The first step in any programming problem is to refine the problem definition into a well-defined problem specification. We must be more specific about the conditions that the input and output must satisfy. Since the problem statement is so vague, the first step is to determine the generality of the solution.

We choose to generalize this particular problem to represent a class of planning problems involving a self-propelling seeker (the monkey), physical objects (the couch, ladder, bananas, and blanket) placed in a three-dimensional physical space (the room), and a particular object (the bananas) identified as the target. The difficulty of the problem depends on the richness with which the environment is described, the amount of detail expected of solutions, the complexity allowed in stating the initial and final configurations for each of the objects, and assumptions about what the seeker (the monkey) knows and can see and remember.

If there were a local expert on this problem, we could get the expert to help constrain the problem and determine the appropriate representation. Left to our own devices, we begin building a *Decisions List:*

1. There is exactly one ladder in the room, and it is of the self-supporting variety.
2. The monkey is self propelling, and we assume there is exactly one such creature in our room.
3. The ladder is tall enough that the monkey, when *on* the ladder, can reach the ceiling. It is light enough for the monkey to carry.
4. The size of other physical objects will be ignored.
5. The weight of physical objects must be expressed, since the monkey cannot hold objects of "heavy" *weight*.
6. The monkey can see all objects in the room.
7. The monkey can carry out certain actions without being told in detail how to do these actions: Walk to any location in the room, move an object to any location in the room, climb on or off any object, drop an object being held, and grab an object.
8. The final program will allow the actions just described to be used in planning.

To complete the requirements analysis for this problem, we must define the objects of the domain and their attributes, the actions that can be part of the plan, the problem-solving strategy and objects used to keep track of the planning activity during problem solving, and legal working memory configurations and output sequences. We explicitly choose not to generalize the solution to handle such problems as having the monkey stack or unstack objects, manipulating the ordering of objects on the plane of the floor, or defining proximity. Such generalizations and extensions of the problem require a more sophisticated planning program than we will develop in this chapter.

3.3 OBJECT AND ATTRIBUTE IDENTIFICATION

There are two general classes of objects used in solving this problem: those relevant to the domain of the problem and those that help keep track of the state of the search for a solution. Since the problem-solving objects cannot be identified until after a solution strategy has been developed, this section will concentrate on the objects in the problem domain.

This problem contains six domain objects: the room, the bananas, the couch, the ladder, the blanket, and the monkey. These can be generalized to the physical space of the problem, the physical objects in the problem, and a self-propelling object. To describe the objects properly, attributes such as location in the room and weight must be representable. According to our *Decisions List*, summarized in Section 3.8, we do not need to represent the size of objects.

3.3.1 PHYSICAL SPACE

The physical space of the problem is a single room. The room defines the world for the problem and forms the basis for specifying locations for objects. The first decision to make is whether or not an explicit representation of the room is necessary. Should the room be represented explicitly as an OPS5 element class? If so, the location attributes and name of each object in the room would be attached to a specific OPS5 element class for the room. Alternatively, the location attributes could be associated with the OPS5 element classes representing the ladder, blanket, bananas, and monkey. Finally, the location of objects could be represented redundantly by using both representations.

To make this choice, we examine what kind of data the program will need to access and how it would be easiest to make the accesses. For instance, the objects and their locations are the only attributes of the room that must be represented, and it is not important to be able to find out what object is at a particular location. This is evidence that the room does not need to be represented explicitly. On the other hand, the objects have other attributes besides location that must be represented. Furthermore, data will be retrieved and stored through object reference. The locations of the target object, of the ladder, and of the monkey are of prime importance. This is evidence in favor of associating the locations of objects with the objects themselves. If both types of accesses were important, we might consider a redundant representation. However, this requires changing two working memory elements each time an object changes location. Such a requirement presents many possibilities for error. The programmer or maintainer may forget to change one or the other element when creating or modifying a rule. Since there is no advantage to a redundant representation in this problem, we reject it in favor of the single representation. We will have no direct representation of the physical space of the problem as a separate element class. Instead, the location of an object will be an attribute of the element class representing that object.

Next, we need to decide how to represent a location. The problem does not require a very exact description of the way the space in the room is filled, since the assumption was made that the details of moving the monkey through the room need not be described. The program will need to identify the horizontal location of each object in the room. The program will need to identify whether a physical object is on the floor or on the ceiling or on another object. The program will also need to know whether the monkey is on the floor or on another object. The horizontal location will simply be a point on a two-dimensional grid. The vertical location will be on the floor, the ceiling, or on a physical object. The implications of this decision are severe. There can be no meaningful way to define such concepts as proximity, nearness, or next-to if each object is reduced to a point in the plane. Since such concepts are not needed for the problem as defined so far, the representation is not deemed deficient.

We add the set of decisions about the representation of locations to the *Decisions List* in Section 3.8. A further generalization of the problem might lead to a different set of decisions.

3.3.2 PHYSICAL OBJECTS

The physical objects in the domain — bananas, blanket, couch, and ladder — have similar properties of interest. The exception is that one of the objects is designated as the target object of the problem. A generalization of the original problem specification would allow any object to be designated as the target. Then all physical objects could have the same representations without distinguishing the target object. This decision requires that an initial problem statement designate the target object as well as the room configuration. This decision is added to our *Decisions List*.

The attributes of interest are the name of the object, the horizontal location, the vertical location, and the weight of the object. The name attribute can be used to generalize the problem to an arbitrary number of physical objects. We choose the following attribute names and state their restrictions:

name	Unique physical object's name, such as "bananas," "blanket," or "couch." There must be one "ladder."
at	Physical object's horizontal location, which by programmers' convention will be a Cartesian coordinate of the form "X-Y," where X and Y are integers between 1 and 10, inclusive.
on	Physical object's vertical location, which can be "floor," "ceiling," any physical object's name, or "nil."
weight	Physical object's weight, which can be either "light" or "heavy."

Several additional design decisions are reflected in the attribute value descriptions given above. Since the *at* attribute may not have the value of "nil," and since the *at* attribute is supposed to reflect the physical object's horizontal location, the program must always update this attribute when the object changes physical location. The *on* attribute is allowed to have a "nil" value. The meaning of a "nil" value must be determined. It is intended that the value is "nil" when the monkey is holding the object. These two decisions are added to the *Decisions List*, Section 3.8.

The term "object" has been used to denote any OPS5 object and specifically to denote any physical object in the domain. To avoid confusion, the OPS5 element class referring to the physical objects discussed in this section will be called *phys-object*.

The OPS5 declaration of the element class *phys-object* is expressed with the following **literalize** statement. (Remember that the descriptions following the semicolons are simply comments in the program to help the programmer and maintainer remember the type restrictions and interpretations for the attributes; the restrictions are not visible to OPS5.)

```
(literalize phys-object   ; Description of physical objects
    name     ; value must be unique for each object
             ;  and not "nil," "floor," or "ceiling"
    at       ; the horizontal location of phys-object
             ;  value, by programmers' convention:
             ;  coordinate X-Y location where X and Y are
             ;  integers between 1 and 10 inclusive
    weight   ; one of: "heavy" or "light"
    on       ; if object is held by the monkey: "nil"
             ;  in this case monkey and object must have
             ;  same at value, and value of name
             ;  attribute for this phys-object must be
             ;  value of holds attribute for monkey
             ; else one of: "floor," "ceiling" or the
             ;  value of the name attribute of
             ;  some phys-object instance.
)
```

3.3.3 SELF-PROPELLING OBJECT

The only self-propelling object in this problem is the monkey, and we have already specified that there can be only one instance of the monkey in working memory at any one time. The monkey's attributes are slightly different from those of the *phys-object* element class. As with physical objects, the location of the monkey must be represented. Since the monkey must be able to move the ladder under the bananas, if necessary, it must be possible to represent what the monkey is holding. Limitations related to the fact that the monkey can hold only light objects will be expressed in the rules, since they cannot be specified as restrictions on the attribute values. An implication of the design decision not to represent attributes such as the size of physical objects is that size cannot be a factor in determining what the monkey can hold. The following descriptive attributes are needed for the monkey:

at Monkey's horizontal location, which by programmers' convention will be a Cartesian coordinate of the form "X-Y," where X and Y are integers between 1 and 10, inclusive.

on Monkey's vertical location, which can be "floor" or the value of the *name* attribute of some *phys-object* in working memory. If the latter value, the *at* attribute for the monkey should be the same as the *at* attribute for that *phys-object*.

holds Object being held by the monkey, which can be the value "nil" or the value of the *name* attribute of any *phys-object* with a value of "light" for the *weight* attribute. If the value is not "nil," that *phys-object* should have the same *at* attribute value as the monkey.

Here is the OPS5 declaration for this element class:

```
(literalize monkey  ; Representation for self-moving objects
    at              ; monkey's horizontal location,
                    ;  by programmers' convention, a Cartesian
                    ;  coordinate of the form "X-Y," where X
                    ;  and Y are integers between 1 and 10,
                    ;  inclusive
    on              ; monkey's vertical location, value can be
                    ;  "floor" or the value of the name
                    ;  attribute of some phys-object instance
                    ;  in working memory. If the latter
                    ;  value, the at attribute for the monkey
                    ;  must be the same as the at attribute
                    ;  for that phys-object
    holds           ; object being held by the monkey,
                    ;  one of: "nil" or
                    ;  the value of the name attribute of any
                    ;  "light" phys-object, which must have
                    ;  same at value as the monkey
)
```

3.4 ACTION IDENTIFICATION

The problem definition requires that the program produce a list of actions taken by the monkey to solve the problem. These actions include grabbing or dropping an object, moving an object to a specified horizontal location, walking to a specified horizontal location, and getting on and off objects. Each action requires that specific conditions called ***preconditions*** be met by the objects in the room. After the action has been completed, specific conditions called ***postconditions*** should be true of the objects in the room. The program should print that an action has been taken only if the preconditions are satisfied and if working memory is modified to reflect the postconditions.

In determining the proper preconditions for an action, we must resolve several questions of proximity and movement. How near, horizontally, to an object must the monkey be in order to grab it? How near, vertically, to an object must the monkey be in order to grab it? When an object is dropped by the monkey, where does it land? We have already determined that the monkey can grab the target from the ceiling only if the monkey is on the ladder. Can the monkey hold more than one thing at a time? Can the monkey get on or off a physical object while holding another physical object?

These decisions must be made and added to the *Decisions List*. The criterion we use for this sample problem is simplicity rather than generality of the solution. The following decisions are added to the list:

- The monkey must be at the exact same horizontal location as an object in order to grab it. "Near enough" is simply defined as "at the same place."
- The monkey must be on the ladder to grab a physical object on the ceiling.
- A physical object dropped by the monkey will be at the exact same horizontal location as the monkey, with vertical location "floor."
- The monkey can jump off a physical object while holding an object.
- The monkey cannot climb upon a physical object while holding an object.
- The monkey can hold only one physical object at a time.

The actions to be included in the output of the program, with the preconditions and postconditions, are shown in Fig. 3.1.

The actions as defined so far have simple preconditions that are checked against the *Decisions List* of Section 3.8 for accuracy. As problem solving proceeds, errors or potential problems may be uncovered. These errors or problems may lead to a change in the decisions. Until they are resolved, they are recorded on a *Problems List*, which is also summarized in Section 3.8.

As we check over the actions and the *Decisions List*, a very unnatural situation becomes apparent. In fact, the representation and actions allow many elements to be in the "same" horizontal space at once. This problem is hard to solve with the simple representation of horizontal location chosen. Rather than worry about it now, we record it as the first problem on the *Problems List*.

```
Grab O
    preconditions:
       monkey is not holding anything
       O is of element class phys-object
       O has a light weight
       monkey is at the same horizontal location as O
       either
           the monkey is on the floor and O is not on the ceiling
        or O is on the ceiling and the monkey is on the ladder
    postconditions:
       monkey is holding O
       O is not "on" anything

Drop O
    preconditions:
       monkey is holding O
       O is of element class phys-object
    postconditions:
       monkey is holding nothing
       O is on the floor

Move O to X-Y
    preconditions:
       monkey is on the floor
       monkey is holding O
       O is of element class phys-object not at X-Y
    postconditions:
       monkey is at horizontal location X-Y
       O is at horizontal location X-Y

Walk to X-Y
    preconditions:
       monkey is on the floor not at X-Y
    postconditions:
       monkey is at horizontal location X-Y

Jump onto the floor
    preconditions:
       monkey is not on the floor
    postconditions:
       monkey is on the floor

Climb onto O
    precondition:
       monkey is on the floor
       monkey does not hold anything
       O is of element class phys-object
       O is on the floor
    postcondition
       monkey is on O
```

FIGURE 3.1 Actions and Their Preconditions and Postconditions

The definition of actions and elements will be refined as a set of rules is developed and exercised. The initial set of rules acts as a prototype system with which the adequacy of the requirements analysis, as reflected in the element and action definitions, can be explored.

3.5 PROBLEM-SOLVING STRATEGY AND OBJECTS

The program to solve this problem will use a goal-driven strategy. While there are other problem-solving strategies, including other forms of goal-driven strategies, that can be implemented in a production system, the strategy that we present here seems most appropriate to the problem. The program will start with a goal to achieve some state, such as to be holding the bananas. Corresponding to each state is one or more actions, such as grabbing the bananas, that result in achieving that state. If all the preconditions necessary to carry out the action hold, then the action can be executed immediately. If some conditions necessary to carry out the action expressed in the initial goal are not met by the elements in working memory, then the program will set up ***subgoals*** or ***subproblems*** to establish those conditions. A subgoal in turn may require that other subgoals be established.

For example, if the goal is to hold the bananas and all the preconditions necessary to grab the bananas are satisfied, then the program should simply instruct the monkey to grab and change working memory to reflect the postconditions of the action. The plan for achieving the goal would have one step. The program output can simply be the instruction "Grab bananas." On the other hand, if all the preconditions are met except that the monkey is not *on* the ladder, then a subgoal to get "on" the *phys-object* whose *name* attribute has the value "ladder" should be set up. Satisfaction of this subgoal would now allow satisfaction of the original goal. Since we want to ensure the satisfaction of the subgoal before working on the original goal, we use the MEA conflict-resolution strategy.

The number of goals that might be active at any one time could be large, depending on how many of the preconditions for the original goal were not satisfied by the initial working memory configuration. Working memory provides the mechanism for recording the goals. Thus working memory will serve as the record of the state of the program's problem-solving efforts. To do this, we must create some new element classes.

An element class must be created for representing goals and subgoals. In fact, the program need not distinguish between the concept of goal and the concept of subgoal. Although the subgoal is a useful convention for humans, from a problem-solving point of view, a separate concept is not needed for subgoals so long as the relationships between goals are available. Thus a single element class will be defined for goals.

Next, we need to consider what attributes of a goal object are necessary to define the goals clearly. Since the goals have the purpose of effecting actions, we begin by classifying the actions of the monkey. The classification is based on which attributes of the *monkey* change when the action is carried out. The *grab* and *drop* actions both result in modifying the *holds* attribute of the monkey. They could be expressed as goals of type "holds." The *grab* version of the goal must indicate the physical object to be grabbed. The *drop* version must have as a result that the monkey *holds* "nil," i.e., nothing. The *jump* and *climb* actions both result in modifying the *on* attribute of the monkey. They could be expressed as goals of type "on." The *climb* version of the goal must indicate the physical object to be climbed upon. The *jump* version must express that the monkey is to be *on* the "floor." The *move* and *walk-to* actions both result in modifying the *at* attribute of the monkey. They could be expressed as goals of type "at." For the *move* version of the goal, a physical object to be moved must be indicated. For the *walk-to* version, there is no object to be moved.

To represent the goals discussed above, an element class called *goal* will be created as part of the program. Instances of this element class will record the goals as they are created by the program. To aid in tracing the process of problem solving, goals established in working memory will not be removed during problem solving even if they have been successfully accomplished. To indicate whether or not a goal has been satisfied, we add a *status* attribute to the *goal* element class. It will have the value "active" when a goal is first established and "satisfied" after it has been accomplished. Alternatively, different element classes could be defined for each goal type. If the problem were larger and the plans created were more complex, using different element classes might enhance the efficiency of the solution. Chapter 6 discusses this and other techniques for improving the efficiency of an OPS5 program. The decisions about goals are also added to the *Decisions List* summary of Section 3.8.

We define one element class with the following attributes:

```
(literalize goal
    status        ; goal's operational status:
                  ;  "active" or "satisfied"
    type          ; type of goal, one of: "holds," "on," "at"
    object-name   ; the name of the phys-object
                  ;  involved in the goal, if any
                  ; for "holds" type: the value of the name
                  ;  attribute of a phys-object in working
                  ;  memory whose weight attribute is "light,"
                  ;  or "nil," meaning drop object already held
```

```
                    ; for "on" type: "floor," or the value of the
                    ;  name attribute of the phys-object in
                    ;  working memory that the monkey is to
                    ;  climb on for "at" type: a value of "nil,"
                    ;  indicating the action to walk to,
                    ;  or the value of the name attribute of a
                    ;  phys-object in working memory, indicating
                    ;  that the phys-object is to be moved to the
                    ;  location given as the value of the to
                    ;  attribute.
    to              ; for goal types "holds" and "on": "nil"
                    ; for "at" type: the value expresses the
                    ;  goal location, and the programmers'
                    ;  convention is that the value is a string
                    ;  X-Y where X and Y are integers
                    ;  between 1 and 10 inclusive.
)
```

3.6 PROBLEM INPUT AND OUTPUT

The input required of the user is the initial room configuration and a statement of the goal of the problem-solving session. The initial room configuration is expressed as a collection of instances of the element class *phys-object*, a *monkey* element, and a *goal* element. It is assumed that the initial working memory configuration given is a legal configuration as described in Section 3.6.1. We will not discuss the rules necessary to enforce legal configurations, but they would be a good extension to the program.

3.6.1 LEGAL WORKING MEMORY CONFIGURATIONS

Not all initial situations describing a room configuration are legal. Although any set of *phys-object* elements and the *monkey* element in working memory at any specific time represent a configuration of the room, some configurations simply do not make sense. For example, having the couch "on" the ceiling disturbs most people's sense of gravity.

To simplify the creation of the rules for planning the monkey's actions, we identify a set of restrictions on room configurations. Each rule will be developed assuming that it finds and leaves the room configuration in working memory in a state satisfying the restrictions. The restrictions are both common-sense restrictions and design decisions that were made earlier and recorded on the *Decisions List*. The restrictions on a room configuration are as follows:

- There must be exactly one *monkey* working memory element, exactly one *phys-object* element whose *name* attribute has the value "ladder," and at least one instance of *goal* element.

- All restrictions on the values of attributes specified in the comments in the element-class declarations must be met by the elements in working memory.
- All restrictions on the values of attributes and the relation between instances specified on the *Decisions List* must be met by the elements in working memory.
- If more than one instance of the *goal* element class is in the initial working memory, it is assumed that the intention of the user is to have the goals satisfied sequentially. The program design does not handle conjunctions of goals.

3.6.2 SAMPLE INITIAL CONFIGURATIONS

An initial configuration of the room could be the following:

> The monkey is on the couch, holding the blanket at one location; the ladder and the bananas are at two other locations, both on the floor. The couch is on the floor. The couch is heavy, whereas the ladder and blanket are light. The goal is for the monkey to grab the bananas.

This configuration can be realized by executing the following **make** actions:

```
(make phys-object ↑name bananas ↑weight light ↑at 9-9
    ↑on ceiling)
(make phys-object ↑name couch   ↑weight heavy ↑at 7-7
    ↑on floor)
(make phys-object ↑name ladder  ↑weight light ↑at 4-3
    ↑on floor)
(make phys-object ↑name blanket ↑weight light ↑at 7-7)
(make monkey ↑at 7-7 ↑holds blanket ↑on couch)
(make goal   ↑status active ↑type holds ↑object-name bananas)
```

Note that all the attributes for the physical objects are given explicit values except the *on* attribute for the blanket. Since the blanket is being held by the monkey, the *on* attribute should be "nil." Any attributes not explicitly given a value in a **make** action will have value "nil."

3.6.3 TECHNIQUES FOR INITIALIZING WORKING MEMORY

Section 2.5 discussed several techniques for initializing working memory. These techniques are demonstrated using the top-level environment via a transcript of a session with OPS5. In testing a program, it is necessary to produce many different initial configurations quickly and efficiently. Each initial configuration is a test case for some aspect of the program. We will define special rules whose left-hand side identifies the test case and whose right-hand side contains the **make** actions to initialize working memory to a situation that will test the desired aspect of the program.

Before writing the test case rules, we must define a new element class. It will be called *testcase*. A *testcase* will be identified by the type of test and by the name of the test. The declaration in OPS5 for a *testcase* element class is:

```
(literalize testcase
    type  ; one of: "general," "holds," "at," "to"
          ;  This value indicates which goal(s) are
          ;  being tested by the testcase
    name  ; unique for each testcase
          ;  a descriptive string to indicate which rules
          ;  within the goal category are being tested
)
```

Examples of the three methods for initializing working memory are given in an annotated transcript of an OPS5 session. This section will also demonstrate the use of functions that allow the examination of working memory and creation of initial working memory elements.

The following transcript uses our standard notational conventions:

- All user input is underlined.
- All commentary on the transcript begins on a new line, indented with the comment character ";" as the first character in the line.

```
 ; NOTE: This transcript was obtained using the FRANZLISP
 ;  version of OPS5. In other implementations, the prompts
 ;  and top level functions may have different names. Check
 ;  your user's manual for the equivalent function/command
 ;  names.
% ops5
 ; The "%" is the system-level prompt.
 ; The declarations can either be entered directly or loaded
 ;  from a previously created file. The declarations are in a
 ;  file called "Monkey.dec." The load command allows the
 ;  user to load files containing OPS5 code.
 ; Declarations must be loaded first.

-> (load 'Monkey.dec)
t
 ; Production memory is loaded with the rules by loading a
 ;  file containing them.

-> (load 'Monkey.rul)
***************t
```

```
; Whenever production memory is loaded, OPS5 acknowledges
;  the processing of a rule by printing an asterisk for each
;  rule correctly loaded. A "t" is printed after the file
;  has been completely loaded.
; The next step is to load working memory with a legal room
;  configuration. This cannot be done before a rule is
;  loaded.
; We first illustrate how elements can be added to working
;  memory with the make action. The action is implemented as
;  a FRANZLISP function. As a function, it returns the value
;  "nil" and this value is printed in the output stream.
; We check the results of the command by requesting a
;  working memory dump with the (wm) command.

-> (make phys-object ↑name bananas ↑weight light
        ↑at 9-9 ↑on ceiling)
nil
-> (make phys-object ↑name couch ↑weight heavy
        ↑at 7-7 ↑on floor)
nil
-> (make phys-object ↑name ladder ↑weight light ↑at 4-3
        ↑on floor)
nil
-> (make phys-object ↑name blanket ↑weight light ↑at 7-7)
nil
-> (make monkey ↑at 7-7 ↑holds blanket ↑on couch)
nil
-> (wm)

1:  (phys-object ↑at 9-9  ↑on ceiling  ↑name bananas
↑weight light)
2:  (phys-object ↑at 7-7  ↑on floor  ↑name couch
↑weight heavy)
3:  (phys-object ↑at 4-3  ↑on floor  ↑name ladder
↑weight light)
4:  (phys-object ↑at 7-7  ↑name blanket  ↑weight light)
5:  (monkey   ↑at 7-7  ↑on couch  ↑holds blanket)nil

; The command (wm) returns the value "nil" as seen after
;  the last working memory element.
; Note that attributes with the value "nil" are not printed.
; Note also that each element is preceded by a "time tag."
;  This "time tag" is supplied by the inference engine and
;  indicates the "recency" of working memory elements. The
;  greater the number, the more recently the element was
;  added to working memory.
; Suppose a new configuration is desired, with the monkey
;  on the couch. By using the remove action, elements 4 and
;  5 can be removed. Then a new monkey element can be added
;  with the desired property:
```

```
-> (remove 4 5)
nil
-> (make monkey ↑at 7-7 ↑on couch)
nil
  ; Working memory reflects the change. Note the time tag on
  ;  monkey.

-> (wm)

1: (phys-object  ↑at 9-9  ↑on ceiling  ↑name bananas
↑weight light)
2: (phys-object  ↑at 7-7  ↑on floor  ↑name couch
↑weight heavy)
3: (phys-object  ↑at 4-3  ↑on floor  ↑name ladder
↑weight light)
8: (monkey  ↑at 7-7    ↑on couch)nil

  ; Complete working memory initialization by creating a goal.
-> (make goal ↑status active ↑type holds
        ↑object-name bananas)
nil
-> (wm)
1: (phys-object  ↑at 9-9  ↑on ceiling  ↑name bananas
↑weight light)
2: (phys-object  ↑at 7-7  ↑on floor  ↑name couch
↑weight heavy)
3: (phys-object  ↑at 4-3  ↑on floor  ↑name ladder
↑weight light)
8: (monkey  ↑at 7-7    ↑on couch)
9: (goal    ↑status active  ↑type holds
↑object-name bananas)nil

  ; It was lucky the typist was so good. This is a tedious
  ;  and error-prone way to load working memory.
  ; The other two methods described are easier.
  ; So we empty working memory with the remove action
  ;  in order to examine another initialization method.
-> (remove *)
nil
-> (wm)
nil

  ; The file Sample.Tst contains a sequence of make action
  ;  calls to initialize working memory.
  ; Load the file with the Lisp load command:

-> (load Sample.Tst)
Error: Unbound Variable: Sample.Tst
<1>:
  ; The quote mark was inadvertently forgotten: a common
```

```
  ;  mistake. Return to the top level with a control D and try
  ;  again. This comment applies to LISP implementations only.
-> (load 'Sample.Tst)
t
-> (wm)
15: (phys-object  ↑at 9-9  ↑on ceiling ↑name bananas
↑weight light)
16: (phys-object  ↑at 7-7  ↑on floor  ↑name couch
↑weight heavy)
17: (phys-object  ↑at 4-3  ↑on floor   ↑name ladder
↑weight light)
18: (phys-object  ↑at 7-7  ↑name blanket    ↑weight light)
19: (monkey    ↑at 7-7    ↑on couch    ↑holds blanket)
20: (goal    ↑status active    ↑type holds
↑object-name bananas)nil
  ; Again, working memory is emptied.
-> (remove *)
nil

  ; The file Rule.Tst contains a single rule whose right-hand
  ;  side contains the make action calls to initialize working
  ;  memory. The left-hand side is a condition matching
  ;  a test case of type "general" whose name, for
  ;  simplicity, is "start."

-> (load 'Rule.Tst)
*t
  ; Now we use a single make action to put an instance of
  ;  testcase in working memory. This instance will trigger
  ;  the test.

-> (make testcase ↑type general ↑name start)
nil
  ; Let's check to see if this element is indeed the trigger
  ;  for the rule by printing the conflict set. To do this we
  ;  use the (cs) command. This command will print out the
  ;  name of the rules for all instantiations in the conflict
  ;  set. Then it prints the name of the dominating, or
  ;  selected, rule.

-> (cs)

Test::General:Start
(Test::General:Start dominates)

  ; The initialization rule does match working memory and will
  ;  be selected. The run command instructs the inference
  ;  engine to go ahead and interpret the rule. The run
  ;  command takes an optional integer argument to indicate
  ;  how many cycles to continue. In this case, we want to
  ;  fire just the one rule.
```

```
-> (run 1)

1. Test::General:Start 27
***break***
  ; The output is an integer followed by a period, 1.,
  ;  indicating that this is the first rule fired in this
  ;  session with OPS5, followed by the name of the rule that
  ;  was fired, Test::General:Start, followed by the time
  ;  tag(s) (recency number) of the element(s) of working
  ;  memory that matched the condition of the rule, 27.
  ; Recency numbers are given in a strictly increasing order.
  ;  However, when working memory is printed, you will find
  ;  some values are skipped.
  ; The ***break*** message indicates the execution was
  ;  stopped artificially by some user restriction.
  ; Now print working memory to be certain it has been
  ;  properly initialized.

-> (wm)

29:(phys-object  ↑at 7-7  ↑name blanket    ↑weight light)
30:(phys-object  ↑at 9-9  ↑on ceiling  ↑name bananas
↑weight light)
31:(phys-object  ↑at 4-3  ↑on floor    ↑name ladder
↑weight light)
32:(phys-object  ↑at 7-7  ↑on floor    ↑name couch
↑weight heavy)
28:(monkey    ↑at 7-7  ↑on couch    ↑holds blanket)
32:(goal    ↑status active    ↑type holds
↑object-name bananas)
27:(testcase ↑type general ↑name start)nil

  ; And the system is ready to go.
```

3.6.4 PROGRAM OUTPUT

We would like the program to print a sequence of commands that will instruct the monkey to grab the bananas. These instructions include the following command types:

- Jump onto the floor
- Walk to LOCATION
- Climb onto OBJECT
- Grab OBJECT
- Drop OBJECT
- Move OBJECT to LOCATION

where LOCATION is represented by a valid Cartesian coordinate pair for the room and OBJECT is the value of the *name* attribute of an instance of element class *phys-object*.

In addition, the program should print a few helpful messages if the initial goal is already achieved, and a congratulations message when all the active goals are satisfied. The messages include the following types:

- Monkey is already on OBJECT
- OBJECT is already being held
- The object OBJECT is already at LOCATION
- Monkey is already at LOCATION
- CONGRATULATIONS there are no active goals
- IMPOSSIBLE the goal GOAL cannot be solved

We have decided that the program being designed will not check for violations of the legal working memory restrictions, nor will it give the user any interactive help in establishing the initial working memory configuration. The decision to so restrict the program is added to the *Decisions List* (Section 3.8).

3.7 RULE IDENTIFICATION

The strategy we use for developing rules is based on examining the goals to be achieved and then designing rules to carry out the necessary actions to satisfy the goals or to set up subgoals. Although the specific problem posed in this chapter is to get the monkey to hold the bananas, the same general methodology is used to develop rules for all goals, and it is easier to start with the simpler goals. After describing our design methodology, we will start rule development with the goal type "on."

For each action related to a goal, a set of rules, termed a ***rule cluster,*** is developed. Each of the three goal types determined in Section 3.5 will be chosen, in turn, to generate a rule cluster related to the goal type. After the rule cluster for a goal type is created, the interactions of that rule cluster with other clusters will be examined. Each set of rules will be integrated into the complete set by the development of initial configurations to exhaustively test the rules.

The strategy for maintaining a legal working memory configuration is to assume that the initial configuration of working memory is a legal configuration and maintain the legality of the configuration represented with each rule. Thus each rule should be checked as it is developed to see if it preserves legality:

```
precondition: {configuration of working memory is legal}
  RULE X FIRES
postcondition: {configuration of working memory is legal}
```

A definite procedure will be used to develop the rule cluster for each goal. The procedure assumes that a general model for the problem solution has been defined, including the definitions of objects and actions. For example, Fig. 3.1 gives the action definitions for the monkey-and-bananas problem. This procedure will produce a good first attempt at creating a prototype solution to the given problem.

The procedure gives a method for translating the action descriptions into rules. The preconditions will become condition elements in the rules, and the postconditions will be realized by actions in the rules. The preconditions used to define the actions include conditions to ensure that the action can be carried out and conditions to ensure that the results of the action do not already exist. For example, the *Walk to X-Y* action has a condition that the monkey is on the floor. This is necessary in order to carry out the action. The condition that the monkey is not at X-Y ensures that the results of the action are not already present. The steps in the procedure are shown in Fig. 3.2.

As an example of steps 2 and 3 in this figure, consider the action *Walk to X-Y*. The base rule will be

```
IF   there is an active "at" goal for the monkey to be at X-Y
 and the monkey is on the floor not at X-Y
THEN write "walk to X-Y"
 and modify the monkey's horizontal location to "X-Y"
```

An example of removing a precondition for step 7 is to suppose that the monkey is not on the floor.

The modified rule would be

```
IF   there is an active "at" goal for the monkey to be at X-Y
 and the monkey is not on the floor
THEN set up a goal to get the monkey on the floor
```

Note that if the monkey is not on the floor, it doesn't matter where the monkey is horizontally.

Not all conditions can be removed, of course. It makes no sense to remove the goal to be achieved, and some conditions (such as that the weight of an object be light) cannot be changed by any action of the monkey.

The condition that is relaxed may seem easy to satisfy directly by carrying out an action rather than by setting up a subgoal. Continuing with our previous example, we might be tempted to write

```
IF   there is an active "at" goal for the monkey to be at X-Y
 and the monkey is not on the floor
THEN write "Jump onto floor"
 and write "Walk to X-Y"
 and modify the monkey's horizontal location to be "X-Y"
 and modify the monkey's vertical location to be floor
```

1. Choose an action related directly to the goal. If all actions have been implemented, then the goal is complete.
2. Create an English version of a left-hand side for a rule that includes one condition element related to the goal or action and a condition element for each of the preconditions defined for the action. (See Section 3.4 for the actions in our problem.)
3. Create an English version of a right-hand side for the rule. The right-hand side should include a statement to write a message that the action has been accomplished (one of the output statement types defined in Section 3.6.4). Postconditions can be achieved by removing, adding, and modifying the appropriate elements of working memory. The goal element should be removed or marked as satisfied.
4. Check to be certain that the rule does leave working memory in a legal configuration.
5. Check the interactions of the rule with already existing rules for this goal type, modifying as necessary.
6. Name the rule and translate it into OPS5. The translation should use the **write** action to implement writing a message indicating that an action has been performed.
7. The rule conditions now have three purposes: (a) specifying the goal, (b) ensuring that the action can now be carried out, and (c) ensuring that the results of the action do not already exist. Choose a condition of purpose (b), create a new condition element specifying that the chosen condition is not satisfied, and use this in a new rule in place of the old condition. Check to see whether or not any other conditions need to be modified as a result (they may have become superfluous or incorrect). Create a new RHS that established a subgoal of satisfying the chosen condition. Write the English version of the new rule.
8. If step 7 results in a new rule, go to step 4; otherwise create a rule by modifying the condition of type (c). This rule's LHS should test for all the conditions resulting from carrying out the goal action. The RHS of the rule should print a warning message that a goal is already satisfied and remove the goal or mark it as satisfied. Check this rule with steps 4, 5, and 6. Then go to step 1.

FIGURE 3.2 Steps in Designing Rules for One Goal

As a matter of good software-engineering practice, the rule writer should resist the temptation to short cut the subgoal mechanism. By putting all instances of carrying out an action in one place rather than several, the programmer is assured that the exact message will be printed in all cases and that the action will be carried out consistently. If the implementation details are spread around in multiple rules, there is more opportunity for error and modification is more difficult. Furthermore, when there are multiple preconditions, the programmer who falls into this habit may be tempted to try to write rules to solve all possible combinations of removed preconditions directly. Such a strategy is guaranteed to produce a much larger and less comprehensible set of rules, which will be subject to multiple bugs.

3.7.1 TESTING THE RULES

Rules should be verified as they are developed. As each rule is developed, the procedure set forth in Fig. 3.2 will check for consistency with the rule cluster for the particular goal. A rule cluster is complete if it includes rules to handle all the working memory configurations related to the preconditions of the actions for the goal of the cluster. Completeness of rules is also checked in step 7 of the Fig. 3.2 procedure. If the actions were well defined in terms of the preconditions and postconditions, the rule cluster should be internally consistent and complete. To test this consistency and completeness, a set of initial working memory configurations should be developed and run in conjunction with the rules as each rule cluster is completed. The entire verification process, including program execution, will identify memory configurations that are needed but cannot be reached, memory configurations that can be reached but do not lead to the goal, and other anomalies of rule behavior. This testing technique will be demonstrated as rules for the sample problem are developed.

3.7.2 THE GOAL TYPE "ON"

The first goal type we consider is the type "on." The goal type "on" is closely related to the actions *Jump onto the floor* and *Climb onto O*.

The Action *Jump*

The problem-solving effort will be stymied if the monkey is on an object and cannot get off to move around and solve the problem. So the first rule developed will allow the monkey to jump onto the floor (step 1). *Jump onto the floor* was specified by

```
preconditions:
   monkey is not on the floor
postconditions:
   monkey is on the floor
```

Two conditions must be created for the left-hand side: one relating to the *goal* and one relating to the single precondition for the action. Phrasing the conditions in English (step 2) results in the left-hand side:

```
IF   there is an "active" goal of "on floor"
 and the monkey is not on the "floor"
```

Three actions are needed to describe the completion of the action of jumping to the floor. Phrasing these actions in English results in the right-hand side (step 3):

```
THEN write "Jump onto the floor"
 and modify the on attribute of the monkey to be "floor"
 and modify the "on floor" goal to "satisfied"
```

There are no existing rules in this cluster to check for consistency (step 5). The rule clearly retains a legal room configuration (step 4). Here we note that both the monkey and the object it was previously "on" are now "at" precisely the same location: the floor. We have two objects in the same place. However, we have chosen to ignore this problem (see *Problems List*, Section 3.8). So a meaningful name for the rule is chosen, `On::Floor`, and the rule is translated into OPS5 (step 6). The name is chosen to first reflect the goal type, "on." The second word indicates which action within that goal is being treated by the rule, in this case "floor." The first letter of each word is capitalized and the words are separated with two colons. The resulting name is `On::Floor`.

Coding the first condition (there is an "active" *goal* "on floor") into OPS5 is quite straightforward:

```
(goal ↑status active ↑type on ↑object floor)
```

We will label each condition of the left-hand side with an element variable for easy reference in the right-hand side.

```
{(goal ↑status active ↑type on ↑object floor)      <goal>}
```

In some rules, labels may be left off conditions when the matched object is not referenced later in the rule.

There are two ways to code the "monkey is not on the floor" statement. One way would be to negate the clause that "there is a monkey on the floor." This would lead to the OPS5 statement

```
- (monkey ↑on floor)
```

which would match working memory in just the case that there were no instances of the monkey element class with *on* attribute of "floor." However, in order to change the "on" attribute of the monkey in the left-hand side of the rule, a specific monkey must be matched. The knowledge that no monkey exists that satisfies a condition will not help. Thus the English statement is translated to mean "there is a monkey on some object other than the floor." In OPS5 this would be coded as

```
{(monkey ↑on <> floor) <monkey>}
```

During execution of the program, the condition matches any instances of the monkey element class not on the floor. If the rule is selected and fired, the element variable <monkey> will be bound to the matched monkey element in working memory. The element variable is now available for use in the right-hand side of the rule. The rule in OPS5 is

```
(p On::Floor
   {(goal ↑status active ↑type on ↑object floor)        <goal>}
   {(monkey ↑on <> floor)                                <monkey>}
-->
   (write    (crlf) (crlf) Jump onto the floor (crlf))
   (modify   <monkey> ↑on floor)
   (modify   <goal>   ↑status satisfied))
```

Modifying any of the preconditions would change the action type (if the *object* that the monkey was to be *on* were changed) or create a situation in which the action is already achieved. Later in this section we'll consider changing the action type. We consider the rule that fires when the goal of being on the floor is already satisfied (step 8). The change in the preconditions of the previous rule is that the monkey is on the floor. The postcondition will print an error message and mark the goal satisfied. The rule in English is:

```
IF   there is a goal for the monkey to be on the floor
 and the monkey is already on the floor
THEN write that the monkey is already on floor
 and modify the goal to indicate it is satisfied
```

This rule will never be in the conflict set with the rule `On::Floor` because their second conditions are mutually exclusive. The rule in OPS5 is

```
(p On::Floor:Satisfied
   {(goal ↑status active ↑type on ↑object floor)        <goal>}
   {(monkey ↑on floor)                                   <monkey>}
-->
   (write    (crlf) (crlf) monkey is already on floor (crlf))
   (modify   <goal>   ↑status satisfied))
```

There are no additional rules to develop for this action.

We now proceed to develop test cases for the rule cluster just developed.

Testing the Rule On::Floor

The initial working memory configuration that is created to test the rule should have an active goal of *type* "on" with *object-name* "floor." There should be a monkey on some object other than the floor. The monkey could be holding something or not. Since the rule conditions do not mention a value for the *holds* attribute, its value is not critical to this rule. To make the initial working memory configuration legal, there must be a ladder in the room. The actions needed to initialize the room are these:

```
(make phys-object ↑name ladder ↑on floor ↑at 5-7
    ↑weight light)
(make monkey ↑on ladder ↑at 5-7)
(make goal ↑status active ↑type on ↑object-name floor))
```

The working memory configuration created by these actions is a legal configuration. There is exactly one ladder and one monkey, and the attributes satisfy the restrictions placed on them. There is a goal.

The rule `On::Floor`'s left-hand side should match this working memory configuration. Since the ultimate goal is to create a file with test cases in it, a rule will be created with this set of actions as the right-hand side. The type of test case being created is a test case for the "on" goal. The specific version of this goal being tested is "on floor." Therefore the rule will be named `Test::On:Floor`. The LHS will contain one condition element, a *testcase*.

```
(p Test::On:Floor
   (testcase ↑type on ↑name floor)
-->
   (make phys-object ↑name ladder ↑on floor ↑at 5-7
       ↑weight light)
   (make monkey ↑on ladder ↑at 5-7)
   (make goal ↑status active ↑type on ↑object-name floor))
```

The following transcript of a session with OPS5 demonstrates the use of several OPS5 run-time support tools to test the rule. The rule `On::Floor` is in a file called "Monkey.rul"; the test rule `Test::On:Floor` is in a file called "Monkey.tst." The initial part of the session is similar to the example of creating initial working memory conditions and will not be commented.

```
% ops5
-> (load 'Monkey.dec)
t
-> (load 'Monkey.rul)
*t
   ; Whenever production memory is loaded, OPS5 acknowledges
   ;  the processing of a rule by printing an asterisk. The
   ;  rule can be printed using the pm function.
-> (pm On::Floor)
```

```
(p On::Floor
   {(goal ↑status active ↑type on ↑object-name floor) <goal>}
   {(monkey ↑on <> floor) <monkey>}
-->
    (write (crlf) (crlf) Jump onto the floor (crlf))
    (modify <monkey> ↑on floor)
    (modify <goal> ↑status satisfied))
nil

    ; The test rule is loaded to complete production memory
    ;  for this test.

-> (load 'Monkey.tst)
*t

    ; The make action is used at the top level to create a
    ;  working memory element "testcase" to trigger the
    ;  test rule.

-> (make testcase ↑type on ↑name floor)
nil

-> (wm)

1: (testcase ↑type on ↑name floor)nil

-> (cs)

Test::On:Floor
(Test::On:Floor dominates)

    ; The conflict set contains the instantiations of rules
    ;  that match the current working memory configuration.
    ; As expected, the test rule matches working memory.
    ; To fire the rules, the run command is given an
    ;  integer argument restricting the number of rules to be
    ;  fired.

-> (run 1)

1. Test::On:Floor 1
***break***

    ; The first integer indicates that Test::On:Floor is the
    ;  first rule fired. The final integers indicate the
    ;  working memory elements matched by the rule's
    ;  conditions. In this case, element 1 matched the first
    ;  condition of the rule.
    ; Working memory should now contain a legal room
    ;  configuration.

-> (wm)

1: (testcase ↑type on ↑name floor)
2: (phys-object ↑at 5-7  ↑on floor ↑name ladder
↑weight light)
```

```
3: (monkey    ↑at 5-7    ↑on ladder)
4: (goal  ↑status active  ↑type on  ↑object-name  floor)nil

    ; Finally, the rule can be tested.
    ; First, do the conditions match?

-> (cs)

On::Floor
(On::Floor dominates)

    ; Now for the firing of the rule.

-> (run 1)

2. On::Floor 4 3

Jump onto the floor

***break***

    ; Working memory elements 4 and 3 were matched by
    ;  conditions 1 and 2, respectively, of the rule
    ;  On::Floor.
    ; Inspection of working memory shows that these two
    ;  elements have been deleted and replaced with the
    ;  modified elements, now numbered 6 and 8 respectively.

-> (wm)

1: (testcase ↑type on ↑name floor)
2: (phys-object ↑at 5-7 ↑on floor ↑name ladder ↑weight light)
6: (monkey ↑at 5-7 ↑on floor)
8: (goal ↑status satisfied ↑type on    ↑object-name floor)nil
    ; At this point, no rule should match working memory.
    ; The rule Test::On:Floor could match element 1.
    ; However, since it has already matched and been fired
    ;  with that instantiation, OPS5 does not record a match.
    ; OPS5 will not fire the same instantiation twice.

-> (cs)

(nil dominates)

-> (run)
    ; Since no instantiations are in the conflict set, the
    ;  final statistics will be printed.
end -- no production true
 2 productions 212 // 12 nodes)
 2 firings (9 rhs actions)
 3 mean working memory size (5 maximum)
 1 mean conflict set size (1 maximum)
 1 mean token memory size (2 maximum)
nil
-> (exit)
```

The testing of the rule has not been exhaustive. As with traditional programs, exhaustive testing is rarely feasible or desirable with production-system programs.

The Action *Climb onto Phys-Object*

The next action considered for the "on" goal is *Climb onto O*. The specifications for this action are

```
precondition:
   monkey is on the floor
   monkey does not hold anything
   O is of element class phys-object
   O is on the floor
postcondition:
   monkey is on O
```

In trying to create a rule with all these conditions specified, we encounter the problem of more than one object in one place at one time. Is this precondition really right? The solution to Exercise 3-3 indicates that the precondition did not mention the horizontal locations of the monkey and the object O. This must be included before the rule can be developed.

Another problem is the insistence that the monkey be on the floor. Our representation allows two objects to be at the same place at the same time. If the monkey is "on" some other object at this horizontal location, couldn't the monkey simply move to be on O? The condition that the monkey be on the floor is overly restrictive. We need to know only that the monkey is not on O. We add a note to the *Problems List* that the rule cluster for *Climb onto O* is affected by the two-objects-in-one-place problem and change the precondition for this action.

The new description of the action is

```
precondition:
   monkey does not hold anything
   monkey is not on O
   O is of element class phys-object
   O is on the floor
   monkey and O are at the same horizontal location
postcondition:
   monkey is on O
```

Combining steps 2 and 3 of the rule development procedure, the rule can be stated in English as follows:

```
IF   there is an active goal to be on an object O
 and the object O is at location p on the floor
 and the monkey is at location p, holding nothing, not on O
```

```
THEN write "Climb onto O"
 and modify the monkey to indicate it is on object O
 and modify the goal to be satisfied.
```

The new rule will not interact with the previous rule, `On::Floor`, which specifically related to the goal of being on the floor. The two rules will not match the same instance of a goal element.

Since O must be a *phys-object* element, it cannot be the floor or the ceiling. However, if object O is not on the floor, the rule will not allow the monkey to climb onto it. There is no design decision concerning the situation. We add a note to the *Problems List* that we are restricting the monkey to *Climb onto* only objects that are on the floor. This may need to be addressed later if the prototype program cannot plan properly. The translated, named rule is

```
(p On::Phys-Object
   {(goal ↑status active ↑type on ↑object-name <o>)      <goal>}
   {(phys-object ↑name <o> ↑at <p> ↑on floor)            <object>}
   {(monkey ↑at <p> ↑holds nil ↑on <> <o>)                <monkey>}
-->
   (write    (crlf) (crlf) Climb onto <o> (crlf))
   (modify   <monkey>   ↑on <o>)
   (modify   <goal>     ↑status satisfied))
```

Now, to develop other rules for this action (step 7), you must examine the conditions one at a time and determine the subgoals and intermediate actions that will be generated when the conditions are not met. One way to do this is to consider the time sequence in which the preconditions should be met. If the monkey is at the right location but is holding something, then the monkey must drop the held object in order to satisfy the rule. This is the condition we change to create the next rule. The rule will remove the precondition of holding nothing and will have a single action, establishing a new goal to hold nothing. We note that the monkey might be holding the object it is to climb on. So we relax the condition that the object is on the floor.

The monkey always has a value for all of the attributes. If the monkey does not have the name of a physical object for the *holds* attribute, the value will be "nil." While we think of "nil" as nothing, it is in fact an actual value for the attribute. In creating the English version of the LHS, we must be careful to indicate that whatever the monkey is holding is not "nil."

The English description of the rule is

```
IF   there is an active goal to be on an object, o1
 and the object o1 is at location p
 and the monkey is at location p holding some object, not nil
THEN make a goal to hold nothing
```

The new rule does not interact with the rule `On::Floor` for reasons similar to those for the rule `On::Phys-Object`. The last condition of the new rule conflicts with the last condition of the rule `On::Phys-Object`. Since there can be only one instance of element class *monkey* in working memory at any time, the two rules will never be in the same conflict set if programmed as indicated. The new rule will leave the room in a legal configuration, as defined by working memory, since the only change is to add a well-defined goal. The translated rule is

```
(p On::Phys-Object:Holds
   (goal ↑status active ↑type on ↑object-name <o1>)
   (phys-object ↑name <o1> ↑at <p>)
   (monkey ↑at <p> ↑holds <> nil)
-->
   (make goal ↑status active ↑type holds ↑object-name nil))
```

The next condition to relax stipulates that the monkey be at the same location as the object to be climbed on. In this case, a subgoal is generated to walk to the location of the target. This rule will not match when the rules `On::Phys-Object` and `On::Phys-Object:Holds` match, because the location of the monkey differs. The English version of the new rule would be

```
IF   the goal "on object o1" is active
 and the object o1 is at location p1 on the floor
 and the monkey is not at p1
THEN create a new goal to walk to location p1
```

There is a reason for not being specific about the monkey other than problems with the location. The subgoal of walking to location p1 is desirable so long as the monkey is not at p1. Whether or not the monkey is holding anything, or is on another object, is not important in setting up this subgoal.

The rule does not change the room configuration. It translates to

```
(p On::Phys-Object:At-Monkey
   (goal ↑status active ↑type on ↑object-name <o1>)
   (phys-object ↑name <o1> ↑at <p1> ↑on floor)
   (monkey ↑at <> <p1>)
-->
   (make goal  ↑status active  ↑type at  ↑to <p1>))
```

There are no further conditions to relax or to remove in developing the action under consideration.

This set of four rules constitutes all the rules necessary to carry out the goal of type *on*. One more rule is added to the set to give the user a message when a goal of this type is established and working memory indicates that the goal is already met. The English version of the rule will be as follows:

```
IF   the goal "on object o1" is active
 and the object o1 is at p1 on the floor
 and the monkey is at p1 on object o1
THEN write a message that monkey is already on o1
 and modify the goal to indicate it is satisfied
```

The other rules relating to the *Climb onto* goal do specify that at least one of the conditions of this rule are not met by working memory. Therefore this rule will not conflict with others in the cluster. The OPS5 translation of the rule is

```
(p On::Phys-Object:Satisfied
   {(goal ↑status active ↑type on ↑object-name <o1>)    <goal>}
   {(phys-object ↑name <o1> ↑at <p1> ↑on floor)       <object>}
   {(monkey ↑at <p1> ↑on <o1>)                        <monkey>}
-->
   (write (crlf) (crlf) monkey is already on <o1>)
   (modify <goal> ↑status satisfied))
```

It would be desirable to combine this rule with the `On::Floor:Satisfied` rule and produce one rule to fire in both situations. Exploring this possibility is left as an exercise.

3.7.3 TESTING THE GOAL TYPE "ON"

An analysis of the conditions of the rules developed suggests that at least one test rule per program rule will be needed. Since rules have not been developed for the "at" and "holds" clusters, there can be no chain of rule firing to test the "on" cluster. A separate test rule is therefore necessary for each program rule.

```
; Test situation for Test::On:Phys-Object
;  trigger: testcase type is "on," name is "phys-object"
;  The monkey is on the floor, at the same location as
;   the ladder The goal is to get on the ladder.
;
;
; Rules expected to fire:
;  On::Phys-Object

(p Test::On:Phys-Object
   (testcase ↑type on ↑name phys-object)
-->
   (make phys-object ↑name ladder ↑on floor ↑at 5-5
       ↑weight light)
   (make monkey ↑at 5-5 ↑on floor)
   (make goal ↑status active ↑type on ↑object-name ladder))
```

```
; Test situation for Test::On:Phys-Object:Holds
;  trigger: testcase type is "on," name is "phys-object-holds"
;  The monkey is on the floor, at the same location as the
;   ladder holding the ladder. The goal is to get on the
;   ladder.
;
; Rules expected to fire:
;  On::Phys-Object:Holds       Set up goal to hold nothing
;
;     Note that when the program is finished, other rules
;      will fire.

(p Test::On:Phys-Object:Holds
   (testcase ↑type on ↑name phys-object-holds)
-->
   (make phys-object ↑name ladder ↑at 5-5 ↑weight light)
   (make monkey ↑at 5-5 ↑holds ladder ↑on floor)
   (make goal ↑status active ↑type on ↑object-name ladder))

; Test situation for Test::On:Phys-Object:At-Monkey
;  trigger: testcase type is "on," name is
;   "phys-object:at-monkey"
;  The monkey is on the floor, at a different location from
;   the ladder. The goal is to get on ladder.
;
; Rules expected to fire:
;  On::Phys-Object:At-Monkey   Set up goal to be at the ladder

(p Test::On:Phys-Object:At-Monkey
   (testcase ↑type on ↑name phys-object:at-monkey)
-->
   (make phys-object ↑name ladder ↑at 6-5 ↑on floor
       ↑weight light)
   (make monkey ↑at 3-3 ↑on floor)
   (make goal ↑status active ↑type on ↑object-name ladder))

; Test situation for Test::On:Phys-Object:Satisfied
;  trigger: testcase type is "on," name is
;   "phys-object-satisfied"
;  The monkey is on the ladder and the goal is to be on the
;   ladder.
;
; Rules expected to fire:
;  On::Phys-Object:Satisfied   Goal is satisfied by working
;  memory
(p Test::On:Phys-Object:Satisfied
   (testcase ↑type on ↑name phys-object-satisfied)
-->
   (make phys-object ↑name ladder ↑at 6-5 ↑on floor
       ↑weight light)
   (make monkey ↑at 6-5 ↑on ladder)
   (make goal ↑status active ↑type on ↑object-name ladder))
```

3.7.4 THE GOAL TYPE "HOLDS"

The goal type "holds" is satisfied by the actions *Grab O* and *Drop O*. The *Drop O* action is least complicated and will be developed first. Rules are developed in the next two sections for these actions. Not shown here, but included in the complete program in the appendix, are rules that print warning messages if a goal is established to create a situation that is already satisfied by working memory.

The Action *Drop*

The specification for the action is

```
Drop O
   preconditions
      monkey is holding O
      O is of element class phys-object
   postconditions:
      monkey is holding nothing
      O is on the floor
```

The rule requires that we make certain that the object held by the monkey is not "nil." Otherwise, the English version is straightforward:

```
IF   the goal "holds nothing" is active
 and the monkey is holding object o1, not nil
THEN write a message Drop o1
 and modify the goal to indicate it is satisfied
 and modify the monkey to show it holds nothing
 and modify o1 to show it is on the floor
```

This rule will certainly leave working memory in a legal configuration. Looking at the rule, we notice that the action part of the rule does not specify a horizontal location for the object o1 when it is dropped. This is consistent with item 13 on the *Decisions List* (Section 3.8), which states that whenever an object changes location, the object's *at* value must be updated. The rule does not interact with any other rule developed as this is the first rule for the goal type "holds." The translated version of the rule is

```
(p Holds::nil
   {(goal ↑status active ↑type holds ↑object-name nil) <goal>}
   {(monkey ↑at <p> ↑holds {<o1> <> nil})              <monkey>}
   {(phys-object ↑name <o1> )                          <object>}
-->
   (write    (crlf) (crlf) Drop <o1> (crlf))
   (modify   <goal>    ↑status satisfied)]
   (modify   <monkey>  ↑holds nil)
   (modify   <object>  ↑on floor))
```

It is not really necessary in the second condition to have the phrase

<o1> <> nil,

since <o1> cannot be "nil" and be the name of a physical object. The only condition that could be relaxed is the condition that the monkey is holding a physical object. The action of *Grab* indicates this condition.

The Action *Grab Object*

The specification for the action is

```
Grab O
   preconditions:
      monkey is not holding anything
      O is of element class phys-object
      O has a light weight
      monkey is at the same horizontal location as O
      either
       the monkey is on the floor and
        O is not on the ceiling
      or O is on the ceiling
       and the monkey is on the ladder
   postconditions:
      monkey is holding O
      O is not "on" anything
```

Because of the disjunction in the fifth condition, the action is split into two actions: *Grab O from ceiling* and *Grab O* (*O* not on ceiling assumed). The main reason for doing this is that in OPS5 it is impossible to express a disjunction of conditions in the LHS.

Action *Grab O from Ceiling*

When an object is on the ceiling, this is the English version of the grabbing-action rule's left-hand side:

```
there is an active goal to "hold" some object O
the object O is light, on the ceiling and at location p
the ladder is on the floor and at location p
the monkey is holding nothing and on the ladder
```

The OPS5 translation is direct:

```
{(goal ↑status active ↑type holds ↑object-name <o1> )   <goal>}
{(phys-object
    ↑name <o1>
    ↑weight light
    ↑at <p>
    ↑on ceiling)                                      <object1>}
{(phys-object ↑name ladder ↑at <p> ↑on floor)         <object2>}
{(monkey  ↑on ladder ↑holds nil)                       <monkey>}
```

The rule will not interfere with the previously developed rule for holding nothing because the object being held, <o1>, must be the name of a physical object. Such a name cannot be "nil" according to the restrictions on working memory configurations. The element variables <goal>, <object1>, <object2>, and <monkey> will be bound to elements of working memory when a match of this condition occurs. The variables will be used in the right-hand side of the rule to effect the proper changes to working memory.

To reflect the action of grabbing the bananas, working memory must be changed so that the monkey is holding the bananas and the bananas are no longer on the ceiling. A statement must be printed to indicate that the bananas have been grabbed and the goal must be modified to have a status of satisfied. The English version of the right-hand side of the rule becomes

```
write a message to "grab" the object
modify the monkey to indicate it is holding the object
modify the object to indicate it is not on the ceiling
modify the goal to indicate the status is now satisfied.
```

This set of actions will leave the room in a legal configuration. However, if there is an object *on* the object to be grabbed, there is a problem. We did not define conditions for keeping track of objects on objects. Therefore we add the condition element

```
- (phys-object ↑on <o1>)
```

to the rule's LHS. Using the element variables above, the OPS5 translation of these actions is

```
(write (crlf) (crlf) Grab <o1> (crlf))
(modify <object1>  ↑on nil)
(modify <monkey> ↑holds <o1>)
(modify <goal> ↑status satisfied)
```

The complete rule is as follows:

```
(p Holds::Object-Ceil
   {(goal ↑status active ↑type holds ↑object-name <o1>) <goal>}
   {(phys-object
        ↑name <o1>
        ↑weight light
        ↑at <p>
        ↑on ceiling)                                   <object1>}
   {(phys-object ↑name ladder ↑at <p> ↑on floor)     <object2>}
   {(monkey  ↑on ladder ↑holds nil)                     <monkey>}
  -(phys-object ↑on <o1>)
-->
   (write (crlf) (crlf) Grab <o1> (crlf))
   (modify <object1>  ↑on nil)
   (modify <monkey> ↑holds <o1>)
   (modify <goal> ↑status satisfied))
```

The condition that the monkey does not hold anything is the first constraint to consider in developing new rules by relaxing or modifying constraints. If the monkey is holding something, the proper action is to have the monkey drop that thing. This situation is very similar to the situation when the rule On::Phys-Object:Holds was developed. Modifying the constraint so that the monkey is holding something and changing the action (right-hand-side) jsequence to create a new goal to drop the held object results in the following rule:

```
(p Holds::Object-Ceil:Holds
   (goal ↑status active ↑type holds ↑object-name <o1>)
   (phys-object ↑name <o1>  ↑weight light ↑at <p>
       ↑on ceiling)
   (phys-object ↑name ladder ↑at <p> ↑on floor)
   (monkey  ↑on ladder ↑holds {<o2> <> <o1>})
   (phys-object ↑name <o2>)
-->
   (make  goal ↑status active ↑type holds
       ↑object-name nil))
```

The critical elements of this rule are that there is a goal to "hold" an object different from the object currently being held and the monkey and the goal object are at the same place. These are exactly the critical elements in the On::Phys-Object:Holds rule. They are also the critical elements in developing the similar rule for the "holds" goal when the goal object is not on the ceiling. The other elements in the left-hand side of the rule are not important to the action of dropping the object. Therefore the new rule will not be used. It will be modified to be appropriate for either the action of grabbing an object on the ceiling or grabbing an object that is not on the ceiling. The modified rule is

```
(p Holds::Object:Holds
   (goal ↑status active ↑type holds ↑object-name <o1>)
   (phys-object ↑name <o1> ↑weight light ↑at <p>)
   (monkey ↑at <p> ↑holds {<> nil <> <o1>})
-->
   (make goal ↑status active ↑type holds ↑object-name nil))
```

This rule is less specific than the rule Holds::Object-Ceil:Holds but will be satisfied by every configuration satisfied by Holds::Object-Ceil:Holds. It will also be satisfied by configurations in which <o1> is not on the ceiling. This one rule handles both situations.

To create the last two rules for this cluster, the constraint relating to the monkey's location, both horizontal and vertical, is removed. In English the left-hand side now reads

```
there is an active goal to hold a physical object, O
the object O should be light, on the ceiling and at location p
the ladder should be on the floor and at location p
the monkey is not on the ladder
```

Under these conditions, a new goal must be set up to get the monkey on the ladder.

```
make a new goal for the monkey to get on the ladder
```

If the monkey is not at the right location, the "on" rule cluster will set up a goal for the monkey to walk to the location "p." By chaining the actions of the two rule clusters, we decrease the number of rules that must be written for each goal and ensure that the actions are carried out consistently.

Working memory configurations that match this rule will not also match the rule `Holds::Object-Ceil` or the rule `Holds::Object:Holds`. The new goal of getting the monkey on the ladder will be activated only in those instances in which the monkey is not already on the ladder.

The rule does not change the room configuration, so it does not violate the legal room configuration constraint. In OPS5 the rule is

```
(p Holds::Object-Ceil:On
   (goal ↑status active ↑type holds ↑object-name <o1>)
   (phys-object ↑name <o1>  ↑weight light ↑at <p>
       ↑on ceiling)
   (phys-object ↑name ladder ↑at <p> ↑on floor)
   (monkey ↑on <> ladder)
-->
   (make goal ↑status active ↑type on ↑object-name ladder))
```

Modifying the condition that the ladder be in place yields the last rule for holding an object on the ceiling. This rule is:

```
(p Holds::Object-Ceil:At-Obj
   (goal ↑status active ↑type holds ↑object-name <o1>)
   (phys-object  ↑name <o1>  ↑weight light ↑at <p>
       ↑on ceiling)
   (phys-object  ↑name ladder ↑at <> <p>)
-->
   (make goal ↑status active ↑type at ↑object-name ladder
       ↑to <p>))
```

Review of Rule Conflicts

The rules developed for the "holds" goal are now reexamined for conflicts. The data configurations matching the first rule and the other four are different because of the condition relating to whether or not the monkey is holding an actual physical object. To develop these rules, we use a problem-solving strategy that generates subgoals to satisfy the condition elements for the general rule. Since the MEA conflict-resolution strategy is being used, we always put the *goal* test as the first condition of the rule. This will ensure that the most recent *goal* element in working memory will be satisfied before any previous goals are considered. The rules in this cluster have mutually conflicting sets of preconditions. `Holds::Object-Ceil:At-Obj` requires that the ladder not be at the desired location. The other rules insist that the ladder is in place. The rule `Holds::Object-Ceil:On` requires that the monkey not be on the ladder and thus doesn't conflict with `Holds::Object-Ceil`. The two rules that may interact by being in the conflict set at the same time are `Holds::Object-Ceil:On` and `Holds::Object:Holds`. This could present a problem if the latter were selected first. However, `Holds::Object-Ceil:On` will always be selected first because it is more specific.

The rest of the rule development is not given in detail. The development is continued as exercises. A complete program is given in Appendix 1.1, and test rules are given in Appendix 1.2. The test rules include descriptions of what rules are expected to fire in what order on the sample configurations they set up. The rule `Test::General:Start` describes a complete sample problem with the goal of having the monkey holding the bananas.

3.8 DECISIONS LIST AND PROBLEMS LIST

This section contains two lists: One details each design decision that was made and the other notes the problems that were encountered in the creation of the monkey-and-bananas program.

Decisions List

1. There is exactly one ladder in the room and it is of the self-supporting variety.
2. The monkey is self propelling, and we assume there is exactly one such creature in our room.
3. The ladder is tall enough that the monkey, when *on* the ladder, can reach the ceiling. It is light enough for the monkey to carry.
4. The size of other physical objects will be ignored.
5. The weight of physical objects must be expressed, since the monkey cannot hold objects of "heavy" *weight*.
6. The monkey can see all objects in the room.

7. The monkey can carry out certain actions without being told in detail how to do these actions: walk to any location in the room, move an object to any location in the room, climb on or off any object, drop an object being held, and grab an object.
8. The final program will allow the actions just described to be used in planning.
9. The location of an object will be an attribute of the element class representing that object.
10. The horizontal location of an object will simply be a point on a two-dimensional grid; the vertical location will be on the floor, the ceiling, or on a physical object.
11. All physical objects will have the same representation, without distinguishing the target object.
12. The initial problem statement must designate the target.
13. The program must always update the *at* attribute when a physical object changes physical location.
14. A value of "nil" for the *on* attribute of a physical object means that the object is being held by the monkey.
15. The monkey must be at the exact same horizontal location as an object in order to grab it or climb on it. "Near enough" is simply defined as "at the same place."
16. The monkey must be on the ladder to grab a physical object on the ceiling.
17. A physical object dropped by the monkey will be at the exact same horizontal location as the monkey, with vertical location "floor."
18. The monkey can jump off a physical object while holding an object.
19. The monkey cannot climb upon a physical object while holding an object.
20. The monkey can hold only one physical object at a time.
21. The problem-solving strategy will be goal driven, with the goal *types* of "holds," "on," and "at."
22. *Goal* elements will receive the value "active" for the *status* attribute when placed in working memory.
23. *Goal* elements will receive the value "satisfied" for the *status* attribute when a message is printed out indicating that the goal has been accomplished. *Goal* elements will not be removed from working memory by the OPS5 program.
24. The program being designed will not check for violations of the legal working memory restrictions.
25. The program will not give the user any interactive help in establishing the initial working memory.

Problems List

1. Two objects can be in one physical location at one time. This is called the two-objects-in-one-place problem.
2. The rule cluster for "Climb onto O" is affected by the two-objects-in-one-place problem. The preconditions for the action were changed to eliminate mention of the "on" attribute of the monkey.
3. The rule `On::Phys-Object` will allow the monkey only to climb onto *phys-objects* that are on the floor. This may be too restrictive.
4. The rules implementing the goal *at* have to be certain to change the *at* attribute of anything carried by the monkey. Note that the action of *walk-to* does not mention the location of the object moved or any object that might be carried along.

3.9 EXERCISES

3-1 Some of the preconditions listed for actions are simply common sense. An example is that the monkey must be holding an object before the *move* action can be performed. Other preconditions are a direct result of the design decisions made. For each action and each precondition, list the term "common sense" or the number of the causal design decision from the *Decisions List,* Section 3.8.

3-2 Some of the postconditions listed for actions are simply common sense. An example is that after performing the *grab* action, the monkey should be holding the object that was to be grabbed. Other postconditions are a direct result of the design decisions made. For each action and each postcondition, list the term "common sense" or the number of the causal design decision from the *Decisions List,* Section 3.8.

3-3 Based on the *Decisions List* in Section 3.8, can you identify any preconditions or postconditions that are missing? If so, state them clearly and identify which decision is the causal decision.

3-4 Give the **make** actions necessary to create the following initial working memory configuration:

The monkey is on the ladder holding the blanket; the ladder is on the floor; the bananas are on the ceiling at a location different from the ladder; the ladder, blanket, and bananas are all light in weight. The goal is to grab the bananas.

3-5 Give the **make** actions necessary to create the following initial working memory configuration:

The monkey is on the floor at one location holding nothing; the bananas are on the floor at another location; the ladder is on the floor at a third location; the bananas and ladder are light in weight. The goal is to grab the bananas.

3-6 What restrictions on working memory configurations would be violated if the following **make** actions were used to initialize working memory?

```
(make phys-object ↑name bananas ↑weight light ↑at 7-7
    ↑on couch)
(make phys-object ↑name ladder  ↑weight light ↑at 5-5
    ↑on floor)
(make phys-object ↑name blanket ↑weight heavy ↑at 5-5
    ↑on floor)
(make money ↑at 5-7 ↑holds blanket ↑on ladder)
(make goal ↑type holds ↑object-name couch ↑to 4-4)
```

3-7 Create your own files containing the declarations (including the declaration for element class *testcase*), the rules developed for the goal "on," and the test rules. Test the "on" goal cluster of rules.

3-8 Identify possible working memory situations that are not tested by the test rules. Create your own test rules for these situations, add them to your test file, and execute them.

3-9 Modify the rule `On::Phys-Object:Satisfied` so that it does not have a condition to match the physical object. If you run your tests again, will the results change? If so, how? Create a test rule that will create a working memory configuration that should trigger this rule, but doesn't. Explain the behavior of your program. Can you create one rule `On::Satisfied` to replace the two rules `On::Phys-Object:Satisfied` and `On::Floor:Satisfied`? If so, test your rule.

3-10 Write a sequence of test rules for the "holds" goal rules as developed so far. For each rule, make a list of all the rules that you expect will be in the conflict set for each cycle, and the selected rule.

3-11 Develop rules for the "holds" goal with the action that the object is not on the ceiling. Name the rules as follows: `Holds::Object-NotCeil`, the rule that implements the action if all preconditions are met; `Holds::Object-NotCeil:On`, the rule that relaxes the condition that the monkey is on the floor; and `Holds::Object-NotCeil:At-Monkey`, the rule that relaxes the condition that the monkey and the object are at the same location. Remember the problem of holding one object when another object is on the object being held.

3-12 When will the rule `Holds::Object:Holds` be in conflict set with the three rules just developed?

3-13 Write a sequence of test rules for the "holds" goal rules added to the cluster in the previous two problems. Test the rule cluster.

3-14 Write rules to effect the action of printing the warning message "Object OBJECT is already being held," when there is a goal to hold the OBJECT and the monkey is holding it.

3-15 The following is a design for the cluster of rules to implement the "at" goal. Implement the design and test it.

```
;
; Cluster for goal type "at"
;  Design: There are two actions:
;     Move an object, called At-object
;     Walk-to a location, called At-monkey
;  Expression of subgoals:
;   At-object is expressed by a goal element with a goal
;     type of "at" and a non-nil value for attribute
;     object-name
;   At-monkey is expressed by a goal element with a goal
;     type of "at" and a nil value for attribute
;     object-name
;  At-object subgoal
;   Rule At::Object implements action of moving goal
;     object
;   Rule At::Object:On-floor if goal held, monkey not on
;     floor establishes new goal to get on the floor.
;   Rule At::Object:Holds if goal object not being held,
;     establishes new goal to hold the object.
;   Rule At::Object:Satisfied indicates goal already
;     satisfied
;  At-monkey subgoal
;   Rule At::Monkey implements action of walking to
;     location when the monkey is holding nothing
;   Rule At::Monkey:Object implements the action of
;     walking to location when monkey is holding something
;   Rule At::Monkey:On if monkey isn't on floor,
;     establish goal to get on the floor
;   Rule At::Monkey:Satisfied indicates goal already
;     satisfied
```

Design specifications for Exercise 3-15.

3-16 There are two situations in which a program should terminate. The first occurs when the test case has been completed successfully by satisfying all of the goals. Write a rule that will fire when a test case is completed successfully. The rule should terminate execution after printing this message:

```
CONGRATULATIONS! The goals are satisfied
```

3-17 The second situation in which a program should terminate occurs when it is impossible for the program to satisfy the active goals. Write a rule that will fire when there are no applicable rules to achieve the active goals. The rule should terminate execution after printing this message:

```
Impossible! The goal GOAL cannot be achieved
```

4

Organization and Control in OPS5

When facing production-system programming for the first time, experienced programmers are often at a loss to write programs that would be straightforward in more traditional languages. At first, some problems seem to elude solution in OPS5. And it's true that seasoned programmers who have acquired the habit of solving problems by writing sequences of instructions may be at more of a disadvantage than utterly naive programmers. A common tendency among new users of OPS5 is to exert excessive control over the sequence in which rules fire. Learning how to use production systems effectively is largely a matter of letting the pattern-matcher do the work.

Chapters 4, 5, and 6 describe techniques that a large and growing programming community has found useful in designing, writing, and debugging OPS5 production systems. The techniques presented here are not necessarily appropriate for other production-system architectures, but their underlying principles may be transferable. Among production-system architectures, even minor differences bear a tremendous influence on how a rule set must be designed to perform a given computation. Whereas programs written in different procedural languages may be quite similar to one another, programs written in different production-system languages rarely display such similarity.

Not all the techniques described here have counterparts in procedural programming languages, but an effort is made to identify such correspondences when they do occur. In most cases, only the preferred technique is presented, although sometimes the implications of different control structures and data representations will be discussed — if only to warn the unwary about hidden traps. By investigating how such computations can be expressed as OPS5 programs, we will illustrate the ways in which simple, straightforward computations can be conceptualized as rule sets. Many of these techniques are obvious, but some are quite subtle, and it is unlikely that an inexperienced production-system programmer would stumble upon them unaided. Once mastered, however, they should prepare the OPS5 programmer to tackle problems of any size and complexity.

4.1 THE LOCUS OF KNOWLEDGE

One of the first decisions a programmer must make in solving a problem is how to represent the knowledge that is needed for that solution. By encouraging some problem-solving modes and discouraging others, OPS5 influences the form that the solution will take. In general, OPS5 allows the programmer to deposit problem-solving knowledge in three places: production memory, working memory, and external functions and procedures. In this section, we will discuss these three alternatives for the placement of knowledge and consider the implications of each. First the possibilities will be presented without judgment, then a summary evaluation will follow.

4.1.1 KNOWLEDGE IN PRODUCTION MEMORY

Early work in production systems [Newell 73] was inspired by a model of human memory that characterized long-term memory as a relatively static set of production rules, with a highly volatile short-term "working" memory holding temporary information such as intermediate results. This model has influenced production-system programming as well, so that there is a tradition of placing domain knowledge in production memory and using working memory sparingly for data, intermediate results, and control. Each domain principle was viewed as an item of knowledge to be embodied in a single rule. This strategy worked well in practice, but experience has shown that the uses of production memory go well beyond representing domain knowledge. Let's now examine types of knowledge that can be placed in production memory: problem-solving knowledge, control knowledge, and database information.

Problem-Solving Knowledge in Production Memory

Problem-solving knowledge belongs in production memory; it is unnatural (but not impossible, as we'll see shortly) to put it anywhere else. To give an example of problem-solving knowledge, rules can be used to specify what conclusions can be drawn justifiably from different kinds of data. This sample rule performs a reasoning step by suggesting possible causes for a common problem in baking bread:

```
(literalize problem
    manifestation)    ; what went wrong
(literalize hypothesis
    cause)            ; what might have been responsible
```

```
(p bread-did-not-rise
   (problem ↑manifestation did-not-rise)
-->
   (make hypothesis ↑cause yeast-inactive)
   (make hypothesis ↑cause water-wrong-temperature)
   (make hypothesis ↑cause forgot-sugar))
```

Expert diagnostic systems consist of large sets of similar but more complex rules.

Control Knowledge in Production Memory

Control knowledge is used to direct the sequence in which problem-solving steps are carried out. One reason for imposing such control is to improve efficiency by first considering the most promising potential solutions. A second reason for imposing control is to make the problem-solving process more comprehensible to a human observer. A third reason is simply to coerce a desired sequence of events. The following example is part of a system that makes sure the steps involved in marketing a new product are performed in the proper sequence:

```
(literalize phase
    description     ; e.g., development, in-house-evaluation
    status)         ; active, finished

(p switch-from-development-to-in-house
   (phase ↑description development
       ↑status finished)
 - (phase ↑description in-house-evaluation)
-->
   (make phase ↑description in-house-evaluation
       ↑status active))

(p switch-from-in-house-to-test-marketing
   (phase ↑description in-house-evaluation
       ↑status finished)
 - (phase ↑description test-marketing)
-->
   (make phase ↑description test-marketing
       ↑status active))
```

Somehow phases have to get their *status* field set to "finished." This is the responsibility of other rules in the system, which operate on phases having a *status* field with value "active." When the work occurring in that phase has been completed, a rule will modify its *status* from "active" to "finished."

Database Knowledge in Production Memory

Finally, database knowledge can be kept in rules. This strategy is rational only if database updates are infrequent; it is expensive to alter production memory either at runtime with the **build** action or by modifying the source code between runs. In the following example, a ship is represented by a single working memory element, and the rule `Carl-Vinson-hull-number` fills into the proper slot the hull number (an identification number) of the aircraft carrier U.S.S. Carl Vinson:

```
(literalize ship
    name          ; name of the ship, e.g., Carl Vinson
    hull-number   ; identification number of the ship,
                  ;  e.g., CVN-70
    mission       ; current mission of the ship
    captain)      ; captain of the ship

(p Carl-Vinson-hull-number
   {(ship ↑name Carl-Vinson ↑hull-number nil)  <ship>}
-->
   (modify <ship> ↑hull-number CVN-70))
```

To perform this task for the entire U.S. Navy would require hundreds of rules, all having the same form.

4.1.2 KNOWLEDGE IN WORKING MEMORY

As we noted, the traditional use of working memory has been to store data, intermediate computations, and control flags, uses that tended to keep working memory both small and volatile. Experience with production-system programming has led to the discovery of new uses for working memory, including the storage and maintenance of a variety of tables. Tables are collections of uniformly structured working memory elements that contain both database and problem-solving knowledge.

Database Knowledge in Working Memory

A simple type of table stores nothing but database information. The following example recasts the hull-number program by placing the data in working memory rather than in production memory:

```
(literalize ship
    name          ; name of the ship, e.g., Carl Vinson
    hull-number   ; identification number of the ship,
                  ;  e.g., CVN-70
    mission       ; current mission of the ship
    captain)      ; captain of the ship

(literalize hull-number-table
    ship-name      ; the name of the ship
    hull-number)   ; the hull number of the ship
```

```
(p assign-hull-number
   {(ship ↑name <name> ↑hull-number nil)      <ship>}
   {(hull-number-table
       ↑ship-name <name>
       ↑hull-number <hull-number>)            <table>}
-->
   (modify <ship> ↑hull-number  <hull-number>))

(make hull-number-table
    ↑ship-name Carl-Vinson
    ↑hull-number CVN-70)

(make hull-number-table
    ↑ship-name Will-Rogers
    ↑hull-number SSBN-659)
```

In this example, the single rule `assign-hull-number` will assign the hull number to any ship, provided that the table entry has been added to working memory.

Control Knowledge in Working Memory

Control knowledge of many kinds can also be placed in working memory. In a sense, data and intermediate results serve as control knowledge, because they influence the order in which rules fire. In addition, though, elements in working memory may have attributes that serve as status flags, or the entire element may have control as its exclusive function. This important topic will be discussed at much greater length later in this and the following chapter, but for now we'll use a simple example to illustrate the use of working memory for control. To recast the example of the new product, we can represent the sequence of phases as a set of ordered pairs:

```
(literalize phase-sequence
    phase-1             ; the phase just completed
    phase-2)            ; the phase about to begin

(literalize phase
    description         ; e.g., development,
                        ;  in-house evaluation
    status)             ; active, finished

(p switch-phases
   (phase ↑description <phase-1> ↑status finished)
   (phase-sequence
       ↑phase-1 <phase-1>
       ↑phase-2 <phase-2>)
 - (phase ↑description <phase-2>)
-->
   (make phase ↑description <phase-2> ↑status active))
```

```
(make phase-sequence ↑phase-1 development
    ↑phase-2 in-house-evaluation)

(make phase-sequence ↑phase-1 in-house-evaluation
    ↑phase-2 test-marketing)
```

Once again, there is a direct substitution of working memory elements for rules.

Problem-Solving Knowledge in Working Memory

Finally, even problem-solving knowledge can be taken outside of rules and placed in working memory [Pasik, Schor 84]. To see how this can be done, we'll reconsider the program to diagnose the bread-baking problem. A manifestation leads to several hypotheses. Thus we can have a table, each entry of which links one manifestation to one hypothesis.

```
(literalize problem
    manifestation)    ; what went wrong

(literalize hypothesis
    cause)            ; what might have been responsible

(literalize diagnostic-table
    manifestation
    possible-cause)

(p suggest-hypothesis
   (problem ↑manifestation <manifestation>)
   (diagnostic-table
       ↑manifestation <manifestation>
       ↑possible-cause <hypothesis>)
-->
   (make hypothesis ↑cause <hypothesis>))

(make diagnostic-table
    ↑manifestation did-not-rise
    ↑possible-cause yeast-inactive)

(make diagnostic-table
    ↑manifestation did-not-rise
    ↑possible-cause water-wrong-temperature)

(make diagnostic-table
    ↑manifestation did-not-rise
    ↑possible-cause forgot-sugar)
```

In this way, a large part of the expert system can be reduced to a few rules, with the diagnostic knowledge in tables in working memory.

4.1.3 KNOWLEDGE IN EXTERNAL FUNCTIONS AND PROCEDURES

For the rebellious programmer who resists using OPS5, there is an easy subterfuge: all the problem-solving work can be accomplished by an external routine called from the right-hand side of a single rule. The purist, of course, may take pride in never invoking any external routine, solving the problem entirely within the production-system architecture. Somewhere between these extremes lies the typical situation: judicious occasional use of external procedures and functions for performing stereotyped, complex, or tedious tasks that are not knowledge intensive.

When trying to decide whether to invoke an external routine rather than program the solution with OPS5 rules, you should ask yourself the following questions: *Is it possible to perform the task within OPS5?* (Some tasks, such as accessing the time of day or communicating with a separate process, simply are beyond the capabilities of OPS5.) *Is it rational to perform the task within OPS5?* (Even though one can write production rules to take square roots, for example, the resulting program will be clumsy and most likely inefficient.) *Is it acceptably efficient to perform the task within OPS5?* (Depending on the particular application, it may be advantageous to employ an external database if the data are voluminous or if it is necessary, write specialized code for manipulating complex data structures.) If the answers to all three questions are in the affirmative, it is probably better to use the production-system architecture to do the work.

4.1.4 WHERE SHOULD KNOWLEDGE BE PLACED?

Should knowledge, then, be placed in production memory, working memory, or external routines? Often the question does not arise. If the inference rules have idiosyncratic left-hand sides, varying widely in format, it would be absurdly difficult to try to format the problem-solving knowledge in a table. What is the point of achieving a minuscule production system at the cost of designing a complicated and abstruse table in working memory? Similarly, if a database management system can be used to access only a few items from an enormous database, sanity demands that it be exploited. But sometimes decisions are not inevitable, and competing considerations must be weighed.

Placing Problem-Solving Knowledge

In most cases, problem-solving principles belong in production memory. When problem-solving knowledge is stored in working memory, one of the main advantages of OPS5, its speed, is sacrificed by using OPS5 to emulate another production-system language. Nevertheless, there are some advantages to placing problem-solving knowledge in working memory, and these advantages should be pointed out. One is that the program can use the problem-solving principles as data, giving it ***meta level knowledge*** about its own reasoning. This information would not be available otherwise, since OPS5 compiles rules into a network that cannot be accessed by the application program (see Section 6.1). A second advantage is that the problem-solving knowledge can easily be modified at run time without using the **build** action. Whether or not these advantages are worth the cost depends on the application.

Placing Database Knowledge

Production memory is not well suited to take the place of a database. Although there is no great cost in efficiency when production memory is used, it is better to use working memory because the latter is more easily updated and examined during execution. In particular, information in working memory may be matched by many rules, and thus can be used in a variety of ways, while information in rules can be applied in much more limited circumstances. For large quantities of data, information can be cached in working memory; that is, it is transferred from the external database to working memory only when it is needed, with database updates occurring if the data are changed.

Placing Control Knowledge

It is much harder to lay down the law about control knowledge. The usual approach is to encode high-level, long-term control knowledge in rules, using working memory elements as switches to store only ephemeral control information. OPS5 encourages the use of working memory for control by supplying the MEA conflict-resolution strategy, which assigns a control function to the first condition element in a rule. Nevertheless, the use of tables in working memory to encode control knowledge has not yet received much attention; this approach may prove to be a useful supplement or alternative to rule-based control, although some will argue that any control that can be encoded in tables is bound to be excessive. External routines should not be used to exert covert control over the OPS5 interpreter; production-system programs are difficult enough to understand as is.

4.2 INTRODUCTION TO CONTROL IN OPS5

By exploiting built-in capabilities of OPS5, a programmer can exert any desired degree of control over the execution of a production system. At one extreme, the program can be tailored so that for all anticipated input streams, the sequence of rule firings is fixed. If this is the case, it was probably wrong to choose a production system to program the solution. At the other extreme, the system can be designed so that the rules do not interact at all (except for competing in conflict resolution); that is, the order in which rules fire makes no difference at all to the result of the computation. Most production-system programs occupy a middle position: the programmer exerts control over the sequence of rule firings with a very light touch, the nature of the specific problem having more influence on the sequence of rule firings than the programmer's bias toward control. To exploit the full power of the OPS5 language, application programs should be data-driven; that is, the rule set should be written so that the course of execution is extremely sensitive to the unique characteristics of the data. Of course, it's no crime to write OPS5 programs (backward-chaining systems, for example) in which the sequence of rule firings is insensitive to the input values, but there may be other system-building tools that are more suited to those applications than OPS5 is.

Nevertheless, the programmer has many legitimate reasons for wresting control away from the data and imposing it with rules. First, since OPS5 contains no features for partitioning either the rule set or working memory, the programmer may impose control to implement this capability. Second, sometimes the most straightforward solution to an OPS5 programming problem is unacceptably expensive. In this situation the programmer may decide to intervene and recode the system to perform an algorithm known to be more efficient. Third, for the purposes of having a smooth, pleasant human interface, it is often necessary for the programmer to constrain the order in which certain rules fire. For example, when soliciting input, it is usually desired that the questions be presented in a constrained order. And fourth, the OPS5 architecture is flexible enough to allow the programmer to emulate different production-system architectures by having the rules in production memory assume some of the capabilities of the emulated interpreter. There are many more situations that justify departures from pure data-driven programming and adoption of goal-driven programming. Nevertheless, these considerations should demonstrate that no discussion of production-system programming is complete without considering control.

We will examine control from two perspectives. First, the mechanisms or means by which the programmer can exert control are listed and briefly discussed. This sets the background to further discussion. Second, the distinction between two radically different production-system architectures, forward chaining and backward chaining, is examined from the point of view of control. Two different solutions, embodying the two different architectures, are applied to a single example problem for the purpose of introducing some common control principles that play a prominent role here and in the next chapter.

4.2.1 MECHANISMS OF CONTROL

The production-system programmer may exercise control over the computation by manipulating the three components of a production system: the production memory, the working memory, and the inference engine. OPS5 encourages the programmer and user to exert all necessary control over execution in one of five ways:

1. Construct the rule set in production memory so that the rules interact with one another in prescribed ways; in a word, this is programming.
2. Select the conflict-resolution strategy, either LEX or MEA, with the top-level **strategy** command.[1]
3. Insert elements into working memory with top-level **make** actions, or delete them with top-level **remove** actions.
4. Tailor the input data that the **accept** and **acceptline** functions read into working memory.
5. Control the number of executed cycles by supplying a numeric argument with the **run** command, by setting breakpoints, or by interrupting execution with a standard operating system control character.

Clever programmers can find other means of exerting control, but they are seldom desirable and never necessary. OPS5 was designed to facilitate some mechanisms of control and to discourage others. Obscure and devious control strategies are not only bad programming practice, but are contrary to the design philosophy of OPS5.

4.2.2 INTERACTIONS AMONG RULES

The advantage of rule-based systems over other programming systems is usually said to be their modularity, which gives them a potential for incremental development. In some production-system application programs, individual rules from well-defined subsets can be inserted, removed, or changed without fear that the program will no longer run. That is, the program's knowledge can be modified without affecting the control. Whether the new knowledge is consistent, complete, and correct is a separate issue. Modularity of knowledge in an OPS5 program is not guaranteed; it must be carefully designed into each application program. Rules can interact in very subtle and complex ways, and unless a discipline is meticulously crafted and faithfully followed, the inter-

[1] OPS5 programs should be written with a single conflict-resolution strategy in mind. Changing the strategy in mid-execution will introduce needless confusion, opening new opportunities for errors and making the programs more difficult to test.

actions among rules may exceed the programmer's control and comprehension. It is especially important to understand the interaction of rules in forward-chaining architectures such as that of OPS5, since rules must be used to encode a great deal of control information in addition to domain knowledge.

The extent and nature of interactions among rules can make it extremely difficult to predict the behavior of a production-system program simply by reading listings of its source code. Consider the cognitive task of hand-tracing the execution of a production system. For each cycle, the momentary state of working memory must be monitored in complete detail, and the processes of matching and conflict resolution must be performed in their entirety. The ordering of the rules on the page is not a reliable guide in selecting which rule will fire next; the whole set must be scanned. As you can see, trying to understand how a production system behaves involves quite a bit of effort and can place great demands on human memory. Furthermore, it is no small matter for the production-system programmer to know what a system will do when it is presented with novel inputs or is modified by adding, deleting, or rewriting rules.

The goal of any adequate programming methodology, no matter what programming system is being employed, is to tame the complexity of the programming task. To manage complexity requires an understanding of its sources and manifestations. Once a sound discipline of design and documentation is adopted, thorough familiarity with the ways rules interact becomes the programmer's most effective tool in managing the complexity of large production-system programs; therefore it is essential to the task of designing elegant, efficient, maintainable — and correct — rule-based systems with a minimum of wasted effort.

The sources of complexity in OPS5 programs are not numerous, but they occur very often and in many subtle guises. At root, there are only four different ways in which rules can influence one another, including interactions of a rule with itself:

1. One rule can enable a second rule by creating the previously absent conditions that are necessary for the second rule to fire.
2. One rule can disable a second rule by removing the previously present conditions that are necessary for the second rule to fire.
3. One rule can expedite a second rule by indirectly raising its dominance in conflict resolution relative to other rules, lowering the dominance of other rules relative to it, or removing the previously present conditions for a higher-dominance rule to fire.
4. One rule can defer a second rule by indirectly lowering its dominance in conflict resolution relative to other rules, raising the dominance of

other rules relative to it, or creating the previously absent conditions for a higher-dominance rule to fire.

In short, a rule firing can cause another rule instantiation to enter or leave the conflict set, or within the conflict set it can raise or lower its relative dominance in conflict resolution.

Depending on the application, interactions among rules may determine not only the order in which results are obtained, but even the results of the computation themselves. This is not a cause for concern if there are many correct solutions of equal value. Too often, however, control problems lead to incorrect results. It is easy to see how control affects results when rules selectively enable and disable one another: A rogue rule may fire against the programmer's intentions, changing intermediate results for the worse, or a needed rule may fail to fire. Less easy to see is how influencing the order in which rules fire either by deferring or by expediting them can also affect the result of the computation.

To illustrate how this can happen, consider the effects of timing from two perspectives. One way of looking at it may be called the "sitting duck" scenario. Once an instantiation of a rule enters the conflict set, it may be removed on any cycle if the conditions for its firing are changed. Thus deferring a rule from firing may give another rule the opportunity to disable it. The second scenario may be called "opportunity knocks but once." The cycle on which a rule fires determines what working memory elements simultaneously occupy working memory — that is, what patterns of data exist. Therefore deferring the firing of a rule can change the set of states working memory assumes, and thus the set of rules that may fire. The art of production-system programming consists in part of knowing how to control rule interactions *just enough* so that the system computes the correct results. Needless control should not be imposed.

The most essential mechanism that governs rule interactions is the set of actions called **make, modify,** and **remove,** which alter working memory. The second mechanism is refraction. Once an instantiation fires, it is disqualified from firing again even if its conditions continue to be satisfied; the next instantiation to fire is selected from among those that remain after refraction winnows down the conflict set. It is sometimes said that changing working memory is the *only* mechanism by which rules interact; the present analysis does not so much contradict this assertion as it extends the meaning of interaction to include both self-interaction and changes in dominance. Because of its central role in production-system programming, the influence that rules exert on one another by altering working memory will occupy the next section of this chapter.

4.3 ANALYSIS OF RULE INTERACTIONS

In a typical production-system program almost every rule alters working memory.[2] Thus, even if there were no refraction, the conflict set would change from cycle to cycle. The OPS5 architecture provides three actions that change the contents of working memory: **make, modify,** and **remove.** (For the purposes of discussion, it is best to ignore user-defined actions, which open up the door to all sorts of devious maneuvers such as arbitrarily modifying working memory or even accessing variables in the implementation language.) These three actions provide a convenient system for classifying the ways rules interact with one another by communicating through working memory.

We will limit our discussion to the fundamental mechanism of interaction, that of rule instantiations enabling and disabling one another. The secondary mechanism of interaction, deferring or expediting the selection of an instantiation for firing, will not be considered here; these forms of interaction owe their existence to enabling and disabling. It should be mentioned, if only in warning, that it is possible to promote an instantiation without changing the contents of working memory by vacuously modifying one of the working memory elements that match the rule so that only the time tag of the element is changed. This rejuvenates the instantiation, giving it an edge with respect to recency by making it a new instantiation. Using this trick often indicates that the control problem has not been adequately thought out.

4.3.1 ENABLING RULES BY CHANGING WORKING MEMORY

The enabling of one rule by another drives production systems forward. A complex computation is usually carried out with a chain of enablements in which each rule passes an intermediate result to the next. In fact, it is possible to write production-system applications in such a way that the only means by which rules interact is through enabling one another, although these programs necessarily would have very meager control structures. If enablement is excluded, no new instantiations ever enter the conflict on any cycle after execution begins. Without the ability to pass intermediate results, the resulting program would be very limited in its ability to perform meaningful problem solving.

Enabling With the Make Action

A rule may add to working memory an element that is needed for another rule to fire; if this new element is the last one needed to enable the second

[2] Those rules which do not change working memory have right-hand sides that perform only **write, openfile, closefile, default, halt, build, bind, cbind,** or **excise** actions, or call user-defined functions with no side effects.

rule, it acts as a trigger. The working memory element may constitute a needed datum, such as a result of some prior computation or an input received by means of an **accept** statement. On the other hand, the element may be what is called a ***control element*** [Davis, King 76], existing solely for the purpose of control and serving only to pass a message from one rule to another. In both cases, the right-hand side of the first rule makes a working memory element that is matched on the left-hand side of the second rule. By far, this is the most familiar form of interaction among rules, since most production systems have primitive actions for adding elements to working memory.

The following example shows how a datum can act as a trigger. The rule `compute-net-income` takes the difference of gross income and expenses and places a new element in working memory. The action of this rule creates an element that enables the rule `in-hot-water` to fire.

```
(literalize amount
     name            ; identification field
     value)          ; dollar amount

; This rule sets a debt trigger
;  if expenses are greater than gross income.
(p compute-debt
   (amount ↑name gross-income ↑value <gross> )
   (amount ↑name expenses ↑value {<expense-value> > <gross>})
-->
   (make amount
       ↑name debt
       ↑value (compute <expense-value> - <gross>)))

; If a debt has been established
;  that is greater than the credit limit,
;  then issue a warning.
(p in-hot-water
   (amount ↑name debt ↑value <debt-value> )
   (amount ↑name credit-limit ↑value {<limit> < <debt-value>})
-->
   (bind <uncovered> (compute <debt-value> - <limit>))
   (write (crlf) You have a debt of | $ | <uncovered>
                 that you are currently unable to cover))
```

The use of the **make** action to generate control elements will be treated in depth in Section 5.2.3.

Enabling With the Remove Action

A rule can be enabled when the last working memory element that matches one of its negated condition elements is removed from working memory. The rule `reorder-part` in the following example will fire as soon as a request is received for the next-to-last instance of some part in a stockroom database.

```
(literalize request
    part name)      ; the part being requested

(literalize stock-item
    part-name       ; the name of the part
    id)             ; a unique identifier

(literalize goal
    type            ; type of goal
    what)           ; what object goal refers to

; This rule removes stock items when granting requests.
(p part-request-granted
   (request ↑part-name <name>)
   {(stock-item ↑part-name <name>)        <requested-part>}
-->
   (remove <requested-part>))

; This rule reorders parts when there is exactly one left.
(p reorder-part
   (stock-item ↑part-name <name> ↑id <id>)
 - (stock-item ↑part-name <name> ↑id <> <id>)
-->
   (make goal ↑type reorder ↑what <name>))
```

As you can see, this is a natural way for causing a working memory element to be replenished when it is depleted. This method can also be used to switch from one phase of a multistage process to another when the earlier task is accomplished, as signaled by the earlier task having consumed all of the data it was sent.

Enabling With the Modify Action

If a rule is waiting for one of its data to assume a particular value before the rule can fire, a **modify** action that confers that value will trigger the rule. In the following example, the rule `save-money` causes the savings account balance to grow; when the balance reaches the cost of a new computer, out comes the money.

```
(literalize spare-cash
    amount)         ; a positive number

(literalize savings-account
    balance)        ; a non-negative number
```

```
(literalize computer
    name          ; a computer type
    price)        ; a positive number

(p save-money
   {<cash>        (spare-cash ↑amount { <amt> > 0 })}
   {<s-account> (savings-account ↑balance <balance>)}
-->
   (modify <s-account>
       ↑balance (compute <balance> + <amt>))
   (remove <cash>))

(p have-enough-money-to-buy-computer
   {<object> (computer ↑name <name> ↑price <cost>)}
   {<money>  (savings-account
       ↑balance {<balance> >= <cost>})}
-->
   (modify <money> ↑balance (compute <balance> - <cost>)))
```

The **modify** action will also enable a rule if it removes the last working memory element matching a negated condition element in the rule. Triggering a rule with a **modify** action is similar to triggering with a **make** action, and sometimes the two methods are interchangeable. It is easy to emulate the effects of **make** by using the **modify** action on an element that stays in working memory. All that is needed is a binary switch (true/false, active/inactive, proceed/wait) to be tested in the condition elements. Setting the switch emulates a **make** action, and resetting it emulates **remove.**

4.3.2 DISABLING RULES BY CHANGING WORKING MEMORY

At first glance it may seem unnecessary to have rules to disable other rules; doesn't that impede progress? Yes, but only in the sense that brakes impede the progress of an automobile, or that inhibitory synapses in the brain impede the progress of thought. If rules were unable to disable other rules, control would be nearly impossible.

Disabling With the Make Action

When a rule creates a working memory element, it will disable another rule from firing if the second rule has a negated condition element that matches the newly created working memory element. A negated condition element specifies that the rule that contains it can fire only when working memory contains no element that matches it.

The following rather involved example will show how working memory elements can serve as means by which one rule inhibits another by means of a veto. In psychoanalytic theory, there are three structures of the personality, the *id*, the *ego*, and *superego*, which are in a constant state of dynamic tension. The id, operating according to the pleasure principle, is all appetite, blindly generating wishes; the superego is the internalized voice of social restraint; and the ego, operating by the reality principle, resolves conflicts between the other two factions. If the id generates a desire which is acceptable to the superego, then the ego can go ahead and look for a way to satisfy the desire; otherwise, one of the defense mechanisms, such as repression, projection, sublimation, or reaction formation, must be invoked to transfom the id's unacceptable desire. All this is summarized by the following two-rule system:

```
(literalize id
    wish                ; wish generated by the id
    object)             ; the object of the wish

(literalize superego
    prohibition)        ; a stricture from the conscience

(literalize plan
    goal                ; a goal to be achieved
    object)             ; the object of the goal

(literalize defense-mechanism
    taboo)

(p ego-makes-plan
   (id ↑wish <wish> )
 - (superego ↑prohibition <wish>)
-->
   (make plan ↑goal <wish> ))

(p ego-makes-defense-mechanism
   (id ↑wish <wish>)
   (superego ↑prohibition <wish>)
-->
   (make defense-mechanism ↑taboo <wish>))

(make superego ↑prohibition anger)
(make superego ↑prohibition envy)
(make superego ↑prohibition greed)
(make superego ↑prohibition pride)
```

Another use for this type of interaction is to assure that an initialization step is performed only once. Note in the following example how the rule `make-elephant-counter` disables *itself*, which is necessary in case there is more than one elephant to be counted.

```
(literalize elephant
    status)             ; one of: counted, uncounted
```

```
(literalize elephant-counter
    count)          ; number of elephants found so far

; initialize the elephant counter to 0
;  if there is no counter and an uncounted elephant
(p make-elephant-counter
   (elephant ↑status uncounted)
 - (elephant-counter)
-->
   (make elephant-counter ↑count 0))

; for each elephant not yet counted
;  add 1 to the total count and mark the elephant counted
(p count-elephants
   {<counter>  (elephant-counter ↑count <elephant-count>)}
   {<elephant> (elephant ↑status uncounted)}
-->
   (modify <counter>
       ↑count (compute <elephant-count> + 1))
   (modify <elephant> ↑status counted))
```

Similarly, the creation of a working memory element may serve to terminate iteration by disabling a governing rule: The element carries the information that signals the loop's termination condition.

Disabling With the Remove Action

A rule can be disabled if one of the working memory elements that is needed to match its left-hand side is removed, leaving it unsatisfied. When data have served their purpose, leading to the achievement of a subgoal, erasing the data will prevent unnecessary further processing. Alternatively, rules that are triggered by control elements may end the processing of a subgoal by removing these control elements from working memory after the subgoal is accomplished. Removing triggers may prevent infinite loops, as in the following example:

```
; the stock data base also include records for a number
;  of clients and a status based on their payment record
(literalize client-record
    name            ; name of the client of record
    status)         ; one of: good, probation, terminated

; the system can add new clients, bill them, and terminate
;  clients if they do not pay their bills
(literalize goal
    type            ; one of: enter-new-client,
                    ;  bill-client, terminate-client
    what)           ; name of client to take action on
```

```
(p terminate-client
   {<terminate> (goal ↑type terminate-client ↑what <name>)}
   {<c-record> (client-record ↑name <name>}
-->
   (modify <c-record> ↑status terminated)
   (remove <terminate>))
```

Since the *client-record* element was modified, it would have been infinitely reinstantiated had the *goal* working memory element not been removed.

Another use for this mechanism is to prematurely abandon pursuit of subgoals that have proven to be unpromising. A rule that evaluates subgoal progress simply has to remove the working memory element that enabled the subgoal to be pursued in the first place. Similarly, if a problem has many solutions, the pursuit can be terminated in this way as soon as the first minimally satisfactory solution is found (this is called ***satisficing***).

Disabling With the Modify Action

Modify actions can disable a rule if they cause elements that once matched the left-hand side of the rule to no longer match. For the savings-account example in Section 4.3.1, a rule that made an emergency withdrawal from the savings account could be made to take precedence over the goal of buying the computer:

```
(p emergency-withdrawal
   {<emergency> (goal ↑type emergency-expense
       ↑what <amount>)}
   {<s-account> (savings-account
       ↑balance {<balance> >= <amount>})}
-->
   (modify <s-account>
       ↑balance (compute <balance> - <amount>))
   (make goal ↑type fix-emergency)
   (remove <emergency>))
```

The **modify** action can also disable a rule by causing a working memory element to match a negated condition element in the rule. It should be evident that disabling via **modify** is to disabling via **remove** as enabling via **modify** is to enabling via **make;** note that none of these actions requires any negated condition elements.

4.4 AN EXAMPLE OF PROGRAMMING CONTROL: FORWARD AND BACKWARD CHAINING

To make the discussion of control more concrete, we will consider how OPS5 can be used to build both a forward-chaining and a backward-chaining production system to assist in filing a federal income tax return. We do not intend to suggest that OPS5, or any production-system language, is an appropriate tool for programming this relatively straightforward accounting task; it merely happens to be a conveniently familiar example that is amenable to both architectural approaches. The rules are drawn, with simplifications, from the 1983 U.S. Individual Income Tax Return.

4.4.1 FORWARD CHAINING

First, let us look at the forward-chaining approach. The solution is quite simple. There are two phases. The data are first placed in working memory, and then these values are combined according to the tax formulas to fill in all the lines on the income tax return. These phases may overlap; rules that combine values may fire before all values have been entered. But this overlap does not diminish the reason for distinguishing the two phases.

The most simple way of getting the data into working memory is to program a daisy chain of rules. As each rule fires, it sets up the condition for firing the next one in sequence. A distinguished working memory element of class *start* initiates the chain.

A *start* element triggers the rule `input-filing-status`, which, when finished, inserts into working memory an element of class *amount* with the value of "filing-status" for its *name* attribute. This working memory element then triggers the rule `input-exemptions`, which in turn triggers the rule `input-wages`. It should be clear to all taxpayers how this set of rules continues.

```
(literalize amount
    name        ; the name of the line on the return
    value)      ; number or amount entered on return
                ;  number of dependents or exemptions
                ;  rounded dollar amount

(literalize start)     ; used to initiate production system

; This rule gets the filing status from the user.
(p input-filing-status
   (start)
 - (amount ↑name filing-status)
-->
   (write (crlf) |Enter number representing filing status :|
          (crlf) |   1: Single|
          (crlf) |   2: Married filing joint return|
          (crlf) |   3: Married filing separate return|
```

```
          (crlf) |   4: Head of household|
          (crlf) |   5: Qualifying widow(er)
                        with dependent child|
          (crlf) |Number:|)
   (make amount ↑name filing-status  ↑value (accept)))

; This rule queries the user concerning each type of
;  exemption and calculates the total number of exemptions.
(p input-exemptions
   (amount ↑name filing-status)
 - (amount ↑name exemptions)
-->
   (write (crlf) |For the following questions, if your|
          (crlf) |answer is "yes" enter the number "1,"|
          (crlf) |and if your answer is "no," enter|
          (crlf) |the number "0"|)
   (write (crlf) |Are you 65 or over?|)
   (bind <self-65> (accept))
   (write (crlf) |Are you blind?|)
   (bind <self-blind> (accept))
   (write (crlf) |Do you claim your spouse as an exemption?|)
   (bind <spouse> (accept))
   (write (crlf) |Is your spouse 65 or over?|)
   (bind <spouse-65> (accept))
   (write (crlf) |Is your spouse blind?|)
   (bind <spouse-blind> (accept))
   (write (crlf) |For the following questions,|
          (crlf) |enter the requested number|)
   (write (crlf) |How many dependent children live with
                  you?|)
   (bind <dep-children> (accept))
   (write (crlf) |How many other dependents do you claim?|)
   (bind <other-dep> (accept))
   (make amount
       ↑name exemptions
       ↑value (compute 1 + <self-65> + <self-blind> + <spouse>
                       + <spouse-65> + <spouse-blind> +
                       <dep-children> + <other-dep> )))

; This rule gets the total income from the user.
(p input-wages
   (amount ↑name exemptions)
 - (amount ↑name wages)
-->
   (write (crlf) |Enter wages, salaries, tips, etc. |)
   (make amount ↑name wages ↑value (accept)))

(make start)
```

The rules in the second set fire opportunistically: As soon as the required data, in the form of elements of class *amount*, appear simultaneously in working memory, the rules can do their work. Moreover, they do their work unobtrusively, neither producing output, requiring input, nor affecting the sequencing of the daisy chain. Whether or not these rules fire before the first phase is completed matters not at all; as it happens, they will in fact be interleaved with rules from the daisy chain because of the specificity principle in both OPS5 conflict-resolution strategies.

Some of these rules follow. Three of them merely take sums and differences of various quantities, but the rule `disallow-negative-tax-balance` is different. It adjusts the *value* of the *amount* of the tax balance so that it does not fall below zero. To make sure this rule fires before the rule `compute-other-taxes`, which is favored by the specificity of conflict resolution, the latter rule includes a test in its first condition element to make sure the tax balance is in the correct range.

```
(p compute-credits
   (amount ↑value <line41> ↑name credit-for-the-elderly)
   (amount ↑value <line42> ↑name foreign-tax-credit)
   (amount ↑value <line43> ↑name investment-credit)
   (amount ↑value <line44>
       ↑name political-contributions-credit)
   (amount ↑value <line45> ↑name dependent-care-credit)
   (amount ↑value <line46> ↑name jobs-credit)
   (amount ↑value <line47> ↑name residential-energy-credit)
-->
   (make amount ↑name total-credits
       ↑value (compute <line41> + <line42> + <line43> +
                       <line44> + <line 45> + <line46> +
                       <line47>)))

(p compute-tax-balance
   (amount ↑value <line48>  ↑name total-credits)
   (amount ↑value <line40>  ↑name total-tax)
-->
   (make amount ↑name tax-balance
       ↑value (compute <line40> - <line48> )))

(p disallow-negative-tax-balance
   {<line49> (amount ↑name tax-balance ↑value < 0)}
-->
   (modify <line49>  ↑value 0))

(p compute-other-taxes
   (amount ↑value {<line49> >= 0} ↑name tax-balance)
   (amount ↑value <line50>  ↑name self-employment-tax)
   (amount ↑value <line51>  ↑name alternative-minimum-tax)
```

```
   (amount ↑value <line52>  ↑name investment-recapture-tax)
   (amount ↑value <line53>  ↑name unreported-tip-SS-tax)
   (amount ↑value <line54>  ↑name uncollected-tip-SS-tax)
   (amount ↑value <line55>  ↑name IRA-tax)
-->
   (make amount ↑name total-tax
       ↑value (compute <line49> + <line50> + <line51> +
                       <line52> + <line53> + <line54> +
                       <line55>)))
```

4.4.2 BACKWARD CHAINING

Now let us examine how this task could be coded as a backward-chaining system. The user of the program may be able to detect no difference between these two architectural variants, but the philosophies are quite different. As we mentioned before, three sets of rules are required: control rules for implementing the backward-chaining system, subgoaling rules, and rules for handling the immediately soluble goals.

A backward-chaining system starts with a goal and tries to achieve it. If it is not possible to finish off the goal immediately, the goal is split into simpler subgoals in the hope that solution will be expedited. This splitting recurs until either immediate solution becomes possible or no further splitting is possible. Because the starting point is the assertion of the ultimate goal, with the system unraveling this goal into ever simpler subgoals, the system can be said to work in a backward direction.

The following rules generate the first few subgoals in the income tax example. Since the production system is now goal driven rather than data driven, the fundamental class of working memory element is called a *goal*. When the goal is solved, its *value* field will be assigned an integer value (filing status, number of dependents, or dollars) to replace the default value of "nil." The *parent* field contains the name of the goal that triggered the creation of the previous goal.

```
   (literalize goal
       name    ; the goal to be achieved
       parent  ; the goal which split to yield this one
       value)  ; integer when goal has been solved, else nil

   (p split:file-return
      (goal ↑name file-return ↑value nil)
   -->
      (make goal ↑name amount-owed
          ↑parent file-return)
      (make goal ↑name background-information
          ↑parent file-return))
```

```
(p split:give-background-information
   (goal ↑name background-information
       ↑value nil)
-->
   (make goal ↑name filing-status
       ↑parent background-information)
   (make goal ↑name header-information
       ↑parent background-information))

(p split:amount-owed
   (goal ↑name amount-owed ↑value nil)
-->
   (make goal ↑name total-tax
       ↑parent amount-owed)
   (make goal ↑name total-payments
       ↑parent amount-owed))

(make goal ↑name file-return)
```

Each splitting rule fires only once because the only modifications to the goal elements involve changing the *value* field to something other than "nil." The top-level **make** action starts the system by asserting the ultimate goal of filing an income tax return.

Splitting is not enough; the goals eventually have to be accomplished. There are two ways in which these goals can be achieved. The first occurs when the goal is so simple that immediate solution is possible. The following rule illustrates this circumstance.

```
(p solve:filing-status
   {<goal> (goal ↑name filing-status ↑value nil)}
-->
   (write (crlf) |Enter number representing filing status :|
          (crlf) |   1: Single|
          (crlf) |   2: Married filing joint return|
          (crlf) |   3: Married filing separate return|
          (crlf) |   4: Head of household|
          (crlf) |   5: Qualifying widow(er) with
                      dependent child|
          (crlf) |Number: |)
   (modify <goal> ↑value (accept)))
```

This rule is obviously the backward-chaining counterpart to the rule `input-filing-status` in the forward-chaining system. But note that the backward-chaining rule fires at the end of a chain of splitting rules, not in the middle of a chain of input requests. The data are requested no earlier than they are recognized as needed.

It is worth nothing at this point that the order in which data are requested depends on the order in which the subgoals are generated. In the example given here, the order of the subgoals in the program text is opposite to the structure of Form 1040. The recency rule in conflict resolution causes the subgoals to be selected in reverse order to the sequence in the program text. Thus the order in which the questions are asked to the user corresponds to the order of the questions on Form 1040.

The second mechanism for achieving goals is the reverse of splitting. In contrast to the process of decomposing an unsolved goal into a set of unsolved subgoals, in this circumstance a goal is recognized as solved by fusing its solved subgoals. The following two rules show both the splitting rule and its mirror image, the complementary fusing rule.

```
(p split:adjusted-gross-income
   (goal ↑name adjusted-gross-income ↑value nil)
-->
   (make goal ↑name total-adjustments
       ↑parent adjusted-gross-income)
   (make goal ↑name total-income
       ↑parent adjusted-gross-income))

(p fuse:adjusted-gross-income
   {<goal> (goal ↑name adjusted-gross-income ↑value nil)}
   (goal ↑name total-income
       ↑value {<line22> >= 0})
   (goal ↑name total-adjustments
       ↑value {<line31> >= 0})
-->
   (modify <goal>
       ↑value (compute <line22> - <line31>)))
```

It is by means of these fusing rules that solutions to subgoals are backed up to their parent goals, this process recurring until the original goal is solved.

There ought to be a one-to-one relationship between rules that split and rules that fuse. To fuse without splitting is futile if there is no mechanism for generating the subgoals in the first place. After all, if the system does not know that a subgoal is to be solved, how can it go about working on a solution for it? One important exception must be mentioned: It is quite possible for a fusing rule to match on a set of solved subgoals that originated with different splitting rules. This opportunistic device shows how forward-chaining components can be inserted into a system that has a basically backward-chaining architecture. On the other hand, to split without fusing is always a blunder: It amounts to sending the system on a wild-goose chase; all effort spent in solving the subgoals is wasted because the solutions are not backed up to the original goal. The rule here is, what your system cannot join together, let no rule rend asunder.

Finally, a backward-chaining system may contain rules to implement a number of useful features that make the system more sophisticated. Suppose the user wants to know why a given value is requested. The system accepts the response "why" to any question and in reply explains its actions in terms of the goals it is working on. It knows these goals because each time a goal is split, the subgoals specify their parent. Consider the following rule:

```
(p explain
   {<goal>  (goal ↑name <subgoal>
                  ↑parent <parent-goal>
                  ↑value why)}
-->
   (write (crlf) I am trying to determine <subgoal>
                 because it is necessary to figure out
                 <parent-goal>)
   (modify <goal> ↑value nil))
```

This single rule can explain why any subgoal is being pursued by giving the parent goal as the reason. It may not be much of an explanation, but it's a start, and it requires little additional effort by the programmer.

When should one problem-solving strategy be preferred over another? As we already noted, backward chaining is preferred for diagnostic tasks, whereas forward chaining seems to be better suited for monitoring and interpretation. A useful guideline is to have the system start where there is most focus. If the nature of the data is well understood but the goals are not easily characterized (perhaps because there are many, quite different solutions), a forward-chaining architecture is to be preferred. On the other hand, if there is only one goal and a well-defined subgoal structure but little structure in the input data, it would be better to select a backward-chaining architecture. If both data and goal are highly focused, as in the income tax example, you should ask yourself why you are not looking for an algorithmic solution instead.

4.5 PROGRAM DEVELOPMENT WITH PRODUCTION SYSTEMS

The task of a typical expert system is seldom fully understood at the time an analyst begins the requirements-analysis phase of the project. One of the main advantages of using expert-system technology is the ability to create executable specifications as the results of the analysis phase. In fact, the problems addressed are usually not susceptible to a rigorous and complete analysis on one pass by an analyst. We suggest the method of *iterative enhancement* [Basili, Turner 75] as an ideal programming methodology for building expert systems. The programmer (analyst) begins with a problem statement and, interacting with the domain expert, constructs a set of problem scenarios. A problem scenario is a specific problem and a proposed method of solution by the system. The programmer-analyst identifies the objects, attributes, and relationships of the domain, as specified so far, in much the same fashion suggested in Chapter 3. The problem may ultimately be solved with either forward chaining or backward chaining. The initial stages of problem solving are the same. One iteration is completed by the creation of a small program sufficient in scope to handle the scenarios discussed with the expert. This program is tested and exercised. Future iterations may involve revising representation decisions or problem-solving decisions, enhancing the program by elaboration, or restructuring the solution through generalization or refinement. Each iteration is approached with solid software-engineering principles used to perform and record the results of the mini stages of analyze, specify, design, code, test. However, each iteration may drastically change the nature of understanding of the problem and thus result in major modifications of the program developed to date.

The methodology of *iterative enhancement* allows the expert system to learn and grow much as human trainees do, but it documents and controls that growth. At the beginning of training, incomplete knowledge may lead to some correct behavior, but most of the time the human and the expert system either get stuck or misapply what knowledge they have. Learning to think like an expert is a complex process involving not just acquisition of principles, but also discovery of structure; the system must learn to perceive distinctions and learn where to direct attention. Many of these skills are tacit rather than explicit, hence they are learned slowly. Thus the acquisition of expertise need not proceed from the abstract to the concrete. As abstractions are learned, the program is changed to reflect such learning.

Production systems grow — that is, they incorporate additional knowledge — by processes of differentiation and expansion. As a production system develops, the programmer adds or modifies rules that enable the system to recognize not only new patterns of data, but also increasingly subtler distinctions among existing patterns of data. Thus expanded and differentiated, the system can perform actions that cover the range of situations more completely and are more finely tuned to the distinctive features of the problem.

Once the designer selects a suitable system design that includes data representations and control regimes, new rules that encode domain knowledge often can be added independently. A sophisticated ***knowledge-acquisition*** system (see Section 8.1) can help the programmer explore and manage interactions among rules and, more abstractly, the knowledge that those rules represent. On the other hand, changing a program's data representations and control structures to incorporate a new insight may be considerably more risky than changing domain knowledge; it is possible that one such change may require the programmer to rewrite a large portion of the system.

In the following pages, we'll examine some of the most important ways in which production systems develop. This growth is often — but not always — monotonic; that is, frequently rules can be inserted without removal or modification of other rules, but this is by no means always the case. If the programmer is not meticulously careful, unexpected interactions of new rules with old rules will necessitate backtracking to modify code that once worked properly. With proper design and planning, the programmer can limit the need for backtracking, keeping it local to a small set of rules; but even with discipline and foresight, some new insight into the problem may prompt the programmer to adopt a thorough reorganization.

4.5.1 INCREMENTAL GROWTH BY ELABORATION

The simplest way of making a rule to detect a new situation is to give it a left-hand side that will detect patterns ignored completely by other rules in the system. The new rule will then respond to a situation that the system previously failed to notice. When a system grows this way, we say that its scope is being extended.

The example that follows illustrates this mode of production-system growth. An automated occupational counselor uses as data a client's responses on an occupational interest questionnaire. For each question, the client answers by giving an interest rating ranging from 0 (absolutely no interest) to 100 (extreme interest) in each of several areas: e.g., nature, people, business, and helping. Each item is represented as a single working memory element, and each rule detects patterns of interest that imply possible satisfaction with a certain career.[3] Some of the rules might be as follows:

```
(literalize interest
    area            ; the area of interest
    strength)       ; the degree of interest

(literalize career-possibility
    occupation)     ; an occupational possibility
```

[3] In a real system, such as the *Strong Vocational Interest Blank*, the program would compute some kind of differential strength for each career possibility.

```
(p biologist
   (interest  ↑area academic ↑strength > 60)
   (interest  ↑area nature   ↑strength > 70)
-->
   (make career-possibility ↑occupation biologist))

(p social-worker-nurse-psychotherapist
   (interest  ↑area academic ↑strength {> 20 < 60})
   (interest  ↑area people   ↑strength > 70)
   (interest  ↑area helping  ↑strength > 80)
-->
   (make career-possibility ↑occupation social-worker)
   (make career-possibility ↑occupation nurse)
   (make career-possibility ↑occupation psychotherapist))

(p forest-ranger-game-warden
   (interest  ↑area nature  ↑strength > 80)
   (interest  ↑area people  ↑strength < 30)
-->
   (make career-possibility ↑occupation forest-ranger)
   (make career-possibility ↑occupation game-warden))

(p advertising)
   (interest  ↑area business ↑strength > 60)
   (interest  ↑area creativity ↑ strength > 90)
-->
   (make career-possibility ↑occupation advertising))
```

It is easy to see how this set of rules could be augmented so that new career possibilities would be suggested. There would be no problem at all in adding the following rules:

```
(p manager
   (interest  ↑area business    ↑strength > 50)
   (interest  ↑area people      ↑strength > 60)
   (interest  ↑area responsibility ↑strength > 80)
-->
   (make career-possibility ↑occupation manager))

(p computer-hacker
   (interest  ↑area technical  ↑strength > 90)
   (interest  ↑area creativity ↑strength > 70)
   (interest  ↑area people     ↑strength     0)
   (interest  ↑area nature     ↑strength     0)
-->
   (make career-possibility ↑occupation computer-hacker))
```

When new careers open up (for example, sales representative for personal computers), the system can be modified easily.

This is just one of the ways to improve our example system. As the system developer acquires a more refined understanding of how stated interests are related to career satisfaction, the rules can be rewritten or modified further.

4.5.2 INCREMENTAL GROWTH BY REFINEMENT

Production systems grow by *refinement* when programmers see distinctions they did not see before; their response is to modify the system, now seen as too coarse, by making the left-hand sides of some of the rules more discriminating. Refinement comes in two variants: spinning off special cases and fission.

Special Cases and Exceptions

Sometimes general rules have significant exceptions or special cases, as in the familiar rhyme "I before E except after C . . .," which goes on to state further exceptions. Pairs of rules that have a special case relationship are likely to be found when one action is appropriate in the presence of some piece of information, and a default action is called for in the absence of that information. This type of reasoning has been called ***non-monotonic*** because the set of conclusions drawn from a set of data does not grow uniformly larger as new information is added: conclusions reached by default may have to be retracted.

To capture this situation in a production system, a programmer will write a general rule that signifies the default situation and then write one or more specialized versions of the general rule, which represent the exceptions. The left-hand side of each specialized rule includes all the tests in the left-hand side of the general rule and at least one extra test element as well. Thus the specialized rules require that more stringent conditions be met before they can fire.

Let's look at an example. A psychiatric diagnosis program is given patient data indicating insomnia, anxiety, rapid heartbeat, digestive distress, restlessness, headaches and irritability. The program might reasonably arrive at the diagnosis of anxiety neurosis, and in most cases it would be correct. But there is another possibility, caffeine addiction, which often produces the same symptoms. To educate the program about this exception to the rule, another rule can be added that tests for the special case in which these same symptoms are observed in the presence of excessive caffeine consumption.

The OPS5 interpreter gives preference to special cases in conflict resolution. If two conflict-set instantiations are identical except that one requires more tests than the other, the one requiring the greater number of tests will dominate. The rationale for this strategy is that those actions that are based on more information should be granted precedence. To return to the psychiatric diagnosis example, if the symptoms of anxiety neurosis are observed and the patient is known to consume large amounts of caffeine, caffeine addiction will be the first diagnosis suggested. Lacking evidence of heavy caffeine use, the default would be to diagnose anxiety neurosis right away.

It is important to remember that dominance in conflict resolution — by specificity, recency, or any other means — does not automatically prevent the dominated rule from firing: The conflict-resolution mechanism simply defers the dominated instantiation; it does not delete it. If a special-case rule is meant to supersede its general case rule, the programmer must take care to prevent both from firing on the same data — each special-case rule must disable its general-case default rule.

The following example shows how one can use the specificity conflict-resolution principle to determine how many days there are in a given year. Recall the rules for leap years:

- If the year is not divisible by 4, February has 28 days.
- If the year is divisible by 4 but not by 100, February has 29 days.
- If the year is divisible by 100 but not by 400, February has 28 days.
- If the year is divisible by 400, February has 29 days.

It is worth noting that in this example a separate rule is required to compute the modulus function. In OPS5 only pattern matching, and not computation, can be performed on the left-hand side of a rule. See Section 5.2.1 for a further discussion of this important topic. The last three rules in this example have a linear ordering; each is a specialized case of its predecessor. To assure that only one of the last three rules fires, and that it fires only once, the left-hand sides of each of these rules test to make sure that *year-length* has not yet been assigned a value.

```
(literalize year
    year-length        ; the result is to be stored here
    raw-year           ; the input datum
    year-mod-4         ; an intermediate result
    year-mod-100       ; an intermediate result
    year-mod-400)      ; an intermediate result

(p take-modulus
   {(year ↑year-mod-4 nil) <year>}
-->
   (modify <year> ↑year-mod-4 (compute raw-year \\ 4)
        ↑year-mod-100 (compute raw-year \\ 100)
        ↑year-mod-400 (compute raw-year \\ 400)))
```

```
(p year-not-4-divisible
   {(year ↑year-length nil ↑year-mod-4 <> 0)          <year>}
-->
   (modify <year> ↑year-length 365))

(p year-4-divisible
   {(year ↑year-length nil ↑year-mod-4 0)             <year>}
-->
   (modify <year> ↑year-length 366))

(p year-100-divisible
   {(year ↑year-length nil ↑year-mod-4 0
       ↑year-mod-100 0)                               <year>}
-->
   (modify <year> ↑year-length 365))

(p year-400-divisible
   {(year ↑year-length nil ↑year-mod-4 0
       ↑year-mod-100 0     ↑year-mod-400 0            <year>}
-->
   (modify <year> ↑year-length 366))

(make year ↑raw-year 1984)
```

It is very common for chunks of knowledge to be organized as sets of special cases, each with its own special treatment, along with a default treatment that is to be applied when none of the special cases is recognized. It is possible, but not as common, for the knowledge to be arranged in a multilevel hierarchy, as in the example, so that there is a layered set of rules with each successive stratum having more and more specific left-hand sides, the default of one rule being a special case of another. When this is the case, the process of program development need not follow a single course, either top-down or bottom-up. Many times, general rules are incorporated *after* the special case rules once it is discovered that the set of special cases does not exhaust the breadth of situations encountered. In general, the order in which the rules are entered, whether special case first, general case first, or inside outward, depends on how the problem is analyzed and the domain knowledge acquired.

Incremental Growth By Fission

Knowledge can also be refined by subdividing cases that previously were treated alike. A rule-based system becomes more discriminating when its rules undergo a process of fission: One rule is replaced (not augmented) by rules that are special cases of the original one. The actions then can be more closely tailored to the individual situations that are anticipated. For example, a production system that models an athletic coach may be mistaken in recommending the same training regimes for, say, both sprinters and milers. If so, the remedy might be to split some of the rules into two, one tailored for "sprint" and the other for "middle-distance." An even deeper knowledge of athletic training might lead to responding differentially on the basis of muscle composition, body fat, injury-proneness, and personality factors.

To return to the occupational-counselor example of Section 4.5.1, suppose the programmer wants to refine the following rule:

```
(p social-worker-nurse-psychotherapist
   (interest  ↑area academic ↑strength {> 20 < 60})
   (interest  ↑area people   ↑strength >70)
   (interest  ↑area helping  ↑strength >80)
-->
   (make career-possibility ↑occupation social-worker)
   (make career-possibility ↑occupation nurse)
   (make career-possibility ↑occupation psychotherapist))
```

Perhaps it is known that nurses differ from social workers and psychotherapists in that they have greater technical interests. Then the above rule could be split into two, as shown below:

```
(p social-worker:psychotherapist
   (interest  ↑area academic ↑strength {> 20 < 60})
   (interest  ↑area people   ↑strength > 70)
   (interest  ↑area helping  ↑strength > 80)
   (interest  ↑area technical ↑strength < 70)
-->
   (make career-possibility ↑occupation social-worker)
   (make career-possibility ↑occupation psychotherapist))

(p nurse
   (interest  ↑area academic ↑strength {> 20 < 60})
   (interest  ↑area people   ↑strength > 70)
   (interest  ↑area helping  ↑strength > 80)
   (interest  ↑area technical ↑strength > 40)
-->
   (make career-possibility ↑occupation nurse))
```

When rules are split this way, more than one of the new rules may be able to fire depending on whether or not the newly added condition elements are mutually exclusive and whether or not the right-hand-side actions of one disable any of the others. In the present example, the new rules are neither mutually exclusive nor do they inhibit one another; both rules will fire if the person's technical interest lies between 40 and 70 and all other condition elements are satisfied.

Structured Programming

Fission and (to an extent) special case are the modes of production-system maintenance that most closely resemble the structured-programming ideals of top-down design and stepwise refinement. (The main difference between these two lies in whether or not the more discriminating rules supplant or augment the less discriminating ones.) For production systems that grow predominantly in either of these two ways, an early version of the rule set will consist of a few rules that lump together all cases into a few gross categories, just as infants are prone to calling all medium-sized, four-legged mammals "doggy." As the system is refined, the rules become more and more discriminating; rules that neglected to differentiate on the basis of important patterns in the data are replaced by more selective rules. The system might be said to gain *resolution* rather than scope.

4.5.3 SHRINKAGE BY GENERALIZATION

Generalization is a means by which production systems shrink rather than grow; while keeping the quantity of knowledge constant, generalization refines the representation of knowledge in the direction of simplicity, elegance, and efficiency. Often a production system can be radically simplified by the substitution of a few powerful general rules for many clumsy or overly specific ones. A related improvement is to shorten the right-hand sides of rules by gathering together in one place repeated sequences of actions.

There are many situations for which generalization is the obvious remedy. If two rules have the equivalent right-hand sides, and both their left-hand sides can be expressed in a unified way, the two rules can be collapsed into one. The following example program is part of an automated postal clerk program: Given an address without a zip code, find the zip code. The following three rules differ only in the value given for the *street* attribute of the *address*. the rules set the zip code for the address matched by the LHS.

```
(literalize address
    number     ; building number
    street     ; name of street, road, lane, court, etc.
    city       ; name of the city, town, village, etc.
    state      ; name of the state or province
    zip)       ; five-digit ZIP code

(p Heyden-48219
   {(address ↑number > 16100  ↑street Heyden
       ↑city Detroit    ↑state Michigan
       ↑zip nil) <address>}
-->
   (modify <address> ↑zip 48219))
```

```
(p Kentfield-48219
   {(address ↑number > 16100  ↑street Kentfield
       ↑city Detroit    ↑state Michigan
       ↑zip nil) <address>}
-->
   (modify <address> ↑zip 48219))

(p Vaughan-48219
   {(address ↑number > 16100  ↑street Vaughan
       ↑city Detroit    ↑state Michigan
       ↑zip nil) <address>}
-->
   (modify <address> ↑zip 48219))
```

It should be obvious that the three rules can be collapsed into one rule using a disjunction for the value of *street:*

```
(p Heyden:Kentfield:Vaughan-48219
   {(address ↑number > 16100
       ↑street << Heyden Kentfield Vaughan >>
       ↑city Detroit    ↑state Michigan
       ↑zip nil) <address>}
-->
   (modify <address> ↑zip 48219))
```

Similarly, if a special-case rule performs actions that have the same effect as its general-case counterpart, the special-case rule is redundant and can be deleted without affecting the correctness of the production system.

Another common way to generalize production systems is to look for complex actions that occur in the right-hand side of many rules. When this occurs, it is usually possible to treat this sequence of actions as a unit. One way is to consider the sequence of actions as a subgoal, setting aside a group of rules to achieve this subgoal and spawning the subgoal by creating a working memory element that triggers this group of rules. More generally, any frequently occurring sequence of operations, however complex, can be isolated and treated as a subgoal, and subgoals can be nested or can communicate with one another arbitrarily. There will be an extensive treatment of subgoaling in Section 5.2.

Consider, as an example, the situation in which many separate rules perform the same sequence of right-hand-side actions that place an element onto the tail of a queue. This sequence of actions can be performed by a single rule triggered by a working memory element; each of the rules that once performed its own enqueue operation is rewritten so that instead it creates the triggering element that contains, or points to, the unique information.

Large production systems such as expert systems typically grow in waves, incremental growth alternating with sudden shrinkage. The interval between reorganizations may be short at the beginning of the project and quite long toward the end, because the programmer needs time to understand the domain deeply enough to be able to reconceptualize it. If the domain lacks structure, or if the knowledge engineer discovers its structure piecemeal after considerable programming effort, generalization is likely to play a large role in production-system program development.

4.6 EXERCISES

4-1 An auto-repair shop has a book that gives the estimated required labor for performing various repairs. Assume that this information has been entered into a production system with working memory elements as follows:

```
(literalize estimated-labor
    job-name        ; the name of the job to be performed
    hours)          ; the estimated number of required hours

(literalize job
    job-name        ; the name of the job to be performed
    difficulty)     ; major, moderate, minor

(make estimated-labor
    ↑job-name install-battery
    ↑hours 1)

(make estimated-labor
    ↑job-name install-control-arm-bushings
    ↑hours 5)
```

Write a three-rule production system to categorize a job as "minor" if it requires two hours or less, "moderate" if it requires more than two hours but no more than four hours, and "major" if it requires more than four hours of labor. Store the result in the *difficulty* attribute of the *job* working memory element. Assume that the value of this attribute is initially "nil."

4-2 Solve the previous problem by writing a single rule and storing the boundary values in working memory elements. Assume that no job requires more than 100 hours.

4-3 An input value may be stored dutifully in working memory but have no chance of influencing the control of the program. Give some ways in which this might occur.

4-4 a) Write a production-system program in which no rule ever disables another rule. Make sure that the only way an instantiation ever leaves the conflict set is by refraction.

b) Write a production-system program in which no rule ever enables another rule. Make sure that no new instantiation ever enters the conflict set from the first cycle onward.

4-5 In the backward-chaining production system to fill out the income tax return, answering "why" to the question about filing status yields the unhelpful explanation, "I am trying to determine filing status because it is necessary to figure out background information." Everybody who has ever filled out Form 1040 knows that filing status is necessary for looking up taxes in the schedules and tables. Why is the explanation so far off track?

4-6 It is certainly bothersome and inelegant to write rules in pairs, one to split and one to fuse. What obstacles stand in the way of writing a single rule to fuse all subgoals into their parent?

5 Advanced Programming Techniques for OPS5

Chapter 4 discussed production-system programming in terms of the mechanisms of control and program development. The discussion in Chapter 5 will detail the concrete choices that the production-system programmer has to make, weighing the advantages and disadvantages of several options. The purpose is to give the reader a set of useful tools for programming with production systems, with an emphasis on data structures and algorithms.

5.1 APPLICATIONS OF COMPOUND DATA REPRESENTATIONS

All modern programming systems provide some mechanism for the programmer to impose structure onto collections of primitive data objects. Lists, arrays, strings, and records are examples of such structured data types. In OPS5, the built-in structured data types are element classes and vector attributes.

5.1.1 VECTORS AS LISTS AND ARRAYS

Vectors resemble lists or strings of scalars, both syntactically and in terms of the permissible operations on them. Nevertheless they differ importantly from their counterparts in LISP, SNOBOL, and PL/I. To manipulate these data types, OPS5 programmers must learn to use a set of built-in functions in a disciplined way.

The right-hand-side function **substr** allows subsequences of vectors to be selected in much the same way as the *substr* function in PL/I extracts substrings from variables of type *character*. This function can be used to implement data structures such as arrays, strings, stacks, queues, and dequeues, depending on the set of operations permitted on the vector. However, this is not necessarily the best way to implement these structures.

The **substr** function returns a list of atoms that constitute a subsequence of a vector. This function takes three arguments:

1. The first argument specifies the working memory element that holds the vector and should be an element variable. (It can also be the number representing the condition element, but this is not recommended.)
2. The second argument is the index of the beginning of the subsequence and can be either an attribute name, an integer, or a variable that evaluates to an attribute name or an integer.
3. The third argument is the index of the end of the subsequence and also can be either an attribute name, an integer, or a variable that evaluates to one of the two. It can also be the special symbol **inf** that denotes that the end of the subsequence is the end of the vector.

In all but the simplest cases, the use of the **substr** function requires use of the OPS5 function **litval** and action **bind**, which are discussed in the following paragraphs.

If we want just the first element of the vector attribute, or in fact any attribute, we can use the name of attribute as the second and third arguments (note that the index operator "↑" is not used). For example, assume the following declarations:

```
(vector-attribute sequence)

(literalize string string-length sequence)
```

One could access the first element of the string with the function call

```
(substr <string-variable> sequence sequence)
```

But what if the beginning of the subsequence is some position other than the first? Obviously, something has to be added to the address of the first element of the vector attribute, which must therefore be a number rather than an attribute name.

To retrieve the numeric value of this address, the built-in function **litval** can be invoked to return this value so that an offset can be added to it. The argument that **litval** takes is an attribute name, and the value it returns is the value assigned to that attribute name during compilation. Note that the programmer never has to pay attention to what this value is; it is enough that the **litval** function can get the value when it is needed. The sum of the address and offset then has to be bound to a variable name, which can then be used as the second (or sometimes the third) argument to the **substr** function. We have already seen how values can be bound to variables on the left-hand side, but now we want to do the binding on the right-hand side. All that is needed are a fresh variable name and the **bind** action.

Suppose the subsequence extracted by the **substr** function is to start with the second element of the vector. The following example shows how to put everything together. The rule `tail` shifts each element of a vector to the preceding position, deleting the prior occupant of the first position. Note that this program will execute an infinite loop if it runs at all.

```
(vector-attribute vector)

(literalize vector-holder
    vector)

(p tail
   {(vector-holder) <vector-holder>}
-->
   (bind <first-position> (litval vector))
   (bind <second-position> (compute <first-position> + 1))
   (modify <vector-holder> ↑vector
     (substr <vector-holder> <second-position> inf) nil))
```

Two features of this example should be mentioned. First, the keyword **inf** indicates that the **substr** function should extract all explicitly assigned values from the vector attribute *vector*. Thus the default "nil" acts as a terminating value. Second, the new value of <vector-holder> has a fresh "nil" attached to the end. This forces the prior value of the final element to be overwritten. If this new "nil" were absent, the new vector would be the same length as the old one, with the last element appearing twice.

It is not difficult to make an OPS5 vector attribute behave somewhat like an array. To access an individual array element requires computing its address within the working memory element. The function **litval** can be used to return the address of the first element of the vector; that is, the position of the vector in the working memory element. The array index is then used as an offset to access the desired element for reading or writing.

```
(vector-attribute array-value)

(literalize array
    array-name                  ; the name of the array
    lower-array-bound           ; the lower array index
    upper-array-bound           ; the upper array index
    array-value)                ; the vector representing
                                ;  the array

(literalize array-operation    ; a command to perform
                                ;  an operation
    array-name                  ; the name of the array
    operation                   ; the operation to be performed
    index                       ; the index of the element
    value)                      ; the value read or written
```

```
(p read-array-element
   {(array ↑array-name <name>
       ↑lower-array-bound <LB>
       ↑upper-array-bound <UB>) <array>}
   {(array-operation
       ↑array-name <name>
       ↑operation read
       ↑index {<index> >= <LB> <= <UB>}
       ↑value nil) <read-op>}
-->
   (bind <first-element> (litval array-value))
   (bind <address> (compute <first-element> + <index> - 1))
   (modify <read-op>
      ↑value (substr <array> <address> <address>)))

(p write-array-element
   {(array ↑array-name <name>
       ↑lower-array-bound <LB>
       ↑upper-array-bound <UB>) <array>}
   {(array-operation
       ↑array-name <name>
       ↑operation write
       ↑index {<index> >= <LB> <= <UB>}
       ↑value {<element> <> nil}) <array-operation>}
-->
   (bind <first-element> (litval array-value))
   (bind <address> (compute <first-element> + <index> - 1))
   (modify <array> ↑<address> <element>)
   (remove <array-operation>))
   (make array ↑array-name A
       ↑lower-array-bound 1
       ↑upper-array-bound 10
       ↑array-value 1 1 2 3 5 8 13 21 34 55)
```

To perform a read or write operation on the array, an *array-operation* working memory element is created. The action

```
   (make array-operation
       ↑array-name A
       ↑operation read
       ↑index 3)
```

instructs rule `read-array-element` to extract the value A[3] (if it exists) and return it in the *value* field of the *array-operation*, while the action

```
   (make array-operation
       ↑array-name A
       ↑operation write
       ↑index 5
       ↑value 77)
```

instructs rule `write-array-element` to assign the value 77 to A[5], provided that array A exists. If the array element returned by the rule `read-array-element` has the value "nil," this rule will fire an infinite number of times, since only the time tag of the *array-operation* will be changed, causing the rule to be reinstantiated. In practice, this should not be a problem if the programmer is careful to initialize the array properly.

List operations similar to those available in LISP are equally easy. The following code fragment shows how the list operations head, tail, and append can be implemented using vectors and the functions **substr** and **litval.** The working memory element *list-operation* both specifies the command and returns the result. Recall that OPS5 vectors can contain only scalars, so these lists are not as general as those of LISP.

```
(vector-attribute list-value)

(literalize list
    list-value)             ; a list of symbolic atoms

(literalize list-operation
    operation               ; the operation to be performed
    list-value)             ; list which is the operand or result

(p append
   {(list-operation ↑operation append) <list-operation>}
   {(list) <list>}
-->
   (modify <list-operation>
       ↑list-value (substr <list> list-value inf)
                   (substr <list-operation> list-value inf)))

(p head
   {(list-operation
       ↑operation head
       ↑list-value nil) <list-operation>}
   (list ↑list-value {<val> <> nil})
-->
   (modify <list-operation> ↑list-value <val>))

(p tail
   {(list-operation
       ↑operation tail
       ↑list-value nil) <list-operation>}
   {(list ↑list-value {<val> <> nil}) <list>}
-->
   (bind <first> (litval list-value))
   (bind <second> (compute <first> + 1))
   (modify <list-operation>
       ↑list-value (substr <list> <second> inf)))
```

Note that the append operation concatenates its operand to the end of the list. It would have been just as easy to append the operand at the beginning.

5.1.2 LINKED DATA REPRESENTATIONS

Because production systems access data by value rather than by address, it is easier to create linked data structures in OPS5 than it is using arrays or pointer variables in procedural programming languages. The following program fragment, which shows one way to implement a queue as a singly linked list, is quite a bit clearer than the **substr** implementation of arrays. The purpose of this example is to show the way pointers are implemented: node A points to node B if and only if the *next* field of node A is equal to the *label* field of node B. Links are traced by a process of matching rather than of dereferencing, which makes linked data structures easier to manage. The built-in function **genatom** returns a new symbolic atom each time it is called, thereby guaranteeing that the pointers are unique. In this implementation, there is a distinguished node whose *label* attribute has the value "head" and whose *value* attribute is never accessed.

```
(literalize node
    label          ; the "address" of the node
    next           ; a pointer to the address of the next node
    value)         ; the datum stored in the node

(literalize element
    value          ; the datum to be stored in a node
    operation)     ; the operation to be performed on the list

(p enqueue-element
   {(node ↑next nil) <node>}
   {(element ↑operation enqueue ↑value {<newval> <> nil})
    <element>}
-->
   (bind <link> (genatom))
   (make node ↑label <link> ↑value <newval>)
   (modify <node> ↑next <link>)
   (remove <element>))

(p dequeue-element
   {(node ↑label head ↑next <link>) <head-node>}
   {(node ↑label <link> ↑value <head-value> ↑next <newlink>)
    <next-node>}
   {(element ↑operation dequeue ↑value nil) <element>}
-->
   (modify <element> ↑value <head-value>)
   (modify <head-node> ↑next <newlink>)
   (remove <next-node>))

(make node ↑label head)
```

Another example of a linked data structure will be presented in Section 5.2.4, where recursion is discussed.

Linking allows the programmer to create data representations as complex as needed for any conceivable application. In particular, linking is necessary for implementing instances of graphs such as goal trees, semantic networks, schemas (frames), and other complex structures encountered in artificial intelligence. Whenever the data are characterized by extensive and varied interrelations, linked data representations are likely to be found.

A curious feature of linked data representations in OPS5 is that dangling pointers do not pose the problem that they do in languages such as C and PASCAL, in which pointer variables are (virtual) machine addresses. A dangling pointer in an OPS5 program will never cause a memory fault; the rule that references the pointer simply will not fire. In fact, one can use rules with negated condition elements to test for dangling pointers, and thereby exploit this information within the program's logic.

5.1.3 NONLINKED DATA REPRESENTATIONS

Some simple data representations do not need to be linked or stored as vectors, since the production-system architecture may permit particularly elegant data representations that have no counterpart in traditional programming languages. Sparse arrays, stacks, and priority queues will serve as simple examples, since their members can be created and manipulated independently.

Example: Sparse Arrays

A sparse array is one in which the vast majority of the elements assume some default value such as "0" (zero) and thus do not have to be represented explicitly. A nonlinked OPS5 representation of sparse arrays might represent each element with a nondefault value by a separate working memory element.

```
(literalize operation
    op-name                  ; the operation: read or write
    array-name               ; the name of the array
    index                    ; the array position being accessed
    value)                   ; the value returned by the operation

(literalize array-elt
    array-name               ; the name of the array
    index                    ; the array position of this element
    value)                   ; the value of this element

; the next rule fires if the element is explicitly
;  represented in working memory
```

```
(p modify-nondefault-array-element
   {(operation ↑op-name write
        ↑array-name <A>
        ↑index <INX>
        ↑value <VAL>)                              <operation>}
   {(array-elt ↑array-name <A>
        ↑index <INX>)                              <array-elt>}
-->
   (modify <array-elt> ↑value <VAL>)
   (remove <operation>))

; this rule fires if the element is not explicitly
;  represented in working memory, signifying that
;  it assumes the default value
(p modify-default-array-element
   {(operation ↑op-name write
        ↑array-name <A>
        ↑index <INX>
        ↑value <VAL>)                              <operation>}
 - (array-elt ↑array-name <A>
        ↑index <INX>)
-->
   (make array-elt ↑array-name <A>
        ↑index <INX>
        ↑value <VAL>)
   (remove <operation>))

(p read-nondefault-array-element
   {(operation ↑op-name read
        ↑array-name <A>
        ↑index <INX>
        ↑value nil)                                <operation>}
   (array-elt ↑array-name <A>
        ↑index <INX>
        ↑value <VAL>)
-->
   (modify <operation> ↑value <VAL>))

(p read-default-array-element
   {(operation ↑op-name read
        ↑array-name <A>
        ↑index <INX>
        ↑value nil)                                <operation>}
 - (array-elt ↑array-name <A>
        ↑index <INX>)
-->
   (modify <operation> ↑value 0))
```

This example assumes that no array element may assume the value "nil." If this assumption is violated, the rule `read-nondefault-array-element` may get caught in an infinite loop.

Example: Stacks

A stack is a one-dimensional data structure that obeys a last-in, first-out access discipline. One can push a new item onto the stack or pop the last-entered item, if there is one, from the stack. It is very easy to implement stacks in OPS5 without using links or vectors, or even array indices, because the conflict-resolution strategy has a built-in bias toward the most recently created (or modified) instances of an element class. Note in the following code fragment how recency can be exploited to implement the stack discipline.

```
(literalize stack-element
    value)                          ; the value of the stack element

(literalize stack-operation
    operation                       ; push or pop
    value)                          ; the returned value of pop

(p push-stack
   {(stack-operation ↑operation push
       ↑value <val>)                <stack-operation>}
-->
   (make stack-element ↑value <val>)
   (remove <stack-operation>))

(p pop-stack
   {(stack-element ↑value <val>)    <stack-element>}
   {(stack-operation ↑operation pop
       ↑value nil)                  <stack-operation>}
-->
   (modify <stack-operation> ↑value <val>)
   (remove <stack-element>))
```

The rule `pop-stack` becomes instantiated with every *stack-element* in working memory, but the OPS5 conflict-resolution strategies always select the instantiation containing the *stack-element* that was most recently created. Thus the characteristic last-in, first-out stack discipline is a convenient byproduct of the OPS5 conflict-resolution strategies. The preceding example is not always the best way to implement a stack; since the rule `pop-stack` becomes instantiated (if at all) with every stack element, the conflict set becomes quite congested if there are many elements on the stack.

Example: Priority Queue

Our final example of a nonlinked data representation is very illuminating. Consider the operation of inserting a node into a priority list. The elements in a priority list are ordered according to the value of some *key* or *priority* and are retrieved according to the keying order. In a procedural language, an obvious data structure is a singly linked list. Let us first consider the OPS5 version of this linked data representation.

For simplicity, assume that the first node in the list is a dummy node containing a priority less than that of any legal priority (i.e., negative infinity), and the last node is an analogous dummy with an impossibly large priority value (positive infinity). Insertion into the priority list requires only one rule:

```
(literalize node
    priority          ; the key value
    label             ; equal to the "next" field of the previous
                      ;  element
    next)             ; equal to the "label" field of the next
                      ;  element

(literalize new-node
    priority)         ; the priority of a node to be inserted

(p insert-in-priority-order
   {(new-node ↑priority <new-priority>) <new-node>}
   {(node ↑priority <= <new-priority> ↑next <link>) <follow>}
   (node ↑priority > <new-priority> ↑label <link>)
-->
   (bind <new-label> (genatom))
   (make node ↑priority <new-priority>
       ↑label <new-label>
       ↑next <link>)
   (remove <new-node>)
   (modify <follow> ↑next <new-label>))
```

Since this operation takes only one rule, the programmer may not notice that the links are unnecessary.

Let's try an unlinked representation. New nodes are not inserted into a list; they are simply created. It is easy to access the node with the smallest (or largest) priority value. This is nothing other than the familiar operation of finding the minimum value element of a set.

```
(literalize node
    priority)

(p print-first-node
   (node ↑priority <p>)
 - (node ↑priority < <p>)
-->
   (write (crlf) <p>))
```

It is equally easy to access the first node having a priority greater than (or less than) a specified value, to delete a node from the list, or to traverse the list in priority order. This example should reveal some of the hidden power of production systems.

5.2 FLOW OF CONTROL

Whatever control is not built into the production-system interpreter must be programmed using suitable rules and working memory elements. Production-system languages differ greatly in the amount of freedom that the programmer has in selecting control regimes. At one extreme, the EMYCIN interpreter has built-in data structures and control strategy, while PRISM gives the programmer a great deal of freedom — and responsibility — to hand-tailor the system to the particular application. This section discusses ways the programmer can exploit the features of a general-purpose production system language like OPS5 to implement common control regimes.

Programmers who are familiar only with procedural languages (such as ALGOL, APL, BASIC, C, COBOL, FORTRAN, PASCAL, and PL/I) are accustomed to thinking that flow of control is intimately related to the sequence in which commands appear in the source listing of a program. With the help of a few constructs, such as jumps, loops, conditionals, and procedure and function invocations, they are allowed to moderate the tyranny of sequence. Production systems behave very differently. Flow of control depends not on any explicitly programmed sequence but on recognition of ever-changing patterns in working memory. Learning to exploit the powerful features of production systems is as much a matter of overcoming sequential programming habits as it is of mastering new techniques.

Learning to program control into a production system requires a thorough understanding of the interpreter's recognize-act cycle and conflict-resolution strategy. This understanding not only guides the programmer in selecting the most efficient implementation of the needed control structure, but is fundamental to the programmer's recognition of what can be done. Our discussion of control structures will illustrate this principle.

5.2.1 CONDITIONALS

Since the primary syntactic unit of a production system, the rule, is an *if . . ., then* pair, the role of conditionals in rule-based programming is as prominent as that of the assignment statement in algebraic languages. But rules must not be identified with conditional statements; the pattern-matching process is not simply testing Boolean conditionals on a set of variables. One crucial difference between rules and ordinary conditional statements is that the left-hand side of a rule is a conjunction of (possibly negated) existentially quantified predicates. That is, the match is successful only if there exist working memory elements such that predicates of the positive condition elements are simultaneously satisfied, and there exist no working memory elements that satisfy the predicates of the negated condition elements. Thus the interpreter does not simply test the expressions to determine whether they are true; rather, it engages in a search to determine if it can bind variables in such a way as to make the expression true. It is this characteristic of pattern matching, along with the dynamic size of working memory, that gives production systems their distinctive capabilities.

The programmer may design a production system to ignore existential quantification, thereby making it emulate traditional programming systems. All that is necessary to nullify the effect of the implicit existential quantifier is to assure that there exists exactly *one* copy of each working memory element class at all times. Under this constraint, it is easy to see that matches depend on the values stored in working memory and not on the existence of the elements. Under these conditions, working memory elements become the production-system equivalents of global, static variables. Similarly, it is not difficult to emulate more advanced memory management features, such as automatic allocation and nested scope rules, but to do so is pointless. If that is what is needed, the program should have been written in a language which provides those features.

In procedural languages the *if* part of *if* . . ., *then* statements is called a Boolean (or logical) expression and is built up from relational and Boolean operators. Common relational operators are = (equal to), < (less than), > (greater than), >= (greater than or equal to), <= (less than or equal to), and <> or ~= (not equal), all of which are provided in OPS5. These are binary operators, and when applied to their arguments (literals or values stored in working memory elements), they yield a Boolean (logical) result. Boolean operators such as *and*, *or*, and *not* take Boolean arguments and yield Boolean results.

There is no simple correspondence between Boolean operators and the syntactic units of OPS5. There are no key words such as *and*, *or*, and *not*, nor are there built-in logical data types (as there are numeric and symbolic atoms). Conditional tests have many different uses in production systems, and how these tests are programmed varies with the usage. We'll look now at the many different ways to effect conditional tests in rule-based programming.

And

OPS5 uses conjunctions in four different ways; three have syntactic counterparts within the OPS5 language definition, while the fourth depends on program design.

The first way to program conjunctions involves multiple conditions on the same attribute. If a single value must simultaneously satisfy two or more conditions, these conditions may be grouped within curly braces:

```
(p octogenarian
   (person
       ↑age {>= 80 < 90}
       ↑name <name>)
-->
   (write (crlf) <name> is an octogenarian)
```

This rule tests the attribute *age* for simultaneous satisfaction of two conditions: that the value be less than 90 and no less than 80.

The second use of conjunctions in OPS5 is between attributes within a single condition element. More generally, any number of attributes within a condition element may be tested for simultaneous satisfaction of any number of conditions:

```
(p nominate-for-senior-class-president
   (student
       ↑name <name>
       ↑class senior
       ↑popularity high
       ↑number-of-scandals 0
       ↑grade-point-average >= 2.0)
-->
   (make nomination
       ↑office senior-class-president
       ↑name <name>))
```

Binding of values to variables is necessary if the values of different attributes are to be compared:

```
(p raise-prices
   (stock-item
       ↑item-number <item-number>)
       ↑supply <supply>
       ↑demand > <supply>)
-->
   (write (crlf) Raise the price of item <item-number>))
```

Since the same attribute may be referenced any number of times in a condition element, curly braces are unnecessary; they can be replaced by repeated tests on the same attribute. To illustrate, the rule that detects octogenarians can be rewritten without the curly braces:

```
(p octogenarian
   (person
       ↑age >= 80
       ↑age < 90
       ↑name <name>)
-->
   (write (crlf <name> is an octogenarian))
```

Nevertheless, curly braces serve as a useful notational convenience and should not be avoided just because they are unnecessary.

Conjunctions appear in a third form as the implicit operator between condition elements on the left-hand side of a rule. If predicates on the values stored in more than one working memory element must be satisfied simultaneously, the several elements can be tested with one condition element each on the left-hand side of a rule. When values must be compared among separate elements, variable binding is again required. So long as there is at least one non-negated condition element per rule, any number of condition elements may be negated, meaning that *no* working memory elements must satisfy their conditions if the rule is to fire. In the following example, the conjunction of good weather, good training, flat course, and lack of injury allows the runner to set a goal that's ten minutes faster than the current personal record for that distance.

```
(p set-marathon-time-goal
   (race ↑distance 26)
   (personal-best ↑distance 26 ↑time <PR>)
   (training ↑intensity heavy ↑regularity regular)
   (course ↑terrain flat)
   (weather ↑temperature < 60)
 - (injury)
-->
   (make goal ↑time (compute <PR> - 10)))
```

This rule will fire only if all conditions are satisfied simultaneously; this is just another way of saying that it can fire only if the conjunction of the conditions is true.

Finally, conjunctions can be distributed among two or more rules. Splitting is useful when a test is performed on *functions* of values rather than on the raw values themselves. Recall that OPS5 does not permit function invocations on the left-hand side of a rule. If it is necessary to perform a test on a function of values, two (or more) rules are needed: First, the value to be tested must be computed on the right-hand side of one rule; and second, the value so computed must be tested in a different rule.

The following example depends on the result from elementary algebra that for a quadratic equation $ax^2 + bx + c$, the quantity $b^2 - 4ac$ (the discriminant) determines the number (one or two) and type (real or complex) of roots to the equation: The conjunction being tested is that both $a \neq 0$ and $b^2 - 4ac = 0$ be simultaneously true.

```
(literalize coefficients
    a                              ; coefficient of quadratic term
    b                              ; coefficient of linear term
    c)                             ; constant

(literalize discriminant
    value)

(p compute-discriminant
   (coefficients ↑a {<a> <> 0} ↑b <b> ↑c <c>)
-->
   (make discriminant
       ↑value (compute (<b> * <b>) - (4 * <a> * <c>))))

(p one-real-root
   (discriminant ↑value 0)
-->
   (write (crlf) The quadratic equation has one real root.))

(p two-real-roots
   (discriminant ↑value {<d> > 0})
-->
   (write (crlf) The quadratic equation has two real roots.))

(p two-complex-roots
   (discriminant ↑value {<d> < 0})
-->
   (write (crlf) The quadratic equation has two complex
       roots.))
```

The rule `compute-discriminant` computes the discriminant from the coefficients, making an intermediate result named *discriminant*, which appears on the left-hand side of each of the remaining three rules.

Or

From the broadest perspective, all rules can be considered as disjuncts of a single disjunction: *if* rule 1 is instantiated *or* . . . rule N is instantiated, *then* select one instantiation and fire it. Needless to say, this observation is not very helpful to someone who wants to program a production system to take the same action in either of two or more situations, so this narrower view of disjunctions will be adopted here. In particular, the term *disjunction* will be applied only to the case in which a single action is to be taken in any of a number of situations. Given these definitions, there are only two different ways to test disjunctions in OPS5: by testing an attribute against a set of values, and by including separate rules for each disjunct.

There are many ways to test an attribute against a set of values.The relational operators <, <=, >, >=, <>, and <=> test an attribute against a set of values specified by a predicate. In the following condition element, the age of a customer is tested for membership in the set of all numbers greater than or equal to 21.

```
(customer ↑age >= 21)
```

In that example the interval was bounded at one end and unbounded at the other. To designate an interval bounded at both ends, a conjunction of tests is needed. The following condition element tests the age for membership in the set of numbers from 13 up to, but not including, 20.

```
(child ↑age {>= 13 < 20})
```

Finally, an interval that is unbounded at both ends can be tested with the same-type relational operator, <=>. The following example shows how this operator can be used to test whether a value is a number.

```
(unknown-type ↑value <=> 0)
```

Note that any number at all can be substituted for 0 in this test. To test whether the value is a symbolic atom, substitute any instance of a symbolic atom.

An attribute may also be tested for having a value equal to any one of a set of explicitly named constants by listing the constants between the delimiters << and >>. The following example tests whether a state is one of a set that is explicitly specified.

```
(state ↑name << Maine Vermont New-Hampshire
                Connecticut Rhode-Island Massachusetts >>)
```

The constants can be numbers as well, and numbers can be mixed with symbolic atoms, as in the following condition element:

```
(parent ↑number-of-children << one 1 >>)
```

When an attribute is tested for membership in a set of values either by means of a predicate or an explicit list of values, the test is implicitly an *exclusive-or,* since an attribute can have only one value at a time. To test an *inclusive-or* calls for a more generalized specification of disjunctions: separate rules whose right-hand sides are identical and whose left-hand sides specify the disjuncts. In this way both *inclusive-or* and *exclusive-or* can be implemented, depending on whether or not the left-hand sides specify mutually exclusive conditions. The following example is a test for *inclusive-or;* the rules make a plan to carry an umbrella under any of three conditions, which are not mutually exclusive.

```
(literalize weather
    sky                     ; clear, partly-cloudy, cloudy
    precipitation)          ; raining, snowing, sleeting, etc.

(literalize attire
    quality)                ; dressy, work, casual, undressed

(literalize plan
    action)                 ; what is to be done?

(literalize residence
    city)                   ; city of residence

(p currently-raining
   (weather ↑precipitation raining)
-->
   (make plan ↑action take-umbrella))

(p protect-fancy-clothes
   (weather ↑sky cloudy)
   (attire ↑quality dressy)
-->
   (make plan ↑action take-umbrella))

(p it-is-Pittsburgh
   (residence ↑city Pittsburgh)
-->
   (make plan ↑action take-umbrella))
```

In this example it is possible that all three rules may fire, making three identical reminders to take an umbrella. If this is undesirable, the first rule to fire could inhibit the others if the following negated condition element were added to the left-hand side of each rule:

```
- (plan ↑action take-umbrella)
```

In practice, the distinction between *inclusive-or* and *exclusive-or* rarely needs to be made explicit; the terminology of propositional calculus is not as well suited to production-system programming as it is to Boolean expressions in procedural languages.

Not

Predicates in OPS5 may be negated either with complementary relational operators or with negated condition elements. In the first alternative, a comparison involving a relational operator can be negated by substituting for the operator its complement: >= for <, <> for =, and so on. Negated condition elements require that there be no element in working memory that satisfies its predicates. If such an element exists, the rule will not be instantiated and cannot fire. The simplicity comes from not having to cast conditions as Boolean expressions; they are expressed in terms compatible with the chosen knowledge representation. Thus juggling Boolean operators inside conditionals is unnecessary.

5.2.2 ITERATION

The recognize-act cycle of a production-system interpreter is fundamentally a *do-while* loop, and for this reason iteration can be particularly easy to program in production systems. Often a single rule suffices.

Suppose a librarian wants to scan the catalogue with the goal of printing out the titles of all books listed in the catalogue database that were published before 1800. The name *for-each* can be applied to this control structure, since it performs the same operation once on each of a set of elements. In this case one rule will do the job:

```
(literalize book
    title                 ; title of the book
    publication-year)     ; year of publication of the book

(p list-title-of-pre-1800-book
   (book ↑publication-year {<year> < 1800}
         ↑title <title>)
-->
   (write (crlf) <year> <title>))
```

The rule `list-title-of-pre-1800-book` will be instantiated once for each working memory element of type *book* and, because of refraction, each instantiation will fire exactly once. Thus once a title is listed, it is not listed a second time.

There is a subtlety in the implementation of *for-each* that leads to a common bug. Suppose it is necessary to increase each of a set of numbers by one. The following code will not work properly:

```
(literalize number
    value)                ; a number

(p increment-number
   {(number ↑value <val>) <number>}
-->
   (modify <number> ↑value (compute <val> + 1)))
```

The reason is that modifying the working memory element gives it a new time tag, which causes it to be repeatedly reinstantiated, thereby creating an infinite loop. Depending on the application, there are many ways to get around this difficulty; setting switches in the modified elements is one way, and assigning the modified values to working memory elements of another class that are later removed or marked is another. Here is a possible solution, assuming that the attribute *status* is initialized to the value "nil."

```
(literalize number
    status              ; a flag to be set if incremented
    value)              ; the value of the number

(literalize task
    name)               ; the goal: increment or unmark

(p increment-and-mark
   (task ↑name increment)
   {(number ↑value <val> ↑status nil) <num>}
-->
   (modify <num> ↑value (compute <val> + 1)
                 ↑status marked))

(p change-task-to-unmark
   {(task ↑name increment) <task>}
-->
   (modify <task> ↑name unmark))

(p unmark
   (task ↑name unmark)
   {(number ↑status marked) <num>}
-->
   (modify <num> ↑status nil))

(p clean-up
   {(task ↑name unmark) <task>}
-->
   (remove <task>))

(make task ↑name increment)
```

This solution requires two firings for each *number* working memory element. In the special case that the loop be executed only once, the marks need not be reset. It is left as a challenging exercise for the reader to find a solution that handles each *number* working memory element only once and can be applied repeatedly (see Exercise 5-6).

Another application of *for-each* iteration is counting the number of instances of something. All that is necessary is that some counter be initialized to zero, and refraction takes care of the rest. The example that follows shows how to count the number of parent-child pairs among the employees of a given organization.

```
(literalize employee
    name                ; the employee's name
    mother-name         ; the name of the employee's mother
    father-name)        ; the name of the employee's father

(literalize pair)

(literalize pair-count
    pairs)              ; the number of pairs counted so far

(p recognize-another-pair-mother
   (employee ↑name <parent>)
   (employee
       ↑name <child>
       ↑mother-name <parent>)
-->
   (make pair))

(p recognize-another-pair-father
   (employee ↑name <parent>)
   (employee
       ↑name <child>
       ↑father-name <parent>)
-->
   (make pair))

(p count-another-pair
   {(pair) <pair>}
   {(pair-count ↑pairs <pairs>) <pair-count>}
-->
   (remove <pair>)
   (modify <pair-count> ↑pairs (compute <pairs> + 1)))

(make pair-count ↑pairs 0)
```

This example shows that a production system may iterate over arbitrary patterns, not just over working memory elements. Pattern recognition was separated from counting to avoid an infinite loop.

A more restricted form of iteration is like the *do* loop in FORTRAN and the *for* loop in PASCAL: the loop is performed a number of times known at loop entry, with an index that steps through a set of values in a fixed sequence. Such loops consist of an initialization step, a termination test, and a loop-housekeeping step. The following code fragment prints the squares of all integers between *lower-limit* and *upper-limit*, which in this case are set to 1 and 10, respectively.

```
(literalize loop-limits
    lower-limit          ; first value of loop index
    upper-limit)         ; final value of loop index
```

```
(p loop-body
   {(loop-limits ↑upper-limit <U>
       ↑lower-limit {<L> <= <U>})                 <loop-limits>}
-->
   (write (crlf) (compute <L> * <L>))
   (modify <loop-limits> ↑lower-limit (compute <L> + 1)))

(p exit-loop
   {(loop-limits)                                 <loop-limits>}
-->
   (remove <loop-limits>))

(make loop-limits ↑lower-limit 1 ↑upper-limit 10)
```

Firing of the rule `exit-loop` is deferred (because of specificity) until all instantiations of `loop-body` have fired; its function is to clean up the loop's debris.

5.2.3 GROUPING RELATED SETS OF RULES

Among the most useful standard programming constructs are subroutines (sometimes called *procedures*), functions, and coroutines. In procedural languages, subroutine calls can be thought of as a substitute for sequences of statements (that is, as compound statements). Because they return a value, functions have a different role; barring side effects, function invocations substitute for expressions. Coroutines are more complex; two or more coroutines cooperate by passing control back and forth until the task on which they are working is completed; unlike subroutines and functions, the relationship between coroutines is not hierarchical. These (and other) program units allow the programmer to avoid repeated code and, more important, permit the solution of large problems by abstraction and decomposition into a set of smaller tasks. Modular design is an important technique for managing complexity.

Production-system programming can also benefit from modular design and procedural abstraction. As production system applications grow in size and complexity, measures must be taken to keep these programs intellectually manageable. In fact, one can make the case that the characteristic features of production systems (e.g., global working memory and rules capable of interacting in many different ways) make functional decomposition especially critical.

OPS5 does not impose any structure on production memory; rules are neither ordered nor grouped. By the same token, all working memory is global; there are no scope rules and working memory is not partitioned in any way. Any structure that is demanded by the application program must be explicitly programmed. In OPS5, modular structure appears in two forms: user-defined functions and actions that can be invoked as right-hand-side primitives (described in Section 5.2.8), and sets of rules that operate collaboratively on a unique task. Experienced OPS5 programmers will use both of these methods in developing large systems, the mix depending on the nature of the problem, the habits of the designer, and the availability of shareable code.

Contexts as a Grouping Technique

Most production systems of nontrivial size can be decomposed into subsystems. Usually it is easy to identify sets of rules that in concert perform well-defined tasks: interacting with the operator, traversing a data structure, performing a multistage computation according to a fixed template, or operating on all working memory elements that satisfy some condition. It is often useful and sometimes necessary for the programmer to exert control over the firing of these rules — for example, to impose some ordering on the sequence of operations or to limit the portion of working memory on which they are to operate. When treated in this way, these rule sets, called ***tasks*** or ***contexts,*** can be made to behave as subroutines, functions, or coroutines do in procedural languages.

Since the OPS5 interpreter does not impose any grouping on the rules in production memory, contexts are created by programming the control into the rules themselves. Selective activation of contexts is effected by distinguishing a working memory element class that is used to enable and disable all the rules in the context. This ***control element*** (also called a ***context element***) is common to the left-hand sides of each rule in the context.

As an example, suppose that a production system reaches a point at which it needs to get the age of a person before it can continue solving the problem at hand. If error-checking is to be performed, it will take more than one rule firing to complete the task. The rule that recognizes that the context must be invoked may create an element as follows:

```
(make context ↑goal get-age ↑object John-Doe)
```

Then, if the conflict-resolution strategy is MEA, any satisfied rules whose *first* condition element matches this context element will be next in line to fire. The following rules might constitute the "get-age" context:

```
(literalize context
    goal          ; the name of the goal to be achieved
    object)       ; a parameter of the goal

(literalize person
    name          ; Firstname-Lastname
    age)          ; 0 <= age <= 120 or age = unknown

(literalize input
    response)     ; user input
```



```
(p get-age::interact-with-user
   (context ↑goal get-age ↑object <name>)
   (person ↑name <name> ↑age nil)
 - (input)
-->
   (write (crlf) Please enter the age of <name>
                 to the nearest year
          (crlf) or enter it as UNKNOWN)
   (make input ↑response (accept)))

(p get-age::age-acceptable
   (context ↑goal get-age ↑object <name>)
   {(input ↑response {<response> > 0 < 120})              <input>}
   {(person ↑name <name>)                                <person>}
-->
   (modify <person> ↑age <response>)
   (remove <input>))

(p get-age::unknown
   (context ↑goal get-age ↑object <name>)
   {(input ↑response << unknown UNKNOWN unk UNK >>)       <input>}
   {(person ↑name <name>)                                <person>}
-->
   (modify <person> ↑age unknown)
   (remove <input>))

(p get-age::age-unacceptable
   (context ↑goal get-age ↑object)
   {(input ↑response <response>)                          <input>}
-->
   (write (crlf) <response> is not acceptable as a value
          for age)
   (remove <input>))
```

To be noted in this example is the fact that the set of rules is self contained and can be invoked from many places at once.

Because rules inside contexts may themselves create context elements, it is easy to see that nesting can be as deep as necessary. If the MEA strategy is in effect, and all rules that are in contexts test for the context element in their first condition element, then context invocations will be stacked in the familiar fashion. The context most recently invoked is the active one so long as any of its rules are instantiated. At the moment that none of its rules can be instantiated, control will pass to the next-most-recently invoked context, if there is one. Control does not necessarily revert to the context that invoked the just-exhausted context. Consider the situation in which a single rule invokes two or more contexts with a sequence of right-hand-side **make** actions. Control will first go to the final one, since it was most recently invoked. When it is exhausted, control will revert to its predecessor in the sequence. As we will discuss further in Section 5.2.7, this is a technique for controlling the sequence of rule firings. The orderly stacking of context invocations even allows for recursion (see Section 5.2.4).

Contexts can be of any length, even one rule long, as in the following example. Suppose, as part of a cleanup operation, a "marker" field is to be reset on each node in a data structure before beginning the next stage of computation. The sequence can be initiated by creating a context element:

```
(make context ↑goal reset-markers)
```

Then a one-rule context can do the work:

```
(p reset-markers
   (context ↑goal reset-markers)
   {(node ↑marker set) <node>}
-->
   (modify <node> ↑marker reset))
```

The same end can also be accomplished without using a context element, but the sequencing may be trickier. Typical contexts tend to be between three and twenty rules in length.

When the rules in a context complete their task, the context element should be removed so as to avoid cluttering working memory and, more important, to prevent unintentionally reinvoking the context later on. If all context elements are given the same class name, such as *context* in the example above, all can be removed at the earliest permissible time with a single rule:

```
(p return
   {(context) <exhausted-context>}
-->
   (remove <exhausted-context>))
```

This rule works because the left-hand side of any other rule that uses the working memory element class named *context* will contain more tests and thus will be a special case; the rule named `return` will fire only when no other rule that matches the context element can fire.

Alternatively, a single context element may be used for multiple context invocations if one of its attributes, acting as a switch, is modified so as to activate or deactivate the rule set. A context element used in this way will be created before the rules are invoked for the first time. An invocation consists of setting a status switch within the context element, while return is effected by resetting the switch. Rewriting the example of resetting markers, the context may be invoked in the following fashion:

```
(modify <context-element> ↑status active)
```

The context itself would consist of the rule

```
(p reset-markers
   (context ↑goal reset-markers ↑status active)
   {(node ↑marker set) <node>}
-->
   (modify <node> ↑marker reset))
```

And the context may be deactivated with the rule

```
(p return
   {(context ↑status active) <exhausted-context>}
-->
   (modify <exhausted-context> ↑status inactive))
```

One limitation of this approach is that, if there can be at most one context element per context, recursion is impossible, since recursion requires generation of any number of nested self-invocations.

Contexts as Procedures

Contexts can be made to behave in a manner analogous to procedural-language subroutines, functions, or coroutines by programming the rules so that invocation and return follow the required sequence and giving the contexts their own local data. Each subroutine or function call is effected by creating a new context element with the required attributes.

Since the OPS5 MEA strategy puts extra emphasis on the first condition element in the left-hand side of a rule, making the first condition a context element provides a strict last-in first-out time ordering of contexts. This decreases the likelihood that the system will be distracted from a task once it has been initiated. There are other less elegant ways of achieving the same effect, such as by repeatedly removing and then recreating (which is the same as vacuously modifying) the context element, but these methods are not recommended.

By using the MEA strategy, subroutine calls can be nested at arbitrary depth. The rules governed by one context element may generate a new context element, which then takes precedence. The rules governed by the new context element may in turn generate another one, and so on. The recency principle for conflict resolution assures that control will be passed to the proper context element. If nested context elements govern the same set of rules, the result is *recursion*, which we'll discuss in the next section of this sequence.

The context element may be used to pass parameters and return results or pointers to results. In this way the subroutines can work on local copies of the data. In truth, all working memory elements are global; it is the program organization that imposes disciplined access to data. Making local copies of data is especially important in recursion, which requires that the separate invocations be distinguishable lest recursion be infinite.

The following production system computes a function named *index:* Given a vector and a scalar, the value of the function is defined as the ordinal position of the earliest occurrence of the given scalar in the vector, if it is found in the vector, and 0 if it is not found in the vector. A driver rule has been included to demonstrate how the function is invoked and its parameters passed. The function consists of four rules: one to copy the input parameters and initialize local variables, a second to iterate down the vector, a third to terminate upon finding the scalar in the vector, and a fourth to terminate without having found the scalar when the entire vector is scanned. Two assumptions must be satisfied if this function is to give the correct results: (1) the scalar argument in *index-args* may have any value except "nil," and (2) when the function is called, the value of *index* in *index-args* is equal to "nil."

```
(vector-attribute vector)

(literalize context
    task)                ; the function's name

(literalize index-args
    sought               ; the value sought
    vector               ; the vector in which to search
    index)               ; the returned value: the
                         ;  element's position

(literalize index-locals
    sought               ; local copy of value sought
    vector               ; local copy of vector in which
                         ;  to search
    current-index)       ; index being examined

(literalize start)

(p pop-context
   {<context> (context)}
-->
   (remove <context>))

(p index::initialize
   (context ↑task index)
   {(index-args ↑sought {<s> <> nil} ↑index nil) <arg>}
 - (index-locals)
-->
   (make index-locals
       ↑sought <s> ↑vector (substr <arg> vector inf)
       ↑current-index 1))
```

```
(p index::found-it
   (context ↑task index)
   {(index-args) <index-args>}
   {(index-locals ↑sought <s> ↑vector <s> ↑current-index <i>)
       <index-locals>}
-->
   (modify <index-args> ↑index <i>)
   (remove <index-locals>))

(p index::not-in-vector
   (context ↑task index)
   {(index-args) <index-args>}
   {(index-locals ↑vector nil) <index-locals>}
-->
   (modify <index-args> ↑index 0)
   (remove <index-locals>))

(p index::try-next
   (context ↑task index)
   {(index-locals ↑current-index <i>) <local>}
-->
   (bind <curr> (litval vector))
   (bind <next> (compute <curr> + 1))
   (modify <local> ↑current-index (compute <i> + 1)
       ↑vector (substr 2 <next> inf) nil))

(p driver
   (start)
-->
   (make context ↑task index)
   (make index-args
       ↑sought M
       ↑vector A B C D E F G H I J K L M
               N O P Q R S T U V W X Y Z))

(make start)
```

Note the role of the working memory element named *start:* the rule named `driver` needs at least one non-negated condition element on the left-hand side, so a dummy element class was created to fulfill this need.

In this example, the *index-locals* element was not explicitly linked to its context. Since there was no nesting, the relationship between context and arguments was unambiguous. In the general case, however, this will not do. Even if recency in conflict resolution does suffice to link implicitly a pair of otherwise unconnected elements, this is at best bad programming practice. It would be much better either to have an explicit link with pointers or to put the local data into the context element itself.

5.2.4 RECURSION

Recursion is a very powerful programming technique that often proves quite difficult to grasp initially. In algorithmic programming languages, recursion results when a function or procedure invokes itself (with parameters different from its input parameters, one hopes). In production systems, recursion occurs when the rules governed by a context element make yet another copy of the context element that governs them. The new element then seizes control because it is more recently created; the older element is "stacked" to assume control when the newer context elements are removed or deactivated.

No matter how disguised, recursion is always characterized by a two-step organization. The *recursion step* works on its task by splitting it into simpler subtasks, reinvoking itself to solve the subtasks it has created. When the subtasks become so simple that they can be solved without further splitting, the *base step* performs the primitive operations that solve these simplest of subtasks.

By now everybody expects the first example of recursion to be computing factorials — and by golly we are not going to disappoint you! Two rules constitute the recursion step, and one rule forms the base step.

```
(literalize function
    name                  ; name of the function
    input-parameter       ; argument passed to the function
    output-parameter)     ; value returned by the function

(p recursion-step-downward
   (function ↑name factorial
       ↑input-parameter {<N> > 0}
       ↑output-parameter nil)
-->
   (make function ↑name factorial
       ↑input-parameter (compute <N> - 1)))

(p recursion-step-upward
   {(function ↑name factorial
       ↑input-parameter {<IP> > 0}
       ↑output-parameter nil) <current-call>}
   {(function ↑name factorial
       ↑output-parameter {<result> > 0}) <backed-up-value>}
-->
   (modify <current-call>
       ↑output-parameter (compute <IP> * <result>))
   (remove <backed-up-value>))
```

```
(p base-step
   {(function ↑name factorial
       ↑input-parameter 0
       ↑output-parameter nil) <function>}
-->
   (modify <function> ↑output-parameter 1))

(p write-result
   {(function ↑input-parameter <argument>
       ↑output-parameter {<result> > 0}) <function>}
 - (function ↑output-parameter nil)
-->
   (write (crlf) <argument> ! | = | <result>)
   (remove <function>))
```

This example illustrates the use of the context element (in this case named *function*) for passing parameters and returning results.

Since recursion is most appropriate for recursively defined data structures, the second example for recursion will illustrate postorder (depth-first) traversal of an unordered tree. The element class called *traverse* serves as the context element, the rule `visit-children-of-internal-node` is the recursion step, and the rule `visit-node` is the base step.

```
(literalize node        ; a node in the tree
    label               ; the unique "address" of the node
    parent-ptr          ; the same value as the parent's label
    value)              ; the datum associated with the node

(literalize traverse    ; a context element
    node)               ; pointer to the node being visited

(p start-traversing
   (node ↑label root)
-->
   (make traverse ↑node root))

(p visit-children-of-internal-node
   (traverse ↑node <current>)
   (node ↑label <current>)
   (node ↑label <child> ↑parent-ptr <current>)
-->
   (make traverse ↑node <child>))

(p visit-node
   {(traverse ↑node <current>) <traverse>}
   (node ↑label <current> ↑value <val>)
-->
   (write (crlf) <val>)
   (remove <traverse>))
```

```
(make node ↑label root ↑value 0)
(make node ↑label 1    ↑value 1 ↑parent-ptr root)
(make node ↑label 2    ↑value 2 ↑parent-ptr root)
(make node ↑label 3    ↑value 3 ↑parent-ptr root)
(make node ↑label 4    ↑value 4 ↑parent-ptr 1)
(make node ↑label 5    ↑value 5 ↑parent-ptr 2)
(make node ↑label 6    ↑value 6 ↑parent-ptr 2)
(make node ↑label 7    ↑value 7 ↑parent-ptr 3)
(make node ↑label 8    ↑value 8 ↑parent-ptr 3)
(make node ↑label 9    ↑value 9 ↑parent-ptr 3)
```

The top-level **make** actions construct the tree. Be sure you understand why the rule `visit-node` visits the leaf nodes and internal nodes in the proper order.

Also recall that recursion, while elegant, is not necessarily optimal or even acceptably efficient in some applications. Consider once again the factorial example and how it can be rewritten iteratively:

```
(literalize function
    name                  ; name of the function
    argument              ; argument passed to the function
    result)               ; value returned by the function

(p factorial-initialize
   {(function ↑name factorial
       ↑argument >= 0
       ↑result nil) <function>}
-->
   (modify <function> ↑result 1))

(p factorial-step
   {(function ↑name factorial
       ↑argument {<arg> > 1}
       ↑result {<res> > 0}) <function>}
-->
   (modify <function> ↑result (compute <res> * <arg>)
       ↑argument (compute <arg> - 1)))
```

The iterative version of the factorial program is shorter and easier to understand, requires half as many firings as the recursive version, and does not add anything to working memory. Recursion should be reserved for those problems that are not easily solved in any other way.

5.2.5 DEMONS

Not all rules in a production system need to reside within contexts. A ***demon*** is a rule that does not have to wait for a context invocation before it can fire;

this occurs because there is no test for a context element in its left-hand side. Standing outside all contexts, a demon is instantiated as soon as it is matched with the data that it wants, regardless of what the production system is doing at the time. Exactly when a demon is selected for firing, however, depends on the conflict-resolution strategy, the ordering of condition elements in the demon's left-hand side, and competition with other demons.

If the MEA conflict-resolution strategy is in effect, then a demon that is to override contexts must in its first condition element match a working memory element that was recently created. If its first condition element tests for a working memory element that is older than the most recent context element, all its instantiations will just sit in the conflict set and wait their turn. With the LEX strategy, no particular emphasis is placed on the first condition element, so it makes no difference which position in the left-hand side is occupied by the test for a context element. Contexts can be enabled and disabled, but there is much less focus of attention, and demons can interrupt contexts with much greater ease under LEX than under the MEA strategy.

One important use of demons is to alter flow of control. Indeed, the rule named `return` (in Section 5.2.3), which removes exhausted context elements, is a demon. In other situations demons can be used to divert the flow of control when exceptional conditions arise, much like hardware *interrupts* and *traps*. For example, demons can be used as error-handlers to detect bad input, illegal values at any stage of the computation, and violations of protocol in data representations (such as dangling pointers). Another use for demons is to have them respond to emergencies in real-time applications — e.g., when nuclear reactors overheat, when patients in intensive care develop cardiac irregularities, or when military tactical situations change.

5.2.6 GOTO

A powerful but infinitely abusable programming construct is the *goto*. In all languages that provide it, the *goto* is easy to program but difficult to discipline; its anarchic power can easily obscure the structure of a task by imposing an arbitrary and possibly inscrutable sequence of operations. In production systems, rules can designate their successors by passing messages: The action of one rule creates a working memory element that is detected by the condition side of only one other rule, as in the following example, which engages in a fixed-format interactive dialogue with the console operator.

```
(literalize next-step
    task              ; a message passed between rules

(literalize personnel-record
    first-name
    last-name
    age)

(p start-dialogue
   (personnel-record ↑last-name nil)
-->
   (make next-step ↑task get-last-name)
   (write (crlf) Last name:))

(p get-first-name
   {(next-step ↑task get-first-name) <next-step>}
   {(personnel-record) <personnel-record>}
-->
   (modify <personnel-record> ↑first-name (accept))
   (modify <next-step> ↑task get-age)
   (write (crlf) Age at last birthday:))

(p get-last-name
   {(next-step ↑task get-last-name) <next-step>}
   {(personnel-record) <personnel-record>}
-->
   (modify <personnel-record> ↑last-name (accept))
   (modify <next-step> ↑task get-first-name)
   (write (crlf) First name:))

(p get-age
   {(next-step ↑task get-age) <next-step>}
   {(personnel-record) <rec>}
-->
   (modify <rec> ↑age (accept))
   (remove <next-step>)
   (write (crlf) Thank you.))

(make personnel-record)
```

The important feature of this example is that, barring unexpected input, the sequence in which these rules fire is fixed. To show how little this code makes use of the pattern-matching capabilities of production systems, note that the same effect could have been achieved with a single rule. (It should be pointed out, however, that the multirule version is preferable in that it can be modified easily to handle unexpected input, whereas the single-rule version cannot.)

```
(literalize personnel-record
    first-name
    last-name
    age)
```

```
(p complete-personnel-record
   {(personnel-record ↑last-name nil) <personnel-record>}
-->
   (write (crlf) Last name:)
   (bind <last-name> (accept))
   (write (crlf) First name:)
   (bind <first-name> (accept))
   (write (crlf) Age at last birthday:)
   (bind <age> (accept))
   (write (crlf) Thank you.)
   (modify <personnel-record> ↑last-name <last-name>
       ↑first-name <first-name>
       ↑age <age>))

(make personnel-record)
```

For tasks involving interactive input/output or multistage numerical computations, such explicit control over the order in which individual rules fire is often necessary; but when used inappropriately, it is considered bad programming style.

5.2.7 SEQUENCING WITH RECENCY

Sometimes explicit sequencing is necessary in production-system programming [Georgeff 82]. The OPS5 interpreter does incorporate one form of explicit sequencing: Right-hand-side actions are performed in the order they are written. However, this provision is not adequate to cover all possible needs; sometimes it is necessary to control the order in which the system performs larger, multirule units of action. In these situations, sequence must be programmed. For the sake of elegance (and a clear conscience) it is best to avoid using the dreaded *goto*. Luckily, *goto*-less sequencing turns out to be easy; it is just like a sequence of procedure calls.

The programmer can make use of recency in conflict resolution to control the sequence in which the system tackles each of a set of subtasks. A single rule performs a series of **make** actions, creating a set of context elements. If the various contexts do not interact, they will be invoked in strict sequence — in an order opposite that in which they were created. This technique is more general than use of message-passing to perform a *goto*, since goals, not rules, are being sequenced.

To show how this technique works, we'll look again at the personnel-record example. One rule simultaneously sets up all six subgoals by creating the associated context elements in reverse order of invocation, and the remaining rules carry out the desired actions.

```
(literalize next-step
    task)                ; a subgoal to be accomplished

(literalize personnel-record
    first-name
    last-name
    age)

(p start-dialogue
   (personnel-record ↑last-name nil)
-->
   (make next-step ↑task get-age)
   (make next-step ↑task get-first-name)
   (make next-step ↑task get-last-name))

(p get-first-name
   {(next-step ↑task get-first-name) <next-step>}
   {(personnel-record) <personnel-record>}
-->
   (write (crlf) First name:)
   (modify <personnel-record> ↑first-name (accept))
   (remove <next-step>))

(p get-last-name
   {(next-step ↑task get-last-name) <next-step>}
   {(personnel-record) <personnel-record>}
-->
   (write (crlf) Last name:)
   (modify <personnel-record> ↑last-name (accept))
   (remove <next-step>))

(p get-age
   {(next-step ↑task get-age) <next-step>}
   {(personnel-record) <personnel-record>}
-->
   (write (crlf) Age at last birthday:)
   (modify <personnel-record> ↑age (accept))
   (remove <next-step>)
   (write (crlf) Thank you.))

(make personnel-record)
```

In this example, each distinct context element appears in the left-hand side of only one rule, but that is simply a matter of the choice of example; in general, the contexts can govern arbitrarily complex subgoals.

5.2.8 USER-DEFINED FUNCTIONS AND ACTIONS

Strictly speaking, OPS5 is a functionally complete programming language: Its built-in capabilities are sufficient to compute any computable function, subject to resource limitations, without departing from the production-system formalism.

In terms of the mathematical theory of computation, OPS5 is *Turing equivalent.* Given sufficient resources, effort, and ingenuity, one can use OPS5 to program anything that can be programmed in any other language. Nevertheless, OPS5 is much better suited for some computations than for others; in particular, it lacks sophisticated primitives for numerical computations such as square root, exponentiation, and the trigonometric functions. There are also many non-numerical computations for which an algorithmic solution is far superior to a rule-based one.

Luckily, OPS5 permits the programmer to define and call external routines from the right-hand side of any rule. These user-defined routines are categorized as either *functions* or *actions*. The purpose of functions is to return a value, while that of actions is to leave side effects. This escape mechanism allows OPS5 production systems to be shorter, more efficient, and more comprehensible. The following list highlights some fairly common tasks that justify implementation of user-defined functions or actions:

- Computing the certainty factor of a newly asserted proposition as a function of the certainty factors of related propositions.
- Constructing a network in which activation is directed from one node to another node, with nodes represented as individual working memory elements.
- Given the position in latitude-longitude pairs of two points on the globe, finding the distance and angle of one point relative to the other.
- Given a board position in a game such as chess, checkers, Othello, or Scrabble, computing a *static evaluation function* summarizing the strength of that position.
- Ordering a list of symbolic atoms alphabetically.
- Applying multiple validity tests to a line of input, returning an error message if the production system's assumptions regarding input data are violated.
- Accepting character-oriented input.
- Interfacing with large external utilities such as databases or real-time systems.

In each case, it is preferable to step outside the production-system formalism to perform the required computation.

Whether to write an external routine or implement the desired effect within OPS5 depends primarily on the relative ease with which the effect can be programmed using OPS5 rules as compared with using another language. Other important considerations are efficiency, clarity, conciseness, and the value of having the code in a shared user library. If a production-system programmer fails to exploit external functions and actions, the result may be a mass of needlessly inefficient, awkward, tedious, and obscure rules. On the other hand, over-reliance on external procedures squanders the power of production systems and, according to some defenders of the faith, violates their spirit.

Depending on the version of OPS5 available, the programmer may be able to define and invoke an external action or function that calls on the implementation language (MACLISP, FRANZLISP, or BLISS) or indirectly on some other language. It is the programmer's responsibility to declare the action or function as **external** to the OPS5 production system, to write the procedure in obedience to interface conventions, and to pass parameters and extract returned values properly.

User-defined *functions* can be called only from right-hand-side actions, e.g., for the following purposes: inside **make** and **modify** actions to provide a value for an attribute; inside a **bind** action to store an intermediate result; inside a **write** action to yield an output value; inside an **openfile, closefile,** or **default** action to specify a file for input or output; and inside a call of a user-defined action to provide one of its arguments. They cannot be called from built-in functions or on the top level. An external function call has the form

```
(<external-function-name> <argument-list>)
```

where <function-name> is a symbolic atom and <argument-list> is a sequence of zero or more variables or constants.

User-defined *actions* are invoked on the right-hand side of rules in the same fashion as the built-in actions.[1] The invocation of an external action has the form

```
(call <external-action-name> <element-pattern>)
```

where <external-action-name> is a symbolic atom and <element-pattern> is in the same form as the arguments to a **make** or **modify** action.

All communication between OPS5 and the user's external functions is via a restricted set of OPS5 functions that manipulate a special entity called the ***result element.*** The result element is a template for a working memory element that is set up by a **make, modify,** or **call.** All actions except **modify** empty out the result element. A **modify** creates a result element that is filled with the contents of the working memory element that is to be modified, and a **call** sets up the result element according to the <element-pattern> in its argument. The terms in the <element-pattern> are evaluated one at a time and individually inserted into the result element. There is only one result element at any given time, so all changes indicated by the communication functions are made to the current result element. The result element has 127

[1] **Call** can also be used at the top level in some implementations.

fields corresponding to the possible locations for attributes in a working memory element. A pointer is maintained to indicate the field where the next value is to be inserted.

There are four commands that can be called from within the external actions to build up the result element or insert its contents into working memory. The first command, **$assert,** copies the result element into working memory but does not change the contents of the result element. The second, **$reset,** clears all the fields in the result element and sets the default insertion location to be the first field. The third command, **$tab,** controls *where* the next value will be placed. It takes a single argument, which is normally the name of the attribute where the next value is to be inserted. In fact, the argument can also be an integer. The final command, **$value,** puts a value into the result element in the current field and updates the pointer to the one just after the field where the previous item was inserted. The **$value** command also takes a single argument, namely the value to be inserted. If there are no intervening calls to **$tab** to reset the location, then successive calls to **$value** will insert their values into a sequence of adjacent fields. Note that there is nothing preventing an external function from creating more than one working memory element through a series of calls to **$assert** and the other **$** commands.

User-Defined Functions

All user-defined functions and actions must be declared through use of the OPS5 **external** command. For instance,

```
(external makecertainty)
```

would appear at the top of any list of rules using the function "makecertainty." More than one function can be declared in the same **external** command, or multiple commands can be used, as for the **vector-attribute** command. Functions not declared as **external** can cause the following error:

```
? <rule> ..funcname .. function not declared external
```

where `<rule>` is the rule involving the function "funcname" which was not declared.

User-defined functions that are written in a LISP dialect must either take no arguments or take one argument and must be defined as a *fexpr* or *nlambda*. This will ensure that the newly defined function does not evaluate its arguments, since OPS5 will pass the arguments literally (i.e., OPS5 will not quote the arguments).

Now let's look at an example of an externally defined function in use. We'll assume a LISP implementation and consider the task of computing certainty factors for the two-rule case; then we'll generalize. When two rules conclude the same fact, the fact's certainty is increased according to this formula:

```
<new certainty> =  <certainty factor 1> + <certainty factor 2>
                 - <certainty factor 1> * <certainty factor 2>
```

where the certainty factors are non-negative numbers.

Let's make a new working memory element of class *evidence* each time a knowledge source delivers a conclusion about a fact. Recording each instance of a fact in a new working memory element rather than updating a single element avoids the infinite loop problem in the collection phase. We will store the certainty factor for each new contribution of *evidence* in the *factor* field. The overall certainty of each fact is kept in the *certainty* field of a *fact* working memory element. To avoid looping in the computation phase, mark each piece of evidence once it has been incorporated into the overall certainty for the fact. This and other techniques for avoiding looping, such as removing evidence, are discussed in Section 5.2.2.

```
(external makecertain)

(literalize fact           ; summary of evidence for a fact
    fact-ID                ; unique identifier for a fact
    certainty)             ; overall certainty

(literalize evidence       ; single piece of evidence for a type
                           ;  of fact
    fact-ID                ; identifier corresponding to a type
                           ;  of fact
    factor                 ; number representing certainty of
                           ;  evidence
    recorded)              ; "t" if fact has been recorded,
                           ;  otherwise "nil"

; IF   a piece of evidence has been collected but not recorded
;  and there is a corresponding summary fact
; THEN incorporate the certainty of the new evidence
;  into the summary fact and mark it the evidence as recorded
(p gather-evidence
   {(evidence ↑fact-ID <name>
       ↑factor <factor1>
       ↑recorded nil)                    <ev>}
   {(fact ↑fact-ID <name>
       ↑certainty <oldcertainty>)     <fact>}
   -->
   (modify <ev> ↑recorded t)
   (modify <fact> ↑certainty
       (makecertain <factor1> <oldcertainty>)))
```

Thus we will be passing the function a list of two factors in variable form and expecting to update the *certainty* attribute of the fact in question.

We define the function "makecertain" as follows:

```
(defun makecertain fexpr (factors)
   ($value (cf ($varbind (car factors))
               ($varbind (cadr factors)))))
(defun cf (f1 f2)
   (difference (plus f1 f2) (times f1 f2)))
```

The "makecertain" function assumes that it will get a list of exactly two values as an argument. The expression "(car factors)" picks out the first value from the argument and "(cadr factors)" picks out the second. In LISP implementations, the **$varbind** function is needed to get the correct value for the arguments, since either variables or symbolic atoms or numbers may have been passed by the OPS5 expression. **$varbind** returns the value of a variable if given a variable and passes other expressions through unchanged. The function "cf" is called on the two values to compute the new certainty according to the formula given previously. Finally, this result is inserted into the result element with the **$value** command. It is crucial for the function to call **$value** explicitly; the newly computed value will not be inserted into the result element simply because it is returned as the value of the LISP function.

User-Defined Actions

Let's take a simple example of how to use the **call** action before giving a more complex version continuing the certainty factor example.

Suppose we are going to have a list of numbers and print out the sum of the squares of the numbers:

```
(literalize task name)
(external sum-squares)

(p simple-call-example
   (task ↑name do-sum)
-->
   (call sum-squares 3 4 5 2 1 9))
```

When a **call** action is used, the external function it applies must be a function of no arguments. This means we need some way to extract the number of parameters and get their values. **$parametercount** returns the index of the last field that received a value in the result element. Often this is just the number of items in the calling pattern, as in this case. To access the individual items in the argument, we use the **$parameter** function. If the argument to

$parameter is *K*, the returned value is the Kth field in the parameter element. For instance, in the example above, `($parameter 1)` would return 3 and `($parameter 3)` would return 5.

```
(defun sum-squares ()
    (do ((count ($parametercount) (sub1 count))
         (sum 0 (plus sum (square ($parameter count)))))
        ((zerop count) (print sum))))
```

We could also get a variable set of numbers by reading them in from the terminal with the action

```
(call sum-squares (acceptline)))
```

Now let's see how we could implement certainty factors with the **call** action and an arbitrary number of certainties. We assume that some rules not discussed here place all the evidence factors in a single vector attribute *evidence-factors* of element class *fact*. These numbers are combined by the function "makecertainty2" and the overall certainty is recorded in the *certainty* field of a *final-fact* element. This technique is used here primarily to illustrate the **call** action; it is not especially recommended for use with certainty factors since it is not especially efficient. Looping during the collection phase must be avoided with the same techniques discussed previously. We first show the rules, then the function definition.

```
(literalize final-fact fact-ID certainty)

(vector-attribute evidence-factors)
(literalize fact          ; a place to record all the evidence
    fact-ID               ; an identifier for the fact
    evidence-factors)     ; a vector of numbers

; a sample element
; (fact ↑fact-ID fname1 ↑evidence-factors...)
```

There would be a rule with a call

```
(p compute-c-f
   (phase-of-the-moon-happy)
   {(fact ↑name <name>)     <fact>}
 - (final-fact ↑fact-ID <name>)
-->
   (call makecertainty2 (substr <fact> 1 inf)))
```

Let us define our function: Given a working memory element of class *fact* with no value in the *certainty* field, the function "makecertainty2" will be called to find the overall certainty of the values in the vector attribute *evidence-*

factors and put the result in the *certainty* field of a new element of the class *final-fact*.

```
(external makecertainty2)
(defun makecertainty2 ()
  (prog (factname newcertainty num counter)
    (setq factname ($parameter ($litbind 'fact-ID)))
    (setq newcertainty 0)
    (setq num ($parametercount))
    (setq counter ($litbind 'evidence-factors))
    loop
    (cond ((greaterp counter num)
           ($reset)
           ($value 'final-fact)
           ($tab 'certainty)
           ($value newcertainty)
           ($tab 'fact-ID)
           ($value factname)
           ($assert)
           (return)))
    (setq newcertainty (cf newcertainty
                           ($parameter counter)))
    (setq counter (add1 counter))
    (go loop)))
(make fact ↑evidence-factors .9 .5 .7 .6)
```

First we see how to pick out the name of the fact. The OPS5 function **$litbind** can be used to retrieve the integer to which an attribute name was assigned. It takes one argument, which is assumed to be an attribute name; if the argument is not an attribute name, it is simply returned as the value. In this case, **$litbind** returns the number corresponding to the name field (it cannot be assumed to be in the first field, since the whole working memory element was copied). This number is passed to **$parameter,** which gets the actual value of the name attribute. We save this in the variable "factname." Notice that *num* is initialized to the last fields in the <fact> working memory element and *counter* is initialized to the *evidence-factors* field of *certainty*. On each iteration, another factor is included into the *newcertainty*. Eventually, *newcertainty* contains the certainty of the evidence-factors and can be returned. We clear the result element with a **$reset** command, and fill the first field with the value "final-fact" to indicate the element class. `($tab 'certainty)` brings us to the correct field for the certainty and `($value newcertainty)` inserts the value of newcertainty there. Similarly, we set up the name with a **$tab** followed by a **$value.** `($assert)` puts the modified element into working memory.

The correct use of user-defined functions hinges on knowing all the production-system language's capabilities for passing and retrieving parameters as well as a thorough knowledge of the implementation language. When multiple programmers work on a project, they often amass a library of user-defined functions for their application, making use of user-defined functions easier and effectively extending the capabilities of the production-system language. Keep in mind that misuse of user-defined functions can render a system impossible to read, maintain, and document.

5.2.9 BUILDING NEW RULES AT RUN TIME

In selected OPS5 implementations, usually those using LISP as the underlying implementation language, new rules can be constructed during execution. The ability to construct new rules gives a program the capacity to learn and also to improve its own efficiency.

As an example of using the **build** action, consider this hypothetical problem: Suppose a company owns a line of personal computers and buys compatible printers to form packages of different types. Among other things, they have a production system for filling people's requests for a PC-printer pair, given a PC in a particular class and given a maximum cost.

The straightforward way of finding pairs takes two rules to verify that the price is acceptable and is also rather slow if there are many printers and many PCs in the database, since it has to check all possible pairs (see Chapter 6 for a more complete discussion of why this is so). To help understand the problem, let's first look at the declarations and rules for the simple approach.

```
(literalize request ID package)
(literalize package name PC-class maxprice)
(literalize PC name PC-class interface price new)
(literalize printer name interface price)
(literalize potential-pair request maxprice total-cost
    verified)

; IF   there is a request <ReqID> for
;       a package of type <PackageName>
;  and the package involves a PC of class <class> and
;       a maximum price <price>
;  and there is a PC named <PCN> in that class
;       with an interface that is compatible with a printer
;       named <PrintN>
; THEN the make a potential PC-printer pair,
;       record the maximum price for the package,
;       and compute the actual total cost
```

```
(p expensive-way-find-pair
   (request ↑ID <ReqID> ↑package <PackageName>)
   (package ↑name <PackageName> ↑PC-class <class>
       ↑maxprice <price>)
   (PC ↑name <PCN> ↑PC-class <class> ↑interface <PCIF>
       ↑price <PCP>)
   (printer ↑name <PrintN> ↑interface <PCIF> ↑price <PrintP>)
-->
   (make potential-pair ↑request <ReqID> ↑maxprice <price>
       ↑total-cost (compute <PCP> + <PrintP>)))

; A separate rule is necessary to check the cost
; IF   there is a request for a package
;  and there is a an unverified potential PC-printer pair
;       whose total cost is less than maximum price
;       allowed for that type of package,
; THEN mark that pair as verified
(p expensive-way-check-pair
   (request ↑ID <reqID>)
   {(potential-pair ↑request <ReqID> ↑maxprice <price>
       ↑total-cost < <price> ↑verified nil) <ppair>}
-->
   (modify <ppair> ↑verified t))
```

The company has a rather extensive product line in PCs, and new ones are added infrequently, but new printers arrive on the market almost as fast as requests come in. It isn't worth the time to precompute all packages because the printers change so fast; but since the firm has many PCs, it is also expensive to recompute the packages in the obvious way with rules.

By using the **build** action, they can construct specialized rules whenever a new PC is added to their product line. One rule is built for each package that the new PC is appropriate for. The rule that is built will check the database of printers whenever a request is made that might involve the particular PC. Before seeing how to build the rule, let's examine what we want the generated rule to look like. Since we now know both the maximum cost for the package and the cost for the PC, we can set an upper bound on the cost for the printer alone rather than having to check it with a special rule. We will still copy the maximum price of the package and the verification mark into the potential pair for compatibility with our original rules.

Consider the case where a new PC is added:

```
(PC ↑name Whizzy ↑PC-class top-of-line ↑interface RI65
    ↑price 2000 ↑new t)
```

Suppose there is a single package:

```
(package ↑PC-class top-of-line ↑name deluxe ↑maxprice 3000)
```

Then we would like the following specialized rule:

```
; IF   there is a request for the deluxe package
;  and there is a printer with interface RI65 that costs less
;       than $1000,
; THEN make a verified potential pair satisfying the request,
;       record that the maxprice for the package is $3000,
;       and compute and record the actual cost
;       of the pair.
(p printer-checker::Whizzy:deluxe
   (request ↑ID <ReqID> ↑package deluxe)
   (printer ↑name <P-name> ↑interface RI65
       ↑price {<PrintP> < 1000})
-->
   (make potential-pair
       ↑request <ReqID> ↑verified t
       ↑maxprice 3000
       ↑total-cost (compute 2000 + <PrintP>)))
```

To construct this rule, we need another rule, which we will call `build-new-checker-for-new-PC`. This rule must notice when there is a new PC and a package using the new PC's PC-class; then it must call the **build** action to create a specialized rule of the type we just discussed. Before building the new rule, `build-new-checker-for-new-PC` should mark the new PC as no longer new, compute the maximum cost for the printer, and get a name for the new rule. The name for the new rule must be unique, for if the same name were used for all the built rules, their definitions would overwrite each other. We can use the built-in function **genatom** to do this. If we would like our rule names to be more descriptive, we could write a user-defined function that would take the PC name and package name as arguments and produce a mnemonic name for the rule.

The first argument to **build** should be the name of the rule. The next set of arguments should be a sequence of condition elements, terminated by the atom `-->`. The final arguments should be a sequence of actions. Arguments to build are assumed to be constants unless preceded by the evaluation operator \\.

Since our rule name is not a constant but rather is bound to the variable <rule-name>, we must precede it with \\ so that it will be evaluated. Most of the rest of the rule that we want can be written out just as it would be normally, but all those variables that we bound in the left-hand side of the rule concerning the new PC (its name, interface type, and price) and the compatible package (its name and maximum cost) must be filled in as specifics in the constructed rule. Therefore we must precede them with \\. Similarly, we want the actual value of the maximum printer cost that was computed with the **bind,** not the variable that stores the results. In contrast, the items that will really be variables in the constructed rule, the request ID and printer name and price, do not need to be specially treated.

```
(p build-new-checker-for-new-PC
   {(PC ↑name <PCName> ↑PC-class <class> ↑interface <PCIF>
       ↑price <PCPrice> ↑new t)
    <newPC>}
   (package ↑name <PackageName> ↑PC-class <class>
       ↑maxprice <MaxPackageCost>)
-->
   (modify <newPC> ↑new nil)
   (bind <MaxPrinterCost>
   (compute <MaxPackageCost> - <PCPrice>))
   (bind <rule-name> (genatom))
   (build \\ <rule-name>)
       (request ↑ID <ReqID> ↑package \\ <PackageName>)
       (printer ↑name <P-name> ↑interface \\ <PCIF>
           ↑price {<PrintP> < \\ <MaxPrinterCost>})
-->
   (make potential-pair ↑request <ReqID> ↑verified t
       ↑maxprice \\ <MaxPackageCost>
       ↑total-cost (compute \\ <PCPrice> + <PrintP>))))
```

There is one difficulty with building rules. Because of the optimization that allows OPS5 to be efficient, rules notice only working memory elements that are added after the rule is incorporated into the system. Thus, according to the method of processing we've just described, our new rule will not notice any old printers. One way to handle this is to establish separate databases for the PCs, packages, and printers. The first two can be loaded, then the updating rules run, and then the printer database loaded. While we have used this example to illustrate a feature, we do not claim that a production system is the right model for solving this particular problem.

5.3 EXERCISES

5-1 In the sparse array example in Section 5.1.3, the user may want to modify the value of an element from a nondefault value back to the default value. The example as presented forces these values to be represented explicitly in working memory. Modify the program so that working memory does not get filled with explicit representations of elements bearing default values. Assume that the default value for all arrays is "0."

5-2 In the stack example in Section 5.1.3, an attempt to pop an empty stack will result in no action being taken until a push operation is performed. Modify the stack program to print an error message instead of deferring the pop operation.

5-3 Write a production system to implement the following exclusive or (*xor*): If someone is a rock climber whose age is "old" *xor* is a rock climber whose style is "bold," write the statement "that is plausible." You may also write another rule to take care of the impossible situation in which both disjuncts are true.

5-4 The following left-hand side of a rule tests the condition, "There is an elephant whose name is Mnemosyne."

```
(animal ↑type elephant ↑name Mnemosyne)
```

Use this data representation to write the left-hand sides corresponding to the following conditions:

a) There is an elephant whose name is not Mnemosyne.
b) There is a non-elephant animal whose name is Mnemosyne.
c) There is no elephant whose name is Mnemosyne.
d) There is no animal whose name is Mnemosyne.
e) There is no elephant.

Which of these conditions, if any, represents the logical negation of the original condition?

5-5 The following left-hand side of a rule tests the condition, "There is a a dog named Napoleon whose owner is named Wellington."

```
(pet ↑type dog ↑name Napoleon ↑owner Wellington)
```

Use this data representation to write the left-hand sides corresponding to the following conditions:

a) There is a dog whose owner also owns a cat.
b) There is a dog whose owner does not own a cat.
c) There is no dog whose owner also owns a cat. (Equivalently, there is no cat whose owner also owns a dog; or, there is nobody who owns both a cat and a dog.)

5-6 Write a production system which will increment by one each of a set of numbers. It must manipulate each number only once, and must be capable of repeated invocation.

5-7 The *greatest common divisor* (gcd) of two positive integers is the largest integer that evenly divides both given integers. An algorithm for computing the gcd, attributed to the Greek geometer Euclid, employs the identities

```
gcd(x, y) = gcd (y, x mod y)
```

and

```
gcd(x, 0) = x
```

where x *mod* y is the remainder when x is divided by y. A PASCAL program to compute the gcd using Euclid's algorithm follows:

```
program gcd(input, output);
var x,y,temp: integer;
begin
 writeln('Enter the first non-negative integer');  readln(x);
 writeln('Enter the second non-negative integer'); readln(y);
 if (x < y) then begin temp := x; x := y; y := temp end;
 while (y > 0) do begin temp := y; y := x mod y; x := temp end;
 writeln('The greatest common divisor is ', x);
end.
```

Write an OPS5 production system to compute the gcd with Euclid's algorithm.

5-8 A *Turing machine* is one of a large set of well-defined mechanisms that have been shown capable of computing, in a finite number of steps and with a finite amount of storage, any function computable by any of the other mechanisms. It is believed that this set of mechanisms is capable of computing all computable functions.

The machine consists of a *tape* of finite but unspecified length and a *finite-state* control, which takes actions depending on both the *internal state* of the machine, of which there is a finite set, and the character written on the tape position that is being scanned by the *read head*. The tape consists of a finite sequence of cells, each of which contains a single character from a finite alphabet. The finite-state control consists of a set of ordered quadruples (s, c, n, a), whose components are as follows:

s	The current state of the machine
c	The character currently being scanned
n	The next state to assume
a	The action to perform: half, move tape left one cell, move tape right one cell, or write a specified symbol

On each cycle, the machine reads the current cell and, if there is a quadruple corresponding to the current state and the character read, switches to the specified next state and performs the specified action. If there is no such quadruple, the machine halts. The set of quadruples thus acts as a program for the machine.

Show that OPS5 is *Turing equivalent* by implementing a Turing machine with an OPS5 production system. Use any set of quadruples you wish.

6

Efficiency in OPS5

Efficiency is an important consideration in many production-system programs, since expert systems may be expected to exhibit high performance in interactive domains or real-time domains. However, correctness and readability of code, clarity of representation, and good documentation are equally important. Therefore efficiency should be considered only after a system is well thought out.

Producing efficient production-system programs requires both a well-implemented production-system language to maximize efficiency[1] and the knowledge of how to write rules that take advantage of the implementation. OPS5 was designed specifically with efficiency in mind, so if the programmer understands how to exploit its features, quite efficient rules can be written. However, failure to understand the sources of inefficiency can result in disconcertingly slow code. Even without a complete grasp of the implementation of OPS5, the programmer who has some familiarity with the techniques discussed in this chapter should be able to write reasonably efficient rules. Still, making complex OPS5 programs efficient can be a difficult process; the challenge requires patience and experimentation as well as a thorough understanding of the algorithms used in the implementation.

In systems like OPS5 that allow complex pattern matching, the major source of inefficiency is the matching process. Unless the inference engine has been optimized, successive recognize-act cycles will repeat many match computations in determining which rules are applicable. These computations involve finding out which combinations of working memory elements, if any, will satisfy the condition-element patterns in the rules' left-hand sides. Thus fast matchers

[1] Research investigating the efficiency of production-system implementations is reported in [Newell, McDermott, Moore 78].

are a requirement for well-implemented languages of this type, and reducing the amount of matching in individual rules is the best way to make a given program faster.

Most of the examples in this chapter are adapted from a set of rules that interprets aerial photographs of airports. The original rules are part of a system called SPAM.[2] The versions of the rules used here are not taken directly from that system, but rather have been simplified or otherwise modified to highlight efficiency issues.

The SPAM system coordinates and controls image segmentation, segmentation analysis, and the construction of a scene model. While the actual spatial arrangement of typical airport structures such as runways, terminal buildings, and parking lots varies greatly between airports, the types of structures normally found in an airport scene are well understood. Thus the airport task provides a knowledge-rich environment in which functional relationships between structures provide spatial constraints. These constraints help restrict and refine hypothesis formation during analysis. The rule-based interpretation can also accommodate clues based on the layout of specific airports.

SPAM has several phases that gradually transform low-level segmentation data into an interpretation in terms of real-world objects such as terminals and runways. The first phase starts with low-level data segmented into *regions* and produces local hypotheses called *fragments*. The hypotheses represented in the fragments are based solely on attributes of regions: shape, texture, and spectral properties, for example. Fragments can have a general hypothesis about the type of object, such as "large-blob" or "linear," and a more concrete hypothesis, such as "tarmac" or "road." After the first phase is complete, the concrete hypotheses are verified locally by testing consistency with other hypotheses, and mutually consistent hypotheses are collected so the validity of each group can be verified. The last phase tests the consistency of groups of functional areas and collects consistent groups into models. Each model is a separate interpretation of the entire airport scene.

Most examples in this chapter are drawn from the first phase of scene interpretation, the generation of initial weak hypotheses from shape, size, and intensity information. The most common OPS5 declarations used by the example rules are shown here. Additional declarations will be given as needed. SPAM uses the MEA strategy for conflict resolution to allow it to compute control of the different phases and other internal subgoaling.

```
(strategy mea)                ; MEA is used to allow explicit
                              ;   subgoaling
```

[2] SPAM is an acronym for **S**ystem for **P**hoto interpretation of **A**irports using **M**APS.

```
(literalize region
    region-status              ; one of: active, interpreted,
                               ;   uninterpretable, deleted
    region-id                  ; a unique ID for the region
    symbolic-name              ; a human-readable name for the
                               ;   region
    compactness                ; the numerical  compactness of
                               ;   the region
    area                       ; the numerical area of the region
    ellipse-length             ; the length of an ellipse best
                               ;   matching the curvature of the
                               ;   region
)

(vector-attribute frag-list)

(literalize fragment
    fragment-id                ; a unique ID for the fragment
    region-id                  ; the unique ID of the region of
                               ;   which this fragment is an
                               ;   interpretation
    origin                     ; where the fragment came from
                               ;   one of: given, machine
    object-type                ; one of: linear, compact, blob
    hypothesis                 ; a subcategory of object-type
                               ;   for linear:  road, runway,
                               ;     taxiway
                               ;   for compact: terminal, hangar
                               ;   for blob: grassy area,
                               ;     parking lot, tarmac
    confidence                 ; a number between 0 and 1
                               ;   determining the goodness
                               ;   of this interpretation
    frag-list                  ; list of fragment IDs with which
                               ;   this fragment is consistent
)

(literalize context
    task                       ; the current task the system is
                               ;   working on
    datum                      ; used to contain data or a flag
    status                     ; state of processing of context
                               ;   one of: active, pending
)

(literalize constants
    tarmac-compactness         ; The minimum compactness for
                               ;   which a blob region can be
                               ;   considered a tarmac
```

```
    parking-compactness      ; The minimum compactness for
                             ;   which a blob region can be
                             ;   considered parking lot
    road-length              ; The minimum length for which a
                             ;   linear region can be
                             ;   considered a road
)
```

Understanding how to program efficiently in OPS5 requires an understanding of how the matching process is implemented. In the first section of this chapter, we discuss the ***Rete match algorithm*** [Forgy 79; Forgy 82] that OPS5 uses to compute the set of applicable rules. The second section describes how to exploit the Rete algorithm to achieve efficiency at the programming level.

6.1 WHY THE RETE MATCH ALGORITHM IS EFFICIENT

Efficient matching in OPS5 relies on a special internal representation for rules. When rules are first loaded into the system, OPS5 ***compiles*** them into a set of features to be checked. The features are mostly tests of the values of attributes. They are connected in a tree-structured sorting network that efficiently performs the matching process. For added efficiency, each feature is compiled into a small program that checks whether or not it matches a working memory element. This is more efficient than interpreting the original declarative description. Let's see just how the Rete algorithm produces efficient matching with this representation.

The Rete algorithm was developed to eliminate extra work that would be performed by an unoptimized pattern matcher. The most obvious way to compute the set of rules that apply would be to take every rule and match it against all working memory elements at the beginning of each recognize-act cycle. Although this obvious algorithm is guaranteed to work, it does not take advantage of several factors: the persistence of data in working memory across multiple cycles, the similarity of structure in the conditions being matched, and the repetitive nature of the computation that finds consistent combinations of conditions to satisfy productions. The Rete algorithm is efficient because it does not match all elements on each cycle, it shares similar tests in different rules, and it recomputes whether or not combinations of matches are consistent only when necessary.

Figure 6.1 summarizes the implementation of the Rete matcher. Although an understanding of the summary should suffice for the purpose of writing efficient OPS5 code, its points are expanded in the remainder of this section.

- Changes in working memory are mapped directly into changes in the conflict set.
- Rather than repeatedly testing all conditions in all rules on each recognize-act cycle, the Rete algorithm saves match information in a network.
- Additions to and deletions from working memory cause changes in the network data structures.
- The saved information and the new memory changes determine whether or not there are changes in the set of rules that match.
- When a working memory element is checked against a condition element, the attribute tests of the condition are evaluated in the order in which they are written. If the element fails one of the tests, the remaining tests are not evaluated.
- The conditions of a rule are checked in order from first (top) to last (bottom). If no combination of working memory elements matches an initial sequence of conditions, the remaining conditions are not considered.
- Stored with each condition element are two data structures: a right memory containing the set of working memory elements that the condition matches, and a left memory containing the combinations of working memory elements (and, implicitly, variable bindings) that make it and all preceding conditions match consistently.
- The consistency of matches for a condition element is computed from its right memory and the left memory of the previous condition. Thus, whenever a working memory element is added or removed, all conditions that newly match or no longer match are affected, and all memories of consistent bindings associated with conditions following the affected ones may also change. In other words, if something changes early in a left-hand side, it affects everything that follows it in the left-hand side.
- Identical condition elements and sequences of condition elements in different rules are factored out in the network and matched only once.
- Deleting a working memory element has an additional cost when many other working memory elements match the same conditions that it does. It takes a linear search to find the deleted element in the lists of matching elements for a condition, and the cost propagates to removing the combined matches from later conditions.

FIGURE 6.1 A Summary of the Rete Matcher

6.1.1 ELEMENTS ARE NOT MATCHED EACH CYCLE

In a straightforward matcher all working memory elements are compared against all rule conditions on each cycle, but seldom is this action necessary. In most production-system programs, working memory changes little on each cycle. On each succeeding cycle the conflict set (the rule instantiations that match) tends to remain stable because the data change so slowly. This persistence of information in working memory across recognize-act cycles is called ***temporal redundancy.*** In some applications, however, the information in working memory changes constantly. For example, real-time processes such as the monitoring of patients in intensive-care units or the monitoring of chemical factories must integrate a great deal of new data on every recognize-act cycle. In these applications there is not much temporal redundancy to exploit.

The Rete algorithm takes advantage of temporal redundancy by matching only the changed data elements against the rules rather than repeatedly matching the rules against all the data. That is, whenever a rule or top-level command makes, modifies, or removes a working memory element, the resulting change is used to identify the rules that no longer match and the rules that newly match. This explains why top-level **make** commands in OPS5 must follow rule definitions. Since data elements are matched only when they are added, if they are loaded first they will never be seen by the rules and can never provide the impetus for matching.

The ***match cycle*** must therefore be distinguished from the recognize-act cycle, and several match cycles may occur within a single recognize-act cycle. A match cycle takes changes to working memory as input and produces changes to the conflict set as output. One cycle of matching is caused by each **make** or **remove.** Each **modify** causes two cycles: one to remove the old form of the element and one to add the new form.

The recognize-act cycle in OPS5 differs in implementation from the match-rules/select-rules/execute-rules version presented in Chapter 1. The steps are reordered to select-rule/execute-rule/match-rules. This ordering permits the conflict set to be consistent with the contents of working memory between cycles. The first step in each cycle is to select one rule instantiation from the conflict set. The next step is to execute the rule. As the rule actions are carried out, changes are made to working memory, triggering match cycles. Thus the match-rules step is actually interleaved with the execute-rule step.

So that it can exploit temporal redundancy and avoid repeated matching, the Rete algorithm must record the information about previous matches. To this end, associated with each condition element in a rule there is a list that records which working memory elements match the condition element. These lists are attached to nodes representing the condition elements, and the nodes are linked together in a network. When a working memory element is added or removed, its element class is checked and only conditions that concern elements of that class are retested. Only the lists associated with those conditions that newly match or no longer match the working memory element are updated; the other lists remain the same. Finally, only those rules whose lists have had updates are rechecked to determine the current set of consistent matches to all of their conditions. (This final step is discussed in more detail in Section 6.1.3.)

To illustrate how match information is saved, we must describe the network structure in more detail. The following fragment of a left-hand side of an airport rule will serve as an example. Figure 6.2 shows a simplified version of the network into which this rule is compiled.

```
; This set of rule conditions tells when a region that is
;   a large blob can be interpreted as a tarmac,

(p interpret-as-tarmac
   {<context-1>    (context
       ↑task interpret-unknown
       ↑datum large-blob <rid>)}
   {<constant-1>   (constants ↑tarmac-compactness <crit>)}
   {<region-1>     (region ↑region-id <rid>
       ↑compactness <= <crit>)}
...
```

When a rule is first loaded into OPS5, each of its condition elements is translated into a sequence of feature tests corresponding to the different properties of attributes required by the condition. Each test is represented by a ***one-input node.*** Nodes 1 and 2 in Fig. 6.2 are examples of one-input nodes. A chain of one-input nodes representing a condition element is joined to the network structure for the preceding part of the rule by a ***two-input node,*** such as node 3 in the figure. The two-input node may also include tests to find variable bindings that are consistent across condition elements (node 4, for example). The output of a two-input node is connected to the input of the two-input node representing the following condition (except for the last condition element, which is a special case). Also associated with the two-input nodes are the lists that record the set of working memory elements that match the associated condition. For historical reasons, this list is called a ***right memory.***

When working memory elements are added or deleted, they are propagated through the Rete network in the form of ***tokens*** that look somewhat like working memory elements or sequences of working memory elements. The tokens are tagged with + or − to indicate whether the element (or element sequence) is being inserted or deleted. The first step in propagating a working memory element is to find the beginning of the chains of one-input nodes that could possibly match the element by finding the node associated with

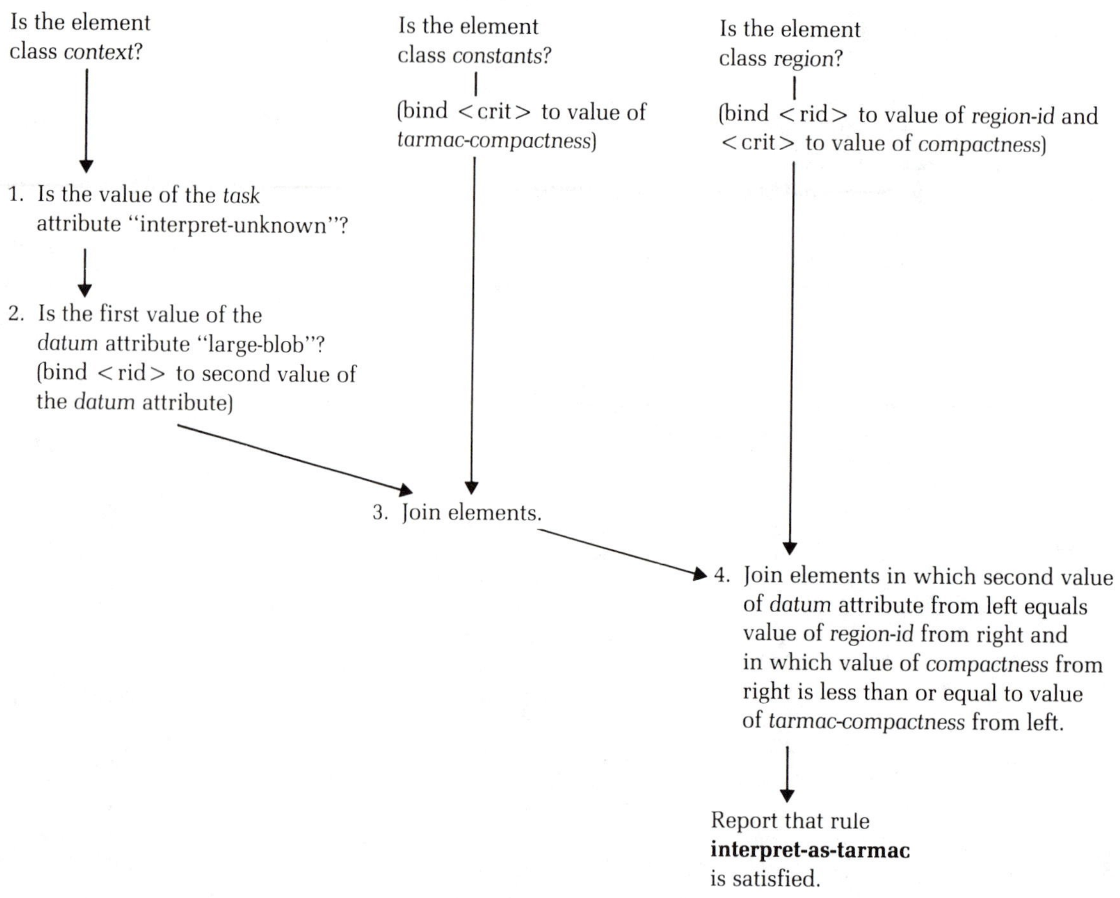

FIGURE 6.2 The Network for Interpret-as-Tarmac

the token's element class. Then, the matcher passes the token on to any tests succeeding the class names that match. Each one-input node applies its test and, if the test is successful, passes copies of the token and its bindings on to the successors of the node. If a test is not successful, the match fails and the token is not passed on for further processing. If a token is passed into the right side of a two-input node, the right memory of that node is updated. A variant of the two-input node is needed to handle negated conditions. It records a count of the number of matches to the unnegated form of the condition element. If no elements match the unnegated condition, this count is zero. Only when the count is zero is a token passed on to the successor nodes. The join process for finding consistent matchings between condition elements is described in Section 6.1.3.

When negative tokens are passed to a right or left memory, the corresponding token in that memory must be removed. When many working memory elements match the same condition element, deleting a working memory element is expensive. It takes a linear search to find the particular element to remove in the list of tokens for a condition.

Suppose the element

```
1: (constants ↑tarmac-compactness .5 ↑road-length .2)
```

is added to working memory. It matches the element class *constants*, so the token +(constants ↑tarmac-compactness .5 ↑road-length .2) is passed to the right memory of the join node 3 with a binding of ".5" for <crit>. We will abbreviate this by saying that the token +1 is passed to node 3 and that the right memory of node 3 contains (1). If a right memory contains matches to working memory elements with time tags x, y, and z, we will represent this by (x, y, z)

If the element

```
2: (region  ↑region-status active ↑region-id region-2
            ↑compactness .7)
```

is added, it matches the element class *region* with bindings of "region-2" and ".7," so the right memory of join node 4 becomes (2).

If the next element added is

```
3: (region  ↑region-status active ↑region-id region-4
            ↑compactness .3)
```

then it also is added to the right memory of node 4, which becomes (2,3).

Adding an element

```
4: (context ↑task region-to-fragment
            ↑datum large-blob region-4)
```

causes the token +4 to be passed to node 1. However, the value of the *task* is not "interpret-unknown," so the token fails the test at that node and no tokens are propagated to the successor node.

If working memory element

```
5: (context ↑task interpret-unknown
            ↑datum large-blob region-4)
```

is added, a token +5 is passed on to node 1. The value of the *task* attribute is indeed "interpret-unknown," so the token is passed on to node 2. The token +5 passes the test at node 2 also, so +5 is passed on to node 3. The first node is handled specially, so it is not stored in the right memory. At this point, consistent matches could be tested and rule `interpret-as-tarmac` reported as satisfied. The handling of the first condition and the checking of consistency are discussed in Section 6.1.3.

If working memory element 3 were deleted, a token −3 would be passed on via the *region* element class test to node 4. The corresponding element in the right memory of node 4 would then be deleted, resulting in a memory of (2). The information about the deletion would be passed on, new consistent matchings would be found, and the fact that `interpret-as-tarmac` no longer matched would be reported.

If the network contained rules whose conditions did not involve the element classes *context*, *constants*, or *region*, those rules would not be affected by any of the working memory element changes just described. Similarly, the addition or deletion of working memory elements not in the network would not cause any updates to the network. For instance, the addition of the element `(fragment ↑region-id region-3 ↑object-type small-blob)` to the network of Fig. 6.2 would not cause any updates.

6.1.2 SIMILAR TESTS IN DIFFERENT RULES ARE SHARED

Even if the identical condition element is repeated in several rules, a simple matcher would perform the test anew for each rule. The concept of having similar conditions is called ***structural similarity.*** Similar condition elements may result from the processes of fission and specialization (see Section 4.5), for example. Structural similarity as well as temporal redundancy can also be exploited in matching algorithms. OPS5 takes advantage of identical condition elements primarily, but rules may be structurally similar at many different levels. Rules may share attribute tests against the same type of object or relations between condition elements in addition to sharing entire condition elements.

As an example of the structural similarity that is relevant in an OPS5 program, consider two fragments from the left-hand sides of rules in Fig. 6.3. The first and third condition elements are identical in the two example rules, as indicated by the labels.

For OPS5 condition elements to be identical, all the same attribute tests must occur in exactly the same order. The Rete algorithm uses this definition because the ordering of tests affects the efficiency of the match process. In other words, OPS5 lets the programmer's judgment on test ordering stand. The variable names need not be identical so long as the bindings are consistent across different condition elements. This is checked when the two chains of one-input nodes representing two condition elements are merged with a two-

```
(p interpret-as-tarmac
   {<context-1>    (context
       ↑task interpret-unknown
       ↑datum large-blob <rid>)}
   {<constants-1> (constants
       ↑tarmac-compactness <crit>)}
   {<region-1>     (region
       ↑region-id <rid>
       ↑compactness <= <crit>)}
...)

(p interpret-as-parking-lot
   {<context-1>    (context
       ↑task interpret-unknown
       ↑datum large-blob <rid>)}
   {<constants-2> (constants
       ↑parking-compactness <crit>)}
   {<region-1>     (region ↑region-id <rid>
       ↑compactness <= <crit>)}
...)
```

FIGURE 6.3 Two Similar Rules

input node. For example, the first two condition elements in the following example would be represented only once in the Rete network, while the second two would be represented separately:

Identical: `names of variables irrelevant if bindings are consistent`

```
(constants ↑parking-compactness <crit>)
(constants ↑parking-compactness <compact>)
```

Not Identical: `tests are identical but test order is different`

```
(context ↑task interpret-unknown ↑datum large-blob <rid> <con>)
(context ↑datum large-blob <rid> <con> ↑task interpret-unknown)
```

Sharing of identical condition elements in OPS5 rules is implemented in the Rete network by using a single sequence of one-input nodes to represent jointly all of the instances of identical condition elements in the rules. However, the single sequence is connected to a number of two-input nodes, one corresponding to each rule sharing the condition element. When an initial sequence of several consecutive condition elements is shared by two or more rules, separate two-input nodes are not constructed until the condition sequences diverge. In this case, the work needed to find the set of working memory elements that consistently match all identical chains of condition elements can be shared above and beyond the work needed to find whether working memory elements match each condition individually. This form of sharing will be discussed in the next section. The Rete network representation of Fig. 6.4 shows that the nodes representing the first and third condition elements of the rules from Fig. 6.3 (marked A and B in the figure) are actually shared rather than being repeated.

When a working memory element such as

```
(context ↑task interpret-unknown ↑datum large-blob road-1 .65)
```

is added or removed in OPS5, the Rete algorithm ensures that it has to be matched against only one instance of the condition element, not two. This speeds up the matching process.

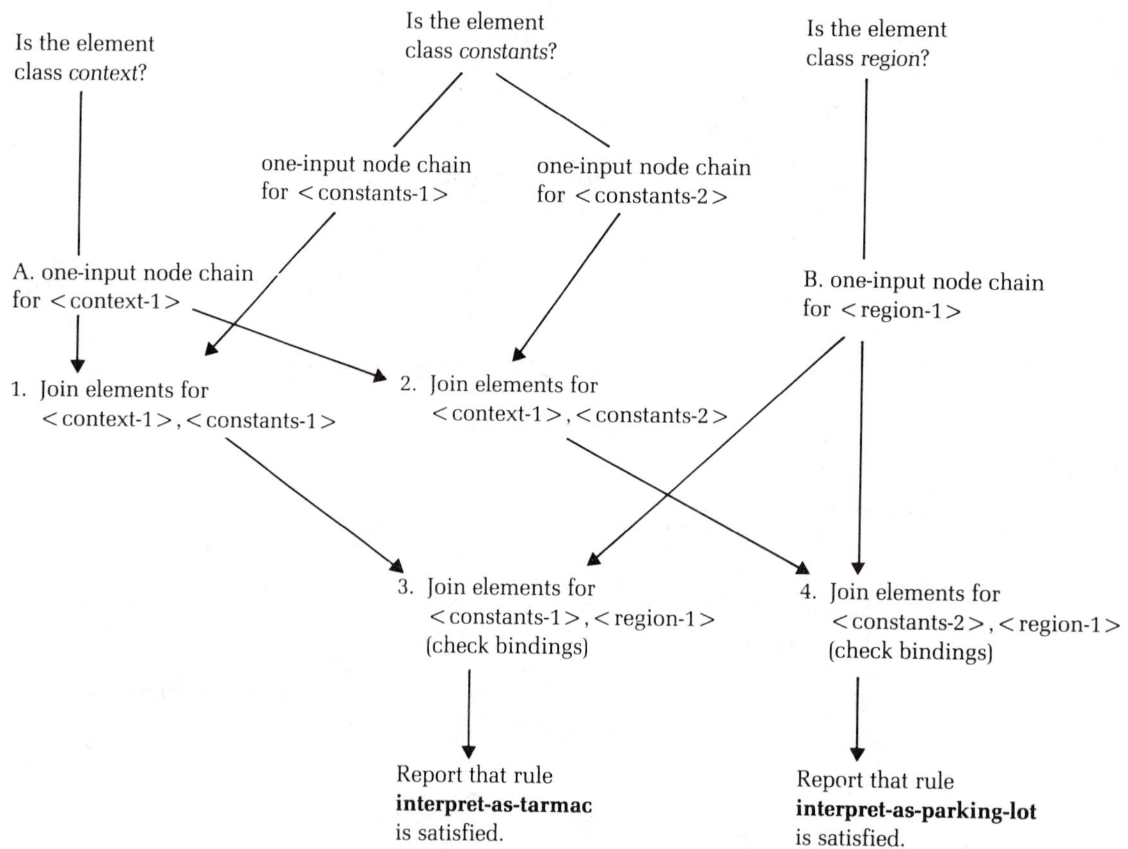

FIGURE 6.4 A Network for Two Similar Rules

6.1.3 CONSISTENT COMBINATIONS OF MATCHES ARE NOT RECOMPUTED

In addition to exploiting the temporal redundancy of data memory and the structural similarity of rules, OPS5 also avoids repetition when computing consistent bindings for variables. Consistent bindings are needed because, although each condition element in a rule may be satisfied individually, the rule may not match as a whole. To match an entire rule, a set of variable bindings that satisfies all tests simultaneously must be found. The matching process was discussed in Section 2.3.1.

The simplest way of computing consistent bindings is more expensive than necessary. The obvious method is to consider the ***cross product*** of all combinations of matches to all condition elements and to do this on every match cycle. If there are n_1 working memory elements that match the first condition element, n_2 that match the second, and n_c that match the last of C condition elements, there would be $n_1 * n_2 * \ldots * n_c$ combinations in the cross product to reconsider on each match cycle. If the n_i average N working memory elements, then the cross product has N^C combinations.

It is not necessary to repeat all the computation that generates a full cross product on each match cycle. Intermediate results of merging bindings can be stored so that they need not be recomputed every time working memory is modified. The description here does not exactly follow the implementation used in OPS5; that implementation does not explicitly save variable names and their bindings but rather makes associations between tests on individual attributes.

A ***linear test and merge*** algorithm can exploit previous computation when combining matches. The algorithm matches each condition in turn and stores the ***partial bindings*** that result from finding the legal combinations of the condition elements so far. That is, associated with each condition element is the set of all working memory elements along with the legal bindings for variables that satisfy all the condition elements up to and including the current one. This information is stored in something called the ***left memory.*** Each condition element, except the first and the last, has a right and a left memory associated with it. The first condition element has no right memory (as defined in Section 6.1.1) since its information would be identical to that in the left memory of the second condition element. The final condition element has no left memory, but instead is merged into the preceding set of consistent matches by an additional network construct called the ***production node.*** Thus only N − 1 two-input nodes are needed to represent N conditions. The right memory of the Nth two-input node contains the matches to condition element N + 1, and matches to condition 1 are not explicitly represented. The left memory of the Nth two-input node contains the consistent bindings for the first N conditions and is therefore associated with the condition element N, but the last set of consistent bindings is not explicitly represented. The **matches** debugging command in OPS5 does not return the final set of consistent bindings because it returns only right and left memories.

For the following reason, the linear test and merge algorithm is more efficient than a straightforward way of finding consistent matches: When a working memory element changes, the right memories of the condition elements that are affected must be updated in any case. Whenever there are changes to any right memories (to a set of working memory elements that matches a condition), then only the left memories (the sets of combined matches) that follow those condition elements have to be updated. Therefore changes in the working memory elements that match the first condition element of a rule result in more expensive updates than changes in working memory elements that match later conditions of a rule.

To illustrate how linear test and merge works, we use the network from Fig. 6.4. Suppose we first add the working memory element

```
1: (constants ↑parking-compactness .5 tarmac-compactness .2)
```

then the right memories of nodes 1 and 2 get the token +1 and are updated to the set (1), indicating a match against the second condition. Since no tokens have come in yet from matches against <context-1>, the left memories for the combined match against all preceding conditions (namely the first one) remain empty. Similarly, all memories on nodes 3 and 4 remain empty.

Next, suppose the element

```
2: (region ↑region-status active ↑region-id region-2
           ↑compactness .7)
```

is added. It matches the third condition, so nodes 3 and 4 have their right memories updated to (2). Again, there are no consistent matches for the first condition because the left memories are empty. Thus none are attempted for the two conditions together or for the rules as a whole.

If the element

```
3: (context ↑task interpret-unknown ↑datum large-blob
                                           region-2)
```

is added next, then the left memories of nodes 1 and 2 would be updated with the matches to <context-1>, resulting in ((3)). We will describe a left memory with a consistent match to x for the first condition and y for the second and also a consistent match z for the first condition element and w for the second as ((x y),(z w)). In this example, the right memories still contain (1), so a token for the combined match, namely +(3 1) is propagated to nodes

3 and 4. The left memories of those nodes are accordingly updated to ((3 1)). However, it is not possible to find a consistent set of bindings for the rules as a whole. Although the <rid> values for a match of element 3 to <context-1> and for a match of element 2 to <region-1> are both "region-2," the *compactness* of region-2, ".7," is not less than the *parking-compactness* value of ".5" or the *tarmac-compactness* value of ".2." As a result, no rule is reported to be matched.

Now suppose the following element is added to working memory:

```
4: (region ↑region-status active ↑region-id region-4
          ↑compactness .3)
```

It, too, matches the third condition, so the right memories of nodes 3 and 4 are updated to (2,4). There are no new combined matches with the left memories of ((3 1)) because the values "region-2" and "region-4" for <rid> are not the same.

Now if the working memory element

```
5: (context ↑task interpret-unknown ↑datum large-blob
                                             region-4)
```

is added, then nodes 1 and 2 are passed the token +5. Their left memories are updated to contain ((5),(3)), and the token +(5 1) for the new combined match is passed on to node 3 from node 1 and to node 4 from node 2. At node 3, there is no new combined match. Although the "region-4" value of <rid> allows elements 4 and 5 to combine, the *compactness* value of ".4" is not less than the *tarmac-compactness* of ".2." However, at node 4, the *compactness* of ".4" is less than the *parking-compactness* of ".5," so a new combined token of +(5 1 4) is to be passed on, and success is reported for the rule `interpret-as-parking-lot`.

If matches to individual conditions change, the combined bindings associated with the condition may no longer be correct. The combined bindings of each condition following the original matched condition may also need to be updated. However, if a set of combined bindings does not have to be changed, then none of the combined bindings following it has to be updated.

6.2 HOW TO WRITE EFFICIENT OPS5 PROGRAMS

Given a basic understanding of the Rete algorithm, the production-system programmer can sometimes make dramatic improvements in the efficiency of a set of rules. Such simple changes as reordering conditions within a rule or adding or regrouping attributes within element classes may noticeably decrease the execution time of a production-system run. In this section, we first note some common causes of system slowness and outline methods for increasing efficiency. Next we discuss how to identify the rules that need to be changed. Finally we give detailed examples of the improvement techniques.

The summary of the Rete algorithm in Fig. 6.1 reveals several possible causes of slowness in a set of rules. The causes are given in decreasing order of effect:

1. When large numbers of working memory elements match successive conditions in the same rule, finding consistent matches is one of the most expensive processes.
2. Frequent changes to elements that match conditions occurring early in rules are more expensive than changes to those that match later-occurring conditions.
3. When a condition matches large numbers of elements, deletions from the set are expensive.

Some techniques for speeding up processing are summarized in Fig. 6.5. Almost all efficiency techniques involve modifying a rule to exploit a constraint as quickly as possible so that complex processing is performed only when necessary. We'll expand on these techniques throughout the remainder of this chapter.

Unfortunately, the principles for improving efficiency are sometimes contradictory. For example, the principle of putting frequently changing conditions later may conflict with the principle of putting restrictive changes earlier if a condition element is both restrictive and matched by working memory elements that change frequently. If the principles conflict, estimates of the costs of alternatives may be used to choose the most effective one.

6.2.1 FIND THE RULES THAT CAUSE TROUBLE

The first step in making any program more efficient is determining why it is slow. When good dynamic efficiency analysis tools are available, they are likely to yield more accurate results than a static efficiency estimation will yield. Unfortunately, although some experimental tools are being developed, neither dynamic nor static analysis tools are currently available to the general public.

If no specific analysis tools are available, the top-level commands of OPS5 (see Section 2.8) can be used to pinpoint rules that slow down the matching process. Then the rules can be improved by the techniques described in this chapter. Some general information is given at the end of an OPS5 run about the number of nodes in the network and the mean and maximum sizes of

1. Avoid conditions that match many working memory elements.
   a) Add attribute tests that change the condition so that fewer working memory elements match it. Tests may be based on restrictions to data or on the state of processing.
   b) Add new element classes or modify the representation to change the data elements so that fewer of them match the condition.
   c) Represent and enumerate sequences carefully.
2. Avoid big cross-products between conditions.
   a) Order the conditions so the more restrictive ones occur first. This limits the number of consistent matches that are passed on to the next condition.
   b) Write rules with a few big conditions rather than many simple conditions by merging the attributes of related element classes into fewer element classes.
   c) Use **build** to specialize rules.
3. Avoid frequent changes to matched conditions.
   a) Put conditions that match frequently changing elements as far toward the end of the rule as possible.
   b) Avoid excessive changes in control elements.
4. Make matching individual condition elements faster.
   a) Put the most restrictive attribute tests first to speed the match of working memory elements against conditions.
   b) Change the representation of data to speed up matching.
5. Limit the size of the conflict set.
6. Call user-defined functions.

FIGURE 6.5 Summary of Techniques for Improving Efficiency in OPS5

working memory, conflict set, and token memory. To get some more specific data, the rule writer should first determine which changes to working memory are slow, then identify the rules that the changes affect, and finally estimate which of the rule matches take the longest time as a result of the numbers of working memory elements matching each condition.

A simple though not very precise method of identifying which changes to working memory slow down a program is to observe a trace after the `(watch 2)` command[3] has been given. The additions and deletions to working memory

[3] `(Watch 3)` in the Bliss implementation is even better.

are printed out when the modifications are started, but a carriage return is not printed until the change has filtered through the network. Thus it is possible to identify those element classes for which changes to working memory take substantial amounts of time.

The next question of interest is which rules are candidates for modification. A clue comes from the element classes of the working memory elements for which changes seem to slow down the system. Rules with conditions matching those element classes should be considered. An editor can be used to find the selected rules.

Once the rules are identified, probable causes of inefficiency should be sought. Not all rules using the element class will contribute to the problem. A single rule is just as likely to be the culprit as a large set is. Ask these questions about each rule:

1. Do the identified element classes contribute to large cross-products in the rule? (See Section 6.1.3)
2. Do the identified element classes change rapidly and get matched in a condition that precedes one or more other conditions that match large numbers of working memory elements?

It also is important to know which element classes have large numbers of instantiations in working memory. Sometimes your knowledge of the problem enables you to make an accurate estimate of this. If not, the `(ppwm <element-class>)` command can be used at any time during a run to determine how many elements of a given class are actually present in working memory.

Costs can be estimated by concentrating on the costs of deletions and of finding consistent matches. Apply the following process to each condition: Estimate the number of elements that match the condition. Multiply this number by the number of combinations that consistently matched the preceding conditions. Add that number to the total cost so far, then add in the costs of deletes if the condition matches large numbers of elements in either memory. Finally, estimate the number of consistent matches following the current condition element, and repeat the process.

After a rule is changed, the system should be run again to check that the functional behavior of the system is unchanged and that the run time has in fact decreased. An important point to note about efficiency testing in OPS5 is that neither removing a rule from rule memory with the **excise** command nor overwriting one rule with another rule of the same name eliminates the nodes representing the original rule from the network. Although the old rule will never be executed, all the work to determine whether or not it matches will still occur. To find the effects of changing or eliminating a rule on run time or network size, it is necessary to reload the entire rule set into a fresh environment.

6.2.2 LIMIT THE NUMBER OF ELEMENTS THAT MATCH A CONDITION

The most common way of increasing execution speed is by reducing the number of working memory elements that match a condition. This helps especially if the condition element is one that is contributing to a large cross-product. Whenever possible, tests that discriminate working memory elements according to existing attributes should be added to condition elements. It also may be useful to add new attributes to a class or to split an element class into several subclasses. Attributes that are added may distinguish objects according to their physical properties or according to the state of processing. Sometimes a representation change, such as from a linked list to a vector attribute, will increase efficiency.

Limit the Range of Elements by Physical Property

Physical objects can always be more and more finely discriminated according to physical properties, but such distinctions need not be made until they are required. Usually it is good programming practice to define broad element classes and to write rules that are as general as possible so that fewer rules are needed. Generic rules make debugging and maintaining a system easier. Nevertheless, it is sometimes more efficient to write more specific rules even if this means writing additional rules.

Suppose a system for airport scene recognition has a single rule to match up pairs of linear fragments into a single linear object. If there are many elements of class *fragment* in working memory, this rule will make the consistency-checking process quite slow.

```
; IF   there are two distinct linear fragments
; THEN call the consistency-checker on them
(p match-linear
   (fragment ↑object-type linear
       ↑fragment-id <id1>)
   (fragment ↑object-type linear
       ↑fragment-id {<id2> <> <id1>})
     ...
-->
   (call consistency-checker <id1> <id2>)
   ...
)
```

In attempting to increase the speed of matching against this rule, the programmer might observe that there are many different types of linear fragments (road, runway, taxiway) and that the types must match for the fragments to be consistent (according to the particular consistency test being performed here). Thus it will be more efficient to postpone consistency checking until there are hypotheses about the types of linear objects to which the fragments correspond. The modified version of the rule shown, `match-linear-2`, adds an additional attribute test for identical hypotheses on fragments. The new rule[4] sends fewer pairs of fragments to the consistency checker.

```
; IF   there are two distinct linear fragments
;         with the same non-nil hypothesis
; THEN call the consistency checker on them
(p match-linear-2
   (fragment
       ↑object-type linear
       ↑hypothesis {<hyp> <> nil}
       ↑fragment-id <id1>)
   (fragment
       ↑object-type linear
       ↑hypothesis <hyp>
       ↑fragment-id {<id2> <> <id1>})
   ...
-->
   (call consistency-checker <id1> <id2>)
   ...
)
```

Still, this rule must consider the same number of pairs of fragments to find those with the same hypothesis. It would be even more efficient to write separate rules for each type of hypothesis. An example for `match-road` follows. The test for linearity of object types is now unnecessary, since such a test was made before classifying the fragment as a road. `Match-runway` and `match-taxiway` will be identical except for the substitution of "runway" or "taxiway" for "road."

```
; IF   there are two distinct fragments with hypothesis road
; THEN call the consistency checker on them
(p match-road
   (fragment
       ↑hypothesis road
       ↑fragment-id <id1>)
   (fragment
       ↑hypothesis road
       ↑fragment-id {<id2> <> <id1>})
   ...
```

[4] Rules that are modifications of previous rules will have the changes highlighted in *italics*.

```
-->
   (call consistency-checker <id1> <id2>)
   ...
)
```

Similarly, additional properties such as color or texture can be used to discriminate between fragments of type "road." Extreme proliferation of rules should be avoided because of diminishing returns in efficiency and increasing difficulty of modification.

Limit the Range of Elements by Processing State

An attribute representing the state of processing can be added to limit the range of elements and avoid having rules unnecessarily or partially satisfied. This reduces the number of matches to a condition element and also avoids large cross-products.

A typical situation in which it helps to add processing status occurs when many goals or contexts are active at the same time. This situation results if one rule sets up several subgoals or subcontexts, as shown in the rule `set-up-contexts-1`. A similar situation arises when the contexts are created one at a time by different rules, but accumulate so that many contexts are active at once. The original contexts may have been created with an explicit *status* field having an "active" value that was modified to some value such as "satisfied" or "deleted," or they may have been created with no explicit *status* field and deleted after processing. Rule `set-up-contexts-1` is an example of a rule that sets up a number of contexts, and rule `process-context` is a sample skeleton of a processing rule.

```
; the MEA strategy allows complete control
;  over context processing
(strategy mea)

; an example of a rule that sets up many contexts
; with the status "active"
(p set-up-contexts-1
   ...
-->
   (make context ↑task g1 ↑status active)
   (make context ↑task g2 ↑status active)
   (make context ↑task g3 ↑status active))

; a skeleton of a processing rule
;  often there will be many such rules
; IF   the current context involves a region
;         that is ready for processing
```

```
; THEN update the region
;  and mark the context as satisfied
(p process-context
   {<cntxt>  (context ↑status active ↑task <name>)}
   {<region> (region ↑region-id <name>)}
    ...
-->
   (modify  <region> ...)
   (modify  <cntxt> ↑status satisfied)
)
```

One problem with these approaches is that all the *contexts* in the "active" state will be unnecessarily matched against the first condition element in the processing rules. Most of the matches are unnecessary because usually only a single *context* element can be processed before any other *contexts* are attempted. The solution described here is an improvement over either of the previous implementations.

Instead of setting up a *context* in the "active" state, the rules that create new *context* elements should initialize them with a *status* of "pending," as in `set-up-contexts-2`. Then a single rule such as `activate-pending-context` can be used to activate the next *context* that is "pending." Because this rule has only one very simple (and therefore unspecific) condition element, it will not fire until all other rules handling the currently active *context* have had their chance. Only one *context* element will be in the active state at any time. With this set of rules, only the active *context* will match processing rules such as `process-context`, so the match will be much quicker.

```
; a more efficient method is to set up contexts
;   with a status of "pending" rather than "active"
(p set-up-contexts-2
   ...
-->
   (make context ↑task g1 ↑status pending)
   (make context ↑task g2 ↑status pending)
   (make context ↑task g3 ↑status pending))

; IF   there is a context with a "pending" status
; THEN modify the status to "active"
(p activate-pending-context
   {<cntxt> (context ↑status pending)}
-->
   (modify <cntxt> ↑status active))

; The processing rules such as process-context
;  need not be changed
```

Create Separate Element Classes

In limiting a match, an alternative to adding attributes is splitting some of the element classes. For example, rather than adding an *hypothesis* attribute to the *fragment* element class in the `match-linear` rule, separate element classes such as *linear-fragment*, *road-fragment*, and *runway-fragment* could be defined. The new element classes can be used for the preliminary filtering of working memory elements in selecting those that match conditions. Filtering by element class is more efficient than filtering by attribute test, but the difference is not great. If the split results in many different-but-similar element classes that require many near-identical rules, the gain in efficiency is not worth the trouble, especially while the program is still in the development phase.

Represent and Enumerate Sequences Carefully

One operation that can be expensive if not properly implemented in OPS5 is enumerating the items in sequences. When the items are explicitly represented in working memory, say by a linked list as described in Section 5.1.1, then finding the next item can require a test proportional to the number of items in the sequence. A more efficient alternative is to store the entire list in a vector attribute in a single working memory element, as described in Section 5.1.1. This option is possible only when the list is short enough to fit in a single working memory element.

Consider representing a list of objects such as the consistency tests for a particular hypothesis about a fragment interpretation. We first consider a straightforward implementation using a linked list. This implementation involves two element-class declarations. Working memory elements in one class represent a test (called a *strategy*) and a pointer to the next *strategy* for that hypothesis. Another working memory element is used to represent a particular fragment's current position in the list of strategies.

```
; there is one set of strategies for each hypothesis
(literalize strategy-list
    label          ; each strategy has a unique ID in each
                   ;  list even if the strategy appears in
                   ;  several lists for different types of
                   ;  hypotheses
    name           ; the name of the strategy
    next-pointer   ; the label of the strategy to be tried next
)

; there is a strategy pointer for each fragment that moves
;  down the list
```

```
(literalize strategy-pointer
    fragment-id    ; the ID of the fragment that is
                   ;   being checked for consistency
    label          ; the label of the strategy to be
                   ;  checked next
)
```

Here are the statements that set up strategies for runways. This same list is used by all fragments with hypothesis "runway." In a real program these statements would have to occur after the rule definitions.

```
(make strategy-list ↑label RS1
                    ↑name runways-parallel-to-terminal-bldg
                    ↑next-pointer RS2)
(make strategy-list ↑label RS2
                    ↑name taxiways-perpendicular-to-runways
                    ↑next-pointer RS3)
(make strategy-list ↑label RS3 ↑name runway-runway-check)
```

Here is a sample rule that sets up a list of consistency strategies. There would be one such rule for each hypothesis.

```
    ; IF   the phase is checking local consistency
    ;  and there is currently no consistency strategy
    ;  and there is a fragment with hypothesis runway
    ;           whose consistency has not yet been checked
    ; THEN set up a strategy pointer for that fragment
    ;    pointing to the standard list of tests
    (p local-consistency-check::check-runway-1
       (global-status ↑phase local-consistency-check)
     - (consistency-strategy)
       (fragment
           ↑fragment-id <fid>
           ↑hypothesis runway
           ↑consistency-flag unchecked
           ↑symbolic-name <symname>)
    -->
       (make strategy-pointer ↑fragment-id <fid> ↑label RS1)
    )
```

The next rule illustrates the general form of rules that check consistency. There can be several such rules for each hypothesis type. If consistency checking is complex, additional rules might be required to compute intermediate results.

```
; IF   there is a consistency pointer for a fragment
;  and the pointer indicates that the strategy to be used
;       next is taxiways-perpendicular-to-runways
; THEN modify the fragment as indicated by the strategy.
;  and make a task to get the next strategy.
```

```
(p taxiways-perpendicular-to-runways-1
   ...
   (consistency-pointer ↑fragment-id <fid> ↑pointer <ptr>)
   (consistency-list ↑label <ptr>
       ↑name taxiways-perpendicular-to-runways)
   {(fragment ↑fragment-id <fid> ...)              <frag>}

   ...
-->
   (modify <frag> ...)
   (make task ↑name get-next-strategy)
)
```

Since each rule makes a task to get the next strategy, we need a rule to carry out this request.

```
; The following rule finds the next strategy in the list
;  as long as there are addition strategies available.
; IF   the current task is to get the next strategy
;       for fragment <fid>
;  and the consistency pointer for fragment <fid> is at <ptr>
;  and the next-pointer is the strategy-list element for <ptr>
; THEN modify the consistency pointer to the next-pointer.
(p local-consistency-check::get-next-strategy
   {(context
       ↑task get-next-strategy
       ↑datum <fid>) <cntxt>}
   {(consistency-pointer
       ↑fragment-id <fid>
       ↑pointer <ptr>) <pointer>}
   (strategy-list
       ↑label <ptr>
       ↑next-pointer {<> nil <nxtptr>)
-->
   (modify <pointer> ↑pointer <nxtptr>)
)

; additional rules are needed to set the consistency-checked
;  flag when all consistency strategies have been checked,
;  change the context, and so on.
```

Since there is only one consistency pointer at a time, finding the next item in the strategy list takes time proportional to the number of strategy lists in memory. The time could be reduced in this particular case by moving the check for the next item into the individual rules for processing each strategy. This is more efficient because the number of *strategy-list* elements that have to be matched is proportional to the number having that test as the *name*, which is likely to be very small.

```
(p taxiways-perpendicular-to-runways-2
   ...
   {(consistency-pointer ↑fragment-id <fid>
       ↑pointer <ptr>)                                  <cp>}
   (consistency-list ↑label <ptr>
       ↑name taxiways-perpendicular-to-runways
       ↑next-pointer <next>)
   {(fragment ↑fragment-id <fid> ...)                   <frag>}
   ...
-->
   (modify <frag> ...)
   (modify <cp> ↑pointer <next>)

)
```

A disadvantage in this approach is the loss of modularity. If moving to the next strategy or handling the end of the list requires more processing than simply resetting the pointer, then that processing has to be repeated in all strategy-handling rules. Also, in many list enumerations for other tasks there will be no constant such as "taxiways-perpendicular-to-runways" that reduces the number of list elements that have to be considered.

An alternative approach is to use the vector-attribute representation for lists and keep all the consistency tests in a single list.

```
(vector-attribute strategy-list)
(literalize consistency-strategy
    id                ; ID of fragment being processed
    strategy-list     ; list of strategies not yet tried
                      ;  on the fragment being processed
)
```

The rule that sets up the strategy list is similar, but it explicitly puts all the items into a vector attribute associated with the fragment rather than just storing a pointer to the front of a list.

```
; IF   the phase is checking local consistency
;  and there is currently no consistency strategy
;  and there is a fragment with hypothesis runway
;           whose consistency has not yet been checked
; THEN make a consistency strategy for that fragment
;    with the standard list of tests
(p local-consistency-check::check-runway-2
   (global-status ↑phase local-consistency-check)
 - (consistency-strategy)
   (fragment
       ↑fragment-id <fid>
       ↑hypothesis runway
       ↑consistency-flag unchecked)
```

```
-->
    (make consistency-strategy
        ↑id <fid>
        ↑strategy-list runways-parallel-to-terminal-bldg
                taxiways-perpendicular-to-runways
                runway-runway-check)
)
```

The rules that process the strategies can simply check the beginning of the *strategy-list* to see if they apply. This activity takes constant time.

```
(p taxiways-perpendicular-to-runways-3
    ...
    (consistency-strategy
        ↑id <fid>
        ↑strategy-list taxiways-perpendicular-to-runways)
    {(fragment ↑fragment-id <fid> ...)              <frag>}
    ...
-->
    (modify <frag> ...)
    (make task ↑name get-next-strategy)
)
```

Finding the next strategy in the list also takes constant rather than linear time:

```
; The following rule pops that element off the
;  strategy list as long as there are addition strategies
;  available: which allows the other rules in the cycle
;  to fire.
(p local-consistency-check::pop-test-list
    {(context ↑task pop-test-list ↑datum <fid>)   <cntxt>}
    {(consistency-strategy
        ↑test-list <> nil
        ↑id <fid>)                                 <cycle>}
-->
    (remove <cntxt>
    (bind <index> (litval test-list))
    (bind <rest> (compute <index> + 1))
    (modify <cycle>
        ↑test-list2 (substr <cycle> <rest> inf) nil)
)

; additional rules are needed to set the
;  consistency-checked flag when all consistency strategies
;  have been checked, change the context, and so on.
```

6.2.3 AVOID BIG CROSS-PRODUCTS

A major cause of inefficiency in production systems is rules that have several conditions, each of which matches many working memory elements. The techniques we've noted for reducing the number of elements that match a condition can, of course, help reduce the size of the cross-product. Additional techniques include reordering the condition elements, avoiding data structures that separate attributes of one object into separate element classes, and using **build** to specialize rules.

Reorder Condition Elements

The ordering of the condition elements in a rule affects the match time because OPS5 evaluates conditions sequentially as they appear in the rule, stopping when there are no consistent matches to an initial subsequence of conditions. Thus, if more restrictive condition elements are placed earlier in the rule, they reduce the number of consistent matches that are passed on to the remainder of the rule. In the extreme case, a restrictive condition may reduce the number of matches to zero and shield the rest of the rule from any consistency tests. A caution on reordering condition elements: If the MEA strategy is being used, the recency of the first element affects conflict resolution, so reorderings based solely on efficiency may not be possible. However, since goal elements are very restrictive, placing them first *is* often most efficient.

In the rule `taxiways-perpendicular-to-runways::consistent-taxiway`, two fragments that have been predetermined to be a perpendicular pair (taxiway, runway) must have their confidence values updated. This processing takes place as part of a series of consistency tests performed on each fragment. A *results* element holds some values determined by previous computation on the fragment.

```
(vector-attribute strategy-list)
(literalize consistency-strategy
    id                    ; ID of fragment being processed
    strategy-list         ; list of strategies not yet tried
                          ;   on the fragment being processed
)

(literalize store-results
    result-one            ; holds the first result value
    result-two            ; holds the second result value
    result-list           ; holds additional result values
    element-id            ; the ID of the fragment processed
)

; fragtovlist keeps the fragment list ordered
; chg-confidence updates the confidence values
; testscore computes some preliminary confidence values
(external fragtovlist chg-confidence testscore)
```

```
; IF   there is perpendicular orientation of a fragment <fid>
;  and it is being compared with
;       another perpendicular fragment <tid>
;  and the current consistency strategy test for <fid> is
;          taxiway-perpendicular-to-runways
;  and fragment <fid> has confidence <con>
;  and fragment <tid> has confidence <tcon>
; THEN remove the intermediate results
;  and update the confidence values and fragment lists
;          for the two fragments
(p taxiways-perpendicular-to-runways::consistent-taxiway
   {<results> (store-results
       ↑result-one oriented-perpendicular
       ↑result-two <tid>
       ↑result-list <low> <high> <value>
       ↑element-id <fid>)}
   {<strat>   (consistency-strategy
       ↑strategy-list taxiways-perpendicular-to-runways
       ↑id <fid>)}
   {<frg1>   (fragment ↑fragment-id <fid> ↑confidence  <con>)}
   {<frg2>   (fragment ↑fragment-id <tid> ↑confidence <tcon>)}
   ...
-->

   (remove <results>)
   (bind <score> (testscore <low> <high> <value>))
   (modify   <frg1>
       ↑confidence (chg-confidence <con> 0.6 <score>)
       ↑frag-list (fragtovlist <tid>))
   (modify   <frg2>
       ↑confidence (chg-confidence <tcon> 0.6 <score>)
       ↑frag-list (fragtovlist <fid>)))
```

The order of condition elements given in this rule is a good one. Other rules in this example guarantee that there is only one *store-results* element and one *consistency-strategy* element in working memory at any time. So although all fragments must be matched in condition <frg1> to find the one with the right <fid>, only that single matching fragment is passed on to the <frg2> condition. Thus when a new fragment is processed for consistency, the time to update the matches to this rule is linear in the number of fragments. However, if the conditions had been reordered so that the <frg1> and <frg2> conditions were first, then all pairs of fragments would have to be matched against the new *results* and *consistency strategy*, and this would take time proportional to the square of the number of fragments. If there are no *store-results* elements in working memory, the rule consistencies do not have to be computed.

Avoid Big Conditionals

Another way to avoid big cross-products is to reduce the number of different condition elements in a rule by changing or adding associations between attributes and element classes. Given a particular representation, a rule may need several condition elements to pick up all the information from different attributes on different element classes. If this is expensive, one of the condition elements can sometimes be eliminated by adding a new attribute to another condition element, repeating some information in another condition, or completely merging two element classes. We give several illustrations of avoiding big conditionals.

Add new attributes. The rule `interpret-as-road-1` creates a fragment with the hypothesis that a given region could be interpreted as a road. It requires that there be no road interpretation for the region already present and that certain shape conditions be met. The obvious way of testing for the absence of road interpretations for that region requires a negated condition element that looks at all fragments. Since there is only one element of class *constants*, and since the number of *contexts* active at any one time is insignificant, the time for matching this rule is roughly proportional to the number of regions times the number of fragments. In a large scene, determining whether this rule matches is expensive.

```
; IF   there is a task to interpret an unknown linear region
;  and the region has ellipse length greater than the
;        threshold for roads found in the list of constants
;  and there is no fragment interpretation for that region
;        with a hypothesis of "road"
; THEN make such a fragment
(p interpret-as-road-1
   (context ↑task interpret-unknown ↑datum linear <rid>)
   (constants ↑road-length <thresh>)
   (region ↑region-id <rid> ↑ellipse-length > <thresh>)
 - (fragment ↑region-id <rid> ↑hypothesis road)
-->
   (make fragment ↑hypothesis road ...))
```

It is possible to cut the matching time of this rule quite substantially. The only use of the negated condition is to ensure that there is not already a fragment of the type road. This check can be accomplished more efficiently by adding a *road* attribute to the *region* element to note this. This attribute functions as a flag; when its value is not "nil," there is already a road interpretation for the region. Using this flag, as in the rule `interpret-as-road-2`, eliminates the need for the negated condition element.

```
(literalize region
    ...          ; as before
    road         ; flag indicating whether there is already
                 ;   a road interpretation for the region
    runway       ; flag indicating whether there is already
                 ;   a runway interpretation for the region
    taxiway      ; flag indicating whether there is already
                 ;   a taxiway interpretation for the region

        ...
)

; IF   there is a task to interpret an unknown linear region
;  and the region has ellipse length greater than the
;       threshold for the roads found in the list of constants
;       but no road flag indication a fragment interpretation
;       with a hypothesis of "road"
; THEN modify the road flag to T
;  and make such a fragment
(p interpret-as-road-2
   (context ↑task interpret-unknown ↑datum linear <rid>)
   (constants  ↑road-length <thresh>)
   {(region
       ↑region-id <rid>
       ↑ellipse-length > <thresh>
       ↑road nil) <r-region>}
-->
   (modify <r-region> ↑road t)
   (make      fragment ↑hypothesis road...))
```

Since there are `interpret-as-X` rules for all hypotheses X, it would appear to require an excessive amount of space to have a flag for each hypothesis. If there were to be more than 127 flags and other attributes, it would not be possible to use this technique. But so long as there are fewer than 127 attributes for the *region* element class, the space taken by the extra attributes is insignificant compared to that taken by the network and tokens.

Repeat attributes. Repeating attributes in more than one element class may also enable condition elements to be eliminated from some rules. For example, when cross-product matching is expensive and is needed only to pick up trivial fields from other elements, it is worth trading off some space and repeating fields.

In the rule set for airport interpretation, there are many fragments (local interpretations) for each region. Each region has a *symbolic-name* attribute as well as a unique ID in the *region-id* attribute. Each fragment has a *region-id* attribute to tie it to the region for which it is an interpretation. A first design of the system might well assume that if the symbolic name of a region were desired in processing a fragment, it could be picked up from the region as in the rule `evaluate-linears-1`.

```
(external enlarger)
            ; Try to find adjacent regions with the
            ;  same hypothesis type to extend the area.
            ; Additional constraints may be tested, e.g.
            ;  adjacent linear areas should be colinear.
; IF   the current phase is building fragment interpretations
;          of regions in the current image
;  and there is a linear fragment corresponding to a region
;  and the region has symbolic name <symname>
; THEN try to enlarge region <symname>
(p evaluate-linears-1
   (global-status
       ↑phase region-to-fragment
       ↑current-image <cimg>)
   (fragment
       ↑object-type linear
       ↑region-id <rid>
       ↑hypothesis <hyp>)
   (region
       ↑region-id <rid>
       ↑symbolic-name <symname>)
-->
   (call   enlarger <symname> <hyp> <cimg>))
```

The cross-product of *fragment* and *region* elements is expensive if there are many regions and fragments in working memory, which there will be in this case. This large cross-product can be avoided if the symbolic name field is repeated in all fragments, as in `evaluate-linears-2`. To do this, we must modify the rules that create fragments to copy the *symbolic-name* field, as in the rule `interpret-as-road-3`. So long as the value of the attribute is the same, it is not necessary to use the same attribute name, but it is much less confusing to do so.

```
(literalize fragment
    ...             ; as before
    symbolic-name   ; symbolic name of the region for which
                    ;   this fragment is an interpretation
)

; IF   the current phase is building fragment interpretations
;          of regions in the current image
;  and there is a linear fragment corresponding to a region
;       with symbolic name <symname>
; THEN try to enlarge region <symname>
```

```
(p evaluate-linears-2
   (global-status
       ↑phase region-to-fragment
       ↑current-image <cimg>)
   (fragment
       ↑object-type linear
       ↑region-id <rid>
       ↑hypothesis <hyp>)
       ↑symbolic-name <symname>)
-->
   (call   enlarger <symname> <hyp> <cimg>))

; Rules such as the following that create new fragments
;   must be sure to pick up the symbolic name from the region
;   and copy it into the symbolic name for the fragment
(p interpret-as-road-3
   {<cntxt>       (context
       ↑task interpret-unknown
       ↑datum linear <rid>)
   {<cnstnts>     (constants ↑road-length <thresh>)
   {<road-region> (region
       ↑region-id <rid>
       ↑ellipse-length > <thresh>
       ↑road nil
       ↑symbolic-name <symname>)}
-->
   (modify <road-region> ↑road t)
   (make fragment
       ↑hypothesis road
       ↑symbolic-name <symname>...))
```

SPAM, the airport scene interpretation system on which these examples are based, was running rather slowly at one point when it contained approximately 100 regions and gradually built up 300 fragments. It was improved to run fifty times as fast when the *symbolic-name* attribute was repeated and flags (such as *road*) were added to indicate whether or not hypotheses already had been generated.

Merge element classes. It is more efficient to associate information about one object with a single element class than to spread it across a number of classes. We must resist the temptation to spread information if more than one vector attribute is desired, for example, or if a simple object-attribute-value tuple is the chosen representation. Suppose information about fragments were spread into classes; we would have *fragment-hypothesis, fragment-history,* and *fragment-status*, each with the attribute *fragment-id* for correlation. If all this information were wanted within a single rule, there would be a large cross-product. Clearly, big conditionals and widely dispersed information should be avoided.

Use Build to Specialize Rules

If a set of rules is very inefficient, perhaps because of large cross-products, special-purpose rules can be designed with the **build** action (see Section 5.2.9). These rules will match only specific objects rather than any object in a class. For example, if it often is necessary to match fragments against regions, a matching rule specialized to a fragment can be built when the fragment is created. The rule `build-rule-for-taxiway-checking` could substitute for `check-taxiway-fragments` in the rule set for hypothesis checking and should fire right after a fragment is created. To ensure that no other rules fire first, however, we may have to modify the context-handling rules.

```
(external check-taxiway)
; the original checking rule
; IF   there is a fragment with hypothesis taxiway
;  and the corresponding region has area <area> and
;          compactness <comp>
; THEN check the region/fragment pair
(p check-taxiway-fragments
   ...
   (fragment
       ↑hypothesis taxiway
       ↑region-id <rid>
       ↑fragment-id <fid>)
   (region ↑region-id <rid> ↑area <area>  ↑compactness <comp>)
-->
   (call check-taxiway <rid> <fid> <area> <comp>))
; end of original rule

; beginning of a rule to build special checking rules
(external ops5concat)  ; a function to concatenate strings
                       ;  inside a $value to return the
                       ;  result used to build mnemonic names
; IF   there is a fragment which has no check rule
; THEN mark the fragment with a check-rule-built
;  and construct a unique name for the rule
;  and build a rule to check the pair
(p build-rule-for-taxiway-checking
   ...
   {<frag>    (fragment
       ↑check-rule-built nil
       ↑hypothesis taxiway
       ↑region-id <rid>
       ↑fragment-id <fid>)}
```

```
-->
   (modify  <frag> ↑check-rule-built t)
   (bind    <prodname1> (ops5concat |CHECK-TAXIWAY::|  <fid>))
   (build   \\ <prodname1>
        ...
       (fragment
           ↑hypothesis taxiway
           ↑fragment-id  \\ <fid>)
       (region  ↑region-id \\ <rid> ↑area <area>
           ↑compactness <comp>)
        -->
       (call check-taxiway \\ <rid> \\ <fid> <area> <comp>)))
; end of building rule

; a sample rule that would be built for fragment F197
;  and region R33
(p CHECK-TAXIWAY::F197
   ...
   (fragment
        ↑hypothesis taxiway
        ↑fragment-id  F197
   (region  ↑region-id R33 ↑area <area> ↑compactness <comp>)
-->
   (call  check-taxiway> R33 F197 <area> <comp>))
```

The rules that result from executing the build rule, such as `CHECK-TAXI-WAY::F197`, have the *fragment-id* and *region-id* specialized to constants. Thus only one region and one fragment will match, and there will be only one combination in the cross-product. The savings in match time is paid for in space; there are more rules and therefore a larger network.

6.2.4 AVOID FREQUENT CHANGES TO MATCHED CONDITIONS

Whenever there is a change in the set of working memory elements that matches a condition, all matchings associated with the condition plus all consistent matchings associated with all the following conditions must be changed. Thus it makes sense to place conditions whose matches change frequently as far toward the end of the rule as possible or otherwise reduce the frequency of change of matching.

Place Changing Elements Late in the Left-Hand Side

An example of when it might pay to move a condition is shown in the rule `interpret-as-road-4` when a count must be maintained of the number of regions hypothesized to be roads. This count is kept in the *road-count* field of the *global-status* element. The *global-status* element also has a number of other fields such as *phase*, *image*, and number of new fragments. If this element is arbitrarily matched at the beginning of the rule, perhaps because all global objects such as contexts and constants are matched there, it may be unnecessarily expensive.

```
(literalize global-status
    ...                            ; as before
    road-count                     ; the total number of regions
                                   ;   interpreted as roads so far
)

; IF   the current task is to interpret a linear region
;  and there are currently <rc> road fragments
;  and the road-length threshold is <thresh>
;  and the region ellipse-length is greater than <thresh>
;          and the region has no road interpretation
; THEN mark the region as having a road interpretation
;  and increment the road count in the global status
;  and make a fragment with hypothesis road,
;          copy the symbolic name, etc.
(p interpret-as-road-4
   {<cntxt>    (context
        ↑task interpret-unknown
        ↑datum linear <rid>)
   {<g-stat>   (global-status ↑road-count <rc>)
   {<cnstnts>  (constants ↑road-length <thresh>)
   {<r-region> (region
        ↑region-id <rid>
        ↑ellipse-length > <thresh>
        ↑road nil
        ↑symbolic-name <symname>)
-->
   (modify     <r-region> ↑road t)
   (modify     <g-stat> ↑road-count (compute <rc> + 1))
   (make       fragment
        ↑hypothesis road
        ↑symbolic-name <symname>...))
```

Whenever the *global-status* element is modified, the time tag on the working memory element changes and the remainder of the rule must be reevaluated to find all sets of consistent matches. Even if the change is not substantial, the new version of the *global-status* working memory element must be incorporated and the old one removed. Since the changes to *global-status* do not affect the match and <rc> is not used anywhere in the left-hand side, there is no reason why this condition cannot be checked last. Regions and contexts change more frequently than the status, but those changes affect the match and are necessary. Also the <cntxt> element must go first as part of the MEA strategy. There is only one working memory element of class *global-status*, so it does not create large cross-product terms that have to be recomputed if the condition element is moved. Thus the condition element could be moved as shown in `interpret-as-road-5`. The more cycles that occur between the time that interpret-unknown tasks are created and the time they are removed (at which point consistent matches no longer need be checked), the greater the savings in match time.

```
; this rule is the same as interpret-as-road-4 except that
;   condition 4 was moved for efficiency
(p interpret-as-road-5
   {<cntxt>        (context
       ↑task interpret-unknown
       ↑datum linear <rid>)
   {<cnstnts>      (constants ↑road-length <thresh>)
   {<road-region> (region
       ↑region-id <rid>
       ↑ellipse-length > <thresh>
       ↑road nil
       ↑symbolic-name <symname>)
   {<global-stat> (global-status ↑road-count <rc>)
-->
   (modify       <road-region> ↑road t)
   (modify       <global-stat> ↑road-count (compute <rc> + 1))
   (make         fragment
       ↑hypothesis road
       ↑symbolic-name <symname>...))
```

Sometimes there are conflicting demands on the position of a condition element. If a condition rules out many data elements or defines a variable that is used in a comparison by another condition, it may not be possible to place it as far toward the end of the rule as frequency of change suggests.

Avoid Excessive Changes in Control Elements

Avoid changes in unrelated attributes. When working memory elements are used for control, it is important from the standpoint of efficiency to avoid changing them too often. For example, a *global-status* element such as the one containing *road-count* is one example of a control element. An alternative to changing the position of the condition element <g-stat> in the rule `interpret-as-road` would be separate working memory elements for each different control attribute (such as *road-count*). If the attributes are independent or if there will be only one instance of each of the new working memory elements, then no matching will be necessary; hence there will be no need to combine them all in one working memory element whose changes affect many rules for unimportant reasons.

Although splitting up such attributes as *road-count* does speed up the matching process, this same principle cannot necessarily be used to split up any element class in which one frequently changing attribute causes excessive changes to many unrelated conditions. The splitting up of attributes that are sometimes needed in one rule usually requires unique labels or identifiers to correlate the corresponding working memory elements. Such a split conflicts with the principle of avoiding big conditions and may result in large cross-products. Thus the exact amount of data and frequency of change in the two alternatives must be considered carefully in each case and reevaluated if the relevant rules change.

Carefully consider deleting old elements. Obsolete information in an OPS5 program is usually deleted for safety (so that it does not inadvertently trigger rules) unless it is helpful for another purpose (such as an explanation system). However, if efficiency is critical, it may be worth considering whether or not deletion is necessary. In systems like OPS5 that take advantage of the temporal redundancy of information, deleting obsolete information may actually slow things down. On the other hand, in systems that don't take this advantage, leaving information in working memory can cause the system to run slowly. Because obsolete information may be rematched or recombined every cycle, deleting unused contexts, control elements, and other redundancies helps these systems run faster.

Consider a goal organization in which the current goal is explicitly represented by an element class different from that of the other goals. A goal-switching rule might then be

```
(literalize current-goal  ; there is only one current-goal
    status                ; one of: success, pending, active
    name                  ; name of the goal
    id                    ; unique ID for the goal
)

(literalize goal
    status                ; one of: success, pending, active
    name                  ; name of the goal
    id                    ; unique ID for the goal
)

; IF   the current-goal element has status success
;   and there is another goal with status pending
```

```
; THEN modify the current-goal element to have the name and
;         ID of the pending goal and status active
;  and change the status of the new goal's element to active
(p switch-goal
   {<current>   (current-goal)
       ↑status success
       ↑name <oldname>
       ↑id <id>)}
   {<new>       (goal
       ↑status pending
       ↑name <name>
       ↑id <newid>)}
-->
   (modify <current> ↑name <name> ↑status active ↑id <newid>)
   (modify <new> ↑status active))
```

The right-hand side of the rule `switch-rule` is equivalent to

```
(remove <current>)
(make current-goal ↑name <name> ↑status active ↑id <id>)
(remove <new>)
(make goal ↑name <name> ↑status active ↑id <newid>))
```

Deleting the elements <current> and <name> takes more time than adding the new elements if there are many goals in the system. Therefore we might consider rewriting the right-hand side as follows:

```
(make current-goal ↑name <name> ↑status active ↑id <newid>)
(make goal ↑name <name> ↑status active ↑id <newid>))
```

However, this adds two instantiations to each rule that could match <oldname> and <name>. It also requires the programmer to keep track of all fields in a *current-goal* element and make sure they are all copied. The principle of recency will cause the right one to be selected, but the matching time is increased because the size of the cross-product increases. Conflict-resolution time increases also, and keeping all four goals and their matches in memory requires much more space. A better way would be to use the *status* of "pending," as described in Section 6.2.2, to keep only a single goal active.

Reduce numbers of control elements by composition. Another cause of system slowness can be that many rule firings yield little knowledge because control elements and partial results are used too often. If the application is an expert system in which the right answer is desired in the least amount of time and no complex explanation facility is required, then it might be profitable to compose some rules into larger sets that yield the same result. The composition procedure is essentially a hand-executed version of the learning mechanism described in Section 8.3.3.

If several rules always fire in a row, there is no reason to have separate rules. A composed rule can add the information that appears on the right-hand sides of its component rules without using control elements. The result of composition is an increased speed of application of rules and a reduction in the number of matches stored in the network. Unfortunately, composing rules can produce rules that are clumsy and unreadable. In addition, if the composed rule replaces its component rules, then the component rule cannot be used as part of a different inference. In systems that take advantage of structural similarity in the rules, keeping both rules in rule memory is not so inefficient.

Another argument against composition is that modifications need to be made in only one place when control elements are used, which makes rules easier to understand and less prone to error. This argument would be invalidated, however, if a preprocessor or macro facility were available. Such a facility would allow the programmer to write modular rules for clarity and ease of modification but would then compose the rules, if so directed, to allow gains in efficiency.

6.2.5 MATCH INDIVIDUAL CONDITION ELEMENTS MORE QUICKLY

Some smaller efficiencies can be gained by speeding up the matches to individual condition elements. To accomplish this, we either place restrictive tests earlier in the conditions or change the representation.

Place Restrictive Tests Early

Since OPS5 evaluates tests in the order in which they appear in the condition and stops when there are no working memory elements that satisfy all tests, the ordering of the tests affects the system efficiency. The test that rules out the greatest number of elements should be performed first, followed by the test that rules out the second-greatest number, given that the first test had successful bindings, and so on. The same principles of ordering and frequency of change that apply to conditions within a rule also apply to attribute tests within a condition, but the effect on efficiency is usually negligible.

Consider the region condition element in the following rule:

```
(p interpret-as-road-6
   (context
       ↑task interpret-unknown
       ↑datum linear <rid> <con>)
```

```
    (region
        ↑region-status <> deleted
        ↑road nil
        ↑region-id <rid>
        ...)
    ...)
```

If there are fewer regions with a "nil" value of the *road* attribute than with a *region-status* that is not "deleted," it saves time to have the *road* test first in the region condition.

```
(p interpret-as-road-7
    (context
        ↑task interpret-unknown
        ↑datum linear <rid> <con>)
    (region
        ↑road nil
        ↑region-status <> deleted
        ↑region-id <rid>
        ...)
    ...)
```

Change the Representation of Data

Sometimes a change in representation can lead to increased speed in the match cycle. Several types of change have already been described here: adding new attributes or values, repeating attributes on related elements, and merging element classes. Additional techniques are changing vectors or vector attributes to regular attributes, and changing attributes to element classes.

Changing vectors or vector attributes to regular attributes can speed up the time it takes to match a single condition. Any condition element matching a vector must specify the vector's form completely up to the element needed. Sometimes this complete specification can result in many variables being used as placeholders for the information desired.

For example, it makes little sense to store the information about a region in a vector of the form

```
(region region-id texture shadow-type location orientation
        height road taxiway linear....)
```

because only a few elements are needed at a time. Picking up the *region-id* and the *road* flag would require a condition of the form

```
(region <rid> <ignore1> <ignore2> <ignore3>
        <ignore4> <ignore5> <rflag>)
```

or

```
(region <rid1> {} {} {} {} <rflag>)
```

The ability to reference only particular pieces of an element is an advantage of the attribute-value representation. The well-defined nature of the representation and the ability to selectively address attributes makes the vector attribute the best representation to use for most applications. Some exceptions are user input and other situations where the form of the input cannot be predetermined.

Some decisions about representing vectors are matters of style rather than efficiency. For example, a vector attribute can be used to hold an arbitrarily long list:

```
(vector-attribute results)
(literalize store-results results)
```

However, if a vector attribute is to contain a list that is known to be smaller than some threshold length, then an enumeration is an alternative implementation:

```
(literalize store-results result-one result-two result-three)
```

At times vector attributes are useful when the length of the vector is not known ahead of time but the first elements are the ones of most interest. In this case, if some rules match particular elements within a list, an indexed set plus a list might be useful:

```
(vector-attribute rest)
(literalize store-results result-one result-two
    result-three rest)
```

There is no algorithm for choosing the right representation. The rule writer must explore multiple representations. The best representation is usually the one that's most readable and that best organizes the system. The representation should be kept general and expandable during the development process. After the system has been shown to execute correctly, the programmer can try changing the representation for faster matching. Efficiency should nearly always be considered last. Correctness, documentation, code readability, and clarity of representation should come first.

6.2.6 LIMIT THE SIZE OF THE CONFLICT SET

Having too large a conflict set can lead to inefficiency. While conflict resolution should be used to control which of the applicable rules fire, sometimes rules can be made inapplicable via greater use of matching, goals, and contexts. Replacing conflict resolution by another form of control may result in a more transparent and more efficient system.

There are no significant ways to speed up conflict resolution other than by reducing the size of the conflict set. In OPS5, all the instantiations in the conflict set are compared and the most recent or most specific is chosen. Although recencies of elements and specificities of rules are not recomputed when resolving conflicts, the values for each rule instantiation must be compared to some maximum each time. This algorithm is linear in the number of rule instantiations in the conflict set.

One reason for a large conflict set might be that recency or specificity is being used inappropriately for control. For example, suppose several rules match, but the programmer wants to force a particular rule to fire first. One approach is to exploit recency and insert a condition that matches a recent but irrelevant working memory element such as a goal. This type of control is not desirable, since the rule with the goal test would not actually be achieving the goal. Another inappropriate approach is to exploit specificity and insert an additional but irrelevant or repeated attribute test.

Inappropriate and inefficient uses of conflict resolution are illustrated in the next few rules. Suppose it were desirable to generate a fragment with an interpretation as a runway before one with an interpretation as a taxiway. A superfluous condition element in the `interpret-as-runway-bad-1` rule

```
(context ↑task interpret-unknown ↑datum linear)
```

ensures that that rule will fire first. The same effect could be achieved by specificity if, instead of adding an additional condition element, one or more unnecessary attribute tests were added, such as the curvature test in `interpret-as-runway-bad-2`. The curvature test is unnecessary because the region has already been noted as linear in the first condition.

```
(literalize constants
    ...                  ; as before
    taxiway-minlength    ; the minimum length for which a linear
                         ;   region can be considered a taxiway
    taxiway-maxlength    ; the maximum length for which a linear
                         ;   region can be considered a taxiway
    runway-minlength     ; the minimum length for which a linear
                         ;   region can be considered a runway
    runway-maxlength     ; the maximum length for which a linear
                         ;   region can be considered a runway
)

(literalize region
    ...                  ; as before
    curvature            ; one of: straight, curved
)
```

```
; IF   the current task is to interpret a linear region
;  and there is no taxiway interpretation of the region
;          and the region's ellipse-length is between the
;          maximum and minimum allowable for taxiways
; THEN ...
(p interpret-as-taxiway
   {<cntxt>        (context
       ↑task interpret-unknown
       ↑datum linear <rid>)}
   {<cnstnts>      (constants
       ↑taxiway-minlength <minlen>
       ↑taxiway-maxlength <maxlen>)}
   {<t-region> (region
       ↑region-id <rid>
       ↑ellipse-length { >= <minlen> <= <maxlen> }
       ↑taxiway nil)}
...
)

; this rule is basically the same as the rule for taxiway
;  interpretation except for the use of different constants
; an unnecessarily repeated condition, <cntxt-2>, has been
;  inserted to force it to fire before interpret-as-taxiway.
(p interpret-as-runway-bad-1
   {<cntxt-1>      (context
       ↑task interpret-unknown
       ↑datum linear <rid>)}
   {<cntxt-2>  (context
       ↑task interpret-unknown)}
   {<cnstnts>      (constants
       ↑runway-minlength <minlen>
       ↑runway-maxlength <maxlen>)}
   {<r-region> (region
       ↑region-id <rid>
       ↑ellipse-length { >= <minlen> <= <maxlen> }
       ↑runway nil)}
...
)

; this rule is basically the same as the rule for taxiway
;  interpretation except for the use of different constants
; an unnecessary test for ↑curvature straight has been
;  inserted to force it to fire before interpret-as-taxiway.
(p interpret-as-runway-bad-2
   {<cntxt>        (context
       ↑task interpret-unknown
       ↑datum linear <rid>)}
   {<cnstnts>      (constants
       ↑runway-minlength <minlen>
       ↑runway-maxlength <maxlen>)}
```

```
    {<r-region> (region
         ↑region-id <rid>
         ↑ellipse-length { >= <minlen> <= <maxlen> }
         ↑runway nil
         ↑curvature straight)}
...
)
```

The addition of extra conditions or tests is not the best means of achieving the desired ends. A better solution is to introduce another field into the control element. This field, *most-promising*, will tell us which interpretation to examine. Control rules could switch the *most-promising* attribute to the value "runway" or "taxiway" if desired.

```
(literalize context
    ...                 ; As before
    most-promising      ; The interpretation to consider next
)

; this rule is basically the same as the rule for taxiway
;  interpretation except for the use of different constants
; a more appropriate test for which interpretation is most
;  promising has been inserted into the context control
;  element to force the rule to fire before
;  interpret-as-taxiway.
(p interpret-as-runway-better
   {<cntxt>       (context
       ↑task interpret-unknown
       ↑datum linear <rid>
       ↑most-promising runway)}
   {<cnstnts>     (constants
       ↑runway-minlength <minlen>
       ↑runway-maxlength <maxlen>)}
   {<r-region> (region
       ↑region-id <rid>
       ↑ellipse-length { >= <minlen> <= <maxlen> }
       ↑runway nil)}
...
)
```

6.2.7 CALL USER-DEFINED FUNCTIONS

Some operations simply are not efficient in OPS5. These operations include membership tests, concatenation, and arithmetic functions not provided by **compute**: e.g., computing distances, determining whether features are within a specified proximity of one another, determining whether features intersect, determining orientation, and updating confidence values. If a process can be completed more efficiently in a user-defined function, then it should be moved out of OPS5. Section 5.2.8 provides details on how to write user-defined functions.

6.3 EXERCISES

6-1 Draw the network for the following pair of rule conditions:

```
(p Remove-satisfied-goal
   (goal ↑status satisfied)
-->
...)

(p Congratulations
   (goal ↑status satisfied)
 - (goal ↑status active)
-->
...)
```

6-2 Draw the network for the following pair of rule conditions:

```
(p On::Phys-Object
   (goal ↑status active ↑type on ↑object-name <o>)
   (phys-object ↑name <o> ↑at <p>)
   (monkey ↑at <p> ↑holds nil)
-->
...)

(p On::Phys-Object:Holds
   (goal ↑status active ↑type on ↑object-name <o1>)
   (phys-object ↑name <o1> ↑at <p>)
   (monkey ↑at <p>)
-->
...)
```

6-3 Describe what happens to the network discussed in Section 6.1.3 when working memory element 3 is removed.

6-4 Describe what happens to the network of Exercise 6-3 if the following element is added:

```
(context ↑task interpret-unknown ↑datum linear)
```

6-5 Describe what happens to the network of Exercise 6-4 when working memory element 2 is removed.

6-6 Which of the previous three updates requires the most work? The least?

6-7 Consider the following alternative organization of element classes for the monkey-and-bananas problem (compare to the declarations of Sections 3.3.2 and 3.3.3). How would it affect the efficiency of the rules?

```
(literalize on
    top-object      ; the monkey or any physical object
    bottom-object   ; the floor or any physical object
                    ;   cannot be "ceiling" if top-object
                    ;   is "monkey"
)
(literalize at
    object          ; the monkey or any physical object
    location        ; coordinate X-Y location with X and Y
                    ; integers between 1 and 10 inclusive
)
(literalize object-weight
    object          ; one element for each physical object
    weight          ; one of: "heavy" or "light"
)
(literalize holds
    what            ; nil or name of physical object of
                    ; "light" weight that monkey is holding
)
```

6-8 Suppose that in the airport interpretation system there are many working memory elements of type *region*, only a single instance of *constants*, and only a few elements of type *context* for each *region*. Discuss the effects of changing the order of the conditions in the rule `interpret-as-road-2`. Assume that matches to the <cntxt> condition will change two times for each region (when a *context* is added and removed) and that the matches to <road-region> will change whenever any of the interpretations cause the flags such as *road* and *taxiway* to be changed. There are 9 such flags and 9 `interpret-as-X` rules of similar form that change the flags. Only one *region* is processed at a time, so there shouldn't be any changes to *context* or *region* elements other than those related to the current *region*.

```
(p interpret-as-road-2
   {<cntxt>        (context
       ↑task interpret-unknown
       ↑datum linear <rid>)}
   {<cnstnts>      (constants  ↑road-length <thresh>)}
   {<road-region> (region
       ↑region-id <rid>
       ↑ellipse-length > <thresh>
       ↑road nil)}
-->
   (modify    <road-region> ↑road t)
   (make      fragment ↑hypothesis road...))
```

6-9 Consider changing the monkey-and-bananas rules in each of the following ways:

a) Remove the goals after they have been achieved rather than marking the *status* as "satisfied."

b) Set up the goals with a *status* of "pending" and keep only a single goal active at a time, as in Section 6.2.2.

Predict the effect of the change on the number of working memory elements and the run time, then modify the rule and measure the actual effect.

6-10 Discuss the efficiency of the alternative implementations for phase switching presented in Section 4.1. Which is better: storing pairs of phases in working memory or writing rules to change phase?

6-11 The airport interpretation program consists of several phases, one of which involves consistency checking. There is a consistency flag on each fragment that is initialized to "unchecked" and is changed to "checked" after the interpretation of the fragment has been tested. The rule `change-phase-1` illustrates a straightforward way to determine when to complete the consistency-checking phase and start up the next phase. This rule fires when there are no fragments whose consistency flag has value unchecked. If there are many fragments in working memory, matching this rule is very expensive. Suggest a more efficient implementation.

```
(literalize fragment
    ...                       ; Define as before
    flag                      ; Consistency flag
                              ;   one of: unchecked, checked
)

(p change-phase-1
    (fragment ↑origin machine)
  - (fragment ↑origin machine ↑flag unchecked)
          ...
)
```

PART THREE

COMPARATIVE PRODUCTION SYSTEMS

7

Production System Architecture

This chapter is intended for the production-system programmer who wants to gain a deeper understanding of the underlying architecture of production systems. Some important differences among production-system architectures have to do with control structures, which typically are designed either to be as general as possible or to facilitate a particular type of application, such as diagnosis. While the languages with specialized architectures are more restricted in expressibility, when these languages are applied to appropriate problems, they increase the ease of programming and the efficiency of the resulting rule sets. The intended control structure of a production system influences the type of data and rule memory needed, including what features — e.g., certainty factors and activation levels — are to be provided as built-in primitives and what kinds of matching are possible.

Production-system languages also differ in the types of rules that are allowed, particularly in the expressiveness of the matching primitives and the generality of predicates allowed in the conditions of the left-hand side. Allowing complex matching or user-defined predicates makes it difficult to produce efficient implementations of the matching process. Finally, languages may differ in their organization of data memory. Most pure production-system languages differ only slightly in their numbers of memories or representations of data elements, although the representation of data does affect the types of matching possible. Hybrid languages that represent data as schemas or frames and mix schema-based reasoning with rule-based reasoning are not discussed explicitly in this chapter. These hybrid languages usually have rules with very simple matching. They do not have the types of control typical of pure production-system languages or any built-in features such as recency or certainty factors.

OPS5 will serve as the reference architecture in our discussion while other production systems, primarily EMYCIN, YAPS, GRAPES, and PRISM, will help illustrate the range of possible architectures. EMYCIN is an example of a backward-chaining architecture with built-in support for certainty factors but relatively primitive matching facilities. OPS5, YAPS, and PRISM are primarily forward-chaining architectures with built-in support for recency, but they can also be programmed to do backward chaining. The architecture of GRAPES includes a goal-tree mechanism in addition to recency; it is used primarily for goal-based backward chaining but allows some forward chaining. OPS5 has more restrictions on data structures and user-defined predicates, but OPS5 is more efficient than YAPS, PRISM, and GRAPES. Chapter 9 summarizes these and other languages.

In the first section of this chapter, we'll discuss the different organizations of data in these production-system languages. In the second section, we'll examine the range of matching features and right-hand-side actions that are available. The final section focuses on a description of mechanisms for bringing about the desired types of control.

7.1 DATA MEMORY

As we have seen in previous chapters, data memory is used primarily to store current knowledge about the task being performed. Data memory can contain two very different types of entities: facts and goals. Facts embody descriptive information that is used by the rules to make inferences, whereas goals provide a direction to the system's processing. In our earlier discussions we have sometimes referred to goals as "contexts" or "tasks." These three terms can be used interchangeably to mean actions that must be accomplished or situations that must be achieved.

Reasoning with facts and goals requires an organizational scheme and a set of processing mechanisms. We turn now to several different organizational schemes for facts and goals and then to some of the possible properties of facts and goals that may be incorporated profitably into the architecture. Some of these properties can be updated transparently by the production system rather than by the programmer and used by the processing mechanisms to increase the efficiency in typical production-system executions.

7.1.1 ORGANIZATION OF DATA

Because facts and goals serve different purposes, some languages store them in separate memories. In GRAPES, for example, goals are kept in a separate data memory that can be matched against and modified much like working memory. Goal success or failure, subgoal order, and other properties of goals are updated automatically by the GRAPES interpreter.

In other languages, such as OPS5 and YAPS, goals and facts are not distinguished by the architecture and are stored together. Since the architecture does not handle goal interactions in a fixed way, greater flexibility in control is possible at a cost of having to specify the behavior in more detail. In OPS5 and YAPS, goals are usually implemented as control elements (see Section 4.3) that reside in working memory. OPS5 goals are added, deleted, and modified like any other working memory elements.

In EMYCIN, all goals are to fill in the values and certainties of objects leading toward the final diagnosis. These objects, and implicitly the corresponding goals to complete the objects, are kept in a tree structure that is used to direct processing and to explain why a decision was made — as well as to store facts.

PRISM has two related data memories, a working memory and a long-term memory. Although not all elements of working memory must be present in long-term memory, generally the former is considered to be the active portion of the latter. Each of the data elements has an associated activation that can be used during conflict resolution and in determining when an element should be added to and removed from working memory. The problem-solving rules generally match against elements in working memory.

The ease with which problems can be solved in a production-system language often depends upon the ease of representing information in data memory. Thus a rule-based language is not always the appropriate choice for implementing an expert system. For example, if the most important aspect of the implementation is the representation of a variety of closely related objects and their interactions, an object-oriented language with inheritance and message passing (such as SMALLTALK or FLAVORS) might be a closer fit. In addition to these general object-oriented languages, other representation schemes have been proposed for specific classes of applications. Some of these languages employ rules as part of their representation, but none is organized solely around the rule-based formalism, and we do not discuss them here. The remainder of this section describes different representations for data in rule-based languages.

Attribute Values and Triples

The OPS5 structure of objects with attributes and values facilitates organizing applications programs around the objects in the problem domain, since *attribute-value element* representations are good for specifying features of objects. OPS5 stores the values of attributes in contiguous memory locations. As described in Section 2.2, the attribute of an object is converted internally to an offset that specifies how many memory locations from the start of the element one must look to find the value corresponding to that attribute. The element class of the object is stored in the first memory location of the working memory element. Vector attributes are stored following all the other memory locations that have been set aside for the object. The **literalize** commands include all the information that the interpreter needs to compute offsets for storing and retrieving values, so the attribute names are not necessary for internal access once the **literalize** declarations, initial working memory, and rules have been loaded. To allow quicker access to working memory elements, OPS5 uses a bucket hash technique. In the LISP implementations, the working memory elements are stored on property lists associated with the element class (the first item in the working memory element). Then, to find whether or not an element is in working memory, only those elements that start with the same first element need be searched.

Attribute-value triples, which are used in the EMYCIN language, are similar to attribute-value elements except that in the left-hand sides of rules the object name is repeated with each attribute. For example, the OPS5 condition

```
(computer ↑size micro ↑word-size 16 ↑disk-type floppy)
```

would be represented in triples by the following three conditions:

```
(computer size micro)
(computer word-size 16)
(computer disk-type floppy)
```

Nevertheless, EMYCIN internally stores all of the attributes of each object with the object.

Objects in EMYCIN are related to one another in a *static context tree*. The root of the tree is the main object about which the consultation gives advice. Descendents of a node in the tree may structure the evidence required to make conclusions about the parent object, distinguish components of the object, or distinguish events that can happen to the object.

Vectors and Lists

YAPS, GRAPES, and PRISM use the general LISP list structure for their internal representation. A list is a sequence of zero or more atoms or lists, surrounded by parentheses. Here are some examples of list representations:

```
(DNA IS-A nucleic-acid)
(Shari HAS-RELATION sister TO Bob)
(TRANSFER object: contract from: (Carmen Paul) to: Chris)

(D N A is a (nucleic acid))
((Shari) is ((the sister)) of Bob)
((Carmen and Paul) gave (the contract) to Chris)
```

As shown in the examples, lists place little restriction on the form in which the knowledge is represented. This paucity of structure often causes problems if no higher-level knowledge organization is used. Defining key words (such as those in capital letters in the previous example) or punctuation can help structure the representation; a grammar that specifies the syntax of all data memory elements is even better. Any knowledge-representation scheme can be mapped into list structures, since they are so general. Nevertheless, list structures are not necessarily the most efficient way of implementing the higher-level organization.

Production systems like YAPS and PRISM that allow lists of arbitrary length use a recursive function to access the structure of those lists. Since matching, storing, and even comparing lists can be computationally expensive, some systems try to optimize these operations. Each list can have an associated unique key, which is used when operations require comparing data memory elements for equality. Comparing two keys is much cheaper than comparing two lists in most implementation languages. In addition, when the production system matches a pattern against a list, the system can hash on various features of the pattern and the list. For example, the system can use the length of the list to find those patterns that could match, or it can use any constants that are common between the pattern and the list.

The construct corresponding most closely to lists in OPS5 is the *vector element* (not vector attribute). Vector elements are single-level lists of atomic items and do not have to be declared ahead of time with a **literalize** command. They are good for terminal input and file input and output, where the length of the data cannot be determined beforehand. The vector element, like the attribute-value element, is stored in the property list corresponding to the first item in the element. All accessing is done with this first item.

Schemas or Frames

Although object-oriented programming is a different style of programming from rule-based programming, it is possible to include such objects in a rule-based language. It is convenient to be able to declare complex data structures — schemas or frames — whose attributes are strongly typed. Organizing such structures in networks allowing inheritance of attributes, value types, and values can greatly facilitate programming without affecting the reasoning style. YAPS is one example of such a system; it allows FLAVORS as data memory objects.

Networks

Another possible organization of data memory is the *network*. Networks are used for relational databases (see Section 9.1.5), some expert-system applications (see Section 9.1.3), and cognitive modeling (see Section 9.2.2).

A network consists of a set of *nodes*, which represent objects or relationships, and *links* (also called *arcs*), which represent attributes of an object or identify the components of the relationship. If the links have names, the network is *labeled*, and if the links apply in one direction only, the network is *directed*.

In PRISM, each object or component of a data element is a node and the relationships between elements are encoded as labeled, directed arcs. Consider the information represented in the following PRISM data elements (called *propositions*):

```
(Commodore is-a computer-company)
(Commodore company-size small)
(Commodore computer-size micro)
(Apple is-a computer-company)
(Apple company-size large)
(Apple computer-size micro)
(Bell is-a telephone-company)
(Bell company-size large)
```

This would be represented graphically in a network as follows:

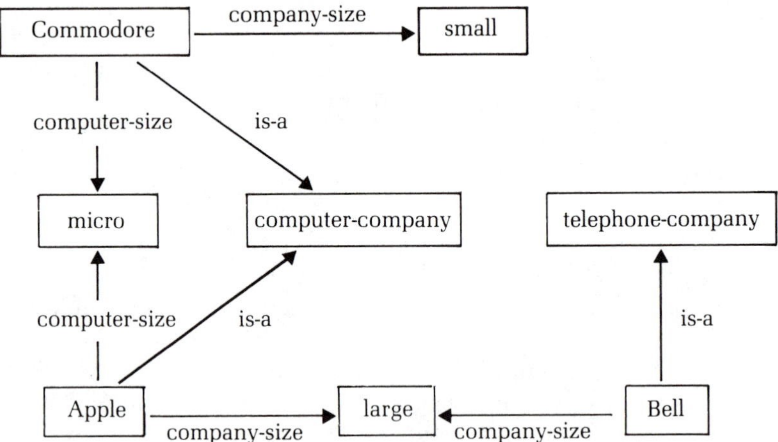

In PRISM, symbols representing predicates such as "is-a" and "computer-size" can be declared to be syntactic elements. All other elements are then assumed to be nodes in the network. Stored with each node are all propositions that apply to that element. This connection also allows the system to find related facts by the internal equivalent of following the directed arcs. Section 7.1.3 describes the use of networks in propagating activation values.

7.1.2 ORGANIZATIONS FOR GOALS

The organization of a set of goals is just as important as the organization of facts. Goals organize what is to be done and what has already been accomplished. Expert systems can also exploit an explicit representation of goals to recognize that a previous solution is applicable again, to merge goals that can be achieved together, and to recognize conflicts among future goals. In the following paragraphs, we will examine some data structures for the organization of goals: trees, queues, stacks, and agendas. Later we'll look at some general attributes of goals that the production system can update independently of their organization.

A *tree* structure often is chosen when an expert system seeks its solution through a strategy of divide and conquer, problem refinement, or problem decomposition. By means of pointers, goals are connected to both their *supergoals* and their *subgoals*. An *or* branch to a set of subgoals specifies that only one of the subgoals must be satisfied, while an *and* branch specifies that all the subgoals must be satisfied. Goals are decomposed into sets of simpler subgoals until goals are reached that are immediately achievable. For example, GRAPES builds a tree of goals and allows rules to match against goals and add new subgoals anywhere in the tree. Goals within a tree can be *visited* and *expanded* in many different orders (e.g., depth first, breadth first, best first) [Nilsson 80], and the rules may implement any of these orderings. The EMYCIN architecture builds a *dynamic context instance tree* when rules fire. The instances of objects in the tree serve as goals that determine what objects and attributes are to be worked on next.

The *queue* is an appropriate data structure to use when all goals must be processed and all goals are of equal importance. A queue is a list in which items stored for later processing enter at the back and items for immediate processing are taken from the front. Goals stored in a queue are pursued in the same order in which they were generated. No manipulation of order is possible. Since the expert-system programmer is rarely indifferent to the order of processing of goals, queues of goals are not commonly built into production-system architectures.

The *stack* is a good data structure with which to implement a pure backward-chaining control strategy. When the goals are pushed onto the stack in the order that they are created, and the most recent goal added to the stack is expanded first, the resulting system will do backward chaining by depth-first search. In programs written in OPS5 or other languages that use recency as a conflict-resolution mechanism, goals frequently are handled by the programmer with an implicit stack discipline. However, goals are not distinguished from other data objects by any built-in treatment.

Agendas are used when relative goal priorities change dynamically. An agenda is like a queue, except that here the goals are rated by priority, which is typically maintained by the rule set. The rules contribute to a goal's overall priority rating by accessing a given property of the goal. An agenda that is ordered strictly by recency leads to a control strategy equivalent to a depth-first tree traversal. A negative recency discipline is equivalent to a queue discipline. While agenda mechanisms are rarely built into production-system languages, they are easy to implement with rules and have been used in a number of expert-system applications.

7.1.3 PROPERTIES OF FACTS

Most production-system programmers prefer to have an architecture that helps ensure that facts relevant to the current task are examined and processed before facts unrelated to the current task. The most common data-element properties in terms of determining relevance are *recency*, *certainty*, and *activation*. Because they suggest, but do not guarantee, relevance, these properties are ***heuristics.*** The ***recency*** heuristic suggests that data elements that were most recently accessed will be relevant to the task at hand. The ***activation*** heuristic suggests that data elements related in some way to recently accessed elements will be relevant. Finally, the ***certainty*** heuristic suggests that facts will be more relevant if it is more certain that they are correct.

Recency

In programming production systems it often pays to give more attention to an element because it has been recently acquired or used. OPS5, YAPS, GRAPES, and PRISM maintain global recency counters that are incremented every time something is added to (and sometimes deleted from) working memory. Recency is maintained by the architecture, not explicitly in the data elements. Some systems (PRISM, for example) provide a *refresh* function to update the recency independently of the data element's modification. This can be simulated in OPS5 by calling the **modify** command on a working memory element without changing any values. Some systems, such as EMYCIN, do not have recency built into them. A production system with a built-in recency principle tends to have high ***sensitivity*** to its changing environment, as discussed in Section 7.3.

Certainty

For some applications, recency alone does not provide enough information about the utility of the data elements. In medical diagnosis, for example, we might want to determine the *certainty* that a patient has a particular disease.

This information is measured on an absolute scale (usually 0 to 1 or −1 to 1) as opposed to the relative scale used in recency computations. Techniques for reasoning about alternative hypotheses include Bayesian posterior probabilities (a variant of which is used in KAS), certainty factors (used in EMYCIN), the Dempster-Shafer theory of belief functions [Buchanan, Shortliffe 84], and confidences (used in EXPERT) [Weiss, Kulikowski 84]. Other techniques that are not incorporated in any current expert system tools are fuzzy reasoning [Zadeh 79], reasoned assumptions [Doyle, London 80], and endorsements [Cohen, Grinberg 83].

In this section we discuss one of these methods. The MYCIN expert system [Buchanan, Shortliffe 84][1] uses subjective certainty factors to express the likelihood that patient has a given disease. Suppose that we gave MYCIN the following beliefs and associated certainties:[2]

Belief	Certainty
(person ↑name George ↑abdominal-pains many)	0.6
(person ↑name George ↑blood-sugar low)	0.4
(person ↑name George ↑previous-appointments 3)	1.0

These memory elements express the belief that George probably has many abdominal pains (he may be a hypochondriac), may have low blood-sugar, and has certainly had three previous appointments.

In MYCIN, rules have numerical factors called *attenuations* that express the inherent reliability of the rule making the inference. Suppose the following rule, expressed in OPS5 syntax, was in MYCIN's rule set:

```
(p patient-has-hypoglycemia      attenuation: 0.8
   (person ↑name <name> ↑abdominal-pains << many several >>)
   (person ↑name <name> ↑blood-sugar low)
   (person ↑name <name> ↑previous-appointments > 0)
-->
   (make diagnosis ↑disease hypoglycemia ↑person <name>))
```

The certainty of a conjunction is the minimum of the certainties of the conjuncts. In this example, min(0.6, 0.4, 1.0) = 0.4. To find the certainty of the conclusion, the certainty of the left-hand side (0.4) is multiplied by the attenuation of the rule (0.8) to yield the certainty of the inference (0.4 * 0.8 = 0.32). Thus the automatic certainty reasoning mechanisms built into MYCIN's architecture would conclude:

[1] EMYCIN is a domain-independent version of MYCIN.

[2] Examples are in OPS5 attribute-value notation. MYCIN working memory elements are actually triples (see Section 7.1.1).

Belief	Certainty
(diagnosis ↑disease hypoglycemia ↑person George)	0.32

When different rules arrive at the same conclusion, the certainty of the conclusion is the result of the combination of independent sources of knowledge. Thus if another rule produced

Belief	Certainty
(diagnosis ↑disease hypoglycemia ↑person George)	0.52

then the certainty of the diagnosis would increase according to the following formula:

```
<new certainty> =    <certainty factor 1> + <certainty factor 2>
                   - <certainty factor 1> * <certainty factor 2>
```

This formula applies only if both certainty factors are positive. There are separate formulas for the other cases. Thus George has hypoglycemia with certainty $0.52 + 0.32 - (0.52)(0.32) = 0.6736$. If certainties are part of the representation of each fact, then each rule in the system has to compute the new certainty for each fact that it concludes. If the architecture does not process certainty factors automatically, then adding a function call to compute the new certainties is desirable. Using OPS5's **compute** function for these calculations would require tedious repetition of the formula and would be more error prone. See Section 5.2.8 for an example of using function calls to compute certainty.

MYCIN certainties can be either positive or negative. Positive certainties denote confidence that the assertion is true, while negative certainties denote confidence that it is false. A certainty of zero indicates that no predominantly positive or negative evidence is available. Certainty values with absolute value below a minimum threshold are treated for some purposes as if they were equal to zero.

Activation

The activation associated with an object is one measure of the amount of attention that should be devoted to the object during a recognize-act cycle. Activation has been used in many cognitive modeling systems [Rummelhart, Lindsay, Norman 72; Anderson 83; Thibadeau, Just, Carpenter 82] but typically is not used in expert-system applications. Activations, represented by numbers, are propagated from elements that are activated to other elements that are related to them. The propagation follows criteria determined either by the architecture or by rules in the system. The activations of elements may be used in conflict resolution to determine which rules are more relevant (have higher activation) and therefore should dominate. Activations also may be used (in PRISM, for example) to determine when to move elements from a long-term to a short-term memory.

One way to represent the relationships between data objects is to construct a network (see Section 7.1.1). A network encodes the strength of the relationship between data memory elements by storing connections, and those connections are used in propagating activation values. Each data memory element (or sometimes each of several attributes of elements) has an associated number representing the activation. A standard mechanism can then be used to propagate activation from one node (data memory element) in the network to all those to which it is linked.

Elements receive activation directly from the environment (through sensors or directly from input statements in the programming language) or from other elements in the network by a process called *flow of activation*. The production system directs activation from one element to another in a single *activation cycle*. It may take several activation cycles for the activation to reach all the elements toward which it is directed. Activation can be directed by rules within a program that explicitly state how to propagate and decay activations [Thibadeau, Just, Carpenter 82], or it can be computed by the inference engine [Anderson 83].

Spreading activation is one method of propagating activation that is computed by the inference engine; spreading activation is used in PRISM. Activation flows from sources to neighboring nodes, then to their neighboring nodes, and so on, until the system reaches a state of equilibrium. The amount of activation received by a node on a given cycle is computed by a spreading algorithm. Anderson's ACT system [Anderson 83] gives one definition of the amount of activation to assign to a node: the sum of its source activation plus the sum of the values of all connected activations. A connected activation is the product of the strength of the connection and the activation of the node. According to this definition, each node receives new activation corresponding to a weighted sum of the activations on the connected nodes. A node can receive additional activation from the environment or it can be marked as a source of activation by a rule.

Activation does not keep increasing as it flows over multiple links, but decays according to some rule. A common rule is to multiply the activation by a decay factor as it spreads out over the network and away from its original source. Theoretically, activation spreads to the entire network, but systems like PRISM allow the user either to set a threshold for the amount of activation that can flow over links or to limit the number of links that are crossed. Alternatively, the spreading can stop when any particular node or any particular data element has reached some predetermined threshold.

7.1.4 PROPERTIES OF GOALS

Properties of goals, like properties of facts, can help ensure that the most relevant aspects of a task are examined and processed first. Whether they are stored in data memory or in a separate goal memory, goals have properties that can be updated by the inference engine, by rules, or by both. Let's turn now to some common properties and see how they are updated. (Section 7.3.3 gives some examples of control rules that use these properties.)

An examination of the properties of goals commonly used in expert systems will be helpful:

Subgoals	A list of goals to accomplish in service of the main goal.
Supergoals	A list of supergoals.
Status	Denotes whether the goal is active, achieved, subsumed, failed, abandoned, or postponed.
Method	A description of how the goal is to be achieved; possibly a history of rules that have tried to achieve the goal.
Preconditions	A set of conditions that must be true before the goal will be attempted. These may be subgoals.
Postconditions	A description of what must be true after a goal has been achieved.
Time	The expected time it will take to accomplish the goal, or the cumulative time spent on the goal so far.
Space	Expected memory requirements to accomplish the goal, or the cumulative memory used in accomplishing the goal so far.
Priority	The importance of a goal relative to other goals.
Recency	The relative or absolute time that the goal was created.

Usually the properties of priority and expected time and space are assigned to goals by the rules, while other properties (method, recency, and cumulative time and space) are best assigned by the inference engine. Subgoals, supergoals, preconditions, postconditions, and status can be specified either way. In GRAPES, for example, a rule may insert a goal anywhere in the *and/or* tree, but the system has defaults for what to do if the rule does not completely specify where to insert the goal. Also, an *and* goal's status is changed to "success" by the inference engine when all the goal's subgoals achieve a status of "success," or a rule may state explicitly that a goal has succeeded.

Priority is used in agenda-based applications to specify an order in which the goals are to be attempted. It can be computed by the architecture or rules from expected time and space, recency, past history of success, and availability of methods.

Properties like recency and cumulative time and space are most easily updated by the architecture, since they are dependent on the underlying implementation and usually are best handled with functions and system variables. For instance, the time can be recorded in number of cycles by a simple counter in data memory. Since the recency and cumulative time and space computations are always the same, including them explicitly on the right-hand side of rules just adds clutter.

The *method* property records the set of rules used to achieve the goal. Some systems, like EMYCIN, keep an audit trail of which rules fired in the attempt to achieve a given goal. This can be used for explanation, knowledge acquisition, or learning.

Preconditions are tests that must be true before a goal may be achieved. In OPS5, preconditions are those conditions that appear on the left-hand side of every rule that might be used to achieve a particular goal. If the architecture provides a mechanism to attach preconditions to goals, then the precondition tests do not have to be attached to each rule. In a backward-chaining system like GRAPES, preconditions are represented as subgoals.

Postconditions describe the desired state of data memory after a goal is satisfied. One use for postconditions in a system that has many rules to achieve the same goal is an automatic updating mechanism. If a stereotyped set of changes to data memory can be abstracted from the right-hand sides of rules, they can be moved to the postconditions. Then, after it is noted that the goal preconditions are satisfied, the standard set of changes can be made.

7.2 RULE MEMORY

Rule memory contains all the condition-action rules that the system uses for reasoning. In keeping with the basic philosophy of production systems, most pure rule-based languages have a single rule memory, although some forms of filtering effectively group rules into related sets (see Section 7.3.2).

In OPS5, rule applicability is specified in terms of conditions that can match individual elements in working memory. The conditions are described by attributes of elements and restrictions on the values of the attributes. In this section, we will summarize the types of left-hand-side matching that are generally available in forward-chaining production-system languages and comment on the structure of the left-hand side of backward-chaining rules. We'll also view the types of actions that the right-hand side of a rule can execute and the types of goals that can be represented.

7.2.1 THE LEFT-HAND SIDE

In backward-chaining production systems, the left-hand side of a rule usually is fairly simple. In EMYCIN, all the conditions have to be expressions that can be established as subgoals if they are not already satisfied in data memory. This means that there can be no complex pattern matching on the left-hand side. The EMYCIN system does allow more than an exact match, however; its dynamic context tree enables rules to apply through different instantiations of the objects mentioned in the rules. The left-hand side may be the site of input and output in EMYCIN. If no rules apply to finding the values of the attributes mentioned on the right-hand side of a rule, or if those attributes are specially tagged, then the user is asked to specify the value and certainty.

Although GRAPES has a backward-chaining architecture in terms of which rules are considered (this decision is based on what actions they will cause), its rules are actually applied in the forward direction. After the initial filtering, all the pattern matching and right-hand-side actions of forward-chaining architectures are permitted.

Forward-chaining systems allow more variety in what can appear on the left-hand side of a rule. As you explore the production-system language features that allow the user to specify which data memory elements should be matched, be aware that while they give the programmer more freedom, they also complicate the implementation of the pattern matcher. For example, if arbitrary functions with side effects are allowed as conditions, these functions must be recomputed on each recognize-act cycle; thus a Rete network implementation is not sufficient, and the time for the match computation is increased. Functions without side-effects can be built into a Rete network.

The features we'll describe here include the general mechanisms for imposing tests on the content of data memory, techniques for limiting the range of values that attributes of data elements may have, the use of variables in describing patterns, and means of specifying relationships that must hold among the data elements that match the conditions. We'll provide a verbal (English) description of each feature, note its availability in OPS5 and other production-system languages, give an example of its use, and offer some hints about how to simulate that feature in those languages where it is absent.

Types of Tests

The left-hand side of a rule is a conjunction of conditions; usually these conditions are descriptions of data memory elements and possibly goal memory elements. The left-hand side checks for the presence or absence of data memory elements and may specify certain tests that elements must satisfy. Tests can be on single elements or sets of elements. A number of methods can be used to test against the contents of data memory: positive tests, negative tests, condition function calls, disjunctions, and partial tests.

Positive Tests

Description — The standard test of a single condition element against data memory. Must be true for the rule match to succeed.

Availability — The default type in all languages.

Example — Is there an element representing a plastic chemical in data memory?
In OPS5:

```
(p find-plastic
   (chemical ↑type plastic)
    ...)
```

Simulation — Unnecessary.

Negative Tests

Description — A test for the absence of an element. If an element satisfying the test is present, then the rule match fails.

Availability — OPS5 and GRAPES: A test preceded by a −; PRISM: <not>; YAPS: ~

Example — Are there no values smaller than <x> in data memory?
YAPS allows tests associated with negated condition elements:

```
(p  smallest
   (-item has-value -x)
(~ (-item2 has-value -y) with (< -y -x))
   -->
   (smallest -item))
```

Variables in YAPS are preceded by − signs. Thus, (−item has-value −y) is a negated condition with two variables.
Variables in PRISM are preceded by = signs. PRISM allows a conjunction of negated conditions that will achieve the same effect as the *with* statement in YAPS:

```
smallest:
  ((=item has-value =x)
   (<not> (=item2 has-value =y)
          (greater-than =y =x))
-->
   (<add> (smallest =item)))
```

where (greater-than =y =x) is an element in data memory.

Simulation — Most languages have negative tests, so simulation is unnecessary.

Condition Function Calls

Description — A call to a function that serves as a condition element and returns success or failure based on its inputs. If it does not return success, the rule match fails.

Availability — YAPS, GRAPES, PRISM

Example — A pair of points in two dimensions is matched in a data memory. We use a function call to test whether both the *x* and *y* coordinates are within a given distance from each other. In YAPS, function calls go in the *test* section of the left-hand side:

```
(p in-close-proximity
   (point -x -y)
   (point -a -b)
test (< (- -x -a) 5)
     (< (- -y -b) 5)
-->
   (fact close (-x -y) (-a -b)))
```

In GRAPES, there is no special place for function calls. Functions are identifiers preceded by a *:

```
(p in-close-proximity
   (point =x =y)
   (point =a =b)
   (*lessp (*difference =x =a) 5)
   (*lessp (*difference =y =b) 5)
-->
   (close (=x =y) (=a =b)))
```

Simulation — Some languages do not allow function calls because of potential side effects as well as decreased portability and understandability. OPS5 allows controlled access to the implementation language through user-defined functions available only on the right-hand side. To perform a test with a user-defined function in a language like OPS5, the user must write a right-hand-side function to compute the result and add it to data memory. An additional rule can then look for that datum in one of its conditions.

Disjunctions

Description	Specifying a set of elements, only one of which need be in data memory. It is also possible to specify disjunctions of negated elements and non-negated elements. If none of the condition elements are matched, the whole rule match fails.
Availability	No availability in languages that we are using as examples.
Example	Is there a super computer that is inexpensive or a personal computer that is moderately expensive in data memory?
Simulation	Write one rule for each element in the condition (see Attributes).

Partial Tests

Description	A minimum number of condition elements (the partial-match threshold) that must be satisfied is specified. If fewer than that number of condition elements match, the rule match fails.
Availability	No availability in example languages.
Example	For a person to be charged with drunk driving, three conditions must hold. Any two of these conditions constitute sufficient grounds to charge the person with impaired abilities. The rule that tests for impaired abilities is a partial matching rule.
Simulation	Write one rule for each subset of condition elements that is sufficient to make the partial matching fire. However, this generally requires an excessive number of rules.

Attributes

Languages often provide ways of placing conditions on the range of values of an attribute. Some techniques used to specify the conditions include relational operators, disjunctions, conjunctions, attribute function calls, negative matching against values, matching components of lists, and partial attribute matching.

Relational Operators

Description — Prespecified functions that test equality or inequality and make numeric comparisons; they return true or false.

Availability — OPS5: <,>, <=, >=, =, <>, <=>;
YAPS, PRISM, and GRAPES have arbitrary left-hand-side function calls that can implement any relational operator.

Example — Is the oil well's depth greater than 2000 feet?

Simulation — Calls to external functions on the left-hand side or right-hand side often can perform the same function as a numeric or comparison predicate.

Disjunctions

Description — An attribute may match any one of a set of values.

Availability — OPS5: << >>

Example — Is the company's name IBM or Apple?

Simulation — Languages such as GRAPES and YAPS allow disjunctions by the use of function calls. In GRAPES, for instance, the following two condition elements implement a disjunction:

```
(company name =name)
(*or (*equal =name IBM) (*equal =name Apple))
```

Conjunctions

Description — Specifying a set of relations about the same value, all of which must match.

Availability — OPS5: { }; PRISM: &

Example — Is the oil well's depth greater than 2000 feet and less than 4000 feet?

Simulation — In languages that do not have conjunctions, information usually can be repeated on the left-hand side in order to put multiple conditions on a single value (e.g., ↑depth > 2000 ↑depth < 4000).

Attribute Function Calls

Description — Arbitrary function calls on the left-hand side, used to test values of attributes.

Availability — GRAPES: *function; PRISM: <function>

Example — Is the air temperature equal to X, some function of the wind-speed and the ground temperature? In PRISM new left-hand-side functions must be declared with the function *predicate*. This declaration must appear before any rules that use this function.

```
(defun <new-air-speed> (windspeed groundtemp)
   (plus (times windspeed windspeed)
         groundtemp))

(predicate <new-air-speed>)
(system
  confirm-plane-airspeed
  ((atmosphere windspeed =wspeed)
   (atmosphere ground-temperature =gtemp)
   (plane speed =plane
       (<new-air-speed> =wspeed =gtemp))
   (plane status unconfirmed) & =p
   -->
   (<delete> =p)
   (plane status confirmed)))
```

GRAPES does not check whether or not the functions used in productions have been defined previously, so this example would look similar except that the declaration would not be present and the definition for the GRAPES predicate (*new-air-speed) could come after the production definition.

Simulation — These can be simulated in OPS5 using two rules. The first rule performs the function computation on the right-hand side and saves the result. The second rule matches against the saved result. In YAPS, function calls can be evaluated in conjunction with a condition element using the *with* construction.

Negative Matching Against Values

Description — Excluding some value for an attribute that is present.

Availability — Not primitive in most languages. The # variable in PRISM can be used to specify that an attribute cannot have some value, but the value must be bound to a variable. These allow tests of the form `(=x bought #x)`. This pattern would match `(Merrill-Lynch bought Coile)` but never `(Merrill-Lynch bought Merrill-Lynch)`. In OPS5 we need to specify that the attribute has a non-nil value and that the value is equal to some constant.

Example   What disease is caused by an ant bite and does not produce swelling of the skin?

Simulation   This can be implemented in OPS5 by

```
(disease ↑cause ant-bite
        ↑skin { <> nil <> swelling })
```

Matching Components of Lists

Description   For an attribute that is a list, specifying some component values that must be in the list.

Availability   GRAPES

Example   Is General Motors before AMC in the list of top-ranked car manufacturers? In GRAPES this match can be done with the following condition:

```
(manufacturers cars
        ($top (General Motors)
        $middle (AMC) $bottom))
```

This condition involves multiple segment variables, which will be described in a later section.

Simulation   In languages with function calls, this can be simulated with a function that performs two searches. One search finds (General Motors) and one ensures that (AMC) is after (General Motors) in the list. OPS5 seriously limits the types of tests that can be done on vector attributes. Doing a membership test, for instance, involves iterating over the vector attribute being searched or writing a user-defined function.

Partial Attribute Matching

Description   There is some predetermined threshold for the number of attributes within an element that must match. Right-hand-side actions that use variables that did not match will not take effect.

Availability   PRISM has activation values that will allow partial matching.

Example   Suppose `(restaurant ↑waiter Italian ↑food Italian ↑table-cloths checkered)` is a prototypical Italian restaurant description. A rule will fire based on a *restaurant* that has at least two of the prototype's features.

Simulation   Partial matching can be achieved by multiple rules that fire on a subset of the features of a data memory element, but this is extremely inefficient. The usual solution to this problem is to represent the prototype in working memory and then compare the instance and prototype with a set of production rules. These rules compare the values of the attributes in the prototype to the values of the same attributes in the instance.

Pattern Matching with Variables

An additional dimension of variation among production-system architectures is the range of pattern-matching facilities available. In this section, we compare the types of variables available and the ways of combining and using those variables in various production-system languages. Usually a particular pattern-matching ability that is missing from a given language can be simulated by using function calls or by changing the representation of elements in data memory.

There are two common variable categories: regular variables and segment variables.

Regular Variables

Description — Matches a single value. The value is usually either a scalar or a list (in languages that support lists).

Availability — OPS5: <symbol>; GRAPES, PRISM: =symbol; YAPS: – symbol

Example — In OPS5 (computer ↑type <comptype>)

Simulation — Available in all languages that have variables. Must write many explicit rules if no variables are available.

Segment Variables

Description — Matches a sequence of items within a data element.

Availability — GRAPES: $symbol; PRISM: !symbol.
In GRAPES, null matches are also allowed; for example, (shop contains $items) can match (shop contains).

Example — In PRISM a data memory element might be:

```
(country is USA with computer-companies
    IBM DEC Univac Three-Rivers)
```

where the computer manufacturers were rated in order of decreasing sales. A condition element with multiple segment variables could match all the companies except the last with the following pattern:

```
(country is =name
    with computer-manufacturers !big
    =last)
```

In this case, =name would bind to USA, =last would bind to Three-Rivers, and !big would bind to all the elements: IBM, DEC, and Univac.

Simulation — The kind of processing performed by segment variables can sometimes be accomplished by the OPS5 **substr** command. Sometimes only a fixed-length prefix must be matched, in which case OPS5 regular variables may be used.

When a variable on the left-hand side of a rule matches an element in data memory, the system usually stores the variable and the value that it matches as a binding. Bindings are generally stored as a list of associations between variables and values.

Most production-system languages do not have typed variables. Nevertheless, typed variables can prevent errors by catching them at compile time. We describe these features of variables here.

Binding

Description	When the variable is matched, the matching process *binds* the variable to the value so that the variable may be used more than once on the left-hand side (for consistent binding, as will be discussed) or the right-hand side (for output or adding to data memory by combining variables bound on the left-hand side).
Availability	OPS5, PRISM, GRAPES, YAPS
Example	See examples throughout this book.
Simulation	Variable binding cannot be simulated unless the language has a pattern-matching facility.

Types

Description	Typing variables provides an additional feature to restrict the values that a variable may assume. The types available may be tied to the language in which the production system was written (e.g., structures and arrays) or the machine architecture (e.g., 32-bit single precision floating-point numbers). The language may also allow *abstract data types* that are defined by the programmer to be tailored to the application.
Availability	OPS83 [Forgy 84]
Example	*Dependent on language:* The *height* attribute has a

variable of type *real* so its value must be of type *real*. *Abstract data type:* IBM-PC is of type *personal* and therefore only matches a variable of type *personal*.

Simulation — The best way to handle this is probably to have the rules enforce the type checking. Alternatively, each attribute can be followed by an additional attribute that states the type of element that can match that variable. Thus `(computer ↑name IBM-PC ↑nametype personal)` would be the data memory element corresponding to a typed variable for ↑name.

Although OPS5 allows little freedom in combining variables and constants to make a pattern, other languages provide a wide variety of pattern-matching abilities, including multiple regular variables, multiple segment variables, and nested patterns.

Multiple Regular Variables

Description — A sequence of regular variables to specify the value of a single attribute.

Availability — OPS5 (vector-attributes only), GRAPES, YAPS

Example — If *companies* is a vector attribute, the match `(country ↑companies <company1> <company2>)` will match <company1> against the first element of the vector attribute and <company2> against the second element.

Simulation — If the production system does not have multiple regular variables, a rule can be written that matches against the first element of the vector and replaces the rest for subsequent checking.

Multiple Segment Variables

Description — Having more than one segment variable to specify the value of a single attribute.

Availability — GRAPES

Example — If we want to determine whether Commodore is in the Fortune 500 this year, we can use GRAPES segment variables (prefaced with $):

```
(descriptor
    of: companies
    publisher: Fortune
    range: (1 500)
    measure: net
    companies:
     ($companies1 Commodore $companies2))
```

In this case the multiple segment variables are used to perform a membership test. Multiple segment variables can also be used to iterate over a set of elements or to select an element with certain properties. For instance, if we wanted to find a company that had assets greater than a billion dollars, we could use the following GRAPES patterns:

```
(descriptor
    of: companies
    publisher: Fortune
    range: (1 500)
    measure: net
    companies:
     ($companies1 =company $companies2))
(descriptor
    of: company
    name: =company
    assets: =assets)
(*greaterp =assets 1000000000)
```

The first condition element would match 500 different companies and then the last condition element would select the company or companies with assets greater than one billion dollars.

Simulation — The fundamental difference between systems with multiple segment variables and systems with single segment variables is that set operations cannot be performed in the latter, since at most a single binding is allowed. The key to simulating multiple segment variables in a language that does not have them is to use right-hand-side functions to extract the needed elements and put them into a separate list for further processing.

Nested Patterns

Description — In languages with lists or some other recursive data structure, nested patterns will match patterns within patterns. In the list representation this means specifying a list structure that contains another list structure that holds variables, constants, and possibly additional lists.

Availability — PRISM, GRAPES, YAPS

Example

For each country we could have an ordered list of large cities also grouped by state:

```
(cities-list USA
    (California
        (LosAngeles SanFrancisco SanJose))
    (Pennsylvania
        (Philadelphia Pittsburgh Harrisburg))
    (Massachusetts (Boston)))
```

In PRISM the first city in the first state could be extracted by

```
(cities-list =country
    (=firststate (=firstcity) !restcities)
    !reststates)
```

Simulation

In languages such as OPS5 that do not have recursive data structures, nested patterns can be represented with explicit pointers:

```
(literalize cities-list
    country    ; The name of the country
    states)    ; A vector of state pointers
(vector-attribute states)
(literalize state-cities
    name       ; The name of the state
    cities)    ; The cities in this state
(vector-attribute cities)
(make cities-list ↑country USA
     ↑states California Pennsylvania
         Massachusetts)
(make state-cities ↑name California
     ↑cities LosAngeles SanFrancisco
         SanJose)
(make state-cities ↑name Pennsylvania
     ↑cities Philadelphia Pittsburgh
         Harrisburg)
(make state-cities ↑name Massachusetts
                   ↑cities Boston)
```

7.2.2 THE RIGHT-HAND SIDE

In a backward-chaining system such as EMYCIN, the right-hand side typically specifies a conclusion to be drawn or possibly adds some data to a local memory. In a forward-chaining system the right-hand side of a rule consists of a (usually ordered) set of actions to perform. These actions include changes to data memories, input and output of information to and from the external environment, and (possibly) changes to rule memory. In this section, we will examine the types of actions available in various production-system languages.

Range and Form of Actions

Although the syntax for right-hand-side actions varies, most systems use function calls to the implementation language. In GRAPES, PRISM, and YAPS these are arbitrary LISP functions; in OPS5 a predefined set of functions and actions are provided, and user-defined functions must follow specific guidelines. The production systems' implementations vary in the amount of error checking they perform. OPS5 checks that all functions called on the right-hand side have been declared by **external.** GRAPES checks the goals added on the right-hand side against the goals matched on the left-hand side to see if they are consistent. Other languages, such as ROSIE and EMYCIN, check the entire set of rules for consistency. OPS5 checks the rules to ensure that all variables used on the right-hand side are bound before they are used. In contrast, PRISM and GRAPES automatically create ***tokens*** — unique atoms that can be used as labels — for variables that are not bound on the left-hand side.

Changes to Data Memory

Data memory can be changed by adding, deleting, or modifying a data memory element. In some languages only addition and deletion are primitive operations, since they can be used to implement modification.

Additions. As described in Section 2.2.3, the OPS5 **make** action adds a new element to working memory. In some languages, such as PRISM and GRAPES, the addition is an implicit action. For instance, in PRISM the action

```
-->
    (acid is h2so4)
```

would add (acid is h2so4) to data memory.

Deletions. Elements to be deleted from data memory are identified by the left-hand-side condition they match. In PRISM elements are removed by calling the function <delete>:

```
get-food
    ((want =food)
     (<not> (have =food))
-->
     (<add> (have =food))
     (<delete> (want =food)))
```

PRISM and OPS5 both allow reference by token. In PRISM removal by token is expressed as follows:

```
get-food
   ((want =food) & =want
    (<not> (have =food))
-->
    (<add> (have =food))
    (<delete> =want))
```

where =want corresponds to an OPS5 element variable. OPS5, GRAPES, and YAPS allow the user to remove items by number. In GRAPES the previous rule would read:

```
(p get-food
   action: eat
   tests:
      (want =food)
    - (have =food)
-->
   (have =food)
   (*remove 1)
   (*pop success))
```

Removal by number has the disadvantage that reordering left-hand-side items causes different items to be removed unless the numbers on the right-hand side are updated.

Modifications. OPS5 implements the **modify** action as a deletion of an element from working memory and a subsequent addition of a new copy of the old element incorporating the necessary changes. This equivalence is one reason why some languages (PRISM and GRAPES, for example) do not support a modify command. In addition, languages such as PRISM and GRAPES that use list structures for data memory elements (see Section 7.1.1) cannot explicitly reference component values of data elements. In contrast, OPS5's attribute-value representation provides an easy way to address memory locations within elements. Thus, the OPS5 **modify** command allows the user to selectively modify attributes of data elements by changing a value of a particular attribute within an element but leaving the remainder unchanged.

Input and Output

Most production systems provide very few functions for file input and output. As with procedural languages, input and output is often dependent on the particular operating system environment or the system implementation language. Some production-system languages that are written in LISP, such as YAPS and GRAPES, allow the user access to all internal LISP functions, including those for input and output. In contrast, the OPS5 syntax for input and output is independent of the particular implementation language.

Changes to Rule Memory

Rules in OPS5 can be prevented from firing with the **excise** action. OPS5 also provides a single action, **build,** for adding new rules during execution. Not all implementations of OPS5 include this action. One problem with building rules in OPS5 is that the newly created rules do not notice elements that are already in working memory. See Section 5.2.9 for a description of the OPS5 **build** action.

Other production-system languages provide commands that modify or remove rules, although these commands are seldom available as right-hand-side actions. Modifying a rule necessitates dynamically recompiling the rule and updating its matches as a result of the changes. YAPS provides the *remp* command for removing rules, but it can be invoked only at the top level of YAPS. EMYCIN provides a rule editor that makes rule modification easy. Dynamic modification of rules is usually confined to learning systems (see Section 8.3) and knowledge acquisition systems (see Section 8.1).

Calling Conventions for User-Defined Functions

In most languages the user-defined functions are simply implementation-language functions that are called with the arguments provided by the rule. There are two common implementation strategies for calling right-hand-side functions; these strategies differ in their placement of responsibility for passing and returning values.

In the first strategy the production-system language assumes all responsibility for creating the function calls with the correct implementation-language syntax. It replaces the variables by their values before the right-hand-side functions are called. Consider the following rule in GRAPES, for instance:

```
(p add-name
   action: list
   item: =item
   tests: (list contains ($elements))
-->
   (*pretty-print (new list contains:) (=item $elements))
   (*pop success))
```

It could match data memory element

```
(list contains (disk cardreader floppy))
```

and goal

```
(goal
  (action: list
   item: CPU))
```

The system would construct a call to the user-defined function "pretty-print" (written in LISP) as follows:

```
(pretty-print '(new list contains:)
    '(CPU disk cardreader floppy))
```

The programmer can be assured that the proper values will be transferred.

The second implementation strategy gives the user the responsibility of constructing user-defined functions so that they correctly retrieve the bindings of variables in rules. In OPS5, for instance, **$litbind** can be used to get the location of an element within a vector attribute and **$parameter** can be called with that location to produce a value. See Section 5.2.8 for a description of how to construct user-defined functions in OPS5.

7.3 CONTROL STRATEGIES

The control strategies in a production-system language dictate which rules should participate in matching and which instantiation should be chosen if more than one exists. Control mechanisms range from nearly complete control of rule firings to arbitrary selection. Our discussion of control starts with simple control mechanisms and works toward more complicated forms of control. ***Conflict resolution*** dictates which rule or instantiation to use if many are applicable. ***Filtering*** decides which rules and data to try to match in the first place. ***Metarules*** provide a more complex way of specifying control.

Some systems have built-in control strategies that separate control knowledge from the domain knowledge expressed in the rules (for example, EMYCIN) so that the user can concentrate on the knowledge rather than on how the knowledge is accessed and used. Among the advantages for constructing or using a system with built-in control strategies and memory properties are (1) the processing is usually faster than can be done through explicit control in the rules; (2) all data elements or goals are treated uniformly by the production system; (3) programming time is not wasted writing repetitive control constructs; and (4) some coding errors can be prevented. However, as with any built-in feature, there are disadvantages: The control mechanisms or properties provided may be ill-suited to the task; exceptions to the predominant mechanism are generally not allowed; often the information processed by the system becomes inaccessible to the user just when the person needs to examine or understand it; and the system may be inefficient, since the production system can (and often does) process information that is superfluous to the execution of the task.

Following the philosophy that flexibility is best, systems like OPS5 and ROSIE provide very few built-in control strategies. In OPS5 the control strategies are programmed as part of the rule set, whereas in ROSIE the user writes the program that controls the access to sets of rules. In OPS5 many rules serve only a control function, and many rules that do incorporate domain knowledge contain condition elements that serve only a control function. In addition, working memory elements that hold data may also hold control switches.

7.3.1 CONFLICT RESOLUTION

A ***conflict-resolution strategy*** is a coordinated set of principles for selecting among competing instantiations. A single principle does not always determine a unique instantiation to fire or provide the right decision criteria for all situations. OPS5's MEA and LEX conflict-resolution strategies are composed from a combination of the principles described in this section.

An expert system's performance depends on the conflict-resolution strategy for both ***sensitivity*** and ***stability*** [McDermott, Forgy 78]. Sensitivity is the system's quickness of response to the dynamically changing demands of its environment, while stability is the system's continuity of behavior. Sensitivity and stability are often contradictory aims, but a system should have both features if it is to perform well in a noisy and changing environment. In this section, we describe refraction, data ordering, specificity ordering and rule ordering as components of a conflict-resolution strategy and consider how they influence the sensitivity and stability of an application system. We describe parallelism and arbitrary choice as possible final decision steps. While these principles are not all incorporated in the production systems we discuss, they are possibilities that have been explored and experimentally compared [McDermott, Forgy 78].

Refraction

The conflict-resolution principle of refraction requires that rules fire not more than once on the same data. This is intended to prevent a trivial form of infinite looping that could occur if a rule did not change the contents of working memory. Without refraction, control flags could be used to prevent such trivial loops, but this solution is so tedious that refraction is universally accepted as a useful component of conflict resolution.

Two rule instantiations are said to be identical if the data memory elements matched by the condition elements are exactly the same for each condition. The elements must be exactly the same, not just look the same; in LISP this is the distinction between *eq* and *equal*. For example, there can be two instances of `(computer ↑type VAX ↑model 780)` created at separate times in a database, and any rule that matches this pattern will have two different instantiations. In OPS5, as in many languages, modifying any part of a data item, even if it is modified to the same value (or if a part not looked at in a match is modified), updates the recency of that item and therefore produces a different item. Sometimes this is desirable, and sometimes this produces the unwanted looping that refraction is intended to prevent.

One way to implement refraction is to store a list of all rule instantiations that have fired and prevent instantiations on this list from entering the conflict set again. OPS5 uses this technique. An alternative technique, used in OPS83, is to store instantiations that have fired only as long as the instantiations remain in the conflict set and to use the stored list to filter instantiations during conflict resolution. Systems often have a function, *refresh*, that produces a new copy of a data memory element (in OPS5, a **modify** of an attribute to its current value achieves the same effect) so that refraction can be subverted if necessary. There are other good reasons for having a refreshing mechanism, such as purposeful loops that make selected items more recent in order to divert attention to them if the recency principle is also in effect.

Another possibility for approximating refraction is to forbid the firing of identical instantiations on *consecutive* cycles. This weaker principle (which also requires less storage to implement) is designed specifically to avoid single-rule loops, which are the most common kind. Another approximation is to save the last *N* instantiations of each rule.

Data Ordering

A powerful way of adding sensitivity to a conflict-resolution strategy is to include a principle that orders the data by recency or activation. A recency or activation ordering gives preferences to rules that match elements most recently added to data memory or that are strongly related to recently added data. Thus any sudden changes in the environment will be noticed immediately.

Recency of data elements can be measured by the number of recognize-act cycles elapsed, by the number of **make** or **remove** actions performed (in OPS5), or by the position of an object or goal in a tree (EMYCIN and GRAPES, respectively). A rule can be selected on the basis of recency in several ways. It can be chosen because it contains a match to the most recent data element or because it matches data elements that sum to a number greater than the sum for any other rule. Alternatively, when element recencies are compared condition by condition, the rule highest on the list may be picked, as in OPS5's LEX and MEA strategies.

The activation of an object or proposition is usually a real number associated with the element that is a measure of its current relevance or importance (see Specificity Ordering, which follows). To provide a measure of recency, systems such as PRISM that use activation values for data elements can use a sum of activations of all data elements that match the conditions in a rule.

None of these principles is guaranteed to produce a unique dominating instantiation. Therefore a data-ordering principle is usually combined with other principles to narrow down the choice of an instantiation to fire next.

Specificity Ordering

Specificity favors rules that are special cases of other rules or are more specific according to some measure. Specificity can be measured in a variety of ways.

One specificity principle depends on a specificity function that is correlated with the degree of complexity of the condition side of the rule. The principle is to prefer those rules that are maximally complex. This is the approach taken in GRAPES and OPS5. In GRAPES constants are weighted most specific, regular variables are less specific, and segment variables are least specific. Each condition element has an associated specificity number, and specificities of rules are computed by adding the specificities of the condition elements. In OPS5 the measure is a simple count of the number of attribute tests that must be made in finding an instantiation. Such specificities are based purely on the rule and not on the data; thus they do not contribute to the sensitivity of the conflict-resolution strategy.

Another specificity principle is to delete from the conflict set instantiations of those rules whose condition sides are proper subsets of the condition sides of other instantiated rules. The rules deleted need not contain any more condition elements than the more specific rules, but they may have variables in place of the constants appearing in the more specific rules. Ordering by specificity of the rules rather than instantiations is not very sensitive, since it depends only on the rules and not on the data. Its advantage is that it is relatively easy to compute. (See also the similar principles of rule ordering, which we'll discuss next.)

Element specificity, a more sensitive principle, compares the sets of data memory elements that match the conditions of all rule instantiations in the conflict set. If one instantiation's set of data memory elements is a proper subset of the data elements matched by another rule, then the first instantiation is ruled out. In OPS5 this is the principle of recency specificity that is incorporated into the recency tests. This kind of specificity cannot be precomputed, since it depends on the data memory elements that match. It frequently results in only a small reduction of the number of instantiations in the conflict set. For a more discriminating specificity strategy, element specificity often is combined with some form of specificity based on rules.

Rule Ordering

Rule ordering strategies provide a static ordering of the rule set independent of the way the rule is instantiated by data. The ordering may be specified by the user or may be computed using some feature of the rules. Systems using static ordering principles tend to be less sensitive, since priorities are independent of the instantiations of the rules, and are more stable.

Either a total or a partial ordering can be given by a relation on rules. If a total rule ordering is given, the rules can be stored in the desired order and scanned linearly until one is found that matches. Programmers often use this technique to write a simple rule-based system in an arbitrary language if that is all that is needed, or if a production-system language is not available. If only some relationships between rules are given, the rules in the conflict set must be inspected pairwise to determine whether or not any can be eliminated.

An ordering can also be a relation that indicates that one set of rules has priority over another set. Rules within a set all have the same priority. If only one rule firing per cycle is desired in such a rule set, additional conflict-resolution principles are needed. The learning mechanisms in GRAPES use classes of rule strengths.

One way to implement the static ordering is to assign numerical strengths to rules. These strengths can be used to select the set of rules with the highest rank.

Arbitrary Choice and Parallel Selection

None of the principles described guarantees that only a single instantiation will remain in the conflict set. If a single firing is desired on each cycle, an arbitrary decision can be made among rule instantiations that remain after all other conflict-resolution principles have been applied. This technique is used in OPS5, for example. The instantiations remaining in the conflict set should be strategically equivalent, and it will not matter which rule fires. It should be noted that firing one rule may prevent other instantiations from firing on subsequent cycles even if some of the removed instantiations have relevant information to add to memory.

An alternative to arbitrary selection is the firing of all the instantiations in one cycle, as is done in XAPS [Rosenbloom 79] and CAPS [Thibadeau 82]; this is called ***parallelism*** in firing. Production systems theoretically lend themselves well to parallel applications because of their modularity and non-interaction. Parallel operations can be done very quickly on special-purpose hardware, and if tree-structured and graph-structured parallel processors are developed, parallelism in firing may become more popular.

A major problem with parallel production systems is that rules firing in parallel may add conflicting information. One rule in the parallel set may add a proposition directly refuting a proposition added by another rule in the set. One rule in the parallel set may also remove some data that matches another rule's tests. Similarly, an added element may match a negative test in some other rule in the parallel set. Thus a group of rules that would not fire serially could fire in parallel if their conditions were met simultaneously. Some systems look for conflicts among added information and others (e.g., CAPS) leave it up to the user to make sure that rules that could fire in parallel never contain conflicting information.

7.3.2 FILTERING

Filtering is a technique for selecting which rules and data participate in matching. ***Rule filtering*** reduces the number of rules that may be matched and ***data filtering*** reduces the number of data elements that may be matched. The filters described in this section can be built into a production-system architecture, yet the power and range of their application is up to the user.

Rule Filtering

While some production systems, such as OPS5, match data memory against the entire set of rules on each recognize-act cycle, this is not always necessary or desirable. Rule filtering is a form of control that helps identify a subset of the rules to match. Rule filtering precedes matching and conflict resolution in the recognize-act cycle.

We will consider three methods of rule filtering: *Controlled production systems* filter rules by referring to a program provided by the user. *Goal-restricted systems* filter rules according to a currently active goal; only rules instrumental to achieving that goal can be matched to data memory. Some systems use *context restriction* and select rules based on information in data memory. Rules applicable in a current context[3] can be stored with that context. When a new context is entered, the rule set is automatically updated to be matched against elements in only that context.

In controlled production systems [Georgeff 82], the user writes a program that specifies which subset of the rules to try in the following cycle. The program is equivalent to a finite-state automaton, with states representing sets of rules to try and arcs representing recognize-act cycles. Controlled production systems offer a mixture of conventional programming and the parallel matching found in normal rule systems. If no rules within the set specified by the control program apply on a given cycle, the system goes into an error state. If the production system reaches a halt state in the control program, or if a particular rule has a halt symbol on its action side, then the system stops without declaring an error.

[3] In this section, the term *context* refers to a group of data memory elements that are organized according to some principle such as a period of time, hypothetical world, or a branch of a consultation tree.

Goal-restricted filtering offers an alternative technique for adding control to a production system. In goal filtering, rules are organized into subsystems by the type of goal that they help to solve. This functional decomposition of the production system makes matching faster, since a good deal of the applicability information is precoded in terms of the goals that various rules reference. The use of goals as an architectural principle is similar to the use of goals as a programming paradigm. The difference is that operations such as subgoaling, goal pursuit, and goal abandonment are built into the architecture. Production systems that have a goal-restricted architecture (e.g., GRAPES) match the rules' goal statements against the current goal before performing any data memory tests. This same effect can be achieved in the OPS5 architecture by always putting the goal test in the first condition element and using the MEA conflict-resolution strategy to pick applicable rules. Because of the Rete match algorithm, OPS5's goal processing is no slower than it would be if the goal matching were built into the system.

Contexts based on data memory also can be used to filter the set of rules. Contexts can group rules into subsystems by their similarity, time of proper application, or some other feature such as location in a consultation tree. In EMYCIN, for example, rules that apply to a type of consultation context are precomputed. Another application for contexts is in systems that store large amounts of knowledge that may be inconsistent. However, since items are added to a single context at a time, the information can be hidden from other contexts. Reasoning is performed within contexts, but control elements can move the system's attention to other contexts. For instance, contexts can be nested so that if no rules in a subcontext are applicable, then rules in the surrounding context will be considered next.

As described in Section 5.2.3, contexts can be implemented in a production-system language without a built-in context mechanism by creating a special data memory element (called a *context element*) that is added when a context is entered and removed when the context is exited. All the rules in a context must then test the context element in their first condition, and a strategy such as MEA that favors recency in the first condition element must be used. If such a strategy is not available, it can be simulated by adding a level number to each context and testing for the greatest level number with a negated condition element. A programmed context mechanism loses much of the efficiency of a built-in context mechanism, because elements added while the system is processing one context must still be matched to all the rules.

Data Filtering

Data filtering reduces the number of data elements that are matched against the rule set by considering only those elements above a given activation threshold or certainty. Any elements that fall below the threshold are not matched. In some systems, such as PRISM, the below-threshold elements are deleted from (or never added to) data memory. PRISM has a limit parameter that determines this threshold. Other systems allow elements to stay in data memory forever, since activation or certainty can increase independently of rule firings and there is always a chance that an inactive or uncertain element can become active again or more certain over time.

Activation filtering identifies a subset of the data memory elements that are relevant or interesting and passes that subset on to the matching algorithm. In PRISM, for example, the user specifies an activation threshold and items below that threshold are simply not matched. If spreading activation is used, the elements may subsequently gain activation and again be used in the matching process.

Certainty filtering identifies a subset of believable or reliable data memory elements and passes that subset on to the matching algorithm. The user specifies a minimum certainty and items that are less certain are not matched. As in activation filtering, if rules control the certainty computation, elements can never again become reliable once they fall below the threshold; they will not be accessible to the matching algorithm.

7.3.3 METALEVEL CONTROL

A more explicit way to specify control is to write rules about the control strategy. These rules, which determine how to apply other rules, are called ***metarules*** [Davis 80]. Metarules can be written in the same language as the rules themselves [Stefik, Bell, Bobrow 82; Genesereth, Greiner, Smith 81], or they can be written in a separate control language; for instance, S.1 represents control information in a block-structured language.

Metarules are needed when no small, fixed set of control principles can effectively determine which of the applicable rules should be applied. Recency, specificity, and refraction can all be coded quite easily as metarules. The recency strategy, for instance, assumes that more recent information will produce more reliable results. A metarule might state that if two rules seem equally good on other grounds, then the rule that matches the most recent elements should be selected.

Section 7.1.4 listed a number of properties of goals that can be used by metarules. Now we illustrate some possible control rules that use those goal properties.

The first example metarule might be used in a robot planning system when the robot has found a method of moving through a particular kind of rough terrain and now finds itself in a similar terrain.

Learn-from-success

```
IF   there was a previous goal
       that has roughly the same aim as the current goal
 and the method for that goal was <m1>
 and the goal was achieved
THEN try method <m1> for the current goal
```

The next example metarule might be used by the same robot planning system to rule out a particular method of crossing rough terrain if the previous method caused the robot to fall or retreat from the area.

Learn-from-failure

```
IF   there was a previous goal
       that has roughly the same aim as the current goal
 and the method for that goal was <m1>
 and the goal failed
THEN rule out method <m1> for the current goal
```

See Section 8.3 on machine learning for a more general discussion of methods that allow a system to improve its performance over time.

The following metarule might be used in a satellite expert system that must run in a specified amount of computer storage space. It might cause the expert system to switch goals from measuring atmospheric conditions to measuring radiation readings because atmospheric conditions generate more data.

Not-enough-space

```
IF   the expected space to accomplish a goal
       is larger than the space left
THEN try to accomplish another goal that takes less space
```

Another metarule might be used in the same satellite expert system in an emergency situation. If the satellite were about to reenter the atmosphere, it would want to switch goals to something that it could finish before it began to burn up.

Not-enough-time

```
IF   the expected time to accomplish a goal
       is larger than the time left
THEN try to accomplish another goal
       that can be finished faster
```

The next metarule might be used to cause any system to create subgoals. Suppose a computer configurer had a high-priority goal to calculate the amount of memory needed for the system. This goal might cause the system to ask the user some questions or to gather relevant facts about the memory size needed.

Do-preconditions

```
IF   a goal has a high priority
 and some of its preconditions are not satisfied
THEN try to satisfy its preconditions
```

The next example metarule is similar to the recency focus in the control strategy that OPS5 uses when the conflict resolution is type MEA (see Section 2.4.2). The recency principle favors more recent elements and the goal is usually the first condition element in the rule. Keeping the focus is important in diagnosis tasks where a user must be asked questions and in tasks where information is being stored in a short-term, fast memory (a cache).

Keep-focus

```
IF   a goal is the one most recently created
THEN try to accomplish that goal
```

There are several additional situations in which metarules may be used in expert system tasks: In a diagnosis system, if several tests are needed to continue the diagnosis, prefer tests with the least risk of injury to the patient. In a business advisor, choose rules that result in the least money being spent. In a nuclear plant disaster-recovery system, choose rules that can be applied most quickly; this includes applying compiled rules before interpreted ones and applying rules with shorter right-hand sides.

To avoid confusion, metalevel processing should not be mixed with normal processing unless it is controlled strictly by tasks, goals, or some other device. Mixing levels of processing makes explanation and modification of rules more difficult. Part of the challenge in designing current artificial intelligence tools is to write systems that factor out domain-independent control knowledge from domain-dependent task knowledge as much as possible.

7.4 EXERCISES

7-1 What would be the best data structure to store goals if goals were ordered by their time of creation and only the most recently created goal could be examined?

7-2 Suppose MYCIN were given the following data:[4]

```
(organism-1 gram-stain gramnegative) 0.8
(organism-1 infection-type primary-bacteremia) 0.3
(organism-1 culture culture-A) 1.0
(ChrisJohnson sex female) 1.0
(ChrisJohnson age 55) 1.0
```

[4] The data and rules in this example are fabricated. They do not represent true domain principles about medicine.

```
(culture-A site throat) 1.0
(throat isa sterile-site) 0.9
(organism-1 growth aerobic) 0.75
```

and the following rules:

```
RULE1: culture-tells-infection-is-bacteroides
attenuation: 0.7
IF: (<DIS> portal-of-entry gastrointestinal-tract)
    (<DIS> culture <CUL>)
    (<CUL> site <SITE>)
    (<SITE> isa sterile-site)
THEN;
    (<DIS> infection-type bacteroides)

RULE2: patient-info-tells-infection-is-bacteroides
attenuation: 0.4
IF (<DIS> bacteria-type coccus)
   (<DIS> growth aerobic)
   (<PER> sex female)
   (<PER> age > 25)
THEN
   (<DIS> infection-type bacteroides)

RULE3: organism-tells-bacteria-type
attenuation: 0.5
IF (<ORG> gram-stain gramnegative)
   (<ORG> growth aerobic)
THEN
   (<ORG> bacteria-type coccus)

RULE4: bacteria-type-tells-portal-of-entry
attenuation: 0.7
IF:  (<DIS> bacteria-type << coccus rod >>)
THEN:
     (<DIS> portal-of-entry gastrointestinal-tract)
```

With what certainty could we conclude that organism-1 had the infection type *bacteroides*?

7-3 Suppose a production system represents data in data memory as vectors that start with symbols indicating the names of objects. This production system has the following matching features:

- Positive matches and variable binding
- Regular variables: symbols preceded by #
- Segment variables: symbols preceded by %
- Multiple regular variables only
- Relational operators: >, =, and <
- Conjunction of attributes: { }

The { } symbol can be used to specify a single relation that must be true, such as (Arleen age { < 50 }) (i.e., Arleen's age is less than fifty). Assume that there is no typing and no set variables. Suppose we were given the following data memory elements:

```
(walls size 10 20)
(house components walls floors ceilings)
(floors size 400 type hardwood)
(objects walls ceilings floors)
(ceilings red blue green)
(inhabitants Arleen Mark Arleen)
(house cost 100000)
(house age 10)
```

Which of the following condition elements would match the given data? Assume that variable bindings must be consistent across the two condition elements given.

a) (house components %things) & (objects %things)
b) (inhabitants #x #x #x) & (house age {< 10})
c) (inhabitants #x #y #z) & (floors size { > 200} type %floortype)

7-4 Given an OPS5-style syntax for rules plus the condition-element syntax and matching features given in the last example, write a rule called "house-high" that will conclude that a house's quality is high if its cost is between $50,000 and $150,000 and its age is less than 5. Use the implicit addition of elements to working memory instead of **make.**

7-5 If your production system has a Rete match algorithm (see Section 6.1), a conflict resolution strategy of *specificity* along with *refraction*, and no negative matching or removing of elements from data memory, then which of the following data structures would most efficiently store the conflict set so that the match cycle takes the least time? Why?

- A queue
- A stack
- A priority queue or agenda ordered by specificity
- A binary tree with the specificity as keys

7-6 Suppose the following goal is present in memory:

```
(goal ↑type move ↑object brick ↑from table ↑to floor)
```

Which of the following rules would be considered for matching if the production system filtered rules by the goal type and then by the object?

```
(p clear-before-moving
   (goal ↑type move ↑object <obj>)
   ...)
```

```
(p find-place
   (goal ↑type <typ> ↑object brick ↑from <place1> ↑to <place2>)
   ...)

(p replace-item
   (goal ↑type replace ↑object brick ↑from <place1>)
   ...)

(p stable-movement
   (goal ↑type move ↑object table ↑from <place>)
   ...)

(p generic-goal
   (goal ↑type <typ> ↑object <obj>)
   ...)

(p table-movement
   (goal ↑type <typ> ↑from table ↑to floor)
   ...)

(p throw-rock
   (goal ↑type harm ↑who <person>)
   ...)
```

8 Knowledge Acquisition, Learning, and Explanation in Production Systems

The ultimate goal of research in the areas of knowledge acquisition, explanation, and learning is to build language systems that will (1) allow the domain expert to enhance the domain knowledge of the program with only a little help from the knowledge engineer; (2) allow the user of the program to obtain pertinent and responsive explanations for system behavior; and (3) enable the program to modify itself so as to improve its performance over time. The goals are not independent: A sophisticated explanation system can facilitate the domain expert's understanding of system modifications and enhancements. A system that can add to its own knowledge (or point out potential areas for expansion) through a learning utility will also facilitate the domain expert's task of adding domain knowledge. This chapter reviews the functionality in run-time support systems needed to achieve these goals and describes techniques currently available to the programmer. Examples will be taken from the systems described in Chapter 9.

8.1 KNOWLEDGE ACQUISITION

The term *knowledge acquisition* has many meanings in computer literature. Knowledge acquisition can be defined as the accumulation, assimilation, and accommodation of new facts with respect to an existing program. The definition of knowledge acquisition can be extended to include the general task of knowledge engineering, the transfer of domain expertise from a knowledgeable human to a computer program (usually via a knowledge engineer), as well as the enhancement and general maintenance of existing computer programs. Self-modifying programs are also examples of programs with knowledge-acquisition capabilities. This section will concentrate on the process of enhancing and maintaining an existing rule-based program, assuming that the following things have been accomplished:

- one complete iteration of requirements analysis
- specification of the domain world model, including definition of the objects, attributes, and operations for that model
- design of the rule-based program
- implementation
- testing

On succeeding iterations of system development, one could concentrate at any of the levels of implementation, design, and modeling. At the implementation level, incremental program growth through elaboration and refinement as well as program shrinkage through generalization (discussed in Section 4.5) are knowledge-acquisition techniques amenable to automated support. Further, support systems can facilitate the extension of a design to add functionality compatible with the existing design and model. But while support systems can demonstrate the need for design reformalization for extensions that are hard to make, the reformalization itself is generally beyond the capabilities of currently available tools. Similarly, as a new view of the domain world is gained by using and developing the program, the systems can facilitate expressing and testing the new model, but they cannot replace the creative discovery process.

The goal of having a domain expert with little computer expertise modify and enhance an expert-system computer program is unrealistic at the present time. Certain types of knowledge, such as new values for attributes or new attributes for objects, could indeed be added by a domain expert who lacked understanding of the internal storage or representation techniques. A general rule could be given; but how would that rule be interpreted by the system? The domain expert needs to know the basic inference strategy of the language in order to properly phrase rules. Even — perhaps *especially* — with a natural language interface, the domain expert may not realize that the system has misunderstood the intention of an addition until long after the addition has been integrated into the program. However, many domain experts are willing and able to learn the basics of the inference and representation techniques. For such experts, a well-structured, easy-to-access set of run-time support tools for knowledge acquisition can be as helpful as it is for the knowledge engineer. Today's available tools include type checkers, editors, static analyzers, and a few simple dynamic analyzers for knowledge enhancement.

8.1.1 TYPE CHECKERS

Even though many of the production-system languages are not strongly typed, most programmers today appreciate the ability to specify the range and type of values permitted for each attribute of an element and rely on a type checker to find potential type errors in a program. Many of the languages we'll discuss in Chapter 9 include type checkers as mandatory or optional parts of the program environment. Many difficult-to-find errors are the result of typos or inconsistent treatment of values. Type checking helps discover the bulk of such errors and is particularly easy to implement. Because of the interactive nature of building a rule-based system, flexibility in type checking is desirable. OPS83 is even more strongly typed than PASCAL. Both EMYCIN and DUCK allow the programmer to declare symbols before using them in rules or to interactively add a new definition if a rule includes symbols that are not yet defined. The programmer can either define the symbol immediately or postpone the definition. Whereas EMYCIN insists that all symbols be defined, DUCK simply gives a warning if an attempt is made to save a program that does not define all the symbols used. Compared with most OPS5 implementations, which do little type checking, both systems give important information to the person adding rules to a program. Usually type checking is a feature of a language editor, which we'll discuss next. We consider type checking separately because it is so useful, so often neglected in the environment of a rule-based language, and the easiest tool to add to one's own environment. Even a language whose definition does not allow typing of attribute values can be augmented to allow strong typing when desired by the user.

8.1.2 EDITORS

Language editors with a knowledge of the specific syntax are available for some of the rule-based languages, such as EMYCIN and KAS. Used interactively, the editors prompt the user for portions of a rule or declaration, supply defaults, correct spelling, and perform type checking as necessary. Such an editor can remove the drudgery of discovering and correcting syntax errors in a new rule as well as expedite the process of adding new rules and types to the program. Languages with relatively simple and fixed syntax, such as EMYCIN, have editors that find all syntax errors. Languages like OPS5 and PROLOG, for which the definitions allow a variety of syntactic forms, generally do not — but could — have editors that warn about unusual constructs, even though the construct might be syntactically correct. Experienced programmers using special constructs are often irritated by such warnings, but they are invaluable in other cases. Providing switches to turn off various editing features would alleviate the irritation.

The trend in editors is to have them perform other analysis functions of a program as new rules are added. This is known as *static analysis*. A major source of errors during program enhancement is the unexpected interaction of new rules with existing rules. A language editor could analyze new rules to help find undesirable rule interactions. While editors that compare rules for direct interactions do exist, there has been very little work done on techniques for the more complex interactions represented in a static flow analysis of a rule-based program. In backward-chaining languages such as EMYCIN, the rules are often stored according to the goal of the consequent. Editors for such languages usually provide tables of the rules concluding each goal type. A comparison of the newly added rule with existing rules of the same goal type could warn the user when a new rule is directly inconsistent with an existing rule (as in the EMYCIN editor), when it subsumes or is subsumed by an existing rule, or when it is missing a predicate normally included in the premise of rules of the same goal type (as in the TEIRESIAS editor).

Another static analysis function is the creation of a cross-reference table showing which objects, attributes, and values are referenced in which rules — both left-hand and right-hand sides. This would be of service for backward- and forward-chaining rule systems. The cross-reference table is useful in determining that particular objects appear only in the portions of the program appropriate to them and in keeping track of changes in symbol usage as the program is modified. A more specific cross-reference table that shows when rules can be in the same conflict sets (when the left-hand sides are satisfied by the same data configurations) would be useful for checking rule interactions. The data configurations that could satisfy the left-hand side of a rule form a set. For two rules, these sets could be identical, implying that the rules might allow inconsistent or conflicting conclusions from the data. The sets could have no elements in common, implying that the rules probably have no interaction. The cases that are not so obvious, and are often overlooked in enhancing a program, are those in which the intersection of the two sets is a non-empty proper subset of one or both of the sets. Such rules need to be examined for inconsistencies and assurance that they are not inappropriately enabling or disabling one another. Additional techniques could examine the rule to see if it created an infinite loop in and of itself.

The static analysis of a program should be available in two modes: *interactive mode* when a new rule is added and *batch mode* to analyze a complete program or program segment. In interactive mode the editor helps focus attention on the appropriate part of a program following the addition of a new rule. In batch mode the editor provides a summary view of the program's data and rules. EXPERT has the capability of summarizing the rules, findings, and hypotheses of a model in a variety of tables to help the model designer find the types of errors discussed in this section. Most of the existing rule-based language editors have some capabilities in both modes.

8.1.3 KNOWLEDGE-ENHANCEMENT TOOLS

While in theory the system designer should not need to execute a program to determine its behavior, static analysis is insufficient as a knowledge-enhancement tool. In enhancing a rule-based program, dynamic analysis tools — tools that perform analysis on the program dynamically during execution — are invaluable. Such tools include traces of rules fired, conflict sets, and working memory modifications; summaries of rule execution statistics; the ability to step forward and backward through an execution, examining the state of working memory and the program; automatic testing tools; and performance-evaluation monitors. In performing an inference the designer needs to be able to determine what rules actually fired, what rules were candidates for firing at each step of the inference, and how the data configuration changed as the rules fired. From this information, the designer can examine several questions: (1) Are there rules that should have been candidates and were not? (2) Were some of the candidate rules erroneous candidates? (3) Are there missing rules for some of the data configurations generated? (4) Should some data configuration have been generated that was not? The same tools that help in debugging a program will help in maintaining and enhancing that program. OPS5 allows the designer to step through the execution dynamically, collecting the information in a file for later examination or on-line for immediate evaluation. EMYCIN provides more help by guiding the designer through the program's reasoning and helping him or her locate and fix the types of problems listed above.

Traditional analysis tools for performing regression testing can be modified to analyze the consistency of modified rule-based programs. Given a database of test cases for the system, the rules expected to fire, and the final data configuration anticipated, a regression test analysis tool can execute the modified program on the same test cases, comparing the performance of the new program with that of the original. Any differences can be displayed to the designer with interactive help to trace the causes of unexpected results. A tool available with the EXPERT system allows the designer to interact with the regression test database using a query facility to retrieve all tests with specified results and summary statistics of the results of the tests. The ability to have test cases added to the database automatically is an important feature of test regression analysis tools.

The most sophisticated existing knowledge-enhancement tools actually evaluate the performance of the program, suggesting areas that need a generalization of rules, specialization of rules, or new rules to fill reasoning gaps. TEIRESIAS was able to provide some advice on the contents of new program rules based on several of its own rule heuristics containing information about reasonable changes to make in rules. More recently, the SEEK system [Politikas, Weiss 84] provides a performance-analysis function that greatly augments the EXPERT designer's tool kit.

8.2 EXPLANATION

An explanation system is a system that attempts to answer the program designer's or user's questions relating to system behavior. In the simplest of systems the answers to questions are canned responses triggered by key words or slightly edited dumps of system traces. More sophisticated systems can paraphrase rules in English and describe motivations based on program self-knowledge. Two types of questions are answered by explanation systems: "Why are you [the program] doing what you are doing now?" "How did you [the program] come to the conclusions you have reported?" Both questions could be interpreted on many levels, creating the justification for program behavior from the actual code embodied by a rule or from some representation of the intention of the system analyst in structuring the original model. While some experimentation with justification based on a model of the domain has been completed successfully [Swartout 83], the programming languages currently available give explanations based on the actual code embodied by the rules.

8.2.1 USES OF EXPLANATION

If the advice given by expert systems is to be accepted by domain experts, it is necessary for these systems to explain the reasoning that led them to their conclusions. Professionals such as medical doctors, mining geologists, and military tacticians will justifiably be very skeptical of any advice (either human or automated) unless a plausible explanation is available on demand. These experts are entirely right to refrain from taking any risk whatsoever on the basis of advice given without such justification. But interestingly enough, experience with rule-based programs for technicians and other nonexpert users indicates that most explanations are superfluous and ignored. The technician wants to be told what to do — not why it should be done.

A related use for explanation is its assistance to the knowledge engineer in debugging the knowledge base. In this case the knowledge engineer is assumed to know the domain of expertise and the design of the expert system. If the expert system can explain to the knowledge engineer how it arrives at recommendations, faulty decisions can be traced to specific gaps or misconceptions in the knowledge base.

Another important use for explanation is in tutoring. The knowledge base of an expert system, if it is effective in supporting high-quality expert judgments, should be able to exploit the expertise to train humans to make the same decisions. However, presenting this knowledge in a form conducive to effective teaching is not as straightforward as it seems [Clancey 82]. The heuristics encoded in the knowledge base may be ad hoc and obscure, or may even serve control functions rather than embody domain knowledge. It is rare that a knowledge base constructed solely for use by a high-performance expert system will serendipitously be adequate for tutoring.

8.2.2 IMPLEMENTATION ISSUES

At the least sophisticated level of explanation is *canned text*, which is human-generated text inserted into the program for the purpose of display when the appropriate question is asked. Although this has the advantage of permitting the explanations to be as elegant as desired, there are some important limitations: The explanations must be revised every time the knowledge base or heuristics change, and the explanation can be adapted to the individual user only with great difficulty.

The next level of sophistication is *execution traces*, traversing a goal tree in response to inquiries. Based on the goal tree, the system can explain how a conclusion was reached by summarizing the goals that were satisfied to reach the conclusion. When asked for more detail, the system can repeat each of the rules that fired in stylized English. Asked which rules did not contribute to the conclusion but could have, the system can paraphrase rules relating to the specific goal. If the program has asked the user for information and the user wants to know why the information is needed, the system can explain which goal is being worked on and how the information will contribute to the satisfaction of the goal. From this discussion, it should be obvious that explanation is much easier in a goal-driven, backward-chaining, rule-based language than in general-purpose, forward-driven, rule-based languages such as OPS5, or applicative languages such as LISP, or object-oriented languages such as FLAVORS. The major disadvantage of the technique described is that the granularity of the trace or explanation is the same as that of the rules; if the rules are obscure or implementation-specific, the explanation will be also.

8.2.3 EXPLANATION IN OPS5

Unfortunately for OPS5 programmers, most reasonable explanation systems are best implemented at the level of the interpreter and not at the level of production rules. While a general-purpose explanation system could be built into OPS5, it is questionable whether the cost in storage and time would be offset by the quality of the explanations. To show how one might go about augmenting a program to provide its own explanation system, a simple forward-chaining deductive database will serve as an example. The database contains relation elements stating relations between two people — e.g., father, mother, aunt. When a new relation is added to the database, the program should immediately deduce all possible additional relations. In general, such a data-driven database would be impractical. The size of working memory would cause storage problems and inefficiency in the rule-matching process. Because there are so many elements of the same type, the time to compute matches may become unreasonably large. The alternative is to recompute a relation whenever it is needed, as the example in Section 2.4.3 demonstrated. Our initial program contains two sample rules for computing the "aunt" relation and the "cousin" relation.

```
(literalize relation
    person-1 ; This person is related by i.e. Alexandra is the
    relation ;  this relationship         i.e. mother of
    person-2 ;  to this person            i.e. Caroline
  )

; The rule aunt-by-blood establishes a working memory element
;  for the relation "aunt." The rule in English is:
;  IF    the <aunt> is the "sister" of the <parent>
;   and  the <parent> is the mother or father of the <target>
;   and  there isn't already a relation of "aunt" between
;          the <aunt> and the <target>
;  THEN  make a relation of "aunt" between the <aunt> and
;        the <target>

(p aunt-by-blood
   (relation ↑person-1 <aunt> ↑relation sister
             ↑person-2 <parent>)
   (relation ↑person-1 <parent> ↑relation << mother father >>
             ↑person-2 <target>)
 - (relation ↑person-1 <aunt> ↑relation aunt
             ↑person-2 <target>)
-->
   (make relation ↑person-1 <aunt> ↑relation aunt
                  ↑person-2 <target>))

;The rule cousin establishes a working memory element
;  for the relation "cousin." The rule in English is:
;  IF    the person-1 is the mother or father of person-2
;   and  the person-1 is the aunt or uncle of the <target>
;   and  there isn't already a relation of "cousin" between
;         person-2 and the <target>
;  THEN  make a relation of "cousin" between the person-2 and
;         the <target>
```

```
(p cousin
   (relation ↑person-1 <aunt-or-uncle>
             ↑relation << mother father >>
             ↑person-2 <cousin> ↑label <label-1>)
   (relation ↑person-1 <aunt-or-uncle>
             ↑relation << aunt uncle >>
             ↑person-2 <target> ↑label <label-2>)
 - (relation ↑person-1 <cousin> ↑relation cousin
             ↑person-2 <target>)
-->
   (make relation ↑person-1 <cousin> ↑relation cousin
                  ↑person-2 <target>))

;Initializations of working memory

(make relation ↑person-1 Alexandra ↑relation sister
               ↑person-2 Beatrice)

(make relation ↑person-1 Alexandra ↑relation mother
               ↑person-2 Caroline)

(make relation ↑person-1 Beatrice  ↑relation mother
               ↑person-2 Dorothy)
```

When this program is run, it will first infer that Alexandra is the aunt of Caroline (using the rule `aunt-by-blood`) and then will infer that Dorothy is the cousin of Caroline (using the rule `cousin`). After this short chain of reasoning, there will be relationships known in three ways:

1. Given initially (Alexandra is the sister of Beatrice; Alexandra is the mother of Caroline; Beatrice is the mother of Dorothy).
2. Inferred directly from relationships that are given (Alexandra is the Aunt of Caroline).
3. Inferred from a combination of given and inferred relationships (Dorothy is the cousin of Caroline).

An explanation system must be able to distinguish and handle these cases appropriately.

For each assertion that is made by one of the rules (as opposed to those assertions that are assumed without question), an element must be placed in working memory to serve as a trace, indicating how the conclusion is justified. Since OPS5 does not allow a program to examine its own rules directly, these traces must redundantly encode information that is already present in the rules. The trace elements will have to tie together three kinds of information: (1) the inference being justified, (2) the rule that was invoked to assert the inference, (3) the antecedent conditions that enabled the rule to fire. Then, when an explanation is required, the necessary information is extracted and interpreted from the appropriate trace element.

Adding an explanatory capability is not merely a matter of appending new rules; the existing data structures have to be modified to include fields for recording the trace information. The first modification is that assertions must be labeled so that the trace elements can be linked to them. In our example, this can be accomplished by defining an attribute named *label* for the working memory element class *relation*.

```
(literalize relation
    person-1  ;This person is related by i.e. Alexandra is the
    relation  ; this relationship          i.e. mother of
    person-2  ; to this person             i.e. Caroline

    label     ;Unique new atom
    )
```

Each relation, when created by a rule, will be given a unique label using the external function, "gint." We use the external function instead of the OPS5 function, **genatom**, to allow the use of the symbol generated by both the program and the user. You should check your user's manual for the appropriate function to use in your implementation. In the LISP implementations of OPS5, the function "gint" may be defined by:

```
(external gint)
(defun gint fexpr (args)
  ($value (intern (gensym))))
```

Each trace element will then have "pointer" attributes that are given values equal to those of the *label* fields of the associated *relation* elements. The need to *label* elements of working memory causes yet another problem for initialization of working memory. Functions cannot be invoked from a top-level **make** action, so working memory initialization must be accomplished using rules.

```
(p initialize-database
   (start)
-->
   (make relation ↑person-1 Alexandra ↑relation sister
                  ↑person-2 Beatrice  ↑label (gint))
   (make relation ↑person-1 Alexandra ↑relation mother
                  ↑person-2 Caroline  ↑label (gint))
   (make relation ↑person-1 Beatrice  ↑relation mother
                  ↑person-2 Dorothy   ↑label (gint)))
(make start)
```

The element providing the trace information for a working memory element will be of element class *reason*, declared as follows:

```
(literalize reason
    rule        ;Name of the rule creating the assertion
    assertion   ;label attribute of the assertion
    condition-1 ;label attribute of LHS element matched
    condition-2 ;label attribute of LHS element matched
)
```

Each rule that deduces a relation will **make** not only a *relation* working memory element, but an associated *reason* element as well. The attribute *rule* will hold a value that identifies the rule that fired; this value need be nothing more than the name of the rule. At explanation time, a paraphrase of the rule can be recovered and printed for the user. The *assertion* attribute points to the associated *relation* element by having a value equal to that of the *relation* element's *label* attribute. In a similar fashion, the two *condition* attributes contain pointers to the *relation* elements that match the positive condition elements in the left-hand side of the rule. If there is no *reason* element for a relation, that relation was given, not inferred.

With these changes, the `aunt-by-blood` rule will look like this:

```
(p aunt-by-blood
   (relation ↑person-1 <aunt> ↑relation <sister>
             ↑person-2 <parent> ↑label <label-1>)
   (relation ↑person-1 <parent> ↑relation << mother father >>
             ↑person-2 <target> ↑label <label-2>)
 - (relation ↑person-1 <aunt> ↑relation aunt
             ↑person-2 <target>)
-->
   (bind <label-3> (gint))
   (make relation ↑person-1 <aunt> ↑relation aunt
                  ↑person-2 <target> ↑label <label-3>)
   (make reason ↑rule aunt-by-blood
                ↑assertion <label-3>
                ↑condition-1 <label-1>
                ↑condition-2 <label-2>))
```

These modifications will cause the program to construct an explicit *inference network*, rather than a collection of implicitly connected, independent assertions of family relationships.

To support an explanatory capability, we will have to make some changes in control. Up to this point it had been tacitly assumed that "primitive" family relationships would be entered on the top level, and the program would then proceed to make all possible inferences before returning to the top level for more information. The user interaction was confined to top-level **make** actions. For explanation, however, some kind of interface is necessary so that the user can specify an assertion to be explained. Both informing the system about relationships and requesting explanations can be handled with the same interactive mechanism, so these will be developed together.

Contexts will be used to control interaction. There will be four *contexts*, "deduce," "explain," "inform," and "interact," and rules to switch from one *context* to another. Each *context* corresponds to a distinct phase of operation. The "explain" *context* will need an added parameter for communication within the rules implementing the *context*. An element class, *response*, will be used to record the text of the user's response. The program declarations given previously are augmented with the following:

```
(literalize context
    name            ;deduce, explain, inform, interact
    parameter       ;name of a rule for explain
)

(literalize response
    text            ;user's input
)
```

The design of a simplified database program to store, retrieve, explain and deduce simple familial relations is given. The four major functions of the system are defined:

deduce	From known family relationships, deduce all other family relationships using inference rules; return to the "interact" context.
explain	Solicit the specification of an assertion to be explained, and traverse the inference network to provide an explanation of that one assertion; return to the "interact" context.
inform	Solicit a single new assertion about family relationships from the user; transfer to "deduce" context.
interact	Determine what the user wants to do, inform or request an explanation; transfer to appropriate context.

From the user's point of view there are obvious flaws and inefficiencies in the design described. For example, probably the user would like the option of tracing an assertion back to primitive relations. To do this, he or she must exit the "inform" context, enter the "interact" context, and go back to the "inform" context for each step of the trace. Generally it is a good design principle to allow the user a choice of continuing with the current context, returning to the previous context, returning to the top level context ("interact" in this program), saving the state of the program, or ending the session. Such modifications to this example are left as exercises for the reader.

The three rules already developed will need to be modified to include *context* information. The rules `aunt-by-blood` and `cousin` will need a new condition element, (context ↑name deduce), while the rule `initialize-database` will need an additional action, (make context ↑name deduce).

The following code fragment shows some of the new rules that will allow user interaction. It is assumed that the rule that initializes working memory has created a *context* element with the value "deduce" for the *name* attribute. Once all deductions have been made, the rule `deduce::done` will fire to change *context* to "interact."

```
;The rule deduce::done fires when no additional deductions
; can be made. The context is switched to "interact"

(p deduce::done
   {(context ↑name deduce) <deduce-context>}
-->
   (modify <deduce-context> ↑name interact))

(p interact::get-users-choice
   (context ↑name interact)
   (response)
-->
   (write (crlf) Do you want to INFORM or should I EXPLAIN?)
   (make response ↑text (accept)))

(p interact::enter-context:inform
   {(context ↑name interact) <interact-context>}
   {(response ↑text << INFORM inform >> ) <response>}
-->
   (modify <interact-context> ↑name inform)
   (remove <response>))

(p interact::enter-context:explain
   {(context ↑name interact) <interact-context>}
   {(response ↑text << EXPLAIN explain >> ) <response>}
-->
   (modify <interact-context> ↑name explain)
   (remove <response>))

(p interact::invalid-response
   {(context ↑name interact) <interact-context>}
   {(response) <response>}
-->
   (write (crlf)
          Your response was not one of INFORM or EXPLAIN)
   (remove <response>))
```

If no error-checking or help facilities are provided, the task of gathering information about a single relation can be accomplished with one rule:

```
(p inform
   {(context ↑name inform) <inform-context>}
-->
   (write (crlf)
          The first person in the relationship |: |)
   (bind <person-1> (accept))
   (write (crlf)
          The second person in the relationship |: |)
   (bind <person-2> (accept))
   (write (crlf)
          The relationship of the first
          to the second person |: |)
   (bind <relation> (accept))
   (write (crlf) adding the relation:)
   (write (crlf) <person-1> is the <relation> of <person-2>)
   (make relation ↑person-1 <person-1>
                  ↑person-2 <person-2>
                  ↑relation <relation>
                  ↑label (gint))
   (modify <inform-context> ↑name deduce))
```

The purpose of this example is to demonstrate rules that can guide the explanation of the program's actions. The explanation portion of the program presents a number of complications. The user first has to know which relationships the system asserts, and then has to have some way of specifying which assertion the system is to explain. The decision adopted here is to have the system list all relations, along with values of their *label* attributes, and have the user specify which relation is to be explained by entering its label.

Listing the relations requires only one rule:

```
(p explain::list-relations
   (context ↑name explain ↑parameter nil)
   (relation ↑person-1 <person-1> ↑relation <relation>
             ↑person-2 <person-2> ↑label <label>)
-->
   (write (crlf)
          <label> <person-1> is the <relation> of <person-2>))
```

This rule will be instantiated with all *relation* working memory elements, and so each known relationship will be listed (in reverse order with respect to when this relationship became known to the system). After the listing is done, the user can be asked to specify one relation to explain. Again, all that is needed is a single rule, which will fire after all instantiations of the rule `list-relation` have fired because of specificity.

```
(p explain::specify-relation
   (context ↑name explain ↑parameter nil)
-->
   (write (crlf)
         Specify a relation to explain by giving its label)
   (make response ↑text (accept)))
```

This rule makes use of the *response* element class which was used in the "interact" context for user's responses.

At this point the system can start explaining. The explanation will vary, depending on whether the assertion is a primitive (that is, entered directly by the user or the initialization rule) or was deduced by the system, and, if the latter is the case, whether the preconditions are themselves primitives or deductions. There is also the possibility the user made an erroneous response, matching the label of none of the assertions.

The easiest case to explain is that of a primitive. If a relationship was given rather than deduced, it has no associated *reason* element. This can be tested easily using a negated condition element. Notice that the context is immediately switched back to "interact."

```
(p explain::primitive
   {(context ↑name explain) <explain-context>}
   {(response ↑text <to-be-explained>)<response>}
   (relation ↑label <to-be-explained>
             ↑person-1 <person-1>
             ↑relation <relation>
             ↑person-2 <person-2>)
 - (reason   ↑assertion <to-be-explained>)
-->
   (write (crlf) I was given
         that <person-1> is the <relation> of <person-2>)
   (remove <response>)
   (modify <explain-context> ↑name interact))
```

Now we develop rules to explain relationships that were deduced by the system. The left-hand side of the rule that recognizes deduced relationships is more complicated than the left-hand side of the rule that recognizes assumed relationships. The major differences include the following:

- The condition element that tests for an associated *reason* is positive.
- The trace information carried in the *reason* element is extracted by binding the values of the attributes *rule*, *condition-1*, and *condition-2*.
- The relations with labels equal to the values of *condition-1* and *condition-2* are matched, and the values of their attributes are bound.

With this information the entire explanation, except the rule paraphrase, can be generated on the right-hand side. In order to paraphrase the rule used for the deduction, each inference rule must have a matching explanatory rule to print the paraphrase. In the present example this paraphrasing of a rule involves canned text, resulting in the maintenance problem of updating the canned paraphrase when the rule is modified.

Another solution would be to provide a user-defined function that accessed the rule file, found the appropriate rule, and created a paraphrase from the OPS5 code. More efficiently, there could be a preprocessor for the program that created, for each rule creating a relation in the RHS, a new rule whose RHS contained a paraphrase of the original rule. Either solution avoids the maintenance problem but requires very careful construction of all rules to allow reasonable paraphrases.

The explanation in the current program will be performed by two rules: one to list the preconditions, and another to expand the name of the inference rule into a paraphrase of that rule. The *parameter* attribute of the *context* element will be used to communicate the name of the inference rule from the first explanatory rule to the second.

Following is the main explanatory rule, the one that extracts all the trace information, lists the preconditions for the deduction, and spawns a context element for generating a paraphrase of the inference rule:

```
(p explain-deduction
   {(context ↑name explain ↑parameter nil) <explain-context>}
   {(response ↑text <to-be-explained>)<response>}
   (relation ↑label <to-be-explained>
             ↑person-1 <person-1>
             ↑relation <relation-1>
             ↑person-2 <person-2>)
   (reason   ↑assertion <to-be-explained>
             ↑rule <rule-name>
             ↑condition-1 <condition-1>
             ↑condition-2 <condition-2>)
   (relation ↑label <condition-1>
             ↑person-1 <person-3>
             ↑relation <relation-2>
             ↑person-2 <person-4>)
   (relation ↑label <condition-2>
             ↑person-1 <person-5>
             ↑relation <relation-3>
             ↑person-2 <person-6>)
-->
   (write (crlf)
          I inferred that <person-1> is the <relation-1> of
          <person-2> (crlf) because (crlf)
          <condition-1> <person-3> is the <relation-2> of
```

```
          <person-4> (crlf)
          <condition-2> <person-5> is the <relation-3> of
          <person-6> (crlf) and (crlf))
   (remove <response>)
   (modify <explain-context> ↑parameter <rule-name>))
```

Finally, there will be one paraphrase-generating rule for each inference rule. For the two inference rules in our system, `aunt-by-blood` and `cousin`, the two paraphrase rules are:

```
(p explain::aunt-by-blood
   {(context ↑name explain
             ↑parameter aunt-by-blood) <p-context>}
-->
   (write The sister of a parent is an aunt)
   (modify <p-context> ↑name interact ↑parameter nil))

(p explain::cousin
   {(context ↑name explain ↑parameter cousin) <p-context>}
-->
   (write The child of an aunt or uncle is a cousin)
   (modify <p-context> ↑name interact ↑parameter nil))
```

The explanation system presented here is really only a rough sketch of what such a system should be like. In the interest of simplicity, many shortcuts were taken, resulting in a program that may be difficult to maintain and inefficient both in terms of storage space and execution time.

8.3 LEARNING

8.3.1 WHAT *IS* LEARNING?

Learning is any change to a behaving system that alters its long-term performance. The changes of major interest are those that improve performance; any other change is either irrelevant or pathological. Throughout most of this century, experimental and educational psychologists have studied learning by examining how it occurs in humans and other animals.

In recent decades, however, the study of machine learning has become an important research tool. Learning researchers from all disciplines now believe that the studies of human and machine learning illuminate one another. Moreover, machine learning is of interest beyond the theoretical arena because of its potential for automating discovery.

There are many different approaches to machine learning. Early programs effected learning through self-modification of stored parameters. This mechanism is currently used in a sophisticated learning model called the "Boltzman Machine" [Hinton, et al. 84]. Other recent learning systems have adopted the production-system model, in which incremental changes in performance are effected by adding new production rules to an existing rule base. Researchers have also investigated a form of learning that results from changes in working memory and reorganization of existing rules.

Learning is not necessarily a single process, but may be a number of overlapping processes. For centuries philosophers have tried to analyze the sources of our knowledge; today's learning researchers are bringing an experimental approach to the problem. For the purposes of studying machine learning with production systems, researchers have found it convenient to classify learning into a number of conceptually distinct strategies. The following classification is based on that of [Michalski, Carbonell, Mitchell 83].

Learning by rote or direct implanting. The shallowest form of learning requires no inference at all by the learner. A human may memorize material by rote, and a program may be modified manually.

Learning from instruction. Knowledge may be handed down from teacher to learner explicitly, either in spoken or in written form. The learner must transform the new knowledge from the input language to the internal representation language and then integrate it with prior knowledge so that it can be used. The teacher has already performed whatever discovery and organization are necessary. This process is essentially the same as knowledge acquisition (see Section 8.1).

Learning by analogy. The scope of existing knowledge can be extended by applying it to new domains. New rules can be constructed by transforming old rules that were applied successfully in a similar domain. Learning by analogy requires the learner to recognize the similarity between the old and new domains, and to find the transformation that will, when applied to the old rules, yield new rules that work correctly in the new domain.

Learning from examples. The learner abstracts from a set of specific examples and counterexamples a general scheme for classifying future instances. Training examples can be generated by the learner, the teacher, or the environment, so long as there is some accurate source of feedback. Some systems use positive exemplars only, while others use both positive and negative exemplars.

Learning from observation and discovery. The unsupervised learner must focus on the salient features of its environment in order to form rules about what it observes. Some systems classify their observations passively, while others actively experiment by changing the environment and focusing on the effects to generate new rules.

Skill refinement. The learner creates rules which permit more efficient performance. This type of learning is most often applied to systems that repeatedly perform tasks. These systems refine their rules incrementally so that they produce faster or more accurate results. The resulting rules summarize the effects of a problem-solving session, and less search is required to solve similar problems (see [Anderson, Farrell, Sauers 84] and [Rosenbloom, Newell 84]).

A system can generate new rules through one of several mechanisms. Many of these have counterparts in the study of human learning.

Generalization	The term ***generalization*** is used in two distinct senses. In the first it refers to the finding of a general principle to describe specific examples, regardless of the mechanism used to derive the principle. In the second sense it refers to the mechanism of deriving a general principle by abstracting it from a set of more specific principles.
Specialization (Discrimination)	In contrast to the second sense of generalization defined above, ***specialization*** refers to the mechanism of refining a too-general principle by specializing it to apply to fewer cases. Specialization is usually enabled by negative exemplars. Since specialization enhances the system's ability to discriminate situations in which the rule should or should not fire, this mechanism is also known as ***discrimination.***
Designation	The system creates a new rule directly from instruction or observation. In the ***designation*** mechanism an event is observed and the system searches for the appropriate conditions that made that event occur.
Composition	The system creates a new rule that summarizes the behavior of two or more existing rules that fired in sequence. The ***composition*** mechanism can produce rules that proceed more directly to an answer.

The above mechanisms are all *syntactic* learning methods, since they do not analyze the conceptual content of the system that they attempt to change; that is, they are independent of domain knowledge. Any syntactic learning mechanism will tend to produce unstable performance and will make the system learn rather slowly as compared to a more knowledge-driven learning scheme.

8.3.2 WHY SHOULD PRODUCTION SYSTEMS LEARN?

Among the reasons for studying programs that learn is the light that such systems may shed on the mechanisms of human cognition, as well as the possibility that a discovery system will produce powerful new ideas [Simon 83]. From the perspective of current expert-system technology, learning systems are needed when all the possible situations that a system will encounter are not known beforehand. By adding a learning component to a system, the programmer hopes that the user can extend the system's capabilities through interaction with it, rather than by the process of reprogramming.

At the time of this writing commercial applications do not incorporate sophisticated learning strategies; advanced learning systems are confined to research laboratories in cognitive psychology and computer science. An exception is knowledge acquisition (see Section 8.1), which has been explored in both scientific and industrial applications. Researchers in machine learning expect that learning systems will become quite common in future AI technology. They forecast natural-language systems that learn new words and idioms, vision systems that abstract shape schemata for later processing, planning systems that improve as a result of experience, and tutorial systems that learn from human teachers to construct better lessons.

8.3.3 HOW ARE LEARNING SYSTEMS CONSTRUCTED?

Learning can be implemented by maintaining a file of rules and adding manually written rules to that file during the life of the rule set. A knowledge-acquisition tool may make this process independent of the implementation language, and allow for consistency checking before inserting new rules. Alternatively the system itself can produce new rules. Learning can be part of the system architecture (see Section 9.2) or can be implemented by a set of learning rules that perform the task of adding new rules to the system. The latter kind of learning affords more flexibility, but it can be more difficult to implement.

Strengthening and Weakening

One way to implement a learning system is to tune a set of parameters so that they converge on a set of optimal values. In production systems that learn, a number can be associated with each rule to indicate the desirability of its firing. Then the probability that this particular rule will fire can be raised by increasing this number. A number of this type is often called the rule's *strength*. Naturally enough, incrementing the strength is called *strengthening*, and decrementing the strength is called *weakening*. If the system determines that one of its decisions was successful because a particular rule was applied, the system can strengthen that rule under the assumption that actions that lead to success should be attempted more frequently. One problem with implementing a system that strengthens and weakens rules is determining which rule was responsible for a successful or unsuccessful decision. This is known as the problem of *credit and blame assignment;* it also plays a prominent role in learning by specialization, as we'll discuss shortly.

Generalization

A system that learns by generalization starts with a set of overly specific rules and generates new rules that are more general and abstract. These inferred rules may improve performance even if they are incorrect, although they are not guaranteed to do so. If the system overgeneralizes, it may be necessary to backtrack or to specialize some of the rules that are too general. (We'll describe this procedure under Specialization, next.)

One simple way to implement generalization is to delete a test from a rule that has applied infrequently. Because the conditions become less restrictive, the new rule is likely to apply more often. In this way the process of learning by generalization will tend to drive the system toward shorter, more general rules. The problem with deleting entire conditions, or even tests within conditions, is that the new rules thus created may apply in grossly incorrect situations. If the system cannot look ahead to see which tests would be most fruitfully abandoned, it is doomed to create many misguided generalizations for every good one it produces.

A weaker generalization technique is used in PRISM. This generalization process creates a new rule for every pair of rules that are found to be *isomorphic*. Rules are said to be isomorphic when the condition and action sides of the two rules are the same except for some small set of symbols, and a simple transformation maps one rule into the other.

The following example shows two isomorphic rules that might apply in an overly specific algebra problem-solving system. For ease of understanding, the rules are written in OPS5 even though OPS5 lacks these learning mechanisms. The first rule recognizes that the expression $5X + 3X$ can be written as $8X$, and the second rule recognizes that $9X - 7X$ can be written as $2X$. Arithmetic tables are stored explicitly in instances of the working-memory element class *rule*. Algebraic equations are represented by a working memory element of class *equation*, which points to two other elements of class *lhs-rhs*, one of which represents the left-hand side of the equation and the other the right-hand side. Each of the sides consists of a list of operands and an operator. Each of the operands in turn is represented by a working-memory element of class *expr*, which has a coefficient and possibly a variable that may be raised to an integer power.

```
(vector-attribute exprs)

(literalize equation
    lhs             ;id field of the equation's left-hand side
    rhs)            ;id field of the equation's right-hand side


(literalize lhs-rhs
    side            ;left or right hand side of the equation
    id              ;label to link to the equation
    exprs)          ;id field if operand 1, operator,
                    ;id field of operand 2

(literalize expr
    id              ;label to link to the rhs or lhs
    coeff           ;an integer constant, e.g., 5 in 5X
    variable        ;a variable name, e.g., X in 5X
    power)          ;exponent of the variable

(literalize rule
    op              ;the operator: + or -
    leftarg         ;the first integer operand
    rightarg        ;the second integer operand
    result)         ;the result of the operation

(p reduce-5X-plus-3X
   {(lhs-rhs ↑id <lhs>
             ↑exprs <expr1> + <expr2>)                      <side>}
   {(expr    ↑id <expr1>
             ↑coeff 5
             ↑variable <var>
             ↑power 1)                                      <left>}
   {(expr    ↑id <expr2>
             ↑coeff 3
             ↑variable <var>
             ↑power 1)                                     <right>}
   (rule     ↑op +
             ↑leftarg 5
             ↑rightarg 3
             ↑result 8)
-->
   (bind <expr-address> (litval exprs))
   (bind <rest> (compute <expr-address> + 3))
```

```
   (bind <newexpr> (genatom))
   (modify <side> ↑exprs <newexpr> (substr <side>
                  <rest> inf) nil)
   (make expr     ↑id <newexpr>
                  ↑coeff 8
                  ↑variable <var>
                  ↑power 1)
   (remove <left>)
   (remove <right>))

(p reduce-9X-minus-7X
   {(lhs-rhs  ↑id <lhs>
              ↑exprs <expr1> - <expr2>                    <side>}
   {(expr     ↑id <expr1>
              ↑coeff 9
              ↑variable <var>
              ↑power 1)                                   <left>}
   {(expr     ↑id <expr2>
              ↑coeff 7
              ↑variable <var>
              ↑power 1)                                   <right>}
   (rule      ↑op -
              ↑leftarg 9
              ↑rightarg 7
              ↑result 2)
-->
   (bind <expr-address> (litval exprs))
   (bind <rest> (compute <expr-address> + 3))
   (bind <newexpr> (genatom))
   (modify <side> ↑exprs <newexpr> (substr <side>
                  <rest> inf) nil)
   (make expr     ↑id <newexpr>
                  ↑coeff 2
                  ↑variable <var>
                  ↑power 1)
   (remove <left>)
   (remove <right>))

(make rule ↑leftarg 5 ↑op + ↑rightarg 3 ↑result 8) ; 5 + 3 = 8
(make rule ↑leftarg 9 ↑op - ↑rightarg 7 ↑result 2) ; 9 - 7 = 2
```

The PRISM generalization algorithm keeps constant the symbols that are common to the two rules and creates a variable for the symbols that differ. By applying the PRISM generalization algorithm to the above rules, the system derives a new rule, which recognizes that arithmetic operations can be performed on variables. The new rule, here named `reduce-terms`, is guaranteed to fire whenever `reduce-5X-plus-3X` or `reduce-9X-minus-7X` would have fired; it may fire in other cases as well.

```
(p reduce-terms
   {(lhs-rhs  ↑id <lhs>
              ↑exprs <expr1> <op> <expr2>) <side>}; <op> new
   {(expr     ↑id <expr1>
              ↑coeff <term1>                        ; <term1> new
              ↑variable <var>
              ↑power 1)               <left>}
   {(expr     ↑id <expr2>
              ↑coeff <term2>                        ; <term2> new
              ↑variable <var>
              ↑power 1)               <right>}
   (rule      ↑op <op>                              ; <op> new
              ↑leftarg <term1>                      ; <term1> new
              ↑rightarg <term2>                     ; <term2> new
              ↑result <result>)                     ; <result> new
-->
   (bind <expr-address> (litval exprs))
   (bind <rest> (compute <expr-address> + 3))
   (bind <newexpr> (genatom))
   (modify <side> ↑exprs <newexpr> (substr <side> <rest> inf)
                  nil)
   (make expr     ↑id <newexpr>
                  ↑coeff <result>                   ; <result> new
                  ↑variable <var>
                  ↑power 1)
   (remove <left>)
   (remove <right>))
```

Thus, if we execute the following **make** actions:

```
   (make equation ↑lhs lhs1
                  ↑rhs rhs1)

   (make lsh-rhs  ↑id lhs1
                  ↑exprs expr1 + expr2)

   (make expr     ↑id expr1
                  ↑coeff 9
                  ↑variable x
                  ↑power 1)

   (make expr     ↑id expr2
                  ↑coeff 11
                  ↑variable x
                  ↑power 1)

   (make rule     ↑op +
                  ↑leftarg 9
                  ↑rightarg 11
                  ↑result 20)
```

the generalized rule will apply, adding *9X* and *11X* to produce *20X*.

A generalized rule can coexist with the original rules quite easily in a system like OPS5; if both are applicable in some situation, they will yield the same result and only one will fire. The generalized rule will fire in some cases where no specific rules are applicable, possibly leading to incorrect results.

Specialization

Specialization is the learning mechanism that changes the rule set by restricting the applicability of an overly general rule. The specialization algorithm used in PRISM illustrates what can be accomplished. This algorithm compares a good (successful) instantiation and a bad (unsuccessful) instantiation of the rule being specialized. It creates one new rule for each difference that is found between the good and bad instantiations.

Consider the overly general rule `reduce-terms` displayed in the previous section. This rule transforms algebraic expressions in accordance with arithmetic identities that are stored in working memory. Suppose working memory contained the following elements:

```
(equation ↑lhs lhs1
          ↑rhs rhs1)

(lhs-rhs  ↑id lhs1
          ↑exprs expr1 + expr2)

(expr     ↑id expr1
          ↑coeff 3
          ↑variable x
          ↑power 1)

(expr     ↑id expr2
          ↑coeff 5
          ↑variable x
          ↑power 1)

(rule     ↑op +
          ↑leftarg 3
          ↑rightarg 5
          ↑result 8)
```

In this case the rule would correctly add the two new elements

```
(lhs-rhs ↑id lhs1
         ↑exprs g00001)

(expr    ↑id g00001
         ↑coeff 8
         ↑variable x
         ↑power 1)
```

to working memory. However, suppose working memory contained the following elements:

```
(equation ↑lhs lhs1
          ↑rhs rhs1)

(lhs-rhs  ↑id lhs1
          ↑exprs expr1 * expr2)

(expr     ↑id expr1
          ↑coeff 9
          ↑variable x
          ↑power 1)

(expr     ↑id expr2
          ↑coeff 11
          ↑variable x
          ↑power 1)

(rule     ↑op *
          ↑leftarg 9
          ↑rightarg 11
          ↑result 99)
```

In this case `reduce-terms` would fire and transform the equation into the following:

```
(lhs-rhs  ↑id lhs1
          ↑exprs g00001)

(expr     ↑id g00001
          ↑coeff 99
          ↑variable x
          ↑power 1)
```

Thus the system would conclude that $9X * 11X = 99X$. This is incorrect, since the variable X was not squared. We need to specialize the rule so that it applies only when the products of variables and coefficients are being added or subtracted, not multiplied or divided.

Learning programs must have some sort of *feedback* to permit intelligent specializations of rules. In this example, feedback comes in the form of an incorrect answer (for example, by comparing the answer to the teacher's solution). If many rules fired between invocation of the critical rule and feedback of results, the system may have trouble assigning credit or blame to the rule. In PRISM the function "assign-credit" stores the name of the rule that made an inference along with the inference itself (a working memory element). Thus

```
(expr ↑id g00001
      ↑coeff 99
      ↑variable x
      ↑power 1)
```

would have `reduce-terms` stored as the rule responsible for its existence.

Then, when a result is not satisfactory (in our example, if we get the wrong answer), the rule responsible for the mistake may be modified.

Learning programs must also be able to focus on the features that need to be changed. In the example of overgeneralization, the system must determine that the problem rests with the multiplication and not, for example, with the specific values of the coefficients. To achieve this focus, the discrimination mechanism in PRISM creates discriminations only when it has both a good and a bad example of a rule and these examples differ in a way that can be understood.

Let us now examine how PRISM might specialize the overgeneralized rule `reduce-terms`. The good instantiation to be used as a positive example is the one that correctly deduced $3X + 5X = 8X$; the negative example will come from the bad instantiation that incorrectly deduced $9X * 11X = 99X$. The system will create a more restrictive rule such as the one called `reduce-terms-unless-multiply`, below; for this reason, the system can be said to engage in discrimination.

```
(p reduce-terms-unless-multiply
   {(lhs-rhs  ↑id <lhs>
              ↑exprs <expr1> {<op> <> *} <expr2>) <side>}
                 ; new test
   {(expr     ↑id <expr1>
              ↑coeff <term1>
              ↑variable <var>
              ↑power 1                       <left>}
   {(expr     ↑id <expr2>
              ↑coeff <term2>
              ↑variable <var>
              ↑power 1)                      <right>}
   (rule      ↑op <op>
              ↑leftarg <term1>
              ↑rightarg <term2>
              ↑result <result>)
-->
   (bind <expr-address> (litval exprs))
   (bind <rest> (compute <expr-address> + 3))
   (bind <newexpr> (genatom))
   (modify <side> ↑exprs <newexpr> (substr <side>
       <rest> inf) nil)
   (make expr ↑id <newexpr>
              ↑coeff <result>
              ↑variable <var>
              ↑power 1)
   (remove <left>)
   (remove <right>))
```

The new rule `reduce-terms-unless-multiply` will apply in all the situations where the old rule `reduce-terms` would have applied, except in those cases where the operator is *. The specialization process discriminates this new rule by noticing that the unmodified system yielded the correct answer when the operator was + but yielded the incorrect answer when the function was *. The reader may notice that the rule `reduce-terms-unless-multiply` is still not specific enough, since nothing prevents it from applying when the operator is / (i.e., when the function is division), in which case an incorrect result is almost certain. A single negative example involving the / operator would cause the system to refine the rule further.

Another way to specialize rules is to replace variables by constants. Using this method, the overgeneralized rule `reduce-terms` gives rise to the rule `reduce-added-terms`:

```
(p reduce-added-terms
   {(lhs-rhs ↑id <lhs>
             ↑exprs <expr1> + <expr2>)     <side>} ; + constant
   {(expr    ↑id <expr1>
             ↑coeff <term1>
             ↑variable <var>
             ↑power 1)                     <left>}
   {(expr    ↑id <expr2>
             ↑coeff <term2>
             ↑variable <var>
             ↑power 1)                     <right>}
   (rule     ↑op +                                 ; + constant
             ↑leftarg <term1>
             ↑rightarg <term2>
             ↑result <result>)
-->
   (bind <expr-address> (litval exprs))
   (bind <rest> (compute <expr-address> + 3))
   (bind <newexpr> (genatom))
   (modify <side> ↑exprs <newexpr>
                       (substr <side> <rest> inf) nil)
   (make expr      ↑id <newexpr>
                   ↑coeff <result>
                   ↑variable <var>
                   ↑power 1)
   (remove <left>)
   (remove <right>))
```

This specialized rule is now specific to the + operator. It will apply correctly in all simple situations, but all the rules in the system are either too specific or too general. Our understanding of arithmetic tells us a rule is needed that applies when the operator is + or −, but not when it is * or /.

The set of all possible generalizations and specializations of the variable-adding rule defines a *version space* of rules that are partially ordered by their range of applicability [Mitchell 84]. Negative examples restrict this version space by informing the learner that the applied rule was too general, while positive examples inform the learner about some of the situations in which the rule should apply.

Composition

When several rules apply in a sequence, the sequence can be optimized by combining or composing the rules; the term *rule composition* is derived by analogy from the mathematical concept of function composition. The composition mechanism makes a new rule whose right-hand side is the concatenation of the right-hand sides of the rules involved in the composition (except where the second rule deleted an element added by the first rule). The composed left-hand side is the union of the left-hand sides of the rules involved, except for those left-hand-side tests that matched against elements put into memory by a previous rule in the composed sequence. In this way the composed rule yields the same result as the sequential application of the rules contained in the composition.

To continue the algebra example, consider an OPS5 rule that performs such transformations as

if $2X + 5 = 7$ *then* $2X = 2$

if $10X + 5 = 20$ *then* $10X = 15$

so as to isolate the constant terms on the right-hand side of an equation. The rule `isolate-constant-terms` performs this transformation:

```
(p isolate-constant-terms
   (equation ↑lhs <lhs>
             ↑rhs <rhs>)
   {(lhs-rhs ↑side left
             ↑id <lhs>
             ↑exprs <expr1> + <expr2>)                    <lside>}
   (expr     ↑id <expr1>
             ↑coeff <coeff1>
             ↑variable <var>
             ↑power 1)
   {(expr    ↑id <expr2>
             ↑coeff <num1>
             ↑variable nil)                               <left>}
   {(lhs-rhs ↑side right
             ↑id <rhs>
             ↑exprs <expr>)                               <rside>}
```

```
   {(expr      ↑id <expr>
               ↑coeff <num2>
               ↑variable nil)                             <right>}
   (rule       ↑op -
               ↑leftarg <num2>
               ↑rightarg <num1>
               ↑result <result>)
-->
   (bind <newexpr> (genatom))
   (make lhs-rhs ↑side left
                 ↑id <lhs>
                 ↑exprs <expr1>)
   (make lhs-rhs ↑side right
                 ↑id <rhs>
                 ↑exprs <newexpr>)
   (make expr    ↑id <newexpr>
                 ↑coeff <result>)
   (remove <lside>)
   (remove <rside>)
   (remove <left>)
   (remove <right>))
```

By isolating the constant terms on the right-hand side, this rule permits the firing of an additional rule that can isolate the variable on the left-hand side.

Now consider a rule that can be applied to isolate the variable on the left-hand side of the equation. It performs such transformations as

if $5X = 10$ *then* $X = 2$
if $7X = 21$ *then* $X = 3$

so as to isolate the variable on the left-hand side of the equation. The rule `isolate-variable` performs this transformation:

```
(p isolate-variable
   (equation  ↑lhs <lhs>
              ↑rhs <rhs>)
   (lhs-rhs   ↑side left
              ↑id <lhs>
              ↑exprs <expr1> nil)
   {(expr     ↑id <expr1>
              ↑coeff <coeff1>
              ↑variable <var>
              ↑power 1)                                   <left>}
   (lhs-rhs   ↑side right
              ↑id <rhs>
              ↑exprs <expr3> nil)
   {(expr     ↑id <expr3>
              ↑coeff <num>
              ↑variable nil)                              <right>}
```

```
   (rule        ↑op /
                ↑leftarg <num>
                ↑rightarg <coeff1>
                ↑result <result>)
-->
   (modify <left>  ↑coeff 1)
   (modify <right> ↑coeff <result>))
```

This transformation will leave the solution on the right-hand side of the equation.

To start the system with the equation $2X + 5 = 7$, working memory would be initialized as follows:

```
(make equation ↑lhs lhs1
               ↑rhs rhs1)

(make lhs      ↑id lhs1
               ↑exprs expr1 + expr2)

(make expr     ↑id expr1
               ↑coeff 2
               ↑variable x
               ↑power 1)

(make expr     ↑id expr2
               ↑coeff 5)

(make rhs      ↑id rhs1
               ↑exprs expr3)

(make expr     ↑id expr3
               ↑coeff 7)

(make rule     ↑op -
               ↑leftarg 7
               ↑rightarg 5
               ↑result 2)

(make rule     ↑op /
               ↑leftarg 2
               ↑rightarg 2
               ↑result 1)
```

Then the two rules could apply in sequence and make the following reduction:

$\{2X + 5 = 7\}$

Apply rule `isolate-constant-terms`

$\{2X = 2\}$

Apply rule `isolate-variable`

$\{X = 1\}$

This solves the problem in straightforward fashion.

When people perform these types of operations over and over again, the procedure becomes automatic. Thus, given any linear equation like *20X + 10 = 50*, a person may learn to compute that *X = 2* immediately. This type of speedup by automatization can be modeled by the composition process. When applied to the two rules `isolate-constant-terms` and `isolate-variable`, it will produce a new rule, `solve-linear-equation`:

```
(p solve-linear-equation
   (equation  ↑lhs <lhs>
              ↑rhs <rhs>)
   {(lhs-rhs  ↑side left
              ↑id <lhs>
              ↑exprs <expr1> + <expr2>)                <lside>}
   {(expr     ↑id <expr1>
              ↑coeff <coeff1>
              ↑variable <var>
              ↑power 1)                                <left1>}
   {(expr     ↑id <expr2>
              ↑coeff <num1>
              ↑variable nil)                           <left2>}
   {(lhs-rhs  ↑side right
              ↑id <rhs>
              ↑exprs <expr3>)                          <rside>}
   {(expr     ↑id <expr3>
              ↑coeff <num2>
              ↑variable nil)                           <right>}
   (rule      ↑op -
              ↑leftarg <num2>
              ↑rightarg <num1>
              ↑result <result>)
   (rule      ↑op /
              ↑leftarg <result1>
              ↑rightarg <coeff1>
              ↑result <result>)
-->
   (bind <newexpr> (genatom))

   (make lhs-rhs     ↑side left
                     ↑id <lhs>
                     ↑exprs <expr1>)
   (modify <left1>   ↑coeff 1)
   (make expr        ↑id <newexpr>
                     ↑coeff <result>
                     ↑variable nil)
   (make lhs-rhs     ↑side right
                     ↑id <rhs>
                     ↑exprs <newexpr>)
   (remove <lside>)
```

```
    (remove <rside>)
    (remove <right>)
    (remove <left2>))
```

Given any equation of the form $aX + b = c$, where X is a variable and a, b, and c are constants, the rule concludes $X = (c-b)/a$ in one step.

Thus, given the equation $2X + 5 = 7$ from the previous example, the rule concludes $X = 1$ immediately. The final contents of working memory will be as follows:

```
(equation ↑lhs lhs1
          ↑rhs rhs1)

(lhs-rhs  ↑side left
          ↑id lhs1
          ↑exprs expr1)

(expr     ↑id expr1
          ↑coeff 1
          ↑variable x
          ↑power 1)

(expr     ↑id g00000
          ↑coeff 1)

(lhs-rhs  ↑side right
          ↑id rhs1
          ↑exprs g00000)

(rule     ↑op -
          ↑leftarg 7
          ↑rightarg 5
          ↑result 2)

(rule     ↑op /
          ↑leftarg 2
          ↑rightarg 2
          ↑result 1)
```

One question remains: When does the system know that composition should be performed? In ACT, composition is applied every time two rules fire in sequence. Composed rules can themselves be combined into even larger rules. The size of the system's working memory determines how large the left-hand side of a rule can become. In GRAPES, the production system's goals become the focal point of the composition process. The group of rules that was instrumental in achieving a particular goal is stored as subgoals of the original goal in the goal tree. The composition operator collapses the goal tree so that a single rule can achieve a goal that originally could be achieved only by a group of rules firing in sequence. See [Anderson, Farrell, Sauers 84] for a description of the GRAPES composition mechanisms.

Designation

Another way to learn new rules is by recognizing causal relations in the external environment and building them into the production system explicitly. For an example in the best empirical tradition of David Hume, a system can create a causal principle that captures the insight that if two events occur in a sequence, at future times when the first event happens, the second event should be anticipated.

```
(literalize event
    type      ; identifies the event that occurred
    time)     ; a number that increases with time

(literalize expectation
    type)     ; identifies the event that is expected

(p propose-causal-hypothesis
   (event  ↑type <action1>
           ↑time <t1>)
   (event  ↑type <action2>
           ↑time {<t2> > <t1>})
 - (action ↑time { > <t1> < <t2>})
-->
   (<build> (genatom)
     (event ↑type \\ <action1>)
   -->
   (make expectation ↑type \\ <action2>)))
```

Recall that the unquote operation, \\, makes the new rule specific to the value of the variable <action1>.

Consider the following two *events* that may be present in working memory:

```
(event ↑type oil-spill
       ↑time 1500)

(event ↑type explosion
       ↑time 1520)
```

The rule `propose-causal-hypothesis` would fire and add the following rule to the production system:

```
(p g00001
   (event ↑type oil-spill)
-->
   (make expectation ↑type explosion))
```

Note that the name of the rule, `g00001`, is the unique atom returned by the OPS5 function call (genatom).

The new rule is much too general; it was generated on the basis of only a single co-occurrence, and it is not the result of a careful reasoning process.

Perhaps it is accidental that these two events followed one another in time; it is also possible that not all oil spills should arouse the fear of an explosion. If there were a more complex learning mechanism to tease apart cause and effect, it might turn out to be reasonable to assert the above rule after only one oil spill. Such a reasoning process might use knowledge about the flammability of oil to conclude that oil spills cause explosions.

The oil-spill example shows only one form of designation, one that induces causality. Learning by designation can be used to build new rules that are either more general or more specific than the rules in the original system. By itself, designation is neutral with respect to learning theory; it is a production-system learning tool that can be used to build new rules of any type.

Conclusion

We have examined a small set of production-system learning mechanisms that work well together. The real worth of a learning system can be measured by its performance in unexpected situations. If the system solves a problem that it was not designed to solve, or if it discovers a new idea, such as a new proof or theorem in mathematics, then the learning research has yielded a rich dividend. The study of machine learning is at the core of artificial intelligence research, and we can expect major advances in the field in the next decade. These advances will be of value to psychologists, computer scientists, and users of knowledge-based expert systems.

8.4 EXERCISES

8-1 The database program created in Section 8.2.3 has no mechanism for halting. Modify the "interact" context to the user response `"STOP"` and add the necessary rule to handle this response.

8-2 Modify the "explain" context rules for the database program in Section 8.2.3 so that the user can continue tracing the explanation of deduced relations back to primitives without returning to the "interact" context.

8-3 In Section 2.4.3, rules were given for generating all the ancestors of a *Person* in a database. Translate these rules to the database program using the *relation* element class instead of the *Person* element class. Write explanation rules for the rules you create.

8-4 Create a database system that does not store relations explicitly. The basic element class for information concerning people should be the *Person* element class defined in Section 2.1.2. Modify the contexts as follows:

deduce	Ask the user for a person's name and the relationship to be deduced; make the deduction requested and return to "interact."
deduce/explain	Ask the user for a person's name and the relationship to be deduced; make the deduction requested, including an explanation of the steps of the deduction, and return to "interact."
inform	Solicit new *Person* instances, then transfer to "interact" when user indicates that he or she is done with informing.
interact	Determine what the user wants to do — inform, deduce, or deduce with explanation.

9

Related Expert-System Tools

This chapter describes a number of publicly available AI languages that can be used to build expert systems or cognitive models. We concentrate on those languages that have a major rule-based component. While a number of useful object-oriented or frame-based systems also are available to the public [Moon, Stallman, Weinreb 83; Goldberg, Robson 83; Genesereth et al. 81; Wright, Fox 82; Brachman 78], they require programming techniques rather different from those discussed here and deserve to be the subject of a separate book. In addition, new languages and systems are being created monthly, so the present coverage is illustrative rather than complete or current. This chapter should provide some perspective on the possibilities available within the rule-based programming paradigm.

The languages we discuss are EMYCIN, EXPERT, KAS, OPS5, ROSIE, YAPS, GRAPES, PRISM, DUCK, PROLOG, KEE, LOOPS, OPS83, and S.1. For each language we give a brief introduction, describe the distinguishing features of the language's data memory, rule memory, and control; we examine the language's run-time environment and any noteworthy facilities or programming techniques. A source of more information about languages and tools used in building expert systems is [Hayes-Roth, Waterman, Lenat 83]. The OPS5 language is included in this section for completeness despite the fact that it has been described in greater detail in previous chapters.

The languages discussed here are classified primarily as *rule-based expert-system tools, rule-based cognitive-modeling tools, logic-based expert-system tools,* or *hybrid expert-system tools.* These are not rigid classifications; OPS5, for instance, has been used for research in both expert-system construction and cognitive psychology, while several of the tools (PROLOG is one), have been used as general-purpose programming languages. Within each class the languages are presented in alphabetical order.

9.1 RULE-BASED EXPERT-SYSTEM TOOLS

Rule-based expert-system tools are intended for use in the construction of high-performance rule-based systems for applications in industry and business as well as for research. The first three languages, EMYCIN, EXPERT, and KAS, were built as consultation systems for diagnosis tasks in which, given some evidence, the system must reach a conclusion. These languages all have well-developed user interfaces with knowledge-based rule editors, debugging aids, and some knowledge-acquisition tools. The next three languages, OPS5, YAPS, and ROSIE, are characterized by a uniform treatment of rules, flexibility in the choice of control strategies, and generality in the range of problem-solving strategies that are representable. The languages have primitive debugging facilities and few aids for knowledge acquisition.

9.1.1 EMYCIN

EMYCIN (Essential MYCIN) is a rule-based expert-system language best suited for problems involving classificatory reasoning. Classification problems have a finite set of possible solutions, and the expert system's task is to find one or more solutions that fit the current case. Problems of this type are usually solved by collecting, aggregating, and abstracting information about a case, relating this abstract description to a general set of solutions, and then selecting and refining one or more specific solutions. For problems that fit the paradigm, EMYCIN provides a well-developed set of user-interface facilities that make rapid system prototyping possible. EMYCIN is not well suited for other types of problems, including planning, design, constraint satisfaction, or model-driven reasoning. EMYCIN's inference engine supports a nearly exhaustive depth-first, backward-chaining strategy. This control strategy enables the system to maintain a well-structured dialogue with the expert-system user and to explore potential solutions in a structured way, making explanation and knowledge acquisition easier. However, the built-in control structure also makes it difficult to process multiple goals in parallel or handle interrupts from new data, corrections to existing data, or any other form of mixed-initiative dialog. Many successful expert systems have been written in EMYCIN, including the original system MYCIN [Shortliffe 76] from which EMYCIN was actually derived, and PUFF [Freiherr 80]. Related work includes augmentations for knowledge acquisition (TEIRESIAS) [Davis, Lenat 80] and intelligent tutoring (GUIDON) [Clancey 82]. Descriptions of all these systems have been collected in a single book [Buchanan, Shortliffe 84].

Data Memory in EMYCIN

The basic objects, called *contexts* in EMYCIN, can have any number of predefined attributes with a predefined acceptable range of values. New attributes and values may be defined interactively as rules are added to the program. Facts in EMYCIN are represented as attribute-object-value triples with an associated certainty factor. There may be multiple facts for a particular context and attribute, with the certainty factor giving the strength of belief in the value. The certainties range from -1 to $+1$ with negative numbers representing a measure of disbelief in assertions about attribute values and non-negatives representing the strength with which an assertion is believed to be true. The context objects are organized into a hierarchy called the *context tree*, with simple inheritance of attribute values.

Rule Memory in EMYCIN

A rule in EMYCIN typically has an antecedent, the left-hand side, that is a Boolean combination of predicates on tuples, and a single predicate as its consequent, or right-hand side. The antecedent is in conjunctive normal form (a conjunction of disjunctions). Each predicate is either a standard function relating to the values of a particular attribute for a particular context or a user-defined LISP function. Rules can have an associated certainty value that represents the expert's certainty that the inference will be valid, given that the antecedent is known with certainty. This simple format for rules makes a good explanation facility easier to implement. There is no pattern matching in EMYCIN rules other than matching against the current context, so to facilitate iterating over sets of objects that meet certain conditions, the language includes some mapping predicates.

Control in EMYCIN

The control structure of EMYCIN is primarily depth-first, exhaustive backward chaining. The goal of the system at any time is to determine the value of an attribute. To do this, all rules whose right-hand sides relate to that particular attribute are retrieved and applied in turn until the certainty reaches 1 or until all rules have been used. If no rules are relevant, or if the certainty of the conclusion is below a threshold, the user optionally may be asked to supply the attribute's value. The user may also be asked for an attribute value before rules are tried. Often the rule's antecedent requires knowing the value of another attribute that is not yet known with a certainty of 1. In this case, the backward-chaining technique is used to determine the relevant rules to try.

Rule applicability in EMYCIN is precomputed. A list of rules with relevant consequents is maintained for each goal of confirming the value of an attribute.

The rules are applied in an arbitrary order; if necessary, all will be applied eventually, so no conflict resolution is necessary to choose among rules. An attempt is made to find a chain of rules whose conclusions have certainty factors of 1 (such as asking the user about lab-test results) so that unnecessary searching is eliminated.

The Environment in EMYCIN

EMYCIN includes an explanation system, tracing and debugging facilities, and support for maintaining test-case libraries. A special rule language editor makes it easy to specify rules in a high-level language and check them for contradiction and subsumption. The explanations provide answers to questions about *why* the system is requesting a particular attribute value, *how* the system will determine a value, and *what* conclusions were made. Questions about why a question was *not* asked or why a conclusion was *not* made are also allowed. The user can phrase questions in a restricted, English-like language. The answers are facts in EMYCIN's database, English descriptions of the rules, or a trace of previous or potential rule applications.

Information about EMYCIN

EMYCIN is available from the Computer Science Department, Stanford University, Stanford, CA. The user's manual [van Melle et al. 81] illustrates the language with numerous examples and programming suggestions.

9.1.2 EXPERT

EXPERT [Weiss, Kulikowski 81; Weiss, Kulikowski, Safir 78] is a tool for building rule-based systems, especially for consultation programs involving diagnosis and classification. It evolved as a generalization of the CASNET/GLAUCOMA program. Applications include consultation models in ophthalmology, endocrinology, rheumatology, laboratory instrumentation, and oil-exploration advice [Weiss, Kulikowski 84]. EXPERT was designed for efficiency and portability and was therefore implemented in FORTRAN. It has many facilities to help maintain a database of test cases, empirically analyze test cases, and suggest improvements in the rules based on test-case analysis. Also, the user can ask the system for a partial diagnosis or classification interpretation at any time. A program in EXPERT is referred to as a *model*. The ability to partially specify a model facilitates rapid prototyping and model enhancement.

Data Memory in EXPERT

In EXPERT's data memory there is an explicit division between *findings* and *hypotheses*. Findings are observations or measurements with values of true, false, unavailable, or a numerical value. Hypotheses are inferences made by the system, either final classifications or intermediate states, and have a confidence range attached.

Rule Memory in EXPERT

Rules are divided into three classes based on the type of relationship that is being defined: FF rules deduce findings from findings; FH rules deduce hypotheses from findings; and HH rules deduce hypotheses from hypotheses and findings. Hypotheses appearing in the left-hand side of rules have an associated confidence range. Those appearing in the right-hand side of rules have an associated confidence value. Rules are ordered within the rule classification by the programmer. For efficiency, the programmer can group rules according to the context of some finding.

Control in EXPERT

The system designer creates lists of questions that result in observations and measurements supplied by the user. The questions may be organized in questionnaires, which the system will ask in the specified order. Alternatively, EXPERT has a number of heuristics for determining the order. The HH rules are evaluated, in the actual order specified by the programmer, once for each cycle of reasoning. Whenever new findings are received, first the FF rules relating to the new findings are triggered, followed by the FH rules relating to the new findings. Then all the HH rules are reevaluated. If the left-hand side of a rule is satisfied by working memory, the hypotheses of the right-hand side are added to memory. All applicable rules will be executed on a given cycle. If there are several rules concluding the same hypothesis with different confidence levels, the maximum of the absolute value of the levels is associated with the hypothesis in memory. Thus the control strategy is basically data-driven with rules evaluated in order and all matching rules fired. The left-hand sides of rules are matched against memory while the right-hand side findings and hypotheses are added to memory. After a cycle, a decision must be made concerning which questions to ask, or which questionnaire to use. Strategies used by EXPERT include selecting the least costly question or questions related to the hypotheses that currently appear most likely.

The Environment in EXPERT

Rules in EXPERT are written in a high-level language and then compiled into an efficient FORTRAN program. Interactive facilities help maintain a database of test cases, analyze test cases empirically, and suggest improvements in the rules based on test-case analysis; in addition there are editing and explanation utilities.

Information about EXPERT

EXPERT is available from the Computer Science Department of Rutgers University, New Brunswick, NJ. The developers of the language have written *A Practical Guide to Designing Expert Systems* [Weiss, Kulikowski 84], which discusses the language more thoroughly with emphasis on the design of an expert system.

9.1.3 KAS

KAS (**K**nowledge **A**cquisition **S**ystem) is another tool to help construct rule-based diagnosis systems. It evolved from the PROSPECTOR [Duda, Gaschnig, Hart 79] system and has also been used to build a chemical-spill source-location system and a water-flow prediction system [Reboh 81]. Systems built with KAS usually have good user interfaces. In some versions the user communicates in a restricted natural language and can volunteer information at any time during the consultation, define synonyms, and ask for summary and trace information. The design of KAS is particularly suited for the class of expert systems that involve diagnostic tasks, but is difficult to adapt to other uses.

Data Memory in KAS

KAS does not have a distinct data memory. The presence or absence of objects is reflected by numerical values attached to nodes in a semantic net, as described in the next section.

Rule Memory in KAS

KAS does not have rules as such. Rather, numerical probability values (which could be thought of as activations) are propagated through a network of conceptual- and logical-structure nodes. The nodes are, in a sense, the left-hand sides of rules. In some ways they are conceptually similar to EMYCIN rules, but they are represented in partitioned semantic networks, and arbitrary n-ary relationships can be represented. The objects of interest are situations and their probability of being present. A probability value is associated with every assertion. Bayesian reasoning is used to propagate probability values. Because of the fixed-network representation, there is no notion of multiple instantiations of rules. There is however, an *or* node at which the highest probability alternative is taken. This lack of instantiation means that no complex symbolic pattern matching is done. Thus techniques that can be used in OPS5 to find all instances of a structure or rule do not apply. However, the system can call itself recursively on subclassification problems. Also, there can be an enabling context partition that must be satisfied before a rule fires. In some cases where nodes are semantically similar based on semantic-net definition, semantic matching is done so that probabilities are assigned properly and propagated; all possible matches are used in this context.

Control in KAS

The control in KAS is a form of best-first search. Each time the user supplies more information, the consequences of those new facts are propagated forward to give all affected nodes new values. The system tries first to identify the best top-level hypothesis and then to determine the best questions to establish that hypothesis or determine a better value for it. (The user can always overrule the system's choice of the current hypothesis.) This resembles, but is more sophisticated than, backward chaining. If answers to the questions cause the rating of the hypothesis to change, then a new best hypothesis may be selected.

The user can volunteer information at any time but typically volunteers that which is obviously relevant at the beginning of the consultation session. Statements are translated into a semantic net and matched against the network representing the knowledge base. Exact or partial matches (where a specialization or generalization of a concept is matched) are used to update the certainty values, and forward chaining is used to propagate the implications of the new certainty values.

Some rule antecedents are questions that can be asked of the user. Others are more complex situations that must be established by applying other rules. Thus one use of the backward chaining is to set subgoals for establishing other situations. Backward chaining is also used to establish contexts needed before even deciding if a rule about the current hypothesis is applicable.

The Environment in KAS

KAS has a structure-oriented editor to build and modify the rules, which are represented in partitioned semantic networks [Hendrix 79]. The facilities protect against illegal parameter arguments and disconnected sections of the network, provide defaults for some attribute values, and keep track of unfinished work. The editor can be invoked at any time, even in the middle of a consultation system, to modify the knowledge base. It has facilities for running libraries of test cases.

Information about KAS

KAS is available from SRI International, Menlo Park, CA. The final report for the PROSPECTOR system [Duda et al. 79] defines KAS, and more detail is given in a thesis about knowledge-engineering tools in the PROSPECTOR environment [Reboh 81].

9.1.4 OPS5

OPS5 is a general-purpose production-system language that has been described in great detail in previous chapters. The main advantages of OPS5 are its stability and efficiency; it has been used to implement a number of moderately large expert systems. Examples of systems written in OPS5 include R1 and XSEL [J. McDermott 83], MUD [Kahn, McDermott 84], and TALIB [Kim, McDermott, Siewiorek 84]. ACE [Vesoder et al. 83] was written in OPS4, an earlier but fairly similar version of OPS5. The main disadvantages of OPS5 are its lack of a well-developed user interface, special editing or explanation facilities, and aids for maintaining test-case libraries. Some recent implementations have better editing utilities and facilities for maintaining different states of the system, including working memory, to facilitate backtracking and testing. The price of flexible control is that problem-solving methods such as backward chaining have to be programmed explicitly when they are desired.

A whole family of OPS languages has evolved. Each new version of OPS has placed increasing emphasis on speed and on the incorporation of control and data-structuring constructs from traditional imperative languages such as PASCAL and C.

Data Memory in OPS5

The OPS5 language has only one data memory, *working memory*. This memory, which can be of arbitrary size, consists of a set of units called *working memory elements*, ordered by their time of creation or most recent modification. Structured data types are attribute-value elements (scalars with field names) and vectors (sequences of scalars stored in contiguous slots). There can be only one vector attribute in a working memory element.

Rule Memory in OPS5

In OPS5 there is only one uniform space for rules. OPS5 provides moderately complex pattern matching, with predicates for testing equality and magnitude of scalars. Variables are provided to permit matching between conditions and to allow the values to be used on the right-hand side. Variables are not typed. In some versions of the system, rules can be created at run time.

Control in OPS5

Two conflict-resolution strategies are provided, based primarily on the recency of the working memory elements that match rule conditions and on the specificity of conditions (measured by the number of tests performed). The MEA strategy allows the recency of the first condition element to dominate, making it easy to implement depth-first search using goal elements as the first condition. The LEX strategy gives no special preference to the first condition element.

The Environment in OPS5

The OPS5 interpreter has been highly optimized. The Rete algorithm [Forgy 82] efficiently finds all rule instantiations for each cycle by quickly computing bindings between variables on the left-hand side of rules and the elements in working memory.

The OPS5 environment provides modest debugging and tracing facilities. Rules can be printed, all of working memory or any subset matching a specified pattern can be printed, the conflict set can be requested before the selected rule is fired, and the list of matches to a rule can be inspected. There are two levels of tracing — listing the names of the rules that fire, or listing the rules that fire plus all the changes to working memory. Also, the system can be run forward or backward in increments of one cycle (up to a limit in the backward direction).

Information about OPS5

OPS5 is available from the Computer Science Department at Carnegie-Mellon University, Pittsburgh, PA, and from Digital Equipment Corporation as well as several other sources. While each implementation has a user's manual, the most complete definition of the language is in the original manual by Charles Forgy [Forgy 81].

9.1.5 ROSIE

ROSIE (**R**ule-**O**riented **S**ystem for **I**mplementing **E**xpertise) is a programming environment for building expert systems. As a language, it provides both standard programming constructs (e.g., procedure calls, common data types) and special constructs important for expert-systems work (e.g., patterns, classes, demons, predicates). It permits (but does not require) solutions that use the rule-system paradigm; there is no inherent conflict-resolution strategy or inference method, but rule sets may specify one of several execution orders. ROSIE code appears quite English-like, making the system's underlying knowledge easily accessible to both user and programmer. An environment patterned after that provided by INTERLISP also facilitates system building and makes access to the underlying system facilities more convenient than in most expert-system tools.

Data Memory in ROSIE

In ROSIE, data and assertions are stored in a relational database of n-ary relations. ROSIE code maps English-like syntactic structures into database access functions. The database can be accessed directly by specifying ROSIE actions to the top level of the interpreter or by building collections of actions (rules and rule sets) to be run under procedural control. In addition to the global database, the user may define an arbitrary number of mutually exclusive additional databases; the search order among databases is under the user's control.

Rule Memory in ROSIE

Rules can be written as individual pieces of static knowledge that are then applied to the database by a user-provided interpreter. In addition, sequences of "*if . . ., then*" rules and simple or iterative actions can be grouped into rule sets. Rule sets can be treated as normal programs, as recognizers triggered by conditions in the database, as predicates, or as generators of classes of elements.

Control in ROSIE

Little explicit control is provided other than that supported by procedure, generator, and predicate calls. The language does support a fast and conceptually clear mechanism for reasoning over hierarchies of relations.

The Environment in ROSIE

ROSIE is implemented in INTERLISP, and the environment reflects this. Features include a saved history list and a *redo* command, automatic recompilation of edited rule sets, and some file package facilities. The programmer may integrate INTERLISP code into an application system (through system rule sets) when efficiency considerations demand it.

Information about ROSIE

ROSIE is available from the Rand Corporation, Santa Monica, CA. The user's manual [Fain et al. 81] should be supplemented with a later report, *Programming in* ROSIE [Fain et al. 82], which contains numerous examples.

9.1.6 YAPS

YAPS (**Y**et **A**nother **P**roduction **S**ystem) is similar to OPS5 and its predecessor OPS4, but it allows a mixture of data-driven and object-oriented programming. It is a flexible, general-purpose production system but does not have a well-developed user interface.

Data Memory in YAPS

YAPS allows multiple databases whose elements can be any arbitrarily nested list expression — they are not restricted to a flat structure as in OPS5.

Variables can also match against *flavored* objects (complex record-like objects similar to those used in object-oriented languages). There is no type checking.

Rule Memory in YAPS

A set of rules is associated with each database. Rules may be used in multiple databases but are encoded in one discrimination net. A YAPS pattern is an arbitrarily nested list expression with variables. Tests can involve any number of variables and may use any LISP function. Negated conditions are allowed, and LISP functions that return a Boolean value can serve as condition elements. Part of the YAPS philosophy is allowing the user to use whatever LISP expressions are convenient. A new rule can be added to the memory at any time, but, as in OPS5, any fact already in the memory will not be compared with the left-hand side of the new rule.

Control in YAPS

The conflict-resolution strategy in YAPS is similar to MEA in OPS5 except that instead of using the working memory element matching the first pattern on the left-hand side to determine priorities, YAPS uses any elements that have the word "goal" in the first position. The user may change this key word to any other or may indicate that the elements should be considered equally. In the latter case, the control structure is identical to the LEX control used in OPS5.

YAPS allows sets of rules to function as subsystems or *demons*. Another program can be the top-level controller, but whenever there is an outstanding goal to be solved and rules that are ready to fire, the rules that handle the goal run automatically.

The Environment in YAPS

The YAPS run-time environment is similar to that of OPS5. It has trace and break capabilities and can print full matching information about rules in the conflict set, but does not give partial match information. The YAPS interpreter does not use the Rete algorithm as OPS5 does, but it has also been optimized. Identical sequences of condition elements are shared, tests are performed as soon as bindings are available, and an efficient implementation of FLAVORS is used. The rules can be compiled by the normal LISP compiler.

Information about YAPS

YAPS is available from the Computer Science Department of the University of Maryland, College Park, MD. The user's manual [Allen 82] is based on a version of the system slightly older than the one described above.

9.2 RULE-BASED COGNITIVE MODELING TOOLS

In this section we describe two languages that are used primarily to construct models of human information processing. GRAPES is basically a backward-chaining system that has been used for intelligent tutoring systems and modeling students learning to program. PRISM is a general system that provides mechanisms to implement a wide variety of production system models.

9.2.1 GRAPES

GRAPES is a **G**oal **R**estricted **P**roduction **S**ystem constructed for modeling goal-directed problem solving. GRAPES is a backward-chaining system, like EMYCIN. Tasks like physics and mathematics problem solving, tutoring, and modeling student-level programming [Anderson, Farrell, Sauers 84] fit easily into the GRAPES architecture. GRAPES differs from many other rule-based systems in its use of goals as a separate memory, its multiple segment variables in matching, its rule action packets, and its knowledge compilation learning mechanisms.

Data Memory in GRAPES

GRAPES has two distinct data memories, working memory and goal memory. A third data memory, long-term memory, contains a subset of the elements in working memory, namely those that are (relatively) permanent and unchanging. The GRAPES working memory is similar to that of OPS5 except that the only data type is the list. The goal memory is stored as an *and/or* tree. Each goal has a name and a list of attribute-value pairs called *parameters*.

Rule Memory in GRAPES

GRAPES rules are organized into packets according to which goal they achieve. Each rule has a group of *goal parameters* and a group of *tests*. The goal-parameter list of the rule consists of atomic attributes and pattern values that must match the current goal description. All rules that can achieve a given type of goal are grouped together by their *action* parameter. When the system creates a goal to *solve* a problem, it retrieves all the rules that have an action of *solve* and tries to match them. It first matches their goal parameters against the current goal and then matches their tests. There are three types of tests available on the left-hand side: goal tests, working memory tests, and function tests. Goal tests can test against goals other than the current goal. Working memory tests are similar to the left-hand-side tests of OPS5. Like the *test* section of a YAPS rule, function tests in GRAPES are LISP predicates that must return a true value if the rule is to succeed.

GRAPES provides regular variables and multiple-segment variables and is therefore slower than OPS5 and other languages that do not have multiple-segment variables. The matcher is a data-flow matcher similar to the Rete matcher used by OPS5, except that partial bindings between elements are not stored between recognize-act cycles. Negative matching and a primitive form of partial matching are available.

Control in GRAPES

Control in GRAPES is largely achieved through the use of goal tests. There exists one special goal, the *current goal*, which is the focus of attention. All rules that reference the current goal must have the same *action* parameter and must match the rest of the parameters of the goal before working memory matching occurs. Thus GRAPES's control is a good example of rule filtering.

Once matchings are found, the conflict-resolution principles dictate which single instantiation to fire. Because of GRAPES's segment variables, there may be more than one way for a rule to match the same data. Conflict resolution is performed in the following order: refraction, recency computed in number of cycles, working memory and goal test specificity, and then arbitrary choice.

The Environment in GRAPES

The GRAPES environment varies with the implementation, but in most versions users can print out bindings, look at the result of conflict resolution, print out rules, goals, or working memory, display the conflict set, examine partial bindings, break at individual goals or rules, or simply interrupt to create a higher command level. The GRAPES tracer prints the goal tree as it is being constructed, along with the instantiations that fired at each goal. The user can specify several levels of tracing. GRAPES has no rule editor. There is no way to run the system forward or backward a given number of rule cycles, but the user can restore the initial state of the system and restart without reloading the rules and initial memory.

A part of the architecture that makes GRAPES different from most other production systems is its knowledge-compilation learning mechanisms, which are in a separate package and can be loaded when needed. The learning mechanisms are *proceduralization* and *composition*. The proceduralization mechanism automatically produces rules that are more specific and hence involve less matching. The composition mechanism collapses sequences of rule applications according to the structure imposed by the goal tree.

Information About GRAPES

GRAPES was developed at the Department of Computer Science, Carnegie-Mellon University, Pittsburgh, PA. It is being distributed by Advanced Computer

Tutoring (ACT), Inc., Pittsburgh, PA. A manual [Sauers, Farrell 82] is included with each copy of the system.

9.2.2 PRISM

PRISM, **P**rogram for **R**esearch **I**nto **S**elf-**M**odifying systems, is a production system that has a flexible control strategy focusing on psychological modeling and learning mechanisms. The flexibility is accomplished through a set of parameters that affect the system's behavior. In fact, PRISM is best viewed as a *class* of production system languages, with the user specifying the desired architecture through parameter settings. The learning mechanisms include strengthening, designation, generalization, and discrimination, and are very similar in spirit to those found in Anderson, Kline, and Beasley's ACT formalism [Anderson, Kline, Beasley 77]. Several systems have been written in PRISM, including one, SAGE, that learns search heuristics [Langley 83].

Data Memory in PRISM

PRISM has two related declarative memories — working memory and long-term memory; the former is viewed as the active portion of the latter (though elements in working memory need not be present in long-term memory, and vice versa). Both memories contain elements represented as list structures, but links between elements in long-term memory can also be stored, producing a propositional network. Rules match against elements in working memory. Each of these elements has an associated activation, which can be used during conflict resolution and in determining when an element should be forgotten. Each element in long-term memory has an associated *trace strength*, which is used in directing spreading activation, the process for retrieving elements from long-term memory and adding them to working memory. PRISM includes parameters that determine the default level of activation, the default trace strength, the rate at which activation decays, and the details of the spreading activation mechanism.

Rule Memory in PRISM

PRISM has a single rule memory that matches against elements in working memory. Rules may contain not only positive conditions and single negated conditions, but also negated conjunctions and negations embedded in negations. PRISM uses a variant of the Rete matcher that allows tests for constants, length of elements, variable bindings, and single-segment variables occurring at the ends of lists. The user can define new variable types, which are compiled into the Rete network along with other tests. New rules can be learned through *designation* (in which one rule creates another in its action side), through *discrimination* (in which good and bad instantiations of a rule are compared, generating variants based on the differences that are found), and through *generalization* (in which a more general rule is created whenever two specific rules with identical forms are found). Each rule has an associated *strength*, which can be altered during the learning process and used during conflict resolution. Rules can be automatically strengthened whenever they are applied, whenever they are relearned by any of the learning mechanisms, or explicitly by the action side of a rule. Parameters determine the rate at which strengthening occurs as well as the degree to which rules are weakened when they lead to an error.

Control in PRISM

The Rete matcher efficiently computes all true instantiations of all rules, paving the way for flexibility during conflict resolution. The details of the conflict-resolution process are determined by parameters for *ordering* instantiations in the conflict set, for *selecting* one or more instantiations based on the resulting orderings, and for *refraction*. Different functions are available for inclusion in these parameters, making it simple to generate a variety of different strategies. Typical ordering functions are based on rule strength and on the activation of matched elements; typical selection strategies involve choosing the best instantiations along a given ordering dimension and selecting all instantiations above a certain threshold. The default refraction strategy eliminates all instantiations that applied on the previous cycle, though other strategies are available.

PRISM's capability for altering the conflict-resolution process leads naturally to two styles of programming search methods. If rules are allowed to apply only one at a time and the activation of each element decays over time, then a depth-first search (with automatic backup) results. However, if rules are allowed to fire in parallel, then a breadth-first search strategy occurs.

The Environment in PRISM

PRISM provides modest facilities to aid the user in the debugging process. The contents of rule memory, long-term memory, and working memory can be printed out before and after runs. Two parameters control the printing of trace information during runs, allowing the user to examine the contents of working memory and the conflict set, as well as the matched conditions and actions of rules selected for application. PRISM also prints out newly learned rules and the name of the mechanism that generated them. However, no break package is included, and the user cannot examine partial matches of rules.

Information About PRISM

PRISM was developed at the Department of Psychology, Carnegie-Mellon University, Pittsburgh, PA. A user's manual [Langley, Neches 81] and a survey article [Langley 83] are available.

9.3 LOGIC PROGRAMMING TOOLS FOR EXPERT SYSTEMS

PROLOG and DUCK are both examples of a genre of languages that are based on predicate logic. They are known as *logic programming languages*. PROLOG stands for **PRO**gramming in **LOG**ic; DUCK stands for de**DUC**tive retrieval. Logic programs consist primarily of descriptive definitions of the relations and functions to be computed, with the facts or data of the program expressed as predicates. Like the rule-based languages described previously, logic languages view computation as controlled inference. The control mechanisms are based on resolution [Robinson 79] and a pattern-matching operation called unification. Such programming languages have been chosen for a variety of applications including relational databases, mathematical logic, understanding natural language, architectural design, and expert systems.

9.3.1 DUCK

DUCK is a LISP-based language for writing predicate-calculus rules. In contrast with PROLOG, it allows a flexible mixture of problem-solving styles including logic programming with unification and backtracking, and applicative and imperative symbolic processing. DUCK is written in NISP, a portable LISP dialect, allowing full use of NISP macros and the underlying LISP environment for program structure, debugging, and run-time support. DUCK programs using only the NISP macros are highly portable, with system support for modifying a particular program to conform to the various LISP dialect conventions. DUCK can be used as a strongly typed language, although type checking can be suppressed.

Data Memory in DUCK

As in other logic languages, there is no separate data memory. The DUCK database includes all the logic formulas currently believed by the program. Formulas that are not rules, as defined in the next section, are called *literal assertions* and may be predicates on variables or individuals of the program. DUCK allows arbitrary list structures as individuals, including the constants defined for the underlying LISP system.

Rule Memory in DUCK

The rule memory for DUCK is a part of the database. The two basic rule types are forward-chaining rules and backward-chaining rules. A forward-chaining rule follows the pattern *(–> p q)*, where –> indicates the rule is to be treated as a forward-chaining rule, *p* is the premise of the rule, and *q* is the consequent of the rule. The rule is read "*If p, then q.*" Here is an example of a forward-chaining rule:

```
(-> (IS ?X MAN) (MORTAL ?X))
```

This can be read, "If ?X is a man, then ?X is a mortal." A backward-chaining rule follows the pattern *(<– q p)*, where <– indicates the rule is to be treated as a backward-chaining rule, *q* is the consequent of the rule, and *p* is the premise of the rule. The backward-chaining rule is read, "*If* there is a goal, *q*, *then* establish a subgoal, *p*." The premise can be a conjunction of predicates.

Control in DUCK

The control of a LISP/DUCK program is highly program dependent. There are LISP functions for entering DUCK and special predicates in DUCK for entering LISP. Although there are language features that allow the use of DUCK as a general-purpose programming language, the intent is to use DUCK for appropriate deductive inferences and database maintenance and use LISP for the rest of the computation.

The forward-chaining rules are data-driven rules. When such a rule is entered in the database, the premise is checked by the unification algorithm for matches in the database. Each match triggers the firing of the rule, causing the consequent (with appropriate variable substitutions) to be added as a literal assertion to the database. When a new literal assertion is added to the database, all forward-chaining rules that unify with the new assertion are triggered. Each assertion in the database is tagged with a justification describing its origin. The justification is used for truth maintenance and is available to the programmer for creating explanations. Later, if the basis for an assertion is removed from the database, the assertion may be automatically suppressed. In addition to augmenting the database, a forward-chaining rule may have a consequent resulting in the substitution of a new predicate for the matched one.

The backward-chaining rules are executed in response to a request to satisfy a goal. The rules are not considered in the order in which they appear in the program, but may be executed in an arbitrary order or in an order determined by the programmer. Literal assertions matching the goal will be selected before any backward-chaining rules are applied. The unification algorithm is used to obtain the set of rules and assertions that apply to a particular goal. The subgoals are developed in a left-to-right fashion as in PROLOG. DUCK maintains a description of the goal-generation process to control backtracking when subgoals fail or when all answers to a query are desired. Special functions can create side effects such as adding assertions to the database during backward chaining.

There are several other representations for implications in DUCK, combining aspects of the forward- and backward-chaining rules. For example, when a rule in the format *(−<p q)* is asserted, it causes a backward-chaining action to find all instances of *p* and then asserts *q* for each one found. Built-in predicates and pseudo predicates affect both control and the power of the language, extending DUCK beyond the orthodox predicate calculus.

The Environment in DUCK

The DUCK environment includes an editor, a workspace manager, various levels of type checking, and a sophisticated data-management system. The interactive type editor allows the programmer to define new symbols as they are used in assertions, associating English descriptions in addition to class and type information. A *walk* mode allows the programmer to walk though the type hierarchy, the predicates and functions, redefining where necessary. A rule editor allows the in-core editing of a specific rule followed by optional type checking. An explicit instruction must be given to save the results of changing the declarations of the symbols or the rules. The workspace manager, actually a part of NISP, supplies utilities for saving and retrieving programs (rule sets) and the associated types and objects. The *data pool* facility allows the maintenance of local databases used to represent hypothetical worlds, time sequences, and packets of special-purpose information. Finally, rules and predicates may be traced with the trace available for debugging or for explanations of deductions. A DUCK program can be run in LISP mode, DUCK mode, or walk mode. In DUCK mode it is assumed that the user is entering either special commands, general deductive goals, or some special LISP form. In walk mode the user has a wide variety of tracing and editing tools directly available. Walk mode can be entered to trace and understand a particular system behavior encountered in DUCK mode. While the environment is rich with user-friendly utilities, the DUCK programmer is expected to be a good LISP programmer.

Information about DUCK

DUCK, developed at the Computer Science Department of Yale University, is available from Smart Systems Technology in McLean, VA. The user's manual [D. McDermott 83] assumes that the reader is a LISP programmer.

9.3.2 PROLOG

Traditionally, computations in PROLOG are viewed as refutations of a goal, using a rule of inference called *resolution*, which is similar to *modus ponens*. However, PROLOG also can be viewed as a backward-chaining rule-based language with very specific information on what to do next. All computation in PROLOG is a result of queries to a database of facts and "*if* . . ., *then*" rules with a single consequent. Rules by themselves also have a declarative semantics in that each rule is an (implicitly universally quantified) sentence in Horn-logic. While PROLOG works with a depth-first control regime, some other logic programming languages make different commitments: Logic programming does not call for a particular control regime; rather, an implementer can choose any reasonable strategy.

PROLOG has been widely used in Europe as a vehicle for implementing expert systems, especially expert systems in pharmacology. Examples of its use include prediction of biological activities of peptides, prediction of drug interactions, and drug design aids. Small experimental versions of EMYCIN and of a fault-finder program have been developed in PROLOG [Hammond 82], and explanation capabilities have been explored [Walker 83].

For the purposes of this discussion we are considering PROLOG as a production-system language and will examine some of its distinctive features. Please bear in mind, however, that PROLOG is a general-purpose language and so is not committed to a particular memory architecture or recognize-act cycle.

Data Memory in PROLOG

In PROLOG there is only one form of memory: the global memory. Data, called *facts*, are represented as special kinds of rules (logical implications with antecedents equal to "true") that express relationships between objects. Examples of facts are:

```
likes(jessica,jeremy).
father(william, margaret).
human(william).
```

Rule Memory

A rule is of the form

R0 IF *R1* AND *R2* . . . AND *Rn*. $(n >= 0)$

R0 is called the *head* of the rule, corresponding to the consequent or right-hand side of an OPS5 rule, and "*R1* AND *R2*... AND *Rn*" is called the *body*, corresponding to the antecedent or left-hand side of an OPS5 rule.

Each *Ri* is called a *term* and is a function of any number of arguments that can also be terms. A term is a generalized record structure. Examples of rules are as follows:

```
brother-of(X,Y) IF male(X) AND parents-of(X,U,V) AND
  parents-of(Y,U,V)
grandfather-of(X,Y) IF father(X,Z) AND parent-of(Z,Y)
```

If $n = 0$, the rule is considered to assert a fact because the reading of such a rule is simply "*R0* IF *true*."

Control in PROLOG

The heart of PROLOG's inference engine is the unification algorithm. Given any two terms, the *most general unifier* is a set of instantiations for the variables in the two terms such that the two terms become syntactically the same. A variable, once instantiated, can never be changed (unless the object it is bound to contains an uninstantiated variable). In general, unification can lead to the instantiation of variables in either of the two terms and is hence a very powerful form of pattern matching. In PROLOG, unification is the sole mechanism for data selection, data creation, data assignment, and parameter passing.

Given a goal G, the inference engine tries to *prove* G by looking for a rule in its database such that G can unify with the consequent of the rule, say with bindings *s1*. The rules are searched in the order they appear in the program. When the inference engine achieves a unification of a consequent with the goal, it then tries to prove the body (antecedent) of the rule (if any) by proving each of the subgoals in the body from *left to right* after applying the set of substitutions, *s1*, to them. If at any time it is not possible to prove a goal (for instance, if there is no rule in the database with a consequent that matches the goal), then the inference engine backtracks, trying to resatisfy the previous goal to generate a new set of bindings so that the current goal can be called again with this different set of bindings. The result of the computation is simply the composition of the set of bindings introduced until all subgoals are satisfied. This mechanism corresponds to a depth-first search in the *and/or* subtree of goal satisfaction, where the leftmost available branch is taken out of a node. The *and* nodes represent the terms of the antecedent of a particular rule, all of which must be satisfied. The *or* nodes represent all the rules whose consequents unify with the goal, in order of their appearance in the program.

Thus in PROLOG the conflict-resolution strategy is built into the system. At each node (*and* or *or*) the path out of the node (if any) is prescribed. There are syntactic structures that can affect this control and allow a small measure of control to the programmer.

It is worth noting that the use of unification for invoking rules implies that any subset of argument values in the goal could be instantiated. Unification instantiates those that are not and checks those that are.

Primitives are available to control search through the tree by pruning away alternatives at and above a particular node, hence causing the failure of any attempt to resatisfy this goal. This mechanism enables the user to control backtracking and allows introduction of the notions of *if-then-else* rules and *negation* as failure to prove a goal. However, especially for novice programmers, it is sometimes difficult to visualize the behavior of the inference engine when pruning mechanisms are used.

The Environment of PROLOG

Since there is no way in PROLOG to maintain global state across calls to prove top-level goals, it is sometimes necessary to add facts or rules to the database at run time. This is in contrast to OPS5-like systems, where making changes to the working memory is a basic and essential operation. In PROLOG additions to the database are done by calls to the system predicates, which are extremely slow. Even more seriously, changing the database means that the theory from which logical deductions are being made is being changed dynamically. As yet no adequate semantics has been proposed for these operations, so they must be regarded as ad hoc, though very useful, features of the language. There is no truth-maintenance system or tagging of assertions with justifications as in DUCK.

Many versions of PROLOG come with a standard break package and a debugger. Rule invocations can be traced at different levels of detail, breakpoints can be set, and, at times, computation can be reattempted from some previous point. The debugger is very useful and quite extensively used. PROLOG also provides the user with some meta-logical primitives which can be used to query the status of a variable (e.g., whether it is currently bound or not and, if bound, whether it is bound to an atom or a number). PROLOG programs can be run interpretively or can be compiled. Compiled and interpreted code can be mixed.

Information about PROLOG

Versions of PROLOG are available from many sources including the Department of Artificial Intelligence, University of Edinburgh, Edinburgh, Scotland, and Logic Programming Associates Ltd., Milford, CT. While the language varies from implementation to implementation, *Programming in* PROLOG [Clocksin,

Mellish 82] contains a complete description with numerous examples and exercises.

9.4 HYBRID PROGRAMMING TOOLS FOR EXPERT SYSTEMS

Often a domain area is not appropriate for a single representation model and a single inference model. Constructs that are clean and easy to understand in LISP can be very clumsy and obtuse when programmed in PROLOG or another rule-based language. Language designers have recognized this need for multiple forms of representation by creating systems that combine, with varying degrees of integration, the models of applicative programming, rule-based programming, object-oriented programming, and procedural programming. While there are many such systems currently on the market, we discuss only four. The first two systems are primarily combinations of object-oriented programming and rule-based programming, while the last two are combinations of rule-based programming and procedural programming. The first system, KEE™, is a stable, commercial product that takes advantage of the special environments provided by the LISP machine architectures. The second system, LOOPS, while used commercially, is a research vehicle for scientists interested in exploring a wide variety of knowledge representations, their interactions, and appropriate applications. LOOPS also takes advantage of a rich, multi-windowing, graphics interface. New versions of LISP that include an object-oriented extension called FLAVORS provide the environment for a system designer to develop a hybrid environment unique to the needs of an internal problem domain, rather than to adopt a hybrid solution of others. The YAPS system includes a FLAVORS extension, for example. Such a venture is nontrivial, as exploration of existing systems will demonstrate. The third system, OPS83, is based on experience with OPS5 but also includes strong typing and procedural control over rule sets. The fourth system, S.1, is also based on experience with a previous system, EMYCIN, and also includes stronger typing and more procedural control than its predecessor.

9.4.1 KEE

The KEE™ (Knowledge Engineering Environment™) system[1] is a hybrid AI tool that combines frame-based knowledge representation, rule-based reasoning, LISP, interactive graphics, and active values. Object-oriented programming provides a unifying principle for these different methodologies. The KEE system

[1] KEE and Knowledge Engineering Environment are trademarks of Intellicorp.

can be applied to a wide variety of problem types. Problems with rich object spaces that can take advantage of the inheritance of properties of objects are best suited to the object-oriented paradigm.

Data Memory in the KEE System

The KEE system's data memory is a frame system organized by objects. The user can declare generic objects and instances of these generic objects will automatically inherit attributes. The KEE system supports entry of information by prompting for names and attributes of objects. Experienced users can edit objects in a template-based editor. Both rule sets and LISP programs can be used to find the value of an attribute. Like S.1, if no value can be ascertained by a rule set or procedural program, KEE software will ask the user to supply a value.

Rule Memory in the KEE System

Rules are very simple in form. The antecedent is a simple conjunction of predicates on attribute values. The consequent fills in the value of one or more attributes. No variable binding is allowed, and unlike EMYCIN, the KEE system has no certainty calculus. There is no global rule base as exists in OPS5. Rules are stored in the *rules* attribute of each object.

While the KEE system is running, it highlights the active rules. The true-or-false state of premises and conclusions already considered is displayed graphically. The user can examine and change the values of attributes while the system is running, since the user interface runs as a separate process.

Control in the KEE System

The default strategy is backward chaining, but the user can modify the control strategy considerably using graphic displays and active-value mechanisms. Active values are object attributes with attached demons that are invoked when a value is stored or retrieved from the attribute. When a rule concludes a value for an active-value attribute, the active value can signal an interrupt or can cause an icon to be redisplayed. The graphic displays can be activated or modified interactively during program execution, allowing the user to modify the control strategy by forcing attributes to have certain values.

The Environment in the KEE System

The KEE system is implemented on LISP machines with multi-windowing capabilities, graphic displays, and a mouse for activating and reacting to symbols on the screen. The LISP machine graphics allow the user to display and edit rules and objects easily. The user can ask *why* he or she was prompted for an answer, and the system will display the set or rules that conclude a value for the attribute in question. In addition, the line of reasoning for any set of conclusions can be shown graphically.

Information about the KEE System

The KEE system is available commercially from IntelliCorp Knowledge Systems, Menlo Park, CA.

9.4.2 LOOPS

LOOPS is a general tool for assisting knowledge-based program construction. LOOPS combines procedure-oriented (e.g., INTERLISP), object-oriented (e.g., SMALLTALK), and access-oriented (e.g., demons and attached procedures) programming paradigms with rule-based programming. The tool was developed to aid in the design and implementation of expert systems; a first example of its use is as an expert assistant for designers of integrated digital systems. LOOPS combines a good editor with powerful debugging aids. It also has mechanisms for implementing belief revision and uncertainty. The rule-oriented part of LOOPS has a number of restrictions, however. The language has explicit control structures and does not support the implicit iteration possible in OPS5 rules. LOOPS pattern matching requires an explicit function call. Rules can return only a single value or have side effects. Finally, rules must first be compiled into LISP, which must then be compiled to obtain efficient running code.

Data Memory in LOOPS

The advantage of an object-oriented language is the control over the object space of the program. LOOPS has several mechanisms for defining a complex network of object structures with inheritance of features and values. Objects can be viewed from multiple perspectives and group identification, as well as from the hierarchy defined by the network. Rule sets and procedures can be associated with objects in a variety of ways. The representation of knowledge in such a system requires problem-solving strategies and programming mechanisms quite different from those in a language like OPS5, where all current object knowledge is stored in a global working memory.

Rule Memory in LOOPS

The LOOPS rule-based component organizes rules into modular sections called *rule sets*. Rule sets consist of an ordered set of rules and a control structure. A rule's left-hand side is a list of LISP expressions that are evaluated from left to right, and all must be satisfied for the rule to fire. Similarly, a rule's right-hand side is a list of expressions that are evaluated. A rule returns whatever its last expression returns, and a rule set returns whatever the last rule to fire returns. Rules and rule sets in LOOPS return values that can be used by other rule sets or by other parts of the system. Rule sets can call other rule sets on the right-hand and left-hand sides, and rule-set recursion is permitted.

Control in LOOPS

LOOPS provides a set of control structures that is more restrictive than the control allowed by conflict-resolution strategies like those in OPS5. However, because the control information is factored out of the rules, rules tend to be fairly transparent and easy to modify and maintain. The exact set of control strategies available has varied, but basically rule sets are ordered and can be cycled through in a number of ways. Either one cycle or repeated cycles may be specified while some condition holds. On each cycle, either the first rule match found or all matches found are executed. If there are repeated cycles, matching may begin either at the top of the rule set or continuing from the last rule fired. Additional constraints on individual rules, such as "fire this rule only once," can be specified to control their interaction with the strategy global to the rule set.

Rule sets in LOOPS are integrated into a many-paradigm environment. Rule sets can be invoked by sending a message to an object, or alternatively, they can be invoked as a side effect of fetching or storing an active value (a type of value with demons attached). They can also be invoked directly from LISP as functions.

The Environment in LOOPS

LOOPS includes a rule editor that provides a template for rule sets. The rule set is automatically translated into LISP code when the editor is exited. Rule sets can also be compiled into machine code through a rule-set option provided in the template. Also, LOOPS has tracing and breaking facilities for debugging rules and stepping through system execution. The system provides an *audit trail* facility for debugging rule sets, creating an explanation facility, or implementing belief revision. If the user specifies *audit mode* for a particular rule set, an audit function is invoked after a rule's left-hand side has been satisfied but before the right-hand side has been evaluated. This audit information is saved along with other meta-level information about rules and can be accessed to see why particular rules fired.

Information about LOOPS

LOOPS is available commercially from Xerox PARC, Palo Alto, CA. A user's manual [Bobrow, Stefik 83] is available.

9.4.3 OPS83

OPS83 is the latest in the OPS family of production-system languages. It is recognizably related to its predecessors, but departs radically in a number of design features. The purpose behind its design was to enable programmers to write very fast, compact, production-system applications. Rules are translated directly to machine language. An OPS83 program consists of declarations of five classes of entities: types (including the *element* type for working memory elements), global variables, functions, procedures, and rules.

The data-typing features and user-defined functions and procedures in OPS83 resemble those in modern procedural languages such as PASCAL and C. The primitive data types consist of integer, real, char, logical, and symbol. Compound types include arrays, records, and derived types. Type checking is rigorous, and there is no implicit type forcing in assignment statements. Control constructs include *if-then-else, while, for,* and *return*. OPS83 is not block structured; there is no nesting of procedure and function definitions, and the only scoping of variables is a local/global distinction.

Data Memory in OPS83

Working memory in OPS83 is very much like that of OPS5 except that working memory elements are declared with the same syntax as records. The time tag of a working memory element can be accessed by means of a built-in function.

OPS83 also provides global variables that can be accessed for reading or writing from procedures, functions, and the right-hand sides of rules, but not from the left-hand sides of rules. Their primary purpose is to retain values such as file descriptors that otherwise would have to be propagated in the parameter lists of functions and procedures whose calls are nested. Global variables were not intended to store problem-solving knowledge, and the prohibition against referencing them on the left-hand sides of rules excludes them from participating in pattern matching.

Rule Memory in OPS83

The production memory of OPS83, like that of OPS5, is a single unordered set of uniquely named rules. Although OPS83 does not partition production memory, the programmer may write conflict-resolution routines that selectively attend to subsets of the conflict set.

The left-hand side of a rule is a sequence of one or more condition elements, any of which other than the first may be negated. Non-negated condition elements may be bound to element variables. Condition elements consist of a sequence of tests on working memory elements of a specified type. These tests can involve simple comparison of attributes, using relational operators, against constants and variables, or they can be arbitrary logical expressions that may include function calls. All functions that can be invoked from the left-hand sides of rules are forbidden to have any direct or indirect side effects; thus input/output, access to global variables, and calls to external routines are excluded.

The right-hand side of a rule is syntactically identical to a procedure body. It has access to global variables and element variables that were bound on the left-hand side, as well as its own local variables. Any component of the working memory element bound to an element variable can be read anywhere in the right-hand side, but the *modify* command is required to write into an element. The *make* and *remove* commands are much the same as their OPS5 counterparts.

Control in OPS83

One procedure in each OPS83 program must bear the name *main;* this procedure is the entry point of the program. There is no counterpart to the OPS5 top level; any command-line interpreter must be provided by the user, either written in OPS83 or called externally.

OPS83 uses the Rete match algorithm to update the conflict set after each change to working memory, but performs no conflict resolution. Instead, data about the instantiations in the conflict set are made available to the programmer, who can apply any conflict-resolution algorithm to these data. A number identifying the selected instantiation is passed as the parameter to the built-in function *fire,* which executes the right-hand side of the instantiation's rule using the variable bindings established on the left-hand side.

Environment in OPS83

OPS83 is a programming language rather than a programming environment. It provides no tools for system development and debugging, but includes several built-in functions that permit the programmer to tailor a programming environment to the needs of the application.

The *use* command is a compiler directive that specifies dependency relationships among the files constituting a single OPS83 program. By means of this command, type-checking information is made available to the compiler, provided that the modules were compiled in the proper sequence. The *use* relationship is transitive; that is, its effects are inherited.

Information about OPS83

OPS83 is available commercially from Production Systems Technologies, Inc., Pittsburgh, PA. A report describing it is also available from Carnegie-Mellon University [Forgy 84].

9.4.4 S.1

S.1 is a knowledge-engineering tool that integrates a simple procedural language and a frame-based data memory with heuristic rules like those found in EMYCIN. Like EMYCIN, S.1 is best suited for classification problems in which there is a finite set of possible solutions and in which the task is to find one or more solutions for the present case. S.1 provides a more general data-memory representation than EMYCIN and also allows greater flexibility in programming control regimes.

Data Memory in S.1

Facts in S.1 are represented as n-ary functions and relations. As in EMYCIN, facts and rules can have certainty factors that range from from -1 to 1. Thus S.1's representation of facts is a generalization of EMYCIN's <context attribute value certainty> tuples. The objects and values in S.1's data memory are organized into a simple frame system. All objects are of a certain *class* or generic type. During a consultation, new objects can be created by instantiating a class. Classes of objects and hypothesis values can be organized into a hierarchy. Attributes can also be related to one another by the *subsumption relation*. For instance, the attribute *has.disk* might subsume the attribute *has.floppy.disk;* this would mean that if the computer does not have a disk, then it cannot have a floppy disk, and if the computer has a floppy disk, it definitely has a disk.

Rule Memory in S.1

Rules in S.1 are very similar to those in EMYCIN. They can contain logical combinations of conditions involving Boolean, numeric, or symbolic values and can lead to multiple conclusions. Rules can be given a certainty value that will associate a degree of belief with the inference. The certainty-factor calculus used in EMYCIN is used to find the certainty of conclusions, given the certainty of conditions. Rules can be modified independently of other forms of knowledge in the system. As in EMYCIN, there is little pattern-matching ability.

Control in S.1

S.1 contains a block-structured language similar to that provided by conventional programming languages. Control blocks are objects in S.1's frame language, and they contain a sequence of commands that must be done in a specified order. Control blocks can create an object, determine the value of an attribute for an object, seek the value of an attribute by querying the user, invoke rule sets, invoke other control blocks, and display text to the user.

A top-level control block starts off a consultation. An investment advisor, for instance, might break down the process of advising into finding the user's needs, explaining the options, getting input from the user, deciding on a stock, and explaining the results to the user. Each part of this process can be a separate control block, all of which are invoked from the top-level block. The control block that decided on what stock to buy might create an instance of a stock and then try to find out what kind of stock, how much it costs, how much to buy, and so forth. Each attribute of the stock to buy would be determined by a rule set.

The Environment in S.1

S.1 includes a multi-window development environment, multilevel tracing and breaking, consistency checking of rules, saved cases and transcripts, an explanation facility, automatic recognition of abbreviated answers, and a help facility. In most implementations S.1 has three windows: the typescript window for running a consultation, a help window that describes the context and the current options, and a LISP window. S.1 performs strong type checking of knowledge-base objects. In addition, every object includes an English slot that can be used to create a translation. In this way untrained users can get descriptions of rules, objects, attributes, and control blocks in plain English. Like EMYCIN, S.1 contains facilities for explaining *why* a question was asked, *how* any conclusion was reached, and *what* conclusions were made.

Information about S.1

S.1 is commercially available from Teknowledge, Palo Alto, CA.

APPENDIX ONE

Complete Code for Monkey and Bananas

1.1 PROGRAM DECLARATIONS AND RULES

PROBLEM STATEMENT

In a 10′ × 10′ × 10′ room, there is

- a heavy couch on the floor,
- a light ladder on the floor,
- a bunch of bananas (either suspended from the ceiling or on the couch, ladder, or floor),
- one very, very hungry monkey who is incapable of moving heavy objects, and
- the monkey's blanket.

Write a program that will read in a description of the objects and their locations in the room and produce as output a sequence of commands that give the monkey instructions that, if followed, will allow the monkey to grab the bunch of bananas.

DECLARATIONS

```
;Declarations for the Monkey and Bananas Problem
;
;  Four element classes are defined
;    phys-object represents the physical objects in the domain
;           of which there must be at least one instance with
;           name ladder in working memory;
;    monkey represents the self-propelling object in the domain,
;           of which there can only be one instance in working
;           memory at any time;
;    goal represents the goals created during problem solving
;    testcase  represents the testcases to test the program.
```

```
(literalize phys-object  ; Description of physical objects
    name                ; value must be unique for each object
                        ;  and not "nil," "floor," or "ceiling"
    at                  ; the horizontal location of phys-object
                        ;  value, by programmers' convention:
                        ;  coordinate X-Y location where X and Y are
                        ;  integers between 1 and 10 inclusive
    weight              ; one of:  "heavy" or "light"
    on                  ; if object is held by the monkey: "nil"
                        ;   in this case monkey and object must have
                        ;   same at value, and value of name
                        ;   attribute for this phys-object must be
                        ;   value of holds attribute for monkey
                        ;  else one of: "floor," "ceiling" or the
                        ;   value of the name attribute of
                        ;   some phys-object instance.
)

(literalize monkey        ; Representation for self-moving objects
    at                  ; monkey's horizontal location,
                        ;  by programmers' convention, a Cartesian
                        ;  coordinate of the form "X-Y," where X  and Y
                        ;  are integers between 1 and 10, inclusive
    on                  ; monkey's vertical location, value can be "floor"
                        ;  or the value of the name attribute of some
                        ;  phys-object instance in working memory.
                        ;  If the latter value, the at attribute
                        ;  for the monkey must be the same as the
                        ;  at attribute for that phys-object
    holds               ; object being held by the monkey,
                        ;  one of: "nil" or
                        ;   the value of the name attribute of any
                        ;   "light" phys-object, which must have same
                        ;   at value as the monkey
)

(literalize goal          ; Representation for problem-solving objects
    status              ; goal's operational status, "active" or "satisfied"
    type                ; type of goal, one of "holds," "on," "at"
    object-name         ; the name of the phys-object involved in the
                        ;  goal, if any.
                        ; for "holds" type, the value of the name
                        ;  attribute of a phys-object in working memory
                        ;  whose weight attribute is "light,"
                        ;  or "nil" meaning to drop the object already held
                        ; for "on" type- "floor" or the value of the
                        ;  name attribute of a phys-object in
                        ;  working memory - object the monkey is to climb on
```

```
                          ; for "at" type - a value of "nil," indicating
                          ;  the action to walk to,
                          ;  or the value of the name attribute of a
                          ;  phys-object in working memory  indicating
                          ;  the phys-object is to be moved to the location
                          ;  given as the value of the to attribute
    to                    ; "nil" for goal types "holds" and "on,"
                          ; for "at" type the value expresses the goal
                          ;   location and programmers' convention is that
                          ;   the value is a string X-Y where X and Y are
                          ;   integers between 1 and 10 inclusive
)
(literalize testcase         ; Representation for test objects
    type                  ; one of "general," "holds," "at," "to."
                          ;  value indicates which goal(s) are being
                          ;  tested by the testcase
    name                  ; unique for each testcase -
                          ;  a descriptive string to indicate which rules
                          ;  within the goal category are being tested.
)
```

RULES

```
;Program is organized around the rule clusters developed for each
; goal type.
;
; ************************************************************************
;
;
; Cluster for Termination
;
;  Design:  There are two termination actions:
;                Congratulations (all goals met)
;                Impossible (goals cannot all be satisfied)
;
;
;   Congratulations:
;        Congratulations implements terminating the program when
;              all goals have been satisfied.
;
;
;   Impossible:
;        Impossible implements terminating the program when there
;              are active goals and no rules can fire.
;
;
; ************************************************************************
;
```

```
;English version of Congratulations:
;  IF    there is a testcase in working memory
;   and  there is at least one satisfied goal
;   and  there are no active goals
;  THEN  write "Congratulations, the goals are satisfied"
;   and  terminate execution of the rule set
;
(p Congratulations
   (testcase)
   (goal ↑status satisfied)
 - (goal ↑status active)
-->
   (write (crlf) CONGRATULATIONS the goals are satisfied (crlf))
   (halt))

;English version of Impossible:
;  IF    there is an active goal in working memory
;  THEN  write "Impossible the goal GOAL cannot be achieved"
;   and  terminate execution
;
;NOTE:  This is the least specific rule of all, it will fire
;   only if no other rule does.  It will constantly be in the
;   conflict set as it matches any active goal.
;
(p Impossible
   (goal ↑status active ↑type <g1>)
-->
   (write (crlf) (crlf) Impossible the goal <g1> cannot be achieved)
   (halt))

; **********************************************************************
;
; Cluster for goal type "On"
;
;  Design:  There are two actions:
;              Jump on Floor
;              Climb On <phys-object>
;
;    Jump on floor:
;        On::Floor implements jumping on the floor if monkey
;                 is currently on something other than the floor
;
;        On::Floor:Satisfied indicates monkey is already on floor
;
;    Climb on physical-object:
;        On::Phys-Object is general rule, implementing the action
;        On::Phys-Object:Hold if the monkey is holding something,
;                 establish goal to drop it
;        On::Phys-Object:At-Monkey if the monkey is not at the same
;                 location as phys-object, establish goal to walk
;        On::Phys-Object:Satisfied indicates the monkey is already
;                 on the physical object;
```

```
; ************************************************************************
;
; Cluster for action Jump on the floor
;
;English version of On::Floor
;  IF    there is a goal for the monkey to be on the floor
;   and  the monkey is not on the floor
;  THEN  write a message to jump onto the floor
;   and  modify the monkey to indicate it is on the floor
;   and  modify the goal to indicate it is satisfied
;
;Rules always conflicting with this rule:
;   Impossible
;
(p On::Floor
   {(goal ↑status active ↑type on ↑object-name floor)              <goal>}
   {(monkey ↑on <> floor)                                          <monkey>}
-->
   (write (crlf) (crlf) Jump onto the floor (crlf))
   (modify <monkey> ↑on floor)
   (modify <goal> ↑status satisfied))

;English version of On::Floor:Satisfied
;  IF    there is a goal for the monkey to be on the floor
;   and  the monkey is already at that location on the floor
;  THEN  write a message that the monkey is already on the floor
;   and  modify the goal to indicate it is satisfied
;
;Rules always conflicting with this rule:
;   Impossible
;
(p On::Floor:Satisfied
   {(goal ↑status active ↑type on ↑object-name floor)              <goal>}
   {(monkey ↑at <p1> ↑on floor)                                    <monkey>}
-->
   (write (crlf) (crlf) Monkey is already on floor (crlf))
   (modify <goal> ↑status satisfied))

; ************************************************************************
;
; Cluster for action Climb on object
;
;English version of On::Phys-Object
;  IF    there is a goal for monkey to be on some physical object
;   and  that object is at a particular location on the floor
;   and  the monkey is at the same location holding nothing
;              not on the physical object
;  THEN  write a message to climb onto the physical object
;   and  modify the monkey to indicate it is on the object
;   and  modify the goal to indicate it is satisfied
;
```

```
;Rules always conflicting with this rule:
;    Impossible
;
(p On::Phys-Object
    {(goal ↑status active ↑type on ↑object-name <o>)                  <goal>}
    {(phys-object ↑name <o> ↑at <p> ↑on floor)                      <object>}
    {(monkey ↑at <p> ↑holds nil ↑on <> <o>)                         <monkey>}
-->
    (write (crlf) (crlf) Climb onto <o> (crlf))
    (modify <monkey> ↑on <o>)
    (modify <goal> ↑status satisfied))

;English version of On::Phys-Object:Holds
;  IF    there is a goal for monkey to be on  some physical object
;   and  that object is at a particular location
;   and  the monkey is at the same location holding something
;  THEN  establish a goal for the monkey to hold nothing
;
;Rules always conflicting with this rule:
;    Impossible
;
(p On::Phys-Object:Holds
    {(goal ↑status active ↑type on ↑object-name <o1>)                 <goal>}
    {(phys-object ↑name <o1> ↑at <p>)                               <object>}
    {(monkey ↑at <p> ↑holds <> nil)                                 <monkey>}
-->
    (make goal ↑status active ↑type holds ↑object-name nil))

;English version of On::Phys-Object:At-Monkey
;  IF    there is a goal for monkey to be on some physical object
;   and  that object is at a particular location on floor
;   and  the monkey is not at that location
;  THEN  establish a goal for the monkey to be at that location
;
;
;Rules always conflicting with this rule:
;    Impossible
;
(p On::Phys-Object:At-Monkey
    (goal ↑status active ↑type on ↑object-name <o1>)
    (phys-object ↑name <o1> ↑at <p> ↑on floor)
    (monkey ↑at <> <p>)
-->
    (make goal ↑status active ↑type at ↑object-name nil ↑to <p>))

;English version of On::Phys-Object:Satisfied
;  IF    there is a goal for monkey to be on some physical object
;   and  the object is at a particular location on the floor
;   and  the monkey is already at that location on that object
;  THEN  write a message that the monkey is already on the object
;   and  modify the goal to indicate it is satisfied
```

```
;
;
;Rules always conflicting with this rule:
;    Impossible
;
(p On::Phys-Object:Satisfied
   {(goal ↑status active ↑type on ↑object-name <o1>)                <goal>}
   {(phys-object ↑name <o1> ↑at <p1> ↑on floor)                  <object>}
   {(monkey ↑at <p1> ↑on <o1>)                                    <monkey>}
-->
   (write (crlf) (crlf) Monkey is already on <o1>)
   (modify <goal> ↑status satisfied))

; **********************************************************************
;
; Cluster for goal type "Holds"
;
;  Design:  There are three actions:
;              Drop <phys-object> - goal is holds "nil"
;              Grab <phys-object> on the ceiling
;              Grab <phys-object> not on the ceiling
;
;
;    Drop - holds nothing:
;        Holds::nil rule implements dropping whatever is held
;        Holds::nil:Satisfied indicates goal already satisfied
;
;    Grab - holds physical-object that is on the ceiling:
;        Holds::Object-Ceil general rule, implementing the action
;            of Grab object - the monkey is on ladder directly under
;            the object to be grabbed and holding nothing.
;        Holds::Object-Ceil:On  if ladder is under the object to be
;            grabbed, establishes the goal of being on ladder.
;        Holds::Object-Ceil:At-Obj otherwise, establish a goal to
;            move the ladder under the object to be grabbed.
;
;    Grab - holds physical-object that is not on the ceiling:
;        Holds::Object-NotCeil general rule, implementing action
;        Holds::Object-NotCeil:On  establishes goal to get on floor
;        Holds::Object-NotCeil:At-Monkey establishes goal for
;            monkey to walk to location of object
;
;    Grab - general
;        Holds::Object:Satisfied indicates that goal object is held
;        Holds::Object:Holds establishes a goal to drop the object
;            held so monkey can grab the goal object

; **********************************************************************
;
; Cluster for action Drop object
;
```

```
;English version of Holds::nil
;  IF    there is a goal for the monkey to hold nothing
;   and  the monkey is holding something, not nil
;  THEN  write a message to drop the object
;   and  modify the monkey to indicate it is holding nothing
;   and  modify the object to indicate it is on the floor
;   and  modify the goal to indicate it is satisfied
;
;Rules always conflicting with this rule:
;   Impossible
;
(p Holds::nil
   {(goal ↑status active ↑type holds ↑object-name nil)          <goal>}
   {(monkey ↑holds {<o1> <> nil})                              <monkey>}
   {(phys-object ↑name <o1>)                                  <object1>}
-->
   (write (crlf) (crlf) Drop <o1> (crlf))
   (modify <goal> ↑status satisfied)
   (modify <monkey> ↑holds nil)
   (modify <object1> ↑on floor))

;English version of Holds::nil:Satisfied
;  IF    there is a goal for the monkey to hold nothing
;   and  the monkey is already holding nothing
;  THEN  write a message that the monkey is holding nothing
;   and  modify the goal to indicate it is satisfied.
;
;Rules always conflicting with this rule:
;   Impossible
;
(p Holds::nil:Satisfied
   {(goal ↑status active ↑type holds ↑object-name nil)          <goal>}
   {(monkey ↑holds nil ↑at <p> ↑on <q>)                        <monkey>}
-->
   (write (crlf) (crlf) Monkey is holding nothing (crlf))
   (modify <goal> ↑status satisfied))

; ************************************************************************
;
; Cluster for action Grab object when the object is on the ceiling
;
;English version of Holds::Object-Ceil
;  IF    there is a goal for the monkey to hold an object
;   and  the object is on the ceiling
;   and  the ladder is on the floor under the object
;   and  the monkey is on the ladder, holding nothing
;   and  there is no object on the goal object
;  THEN  write a message to grab the object
;   and  modify the monkey to indicate it is holding the object
;   and  modify the object to indicate it is on nil
;   and  modify the goal to indicate it is satisfied
```

```
;
;Rules always conflicting with this rule:
;   Impossible
;
(p Holds::Object-Ceil
   {(goal ↑status active ↑type holds ↑object-name <o1>)                 <goal>}
   {(phys-object ↑name <o1> ↑weight light ↑at <p> ↑on ceiling)    <object1>}
   {(phys-object ↑name ladder ↑at <p> ↑on floor)                   <object2>}
   {(monkey ↑on ladder ↑holds nil)                                  <monkey>}
 - (phys-object ↑on <o1>)
-->
   (write (crlf) (crlf) Grab <o1> (crlf))
   (modify <monkey> ↑holds <o1>)
   (modify <object1> ↑on nil)
   (modify <goal> ↑status satisfied))

;English version of Holds::Object-Ceil:On
;  IF    there is a goal for the monkey to hold an object
;   and  the object is on the ceiling
;   and  the ladder is on the floor under the object
;   and  the monkey is not on the ladder
;  THEN  create a new goal to be on the ladder
;
;NOTE:  The rule doesn't mention the X-Y location of the monkey.
;   The "on" goal will set up a subgoal to move to the location
;   if the monkey is not already there.
;
;Rules always conflicting with this rule:
;   Holds::Object-Ceil:At-Obj
;   Impossible
;
(p Holds::Object-Ceil:On
   (goal ↑status active ↑type holds ↑object-name <o1>)
   (phys-object ↑name <o1> ↑weight light ↑at <p> ↑on ceiling)
   (phys-object ↑name ladder ↑at <p> ↑on floor)
   (monkey ↑on <> ladder)
-->
   (make goal ↑status active ↑type on ↑object-name ladder))

;English version of Holds::Object-Ceil:At-Obj
;  IF    there is a goal for the monkey to hold an object
;   and  the object is on the ceiling at some location
;   and  the ladder is not at that location
;  THEN  create a new goal to move the ladder under the object
;
;NOTE:  This rule doesn't mention the monkey, because until the
;   ladder is in place, the monkey is not important.
;
;Rules always conflicting with this rule:
;   Impossible
;
```

```
(p Holds::Object-Ceil:At-Obj
   (goal ↑status active ↑type holds ↑object-name <o1>)
   (phys-object ↑name <o1> ↑weight light ↑at <p> ↑on ceiling)
   (phys-object ↑name ladder ↑at <> <p>)
-->
   (make goal ↑status active ↑type at ↑object-name ladder ↑to <p>))

; ************************************************************************
;
; Cluster for action Grab object
;         when the object is not on the ceiling
;
;English version of Holds::Object-NotCeil
;  IF    there is a goal for the monkey to hold an object
;   and  the object is not on the ceiling
;   and  the monkey is at location of the object, on floor, holding
;            nothing
;   and  there is no object on the goal object
;  THEN  write a message to grab the object
;   and  modify the object to be on nothing
;   and  modify the monkey to be holding the object
;   and  modify the goal to be satisfied
;
;Rules always conflicting with this rule:
;   Impossible
;
(p Holds::Object-NotCeil
   {(goal ↑status active ↑type holds ↑object-name <o>)                <goal>}
   {(phys-object ↑name <o> ↑weight light ↑at <p> ↑on <> ceiling)  <object>}
   {(monkey ↑at <p> ↑on floor ↑holds nil)                          <monkey>}
 - (phys-object ↑on <o>)
-->
   (write (crlf) (crlf) Grab <o> (crlf))
   (modify <object> ↑on nil)
   (modify <monkey> ↑holds <o>)
   (modify <goal> ↑status satisfied))

;English version of Holds::Object-NotCeil:On
;  IF    there is a goal for the monkey to hold an object
;   and  the object is not on the ceiling
;   and  the monkey is at the location of object, not on the floor
;  THEN  make a goal for the monkey to get on the floor
;
;Rules always conflicting with this rule:
;   Impossible
;
(p Holds::Object-NotCeil:On
   (goal ↑status active ↑type holds ↑object-name <o1>)
   (phys-object ↑name <o1> ↑weight light ↑at <p> ↑on <> ceiling)
   (monkey ↑at <p> ↑on <> floor)
-->
   (make goal ↑status active ↑type on ↑object-name floor))
```

```
;English version of Holds::Object-NotCeil:At-Monkey
;  IF    there is a goal for the monkey to hold an object
;   and  the object is not on the ceiling at some location
;   and  the monkey is not at the location
;  THEN  make a goal for the monkey to go to location of the object
;
;
;
;Rules always conflicting with this rule:
;   Impossible
;
(p Holds::Object-NotCeil:At-Monkey
   (goal ↑status active ↑type holds ↑object-name <o1>)
   (phys-object ↑name <o1> ↑weight light ↑at <p> ↑on <> ceiling)
   (monkey ↑at <> <p>)
-->
   (make goal ↑status active ↑type at ↑object-name nil ↑to <p>))



; ************************************************************************
;
;  General "hold" rules for Grab object action
;
;English version of Holds::Object:Holds
;  IF    there is a goal for the monkey to hold an object
;   and  the object is at some location
;   and  the monkey is at the same location holding an object not
;          the goal object
;  THEN  make a goal for the monkey to  hold nothing
;
;NOTE:  This rule is activated whether the goal object is
;   on the ceiling or not.  It will be activated when the
;   monkey is ready to grasp the object, but finds something
;   already in its hands
;
;Rules always conflicting with this rule:
;   Impossible
;
(p Holds::Object:Holds
   (goal ↑status active ↑type holds ↑object-name <o1>)
   (phys-object ↑name <o1> ↑weight light ↑at <p>)
   (monkey ↑at <p> ↑holds {<> nil <> <o1>})
-->
   (make goal ↑status active ↑type holds ↑object-name nil))

;English version of Holds::Object:Satisfied
;  IF    there is a goal for the monkey to hold an object
;   and  the monkey is already holding that object
;  THEN  write a message that the goal object is being held
;   and  modify the goal to indicate that it is satisfied
```

```
;
;Rules always conflicting with this rule:
;   Impossible
;
(p Holds::Object:Satisfied
   {(goal ↑status active ↑type holds ↑object-name <o1>)               <goal>}
   {(phys-object ↑name <o1> ↑on nil ↑at <p> ↑weight light)          <object>}
   {(monkey ↑at <p> ↑holds <o1>)                                     <monkey>}
-->
   (write (crlf) (crlf) Object <o1> is already being held)
   (modify <goal> ↑status satisfied))

; **********************************************************************
;
; Cluster for goal type "At"
;
;  Design:  There are two actions:
;                Move an object, called At-object
;                Walk-to a location, called At-monkey
;
;    Expression of subgoals:
;        At-object is expressed by a goal element with a goal type
;              of "at" and a non-nil value for attribute object-name
;        At-monkey is expressed by a goal element with a goal type
;              of "at" and a nil value for attribute object-name
;
;  At-object subgoal
;        Rule At::Object implements action of moving goal object
;        Rule At::Object:On-floor if goal held, monkey not on floor
;              establishes new goal to get on the floor.
;        Rule At::Object:Holds if goal object not being held,
;              establishes new goal to hold the object.
;        Rule At::Object:Satisfied indicates goal already satisfied
;
;  At-monkey subgoal
;        Rule At::Monkey implements action of walking to location
;              when the monkey is holding nothing
;        Rule At::Monkey:Object implements the action of walking
;              to location when monkey holding something
;        Rule At::Monkey:On if monkey isn't on floor, establish goal
;              to get on the floor
;        Rule At::Monkey:Satisfied indicates goal already satisfied

; **********************************************************************
;
; Cluster for at-object subgoal
;
;English version of At::Object
```

```
;  IF    there is a goal for monkey to move an object to a location
;   and  monkey is holding object on floor at a different location
;  THEN  write a message to move the object to the goal location
;   and  modify the monkey to indicate it is at the location
;   and  modify the object to indicate it is at the location
;   and  modify the goal to indicate it is satisfied
;
;Rules always conflicting with this rule:
;    Impossible
(p At::Object
   {(goal ↑status active ↑type at ↑object-name <o1> ↑to <p>)        <goal>}
   {(monkey ↑at <> <p> ↑holds <o1> ↑on floor)                     <monkey>}
   {(phys-object ↑name <o1>)                                     <object1>}
-->
   (write  (crlf) (crlf) Move <o1> to <p> (crlf))
   (modify <object1> ↑at <p>)
   (modify <monkey> ↑at <p>)
   (modify <goal> ↑status satisfied))

;English version of At::Object:On-floor
;  IF    there is a goal for monkey to move an object to a location
;   and  the monkey is not on the floor but is holding the object
;   and  the object is not at the location
;  THEN  make a subgoal to get on the floor
;
;Rules always conflicting with this rule:
;    Impossible
;
(p At::Object:On-floor
   (goal ↑status active ↑type at ↑object-name <o1> ↑to <p>)
   (monkey ↑on <> floor  ↑holds <o1>)
   (phys-object ↑name <o1> ↑at <> <p>)
-->
   (make goal ↑status active ↑type on ↑object-name floor))

;English version of At::Object:Holds
;  IF    there is a goal for monkey to move an object to a location
;   and  the object is at a different location
;   and  the monkey is not holding the goal object
;  THEN  make a subgoal to hold the goal object
;
;Rules always conflicting with this rule:
;    Impossible
;
(p At::Object:Holds
   (goal ↑status active ↑type at ↑object-name <o1> ↑to <p>)
   (phys-object ↑name <o1> ↑weight light ↑at <> <p>)
   (monkey ↑holds <> <o1>)
-->
   (make goal ↑status active ↑type holds ↑object-name <o1>))
```

```
;English version of At::Object:Satisfied
;  IF    there is a goal for monkey to move an object to a location
;   and  the object is at that location
;  THEN  write a message that the object is already at the location
;   and  modify the goal to be satisfied
;
;Rules always conflicting with this rule:
;   Impossible
;
(p At::Object:Satisfied
   {(goal ↑status active ↑type at ↑object-name <o1> ↑to <p>)          <goal>}
   {(phys-object ↑name <o1> ↑weight light ↑at <p>)                 <object1>}
-->
   (write (crlf) (crlf) The object <o1> is already at <p> (crlf))
   (modify <goal> ↑status satisfied))

; **********************************************************************
;
; Cluster for at-monkey subgoal
;
;English version of At::Monkey
;  IF    there is a goal for the monkey to walk to a location
;   and  the monkey is at a different location holding nothing
;  THEN  write a message to walk to the location
;   and  modify the monkey to be at the location
;   and  modify the goal to be satisfied
;
;Rules always conflicting with this rule:
;   Impossible
;
(p At::Monkey
   {(goal ↑status active ↑type at ↑object-name nil ↑to <p1>)          <goal>}
   {(monkey ↑on floor ↑at <> <p1> ↑holds nil )                       <monkey>}
-->
   (write (crlf) (crlf) Walk to <p1> (crlf))
   (modify <monkey> ↑at <p1>)
   (modify <goal> ↑status satisfied))

;English version of At::Monkey:Object
;  IF    there is a goal for the monkey to walk to a location
;   and  monkey is at a different location holding a physical object
;  THEN  write a message to walk to the location carrying the object
;   and  modify the monkey to be at the location
;   and  modify the physical object to be at the location
;   and  modify the goal to be satisfied
;
;Rules always conflicting with this rule:
;   Impossible
```

```
(p At::Monkey:Object
   {(goal ↑status active ↑type at ↑object-name nil ↑to <p1>)          <goal>}
   {(monkey ↑on floor ↑at <> <p1> ↑holds <o1>)                       <monkey>}
   {(phys-object ↑name <o1>)                                         <object>}
-->
   (write (crlf) (crlf) Walk to <p1> carrying <o1> (crlf))
   (modify <monkey> ↑at <p1>)
   (modify <object> ↑at <p1>)
   (modify <goal> ↑status satisfied))

;English version of At::Monkey:On
;  IF    there is a goal for the monkey to walk to a location
;   and  the monkey is not at the location and not on the floor
;  THEN  make a goal for the monkey to be on the floor
;
;
;Rules always conflicting with this rule:
;   Impossible
;
(p At::Monkey:On
   (goal ↑status active ↑type at ↑object-name nil ↑to <p1>)
   (monkey ↑on <> floor ↑at <> <p1>)
-->
   (make goal ↑status active ↑type on ↑object-name floor))

;English version of At::Monkey:Satisfied
;  IF    there is a goal for the monkey to walk to a location
;   and  the monkey is already at that location
;  THEN  write a message that the monkey is already at the location
;   and  modify the goal to be satisfied
;
;Rules always conflicting with this rule:
;   Impossible
;
(p At::Monkey:Satisfied
   {(goal ↑status active ↑type at ↑object-name nil ↑to <p1>)         <goal>}
   {(monkey ↑at <p1>)                                               <monkey>}
-->
   (write (crlf) (crlf) Monkey is already at <p1>)
   (modify <goal> ↑status satisfied))
```

1.2 TESTING RULES

```
;This is the test set for the Monkeys and Bananas problem
; The rules are organized by the cluster they were designed to test.
;
```

```
;General Test Rules
;The first test rules test general situations that should
; use many of the rules.  They are used only after the rule set is
; completely tested out, cluster by cluster.

;Test::General:Start
;
;English description of initial configuration for working memory:
;
;The monkey is on the couch, holding the blanket at one location,
; and the ladder and the bananas are at two other locations,
; and the goal is to have the monkey grab the bananas.

;Rules expected to fire (and order of firing):
;  Holds::Object-Ceil:At-Obj          Set up goal to move ladder
;  At::Object:Holds                   Set up goal to hold ladder
;  Holds::Object-NotCeil:At-Monkey    Set up goal to walk to ladder
;  At::Monkey:On                      Set up goal to jump on floor
;  On::Floor                          Action of jumping on floor
;  At::Monkey:Object                  Action of walking to ladder
;  Holds::Object:Holds                Set up goal to drop blanket
;  Holds::nil                         Action of dropping the blanket
;  Holds::Object-NotCeil              Action of grabbing the ladder
;  At::Object                         Action of moving the ladder under
;                                         bananas
;  Holds::Object:Holds                Set up goal to drop the ladder
;  Holds::nil                         Action of dropping the ladder
;  Holds::Object-Ceil:On              Set up goal to get on ladder
;  On::Phys-Object                    Action of climbing on ladder
;  Holds::Object-Ceil                 Action of grabbing the bananas
;  Congratulations                    Final message

(p Test::General:Start
   (testcase ↑type general ↑name start)
-->
   (make phys-object ↑name bananas ↑weight light ↑at 9-9 ↑on ceiling)
   (make phys-object ↑name couch ↑on floor ↑weight heavy ↑at 7-7)
   (make phys-object ↑name ladder ↑on floor ↑weight light ↑at 4-3)
   (make phys-object ↑name blanket ↑weight light ↑at 7-7)
   (make monkey ↑on couch ↑at 7-7 ↑holds blanket)
   (make goal ↑status active ↑type holds ↑object-name bananas))

;Test::General:On-ladder
;
;English description of initial configuration for working memory:
;Monkey is on ladder at different location than bananas; bananas
; are on ceiling; goal is to have monkey grab bananas.
;
; The test type is "general," the name is "on-ladder"
```

```
;Rules expected to fire
;  Holds::Object-Ceil:At-Obj        Set up goal to move ladder
;  At::Object:Holds                 Set up goal to hold ladder
;  Holds::Object-NotCeil:On         Set up goal to jump on floor
;  On::Floor                        Action of jumping on floor
;  Holds::Object-NotCeil            Action of grabbing the ladder
;  At::Object                       Action of moving ladder under bananas
;  Holds::Object:Holds              Set up goal to drop ladder
;  Holds::nil                       Action of dropping ladder
;  Holds::Object-Ceil:On            Set up goal to get on ladder
;  On::Phys-Object                  Action of getting on ladder
;  Holds::Object-Ceil               Action of grabbing bananas
;  Congratulations                  Final message

(p Test::General:On-ladder
   (testcase ↑type general ↑name on-ladder)
-->
   (make monkey ↑on ladder ↑at 5-5 )
   (make phys-object ↑name bananas ↑on ceiling ↑weight light ↑at 7-7)
   (make phys-object ↑name ladder ↑at 5-5 ↑on floor ↑weight light)
   (make phys-object ↑name blanket ↑at 5-5 ↑weight light ↑on floor)
   (make goal ↑status active ↑type holds ↑object-name bananas))

; *********************************************************************
;
; Test cluster for goal "On"
;
;  Design:  two actions, Jump on floor, Climb on physical-object
;
;    Jump on floor:
;        Test::On:Floor rule tests if monkey will jump to floor
;        Test::On:Floor-Satisfied checks conditions already set
;
;    Climb on physical object:
;        Test::On:Phys-Object tests if monkey will climb on object
;        Test::On:Phys-Object:Hold  tests for goal to drop set up
;        Test::On:Phys-Object:At-Monkey tests for goal set up
;        Test::On:Phys-Object-Satisfied checks conditions already set
;
;    If the complete program is in working memory when the
;       rules are fired, rules in the "Holds" and "At" clusters
;       will also be tested.
;
; *********************************************************************

;Test situation for Test::On:Floor
; trigger: testcase type is "on," name is "floor"
; The monkey is on ladder and there is an active goal to be on floor.
;
```

```
;Rules expected to fire
;  On::Floor
;  Congratulations
;
(p Test::On:Floor
   (testcase ↑type on ↑name floor)
-->
   (make phys-object ↑name ladder ↑on floor ↑at 5-7 ↑weight light)
   (make monkey ↑on ladder  ↑at 5-7)
   (make goal ↑status active ↑type on ↑object-name floor))

;Test situation for Test::On:Floor-Satisfied
; trigger: testcase type is "on," name is "floor-satisfied"
; The monkey is on floor and there is an active goal to be on floor.
;
;Rules expected to fire
;  On::Floor:Satisfied
;  Congratulations
;
(p Test::On:Floor-Satisfied
   (testcase ↑type on ↑name floor-satisfied)
-->
   (make phys-object ↑name ladder ↑on floor ↑at 5-7 ↑weight light)
   (make monkey ↑on floor ↑at 5-7)
   (make goal ↑status active ↑type on ↑object-name floor))

;Test situation for Test::On:Phys-Object
; trigger: testcase type is "on," name is "phys-object"
; The monkey is on the floor, at the same location as the ladder.
; The goal is to get on the ladder.
;
;Rules expected to fire:
;  On::Phys-Object
;  Congratulations
;
(p Test::On:Phys-Object
   (testcase ↑type on ↑name phys-object)
-->
   (make phys-object ↑name ladder ↑on floor ↑at 5-5 ↑weight light)
   (make monkey ↑at 5-5 ↑on floor)
   (make goal ↑status active ↑type on ↑object-name ladder))

;Test situation for Test::On:Phys-Object:Holds
; trigger: testcase type is "on," name is "phys-object-holds"
; The monkey is on the floor, at the same location as the ladder
;  holding the ladder.  The goal is to get on the ladder.
;
;Rules expected to fire:
;  On::Phys-Object:Holds        Set up goal to hold nothing
;  Impossible                   Active goals cannot be satisfied
```

```
;If complete rule set in production memory:
;  On::Phys-Object:Holds        Set up goal to hold nothing
;  Holds:nil                    Action of dropping held object
;  On::Phys-Object              Action of climbing on object
;  Congratulations              Final message

(p Test::On:Phys-Object:Holds
   (testcase ↑type on ↑name phys-object-holds)
-->
   (make phys-object ↑name ladder ↑at 5-5 ↑weight light)
   (make monkey ↑at 5-5 ↑holds ladder ↑on floor)
   (make goal ↑status active ↑type on ↑object-name ladder))

;Test situation for Test::On:Phys-Object:At-Monkey
; trigger: testcase type is "on," name is "phys-object:at-monkey"
; The monkey is on the floor, at a different location than
;  ladder.  Goal is to get on ladder.
;
;Rules expected to fire:
;  On::Phys-Object:At-Monkey    Set up goal to be at the ladder
;  Impossible                   Active goals cannot be satisfied
;If complete rule set in production memory:
;  On::Phys-Object:At-Monkey    Set up goal to be at ladder
;  At::Monkey                   Action of walking to ladder
;  On::Phys-Object              Action of climbing on ladder
;  Congratulations              Final message


(p Test::On:Phys-Object:At-Monkey
   (testcase ↑type on ↑name phys-object:at-monkey)
-->
   (make phys-object ↑name ladder ↑at 6-5 ↑on floor ↑weight light)
   (make monkey ↑at 3-3 ↑on floor)
   (make goal ↑status active ↑type on ↑object-name ladder))

;Test situation for Test::On:Phys-Object:Satisfied
; trigger:  testcase type is "on," name is "phys-object-satisfied"
; The monkey is on the ladder, the goal is to be on the ladder.
;
;Rules expected to fire:
;  On::Phys-Object:Satisfied    Goal is satisfied by present wm
;  Congratulations              Final message
;
(p Test::On:Phys-Object:Satisfied
   (testcase ↑type on ↑name phys-object-satisfied)
-->
   (make phys-object ↑name ladder ↑at 6-5 ↑on floor ↑weight light)
   (make monkey ↑at 6-5 ↑on ladder)
   (make goal ↑status active ↑type on ↑object-name ladder))
```

```
; ***********************************************************************
;
; Test cluster for goal "Holds"
;
; Design:  two subgoals, holds nothing, holds physical object
;
;   Holds nothing:
;       Test::Holds:nil  tests the monkey dropping a held object
;       Test::Holds:nil-Satisfied
;
;   Holds physical object that is on the ceiling:
;       Test::Holds:Object-Ceil tests general rule and Object-Ceil:On
;       Test::Holds:Object-Ceil:At-Obj tests At-Obj case
;
;   Holds physical object not on the ceiling:
;       Test::Holds:Object-NotCeil:On-ladder
;       Test::Holds:Object-NotCeil:At
;       Test::Holds:Object-Satisfied checks to see if goal satisfied
;
; ***********************************************************************


;Test situation for Test::Holds:nil
; trigger:  testcase type is "holds" name is "holds-nil"
; The monkey is on the floor, holding the blanket
;  and there is an active goal to hold nothing.
;
; Rules expected to fire:
;   Holds::nil                        Action of dropping the blanket
;   Congratulations                   Final message
;
(p Test::Holds:nil
   (testcase ↑type holds ↑name holds-nil)
-->
   (make phys-object ↑name blanket ↑weight light ↑at 5-5)
   (make monkey ↑5-5 ↑holds blanket ↑on floor)
   (make goal ↑status active ↑type holds))


;Test situation for Test::Holds:nil-Satisfied
; trigger:  testcase type is "holds," name is "nil-satisfied"
; The monkey is on the floor holding nothing with an active goal
;  to hold nothing.
;
;Rules expected to fire:
;  Holds::nil:Satisfied               Goal is satisfied by present wm
;  Congratulations                    Final message
;
```

```
(p Test::Holds:nil-Satisfied
   (testcase ↑type holds ↑name nil-satisfied)
-->
   (make monkey ↑at 5-5 ↑holds nil ↑on floor)
   (make goal ↑status active ↑type holds))

;Test situation for Test::Holds:Object-Ceil
; trigger: testcase type is "holds," name is "object-ceil:on-floor"
; The monkey is on the floor at the location of the ladder.  The
;  bananas are at the same location on the ceiling.  The active
;  goal is to hold the bananas.
;
;Rules expected to fire:
;  Holds::Object-Ceil:On        Set up goal to climb on ladder
;  On::Phys-Object              Action of climbing on ladder
;  Holds::Object-Ceil           Action of grabbing bananas
;  Congratulations              Final message
; EXPECTATION:  "on" cluster is in production memory
;
(p Test::Holds:Object-Ceil
   (testcase ↑type holds ↑name object-ceil:on-floor)
-->
   (make phys-object ↑name ladder ↑at 5-5 ↑on floor ↑weight light)
   (make phys-object ↑name bananas ↑at 5-5 ↑on ceiling ↑weight light)
   (make monkey ↑at 5-5 ↑on floor)
   (make goal   ↑status active ↑type holds ↑object-name bananas))

;Test situation for Test::Holds:Object-Ceil:At-Obj
; trigger: testcase type is "holds," name is "object-ceil-at-obj"
; The monkey is on the ladder: holding the blanket.  The
;  bananas are at a different location on the ceiling.  The active
;  goal is to hold the bananas.
;
;Rules expected to fire:
;  Holds::Object-Ceil:At-Obj   Set up goal to move ladder to bananas
;  Impossible                  Active goals cannot be satisfied
;If complete rule set in production memory:
;  At::Object:Holds            Set up goal to hold ladder
;  Holds::Object-NotCeil:On    Set up goal to be on the floor
;  On::Floor                   Action of jumping on the floor
;  Holds::Object:Holds         Set up goal to hold nothing
;  Holds::nil                  Action of dropping blanket
;  Holds::Object-NotCeil       Action of grabbing the ladder
;  At::Object                  Action of moving ladder to bananas
;  Holds::Object:Holds         Set up goal to hold nothing
;  Holds::nil                  Action of dropping the ladder
;  Holds::Object-Ceil:On       Set up goal to be on the ladder
;  On::Phys-Object             Action of getting on ladder
;  Holds::Object-Ceil          Action of grabbing the bananas
;  Congratulations             Final message
```

```
(p Test::Holds:Object-Ceil:At-Obj
   (testcase ↑type holds ↑name object-ceil-at-obj)
-->
   (make monkey ↑on ladder ↑at 5-5 ↑holds blanket)
   (make phys-object ↑name blanket ↑at 5-5 ↑weight light)
   (make phys-object ↑name bananas ↑on ceiling ↑weight light ↑at 7-7)
   (make phys-object ↑name ladder ↑at 5-5 ↑on floor ↑weight light)
   (make goal ↑status active ↑type holds ↑object-name bananas))

;Test situation for Test::Holds:Object-NotCeil:On-ladder
; trigger: testcase type is "holds," name "object-notceil:on-ladder"
; The monkey is on the ladder, holding nothing.  The goal is to
;  hold the ladder.
;
;Rules expected to fire:
;  Holds::Object-NotCeil:On           Set up goal to jump on floor
;  On::Floor                          Action of jumping on floor
;  Holds::Object-NotCeil              Action of grabbing ladder
;  Congratulations                    Final message
; EXPECTATION:  "on" cluster is in production memory
;
(p Test::Holds:Object-NotCeil:On-ladder
   (testcase ↑type holds ↑name object-notceil:on-ladder)
-->
   (make monkey ↑at 5-5 ↑holds nil ↑on ladder)
   (make phys-object ↑name ladder ↑at 5-5 ↑on floor ↑weight light)
   (make goal ↑status active ↑type holds ↑object-name ladder))

;Test situation for Test::Holds:Object-NotCeil:At
; trigger:  testcase type "holds," name is "object-notceil:at"
; The monkey is on the floor at a location different than that of
;  the ladder.  The goal is to hold the ladder.
;
;Rules expected to fire:
;  Holds::Object-NotCeil:At-Monkey    Set up goal to walk to ladder
;  Impossible                         Active goals not satisfiable
;If complete rule set in production memory:
;  Holds::Object-NotCeil:At-Monkey    Set up goal to walk to ladder
;  At::Monkey                         Action of walking to the ladder
;  Holds::Object-NotCeil              Action of grabbing the ladder
;  Congratulations                    Final message
;
(p Test::Holds:Object-NotCeil:At
   (testcase ↑type holds ↑name object-notceil:at)
-->
   (make monkey ↑at 5-5 ↑on floor)
   (make phys-object ↑name ladder ↑at 7-5 ↑on floor ↑weight light)
   (make goal ↑status active ↑type holds ↑object-name ladder))
```

```
;Test situation for Test::Holds:Object-Satisfied
; trigger:  testcase type is "holds," name is "object-satisfied"
; The monkey is on the floor holding the bananas, the goal is to
;  hold the bananas.
;
;Rules expected to fire:
;  Holds::Object-Satisfied              Goal is satisfied by present wm
;  Congratulations                      Final message
;
(p Test::Holds:Object-Satisfied
   (testcase ↑type holds ↑name object-satisfied)
-->
   (make monkey ↑at 5-5 ↑on floor ↑holds bananas)
   (make phys-object ↑name bananas ↑at 5-5 ↑weight light)
   (make goal ↑status active ↑type holds ↑object-name bananas))

; ***********************************************************************
;
; Test cluster for goal "At"
;
;  Design:  two subgoals, at-object and at-monkey (walk-to and move)
;
;    At-monkey
;        Test::At-Monkey tests the general rule
;        Test::At-Monkey:Object tests rule when
;               the monkey holds something
;        Test::At-Monkey:On tests the rule that
;                sets subgoal of on floor.
;
;    At-object
;        Test::At-Object tests the general rule
;        Test::At-Object:Holds tests rule with monkey
;                not holding object
;
; ***********************************************************************

; ***********************************************************************
;
; Cluster for action Walk to, rules of type "at-monkey"
;
;Test situation for Test::At-Monkey
; trigger:  testcase type is "at," name is "at-monkey"
; The monkey is on the floor at one location. The ladder is
;  at a different location.
; The goal is to walk to the ladder.
;
;Rules expected to fire:
;  At::Monkey                           Action of walking to ladder
;  Congratulations                      Final message
```

```
;
(p Test::At-Monkey
   (testcase ↑type at ↑name at-monkey)
-->
   (make monkey ↑at 5-7 ↑on floor)
   (make phys-object ↑name ladder ↑at 7-7 ↑on floor)
   (make goal ↑status active ↑type at ↑object-name nil ↑to 7-7))


;Test situation for Test::At-Monkey:Object
; trigger :  testcase type is "at," name is "at-monkey-object"
; The monkey is on the floor at one location holding the blanket:
;  ladder is at different location; goal is to walk to ladder.
;
;Rules expected to fire:
; At::Monkey:Object           Action of walking to ladder with blanket
; Congratulations             Final message
;
(p Test::At-Monkey:Object
   (testcase ↑type at ↑name at-monkey-object)
-->
   (make monkey ↑at 5-5 ↑holds blanket ↑on floor)
   (make phys-object ↑name blanket ↑at 5-5 ↑weight light)
   (make phys-object ↑name ladder ↑at 7-7 ↑on floor ↑weight light)
   (make goal ↑status active ↑type at ↑object-name nil ↑to 7-7))


;Test situation for Test::At:Monkey-On
; trigger: testcase type is "at," name is "at-monkey-on"
; The monkey is at one location on couch, the ladder at a different
;  location; goal is to walk to the location of the ladder.
;
;Rules expected to fire:
;  At::Monkey:On                      Set up goal to jump on floor
;  Impossible                         Active goals cannot be satisfied
;Rules to fire if "on" cluster is also in production memory
;  At::Monkey:On                      Set up goal to jump on floor
;  On::Floor                          Action of jumping on floor
;  At::Monkey                         Action of walking to ladder
;  Congratulations                    Final message

(p Test::At-Monkey:On
   (testcase ↑type at ↑name at-monkey-on)
-->
   (make monkey ↑at 5-5 ↑on couch)
   (make phys-object ↑name couch ↑at 5-5 ↑weight light ↑on floor)
   (make phys-object ↑name ladder ↑at 7-7 ↑on floor)
   (make goal ↑status active ↑type at ↑object-name nil ↑to 7-7))
```

```
; ************************************************************************
;
; Cluster for action Move object to, rules of type "at-object"

;Test situation for Test::At-Object
; trigger :  testcase type is "at," name is "at-object"
; The monkey is on the floor at one location, holding the ladder.
; The bananas are at a different location on the ceiling.
; The goal is to move the ladder under the bananas.
;
;Rules expected to fire:
;  At::Object                          Action of moving ladder
;  Congratulations                     Final message
;
(p Test::At-Object
   (testcase ↑type at ↑name at-object)
-->
   (make monkey ↑at 5-5 ↑on floor ↑holds ladder)
   (make phys-object ↑name ladder ↑at 5-5 ↑weight light)
   (make phys-object ↑name bananas ↑at 8-8 ↑on ceiling ↑weight light)
   (make goal ↑status active ↑type at ↑object-name ladder ↑to 8-8))

;Test situation for Test::At-Object:On-floor
; trigger:  testcase type is "at," name is "at-object-on-floor"
; The monkey is on the couch, holding the bananas at one
;  location.  The goal is to move the bananas to a different
;  location.
;
;Rules expected to fire:
;  At::Object:On-floor                 Set up goal to jump on floor
;  Impossible                          Active goals cannot be satisfied
;If complete rule set in production memory:
;  At::Object:On-floor                 Set up goal to jump on floor
;  On::Floor                           Action of jumping on floor
;  At::Object                          Action of moving bananas
;  Congratulations                     Final message

(p Test::At-Object:On-floor
   (testcase ↑type at ↑name at-object-on-floor)
-->
   (make monkey ↑at 5-5 ↑on couch ↑holds bananas)
   (make phys-object ↑name couch ↑at 5-5 ↑weight heavy ↑on floor)
   (make phys-object ↑name bananas ↑at 5-5 ↑weight light)
   (make goal ↑status active ↑type at ↑object-name bananas ↑to 7-7))

;Test situation for Test::At-Object:Holds
; trigger :  testcase type is "at," name is "at-object-holds"
; The monkey is on the floor at one location, the ladder is
;  on the floor at a different location, the bananas on the
;  ceiling at a third location.  The goal is to move
;  the ladder under the bananas.
```

```
;Rules expected to fire:
;  At::Object:Holds                     Set up goal of grabbing ladder
;  Impossible                           Active goals cannot be satisfied
;If complete rule set in production memory:
;  At::Object:Holds                     Set up goal of grabbing ladder
;  Holds:Object-NotCeil:At-Monkey       Set up goal of walking to ladder
;  At::Monkey                           Action of walking to ladder
;  Holds::Object-NotCeil                Action of grabbing ladder
;  At::Object                           Action of moving ladder
;  Congratulations                      Final message

(p Test::At-Object:Holds
   (testcase ↑type at ↑name at-object-holds)
-->
   (make monkey ↑at 5-5 ↑on floor)
   (make phys-object ↑name ladder ↑at 7-5 ↑on floor ↑weight light)
   (make phys-object ↑name bananas ↑at 8-8 ↑on ceiling ↑weight light)
   (make goal ↑status active ↑type at ↑object-name ladder ↑to 8-8))
```

APPENDIX TWO

OPS5 Syntax Grammar

This appendix contains a BNF description of the simplified syntax of OPS5 as described and used in this text including all actions and functions. For completeness we include the additional syntax rules necessary for the original language definition given in the OPS5 *User's Manual* [Forgy 81]. That material is underlined. We would like to thank Charles L. Forgy for permission to use and modify his original BNF description.

Terminals are printed in roman bold-face type, and nonterminals appear in italics. The only nonstandard meta symbol used is the star ("*"). The star indicates that the preceding item is to be repeated zero or more times.

production	::=	**(p** constant-symbolic-atom lhs **-->** rhs **)**
lhs	::=	positive-ce ce*
ce	::=	positive-ce
	::=	negative-ce
positive-ce	::=	form
	::=	**{** element-variable form **}**
	::=	**{** form element-variable **}**
negative-ce	::=	**-** form
form	::=	**(** constant-symbolic-atom lhs-term* **)**
	::=	**(** lhs-term* **)**
lhs-term	::=	**↑** constant-symbolic-atom lhs-value
	::=	**↑** number lhs-value
	::=	lhs-value
lhs-value	::=	**{** restriction* **}**
	::=	restriction
restriction	::=	**≪** any-atom* **≫**
	::=	predicate atomic-value
	::=	atomic-value
atomic-value	::=	**//** any-atom
	::=	var-or-constant

var-or-constant	::=	*constant-symbolic-atom*
	::=	*number*
	::=	*variable*
predicate	::=	**=**
	::=	<>
	::=	<
	::=	<**=**
	::=	>**=**
	::=	>
	::=	<**=**>
rhs	::=	*action**
action	::=	(**make** *rhs-pattern*)
	::=	(**make** *rhs-term**)
	::=	(**remove** *element-designator**)
	::=	(**modify** *element-designator rhs-term**)
	::=	(**halt**)
	::=	(**bind** *variable*)
	::=	(**bind** *variable rhs-value*)
	::=	(**bind** *variable rhs-term**)
	::=	(**cbind** *element-variable*)
	::=	(**call** *constant-symbolic-atom rhs-term**)
	::=	(**write** *rhs-value**)
	::=	(**write** *rhs-term**)
	::=	(**openfile** *rhs-value rhs-value rhs-io*)
	::=	(**openfile** *rhs-term**)
	::=	(**closefile** *rhs-value**)
	::=	(**closefile** *rhs-term**)
	::=	(**default** *rhs-value rhs-default*)
	::=	(**default** *rhs-term**)
	::=	(**build** *quoted-form**)
element-designator		
	::=	*element-variable*
	::=	*number*
rhs-pattern	::=	*constant-symbolic-atom rhs-term**
rhs-term	::=	↑ *constant-symbolic-atom rhs-value*
	::=	↑ *var-or-constant rhs-value*
	::=	*rhs-value*
rhs-value	::=	*atomic-value*
	::=	*function*

rhs-io	::=	**in**
	::=	**out**
rhs-default	::=	**trace**
	::=	**write**
	::=	**accept**
function	::=	(**litval** *var-or-constant*)
	::=	(**substr** *element-designator var-or-constant var-or-constant*)
	::=	(**genatom**)
	::=	(**crlf**)
	::=	(**rjust** *var-or-constant*)
	::=	(**tabto** *var-or-constant*)
	::=	(**accept**)
	::=	(**accept** *var-or-constant*)
	::=	(**acceptline** *var-or-constant**)
	::=	(**compute** *expression*)
	::=	*user-defined-function*
user-defined-function		
	::=	(*constant-symbolic-atom var-or-constant**)
expression	::=	*number*
	::=	*variable*
	::=	*expression operator expression*
	::=	(*expression*)
operator	::=	+
	::=	−
	::=	*
	::=	//
	::=	\\
quoted-form	::=	\\ *rhs-value*
	::=	*any-atom*
	::=	(*quoted-form**)

Several terms have been left undefined: *variable, element-variable, constant-symbolic-atom, any-atom,* and *number*. Symbolic atoms and numbers are described in Section 2.1.1. The two kinds of variables are described in Sections 2.3.1 and 2.3.2. An *any-atom* is an atom that is treated as a constant because it is quoted, usually with // or ≪ ≫. A *constant-symbolic-atom* is an atom that is treated as a constant because it does not have the form of a variable or operator.

References

[Allen 82] Allen, L., *YAPS: Yet Another Production System*, Technical Report TR-1146, Department of Computer Science, University of Maryland, February 1982.

[Anderson 76] Anderson, J. R., *Language, Memory, and Thought*. Hillsdale, NJ: Lawrence Erlbaum Associates, 1976.

[Anderson 83] Anderson, J. R., *The Architecture of Cognition*. Cambridge, MA: Harvard University Press, 1983.

[Anderson, Farrell, Sauers 84] Anderson, J. R., R. Farrell, and R. Sauers. Learning to Program in LISP, *Cognitive Science* 8(2), April–June 1984.

[Anderson, Kline, Beasley 77] Anderson, J. R., P. J. Kline, and C. M. Beasley, *A Theory of the Acquisition of Cognitive Skills*. Technical Report 77-1, Yale University, 1977.

[Barr, Feigenbaum 81] Barr, A., and E. A. Feigenbaum (eds.), *Handbook of Artificial Intelligence*, Vol. 1. Los Altos, CA: William Kaufmann, Inc., 1981.

[Basili, Turner 75] Basili, V. R., and A. J. Turner, Iterative Enhancement: A Practical Technique for Software Development, *IEEE Transactions on Software Engineering*, December 1975, 390–396.

[Bobrow, Stefik 83] Bobrow, D., and M. Stefik, *The* LOOPS *Manual*. Technical Report, Xerox PARC, 1983.

[Brachman 78] Brachman, R. J., *A Structural Paradigm for Representing Knowledge*. Technical Report 3605, Bolt, Beranek, and Newmann, Inc., May 1978.

[Buchanan, Duda 83] Buchanan, B. G., and R. O. Duda, Principles of Rule-Based Expert Systems; in M. Yovits (ed.), *Advances in Computers*, Vol. 22. New York: Academic Press, 1983.

[Buchanan, Shortliffe 84] Buchanan, B. G., and E. H. Shortliffe (eds.), *Rule-Based Expert Systems*. Reading, MA: Addison-Wesley, 1984.

[Clancey 82] Clancey, W., GUIDON; in A. Barr, and E. A. Feigenbaum (eds.), *The Handbook of Artificial Intelligence*. Los Altos, CA: William Kaufmann, Inc., 1982.

[Clocksin, Mellish 82] Clocksin, W. F., and C. S. Mellish, *Programming in* PROLOG. New York: Springer-Verlag, 1982.

[Cohen, Grinberg 83] Cohen, P. R., and M. R. Grinberg, A Theory of Heuristic Reasoning About Uncertainty, *AI Magazine* 4(2), Summer 1983, 17–24.

[Davis 80] Davis, R., Meta-Rules: Reasoning about Control, *Artificial Intelligence* 15, 1980, 179–222.

[Davis, King 76] Davis, R., and J. King, An Overview of Production Systems; in E. W. Elcock and D. Michie (eds.), *Machine Intelligence*. New York: John Wiley, 1976, 300–331.

[Davis, Lenat 80] Davis, R., and D. B. Lenat, *Knowledge-Based Systems in Artificial Intelligence*. New York: McGraw-Hill, 1980.

[Doyle, London 80] Doyle, J., and P. A. London, Selected Descriptor-Indexed Bibliography to the Literature on Belief Revision. *SIGART Newsletter* (71), April 1980, 7–23.

[Duda, et al. 79] Duda, R. O., P. E. Hart, K. Konolige, and R. Reboh, *A Computer-Based Consultant for Mineral Exploration*. Technical Report; Final Report, SRI Project 6415, SRI International, September 1979.

[Duda, Gaschnig, Hart 79] Duda, R. O., J. G. Gaschnig, and P. E. Hart, Model design in the PROSPECTOR consultant system for mineral exploration. In D. Michie (ed.), *Expert Systems in the Micro-Electronic Age*. Edinburgh University Press, 1979.

[Fain, et al. 81] Fain, J., D. Gorlin, F. Hayes-Roth, S. J. Rosenschein, H. Sowizral, and D. Waterman, *The* ROSIE *Language Reference Manual*. Technical Report N-1647-ARPA, The Rand Corporation, Santa Monica, CA, 1981.

[Fain, et al. 82] Fain, J., F. Hayes-Roth, H. Sowizral, and D. Waterman, *Programming in* ROSIE. Technical Report N-1646-ARPA, The Rand Corporation, Santa Monica, CA, 1982.

[Forgy 79] Forgy, C. L., *On the Efficient Implementation of Production Systems*. PhD thesis, Department of Computer Science, Carnegie-Mellon University, February 1979.

[Forgy 81] Forgy, C. L., OPS5 *User's Manual*. Technical Report CMU-CS-81-135, Department of Computer Science, Carnegie-Mellon University, July 1981.

[Forgy 82] Forgy, C. L., Rete: A Fast Algorithm for the Many Pattern/Many Object Pattern Match Problem, *Artificial Intelligence* 19(1), September 1982, 17–37.

[Forgy 84] Forgy, C. L., *The* OPS83 *Report*. Technical Report CMU-CS-84-133, Department of Computer Science, Carnegie-Mellon University, May 1984.

[Fox, Lowenfeld, Kleinosky 83] Fox, M. S., S. Lowenfeld, and P. Kleinosky, Techniques for Sensor-Based Diagnosis; in *Proceedings of the Eighth International Joint Conference on Artificial Intelligence*. Los Altos, CA: William Kaufmann, Inc., 1983, 158–163.

[Freiherr 80] Freiherr, G., *The Seeds of Artificial Intelligence*. Technical Report 80-2071, NIH SUMEX-AIM, 1980.

[Genesereth 82] Genesereth, M. R., Diagnosis Using Hierarchical Design Models;

in *Proceedings of the Second National Conference on Artificial Intelligence.* Los Altos, CA: William Kaufmann, Inc., 1982, 278–283.

[Genesereth, et al. 81] Genesereth, M. R., R. Greiner, and D. E. Smith, *MRS Manual.* Technical Report HPP-81-6, Department of Computer Science, Stanford University, November 1981.

[Georgeff 82] Georgeff, M. P., Procedural Control in Production Systems, *Artificial Intelligence* 18(2), April 1982, 175–201.

[Goldberg, Robson 83] Goldberg, A., and D. Robson, SMALLTALK-*80, The Language and Its Implementation.* Reading, MA: Addison-Wesley, 1983.

[Hayes-Roth, Waterman, Lenat 83] Hayes-Roth, F., D. A. Waterman, and D. B. Lenat (eds.), *Building Expert Systems.* Reading, MA: Addison-Wesley, 1983.

[Hendrix 79] Hendrix, G. G., Encoding Knowledge in Partitioned Networks; in N. V. Findler (ed.), *Associative Networks: The Representation and Use of Knowledge in Computers.* New York: Academic Press, 1979, 51–92.

[Hinton, et al. 84] Hinton, G. E., T. J. Sejnowski, and D. H. Ackley, *Boltzman Machines: Constraint Satisfaction Networks that Learn.* Technical Report CMU-CS-84-119, Department of Computer Science, Carnegie-Mellon University, May 1984.

[Kahn, McDermott 84] Kahn, G., and J. McDermott, The MUD System; in *Proceedings IEEE Conference on Artificial Intelligence Applications,* IEEE, 1984.

[Kant, Barstow 84] Kant, E., and D. R. Barstow, The Refinement Paradigm: The Interaction of Coding and Efficiency Knowledge in Program Synthesis; in D. R. Barstow, H. Shrobe, and E. Sandewall (eds.), *Interactive Programming Environments.* New York: McGraw-Hill, 1984.

[Kim, McDermott, Siewiorek 84] Kim, J., J. McDermott, and D. Siewiorek, Exploiting Domain Knowledge in IC Cell Layout, *IEEE Design and Test Magazine,* August 1984.

[Langley 83] Langley, P., Exploring the Space of Cognitive Architectures, *Behavior Research Methods and Instrumentation* (15), 1983, 289–299.

[Langley, Neches 81] Langley, P., and R. T. Neches, PRISM *User's Manual.* Technical Report, Department of Psychology, Carnegie-Mellon University, 1981.

[Marcus, McDermott, Wang 84] Marcus, S., J. McDermott, and T. Wang, *Knowledge Acquisition in Constructive Tasks.* Technical Report, Department of Computer Science, Carnegie-Mellon University, 1984.

[Martin, et al. 77] Martin, N., P. Friedland, J. King, and M. Stefik, Knowledge-Based Management for Expert Planning in Genetics; in *Proceedings of the*

Fifth International Joint Conference on Artificial Intelligence. Los Altos, CA: William Kaufmann, Inc., 1977, 882–887.

[D. McDermott 83] McDermott, D., DUCK: *A* LISP-*Based Deductive System.* Technical Report, Department of Computer Science, Yale University, May 1983.

[J. McDermott 83] McDermott, J., Building Expert Systems; in Reitman, W. (ed.), *Artificial Intelligence Applications for Business.* Norwood, NJ: Ablex Publishing Corp., 1983.

[McDermott 80] McDermott, J., R1: *A Rule-Based Configurer of Computer Systems.* Technical Report CMU-US-80-119, Department of Computer Science, Carnegie-Mellon University, 1980.

[McDermott, Forgy 78] McDermott, J., and C. Forgy, Production System Conflict Resolution Strategies; in D. A. Waterman and F. Hayes-Roth (eds.), *Pattern-Directed Inference Systems.* New York: Academic Press, 1978.

[Michalski, Carbonell, Mitchell 83] Michalski, R. S., J. G. Carbonell, and T. M. Mitchell, *Machine Learning.* Palo Alto, CA: Tioga Publishing Co., 1983.

[Mitchell 84] Mitchell, T. M., Generalization as Search, *Artificial Intelligence* 18(2), March 1984, 203–226.

[Moon, Stallman, Weinreb 83] Moon, D., R. M. Stallman, and D. Weinreb, LISP *Machine Manual.* Technical Report, Artificial Intelligence Laboratory, January 1983, Chs. 19 and 20.

[Newell 73] Newell, A., Production Systems: Models of Control Structures; in W. G. Chase (ed.), *Visual Information Processing.* New York: Academic Press, 1973, Ch. 10, 463–526.

[Newell, McDermott, Moore 78] Newell, A. N., J. McDermott, and J. Moore, The Efficiency of Certain Production System Implementations; in D. A. Waterman and F. Hayes-Roth (eds.), *Pattern-Directed Inference Systems.* New York: Academic Press, 1978, 155–176.

[Newell, Simon 72] Newell, A., and H. A. Simon, *Human Problem Solving.* Englewood Cliffs, NJ: Prentice-Hall, 1972.

[Nilsson 80] Nilsson, N. J., *Principles of Artificial Intelligence.* Palo Alto, CA: Tioga Publishing Co., 1980.

[Pasik, Schor 84] Pasik, A., and M. Schor, Table-driven Rules in Expert Systems, *SIGART Newsletter* (87), January 1984, 31–33.

[Politakis, Weiss 84] Politakis, P., and S. M. Weiss, Using Empirical Analysis to Refine Expert System Knowledge Bases, *Artificial Intelligence* 22(1) 1984, 23–48.

[Post 43] Post, E. L., Formal Reductions of the General Combinatorial Decision Problem, *American Journal of Mathematics* 65, 1943.

[Reboh 81] Reboh, R., *Knowledge Engineering Techniques and Tools in the Prospector Environment.* Technical Report Technical Note 243, SRI International, 1981.

[Rich 83] Rich, E., *Artificial Intelligence.* New York: McGraw-Hill, 1983.

[Robinson 79] Robinson, J. A., *Logic: Form and Function, The Mechanization of Deductive Reasoning.* New York: North Holland, 1979.

[Rosenbloom 79] Rosenbloom, P. S., XAPS *Reference Manual.* Technical Report, Department of Computer Science, Carnegie-Mellon University, 1979.

[Rosenbloom 83] Rosenbloom, P. S., *The Chunking of Goal Hierarchies: A Model of Practice and Stimulus-Response Compatibility,* PhD thesis, Department of Computer Science, Carnegie-Mellon University, 1983.

[Rosenbloom, Newell 84] Rosenbloom, P. S., and A. Newell, Learning by Chunking: A Production-System Model of Practice; in D. Klahr, P. Langley, and R. Neches (eds.), *Self-Modifying Production Systems Models of Learning and Development.* Cambridge, MA: MIT Press, 1984.

[Rummelhart, Lindsay, Norman 72] Rummelhart, D. E., P. H. Lindsay, and D. A. Norman, *A Process Model for Long-Term Memory.* New York: Academic Press, 1972, 198–246.

[Sauers, Farrell 82] Sauers, R., and R. Farrell, GRAPES *User's Manual.* Technical Report ONR-82-3, Department of Psychology, Carnegie-Mellon University, November 1982.

[Shortliffe 76] Shortliffe, E. H., *Computer Based Medical Consultations:* MYCIN. New York: Elsevier, 1976.

[Simon 83] Simon, H. A., Why Should Machines Learn? in R. S. Michalski, J. G. Carbonell, and T. M. Mitchell (eds.), *Machine Learning.* Palo Alto, CA: Tioga Publishing Co., 1983, 25–37.

[Stefik, Bell, Bobrow 82] Stefik, M., A. G. Bell, and D. G. Bobrow, *Rule-Oriented Programming in* LOOPS. Technical Report KB-VLSI-82-22, XEROX PARC, 1982.

[Swartout 83] Swartout, W. (ed.), Workshop on Automated Explanation Production, *SIGART Newsletter* (85), July 1983, 7–13.

[Thibadeau 82] Thibadeau, R., CAPS: A Language for Modelling Highly-Skilled Knowledge-Intensive Behavior; in *Proceedings National Conference on the Use of On-line Computers in Psychology,* APA, 1982.

[Thibadeau, Just, Carpenter 82] Thibadeau, R., M. Just, and P. Carpenter, A

Model of the Time Course and Content of Reading, *Cognitive Science* 6(2), April–June 1982.

[van Melle, et al. 81] van Melle, W., A. C. Scott, J. S. Bennett, and M. Peairs, *The* EMYCIN *Manual*. Technical Report HPP-81-16, Computer Science Department, Stanford University, 1981.

[Vesonder, et al. 83] Vesonder, G. T., S. J. Stolfo, J. E. Zielinski, F. D. Miller, and D. H. Copp, ACE: An Expert System for Telephone Cable Maintenance; in *Proceedings of the* ACE *International Joint Conference on Artificial Intelligence*. Los Altos, CA: William Kaufmann, Inc., 1983, 116–121.

[Walker 83] Walker, A., PROLOG/EX1, An Inference Engine which Explains Both Yes and No Answers; in *Proceedings of the Eighth International Joint Conference on Artificial Intelligence*, Los Altos, CA: William Kaufmann, Inc., 1983, 526–528.

[Waterman, Hayes-Roth 78] Waterman, D. A., and F. Hayes-Roth, An Overview of Pattern-Directed Inference Systems; in D. A. Waterman and F. Hayes-Roth (eds.), *Pattern-Directed Inference Systems*, New York: Academic Press, 1978, 3–22.

[Weiss, Kulikowski 81] Weiss, S. M., and C. A. Kulikowski, Expert consultation systems: The EXPERT and CASNET projects; in *Machine Intelligence*, Infotech State of the Art Report 9, no. 3, Pergamon Infotech Ltd., Maidenhead Berks, G. B., 1981.

[Weiss, Kulikowski 84] Weiss, S. M., and C. A. Kulikowski, *A Practical Guide to Designing Expert Systems*. Totowa, NJ: Rowman & Allanheld, 1984.

[Weiss, Kulikowski, Safir 78] Weiss, S. M., C. A. Kulikowski, and A. Safir, A Model-Based Method for Computer-Aided Medical Decision Making, *Artificial Intelligence* 11, 1978.

[Wright, Fox 82] Wright, J. M., and M. S. Fox, SRL/1.5 *User Manual*. Technical Report, Robotics Institute, Carnegie-Mellon University, 1982.

[Zadeh 79] Zadeh, L. A., A Theory of Approximate Reasoning; in J. E. Hayes, D. Mitchie, and L. I. Mikulich (eds.), *Machine Intelligence*. New York: John Wiley and Sons, 1979.

Answers to Selected Exercises

ANSWERS FOR CHAPTER 1

Exercise 1-1.

a) The matches found by match-rules are:

Rule 1	-Jess
Rule 2	-Terry
Rule 2	-Robin
Rule 3	-Terry

b) The select-rules algorithm will choose the match of Rule 3 and Terry because three conditions are matched as opposed to two conditions for each of the other matches.

c) Continuing through the cycles, we have Rule 3 firing with Terry. In data memory after Rule 3 is information about Terry, but changed to the following:

```
Terry is a customer
  whose payment record is bad
  who has been a customer 22 years
  whose billing category is set to priority
```

Next either the match of Rule 1 with Jess or the match of Rule 2 with Robin is chosen. Both have two conditions matched, so the select-rules arbitrarily breaks the tie. On the next cycle, select-rules will choose the remaining match and working memory will be:

```
Terry is a customer
  whose payment record is bad
  who has been a customer 22 years
  whose billing category is set to priority

Jess is a customer
  whose payment record is good
  who has been a customer 9 years
  whose billing category is set to priority

Robin is a customer
  whose payment record is bad
  who has been a customer 10 years
  whose billing category is set to normal
```

Exercise 1-2.

Cycle 1 — Match-rules:

Rule 1 -Jess
Rule 2 -Terry
Rule 2 -Robin
Rule 3 -Terry

Cycle 1 — Select-rules: All three rules are selected

Cycle 1 — Fire-rules: (note choice of ordering for Rule 2 — firings are arbitrary)

1. Fire Rule 3 with Terry
2. Fire Rule 2 with Terry
3. Fire Rule 2 with Robin
4. Fire Rule 1 with Jess

Cycle 1 — Data Memory:

```
Terry is a customer
  whose payment record is bad
  who has been a customer 22 years
  whose billing category is set to normal

Jess is a customer
  whose payment record is good
  who has been a customer 9 years
  whose billing category is set to priority

Robin is a customer
  whose payment record is bad
  who has been a customer 10 years
  whose billing category is set to normal
```

Cycle 2 — No Matches!

ANSWERS FOR CHAPTER 2

Exercise 2-1.

- between −1 and 10
  {>−1 < 10} if "between" means "excluding the end-points"
  {>= −1 <= 10} if "between" means "including the end-points"

- in the list: NM MA ME NC
  <<NM MA ME NC>>
- any number or the atom "nil"
  Impossible; a disjunction can only contain constants. To say "any number," we need to use the operator <=>.
- equal to 45
  45

Exercise 2-2. A first approach to the problem might attempt to use the *spouse* attribute to represent the marital status also. We suggest another attribute with coded values to represent marital status.

```
(literalize Person                ; Element class representing
                                  ; people
    name                  ; first name of Person
    mother                ; name attribute of a Person, or nil
    father                ; name attribute of a Person, or nil
    age                   ; positive integer or nil
    sex                   ; male, female, or nil
    spouse                ; name attribute of a Person, or nil
    marital-status        ; M, S, D, W or nil
    street-address        ; represents address, or nil
    city-of-residence)    ; name attribute of a City, or nil
```

Exercise 2-3.

- <thisperson> is the *sibling* of <thatperson>

```
(Person
    ↑name <thisperson>
    ↑mother <mother-name>
    ↑father <father-name>)
(Person
    ↑name <thatperson>
    ↑mother <mother-name>
    ↑father <father-name>)
```

- <thisperson> is the *sister* of <thatperson>

```
(Person
    ↑name <thisperson>
    ↑mother <mother-name>
    ↑father <father-name>
    ↑sex female)
(Person
    ↑name <thatperson>
    ↑mother <mother-name>
    ↑father <father-name>)
```

- <thisperson> is the *maternal grandmother* of <thatperson>

```
(Person
    ↑name <thatperson>
    ↑mother <mother-name>)
(Person
    ↑name <mother-name>
    ↑mother <thisperson>)
```

- <thisperson> is the *paternal aunt* of <thatperson>

```
;Rephrasing the relation we get:
; <thisperson> is the sister of the <father> of <thatperson>
; or
(Person
    ↑name <thisperson>
    ↑sex female
    ↑mother <m-name>
    ↑father <f-name>)
(Person
    ↑name <father>
    ↑mother <m-name>
    ↑father <f-name>)
(Person
    ↑name <thatperson>
    ↑father <father>)
```

Exercise 2-4.

```
(p Find::NH
   (City ↑state NH ↑name <name1>)
   (Person ↑city-of-residence <name1> ↑name <person-name>)
-->
   (write (crlf) <person-name> lives in <name>\, NH))
```

Exercise 2-6.

```
;The rule Find::Oldest
; finds the largest age value in the data base
;   and the second largest age value in the data base
; then  computes the difference in the two values
;   and prints the name of a person with the greatest age,
;      followed by the age and the computed age difference
;
(p Find::Oldest
           ;The first element matches all Person elements.
   (Person ↑name <oldest> ↑age <age-old>)
           ;The next element only matches someone else,
           ; the same age or younger than <oldest>
   (Person ↑name <> <oldest> ↑age {<age-next> <=
           ; <age-old>})
```

```
            ;Finally, restrict the matches so that there is
            ; no one older than <age-next>
            ; except those as old as <oldest>
 - (Person ↑age { > <age-next> <> <age-old> })
-->
   (write (crlf) <oldest>\, aged <age-old>\,)
   (write (crlf) is about (compute <age-old> - <age-next>))
   (write years older than anyone else\.))
```

Exercise 2-8.

```
;  IF    there is a Start element in working memory
;  THEN  remove the Start element
;   and  write a message to input the type of relation
;          to find
;   and  write a message to input the name of the person
;          as target
;   and  make a Request element to find all relations of
;          the person
;
(p Find::Initialize
   {(Start)                        <initialize>}
-->
   (remove <initialize>)
   (write (crlf)
      |Please type the relationship to compute:|)
   (bind <relation> (accept))
   (write (crlf) |If you type the name of <person1>,|)
   (write (crlf) |all people related to <person1> by
      relation|)
   (write (crlf) <relation> |will be printed:|(crlf))
   (make Request ↑type <relation> ↑target (accept)))
```

Exercise 2-10.

```
;  IF    there is a Request to stop
;  THEN  print "That's All Folks"
;   and  halt the program
;
(p Find::Stop
   (Request ↑type stop)
-->
   (write (crlf) That\'s All Folks)
   (halt))
```

Exercise 2-12.

```
;There are three rules:
;  FindDescendant::Mother
;  FindDescendant::Father
```

```
;  FindDescendant::Print
;  IF    there is a request to find a person's descendant
;   and  the person is the mother  of a person <child>
;  THEN  make a request to find the descendant <child>
;
(p FindDescendant::Mother
   (Request ↑type descendant ↑target <mother>)
   (Person ↑name <child> ↑mother <mother>)
-->
   (make Request ↑type descendant ↑target <child>))

;  IF    there is a request to find a person's descendant
;   and  the person is the father of a person <child>
;  THEN  make a request to find the descendant <child>
;
(p FindDescendant::Father
   (Request ↑type descendant ↑target <father>)
   (Person ↑name <child> ↑father <father>)
-->
   (make Request ↑type descendant ↑target <child>))

;FindDescendant::Print
;  IF    there is a request to find a person's descendant
;  THEN  write the name of the person
;   and  remove the request element
(p FindDescendant::Print
   {(Request
       ↑type descendant
       ↑target { <child>) <> nil }             <request1>}
-->
   (remove <request1>)
   (write <child> is a descendant))
```

Exercise 2-14.

```
;First we will create a rule to remove
; requests with "nil" names:
;
(p Find::Clean-up
   {(Request ↑target nil)                       <request1>}
-->
   (remove <request>))

;Now, generalize the old Stop rule.
;  IF    there is only one request of a given type
;   and  the type is not stop
;  THEN  remove the request
;   and  print a termination message for the type
;   and  reinitialize by making a Start element
;
```

```
(p FindType::Stop
   {(Request
       ↑type { <type1> <> stop }
       ↑target { <name1>  <> nil })                  <request1>}
 - (Request
       ↑type <type1>
       ↑target <> <name1>)
-->
   (remove <request1>)
   (write (crlf) No more <type1>)
   (make Start))
```

ANSWERS FOR CHAPTER 3

Exercise 3-1. Answer for actions *Grab* and *Drop*:

```
Grab O
   preconditions:
d20   monkey is not holding anything
d5    O is of element class phys-object
d5    O has a light weight
d15   monkey is at the same horizontal location as O
      either
cs       the monkey is on the floor and O is not on the
         ceiling
d16   or O is on the ceiling and the monkey is on the
      ladder

Drop O
   preconditions:
cs    monkey is holding O
d5    O is of element class phys-object
```

Exercise 3-2. Answer for *Grab* and *Drop*:

```
Grab O
   postconditions:
cs    monkey is holding O
d14   O is not "on" anything

Drop O
   postconditions:
cs    monkey is holding nothing
d17   O is on the floor
```

Exercise 3-3. Design decision 15 states that the monkey must be at exactly the same horizontal location as an object in order to climb onto it. Modify the precondition for *Climb onto* to read:

```
Climb onto O
   precondition:
      monkey is on the floor
      monkey does not hold anything
      O is of element class phys-object
      O is on the floor
      monkey and O at same horizontal location
```

Design decision 13 states that the *at* attribute of a phys-object must always be updated when the object is moved. Problem 4 relates to this design decision and points to a problem with the precondition of the *walk to* action. Create two actions:

```
Walk to X-Y carrying nil
 preconditions:
    monkey is on the floor not at X-Y
    monkey holds nothing
 postconditions:
    monkey is at location X-Y

Walk to X-Y carrying <> nil
 preconditions;
    monkey is on the floor not at X-Y
    monkey holds a phys-object, O
 postconditions:
    monkey is at location X-Y
    O is at location X-Y
```

Design decision 5 states that the monkey cannot carry "heavy" objects. However, if a "heavy" object is on a "light" object, the monkey may pick up the "light" object, and there is no mention of what happens to the "heavy" object. Modify the *Grab O* definition to:

```
Grab O
   preconditions:
      monkey is not holding anything
      O is of element class phys-object
      O is light in weight
      O doesn't have anything on it
      monkey and O at same horizontal location
      either
       monkey on floor and O not on ceiling
      or
       monkey on ladder and O on ceiling
```

Exercise 3-4.

```
(make monkey ↑on ladder ↑holds blanket ↑at 5-5)
(make phys-object ↑name ladder ↑at 5-5 ↑on floor ↑weight
      light)
```

```
(make phys-object ↑name bananas ↑weight light ↑at 7-7 ↑on
      ceiling)
(make phys-object ↑name blanket ↑at 5-5 ↑weight light)
(make goal ↑type holds ↑object-name bananas ↑status active)
```

Exercise 3-5.

```
(make monkey ↑on floor ↑at 7-7)
(make phys-object ↑name bananas ↑on floor ↑at 9-9 ↑weight
      light)
(make phys-object ↑name ladder ↑on floor ↑at 3-2 ↑weight
      light)
(make goal ↑type holds ↑object-name bananas ↑status active)
```

Exercise 3-6.

1. The *monkey* is holding a heavy physical object, the "blanket," and that object is at a location different from the location of the *monkey*.
2. The *monkey* is *on* an object at a location different from that of the *monkey*.
3. The *goal* and the description of the location of "bananas" both refer to a *phys-object* named "couch" that does not occur in working memory.
4. The *goal* has *type* "holds" and doesn't have a "nil" value for *to*.
5. The *phys-object* "bananas" should have a "nil" value for *on* because it is being held by the *monkey*.

Exercise 3-8. You should be sure to develop rules that have goals to grab objects that have other objects on them.

Exercise 3-11. See Appendix 1.1 for one version of a complete program. Note that this version does not have corrections for all the problems identified in this exercise set.

ANSWERS FOR CHAPTER 4

Exercise 4-1.

```
(literalize estimated-labor
    job-name          ; the name of the job to be performed
    hours             ; the estimated number of required hours
)

(literalize job
    job-name          ; the name of the job to be performed
    difficulty        ; major, moderate, minor
)
```

```
(p minor
   {(job
       ↑job-name <job-name>
       ↑difficulty nil)                    <job>}
   (estimated-labor
       ↑job-name <job-name>
       ↑hours <= 2)
-->
   (modify <job> ↑difficulty minor))

(p moderate
   {(job
       ↑job-name <job-name>
       ↑difficulty nil)                    <job>}
   (estimated-labor
       ↑job-name <job-name>
       ↑hours { > 2 <= 4 })
-->
   (modify <job> ↑difficulty moderate))

(p major
   {(job
       ↑job-name <job-name>
       ↑difficulty nil)                    <job>}
   (estimated-labor
       ↑job-name <job-name>
       ↑hours > 4)
-->
   (modify <job> ↑difficulty major))

(make estimated-labor
    ↑job-name install-battery
    ↑hours 1)

(make estimated-labor
    ↑job-name install-control-arm-bushings
    ↑hours 5)
```

Exercise 4-2.

```
(literalize estimated-labor
    job-name          ;the name of the job to be performed
    hours             ;the estimated number of required hours
)

(literalize job
    job-name          ; the name of the job to be performed
    difficulty        ; major, moderate, minor
)
```

```
(literalize boundary
    difficulty      ; major, moderate, minor
    lower           ; the lower boundary in hours
    upper           ; the upper boundary in hours
)

(p categorize
   {(job
       ↑job-name <job-name>
        ↑difficulty nil)                    <job>}
   (estimated-labor
       ↑job-name <job-name>
       ↑hours <hours>)
   (boundary
       ↑difficulty <difficulty>
       ↑lower <  <hours>
       ↑upper >= <hours>)
-->
   (modify <job> ↑difficulty <difficulty>))

(make boundary ↑difficulty minor    ↑lower 0 ↑upper 2  )
(make boundary ↑difficulty moderate ↑lower 2 ↑upper 4  )
(make boundary ↑difficulty major    ↑lower 4 ↑upper 100)

(make estimated-labor
    ↑job-name install-battery
    ↑hours 1)

(make estimated-labor
    ↑job-name install-control-arm-bushings
    ↑hours 5)
```

Exercise 4-3. Most obviously, if the class of a working memory element is never tested in any condition element, it can never have any effect. More indirectly, it may be tested only in the left-hand side of rules that cannot possibly be instantiated (for example, because their conditions are self-contradictory).

Exercise 4-5. The subgoal structure encoded into the program was based on the major structural divisions of Form 1040 and not on the logical relationships among the questions.

Exercise 4-6. Most important, there are varying numbers of subgoals for different parent goals, so a single rule will not work. Perhaps a set of rules, one for each different number of subgoals, will do the trick.

There is also the problem of how the results of the subgoals are to be combined: added, subtracted, etc. This could be solved with an external function call, passing as parameters the name of the parent goal and an ordered list consisting of the *amount* fields of the subgoals.

ANSWERS FOR CHAPTER 5

Exercise 5-1. There are many ways to perform the modification. One way is to add a rule that purges working memory of the superfluous elements. The rule might look like this:

```
(p purge-default-element
   {(array-elt ↑value 0)      <supererogatory>}
-->
   (remove <supererogatory>))
```

The disadvantage of this solution is that unnecessary work must be undone. It is better to nip the problem in the bud by splitting the rule `modify-nondefault-array-element` into two rules: one to create an element if the new value is not the default, and the other to refrain from creating a default value.

```
(p modify-nondefault-array-element-to-another-nondefault
   {(operation
       ↑op-name write
       ↑array-name <A>
       ↑index <INX>
       ↑value { <VAL> <> 0 })       <operation>}
   {(array-elt
       ↑array-name <A>
       ↑index <INX>)                <array-elt>}
-->
   (modify <array-elt> ↑value <VAL>)
   (remove <operation>))

(p modify-nondefault-array-element-to-default
   {(operation
       ↑op-name write
       ↑array-name <A>
       ↑index <INX>
       ↑value 0)                    <operation>}
   {(array-elt
       ↑array-name <A>
       ↑index <INX>)                <array-elt>}
-->
   (remove <array-elt>)
   (remove <operation>))
```

What will happen if there is an operation to modify an element bearing the default value so that the new value is also the default? What are you going to do about it?

Exercise 5-2.

```
(p attempt-to-pop-empty-stack
   {(stack-operation ↑operation pop ↑value nil)    <nogood>}
 - (stack-element)
-->
   (remove <nogood>)
   (write (crlf) |The stack is empty so it can not be
       popped|))
```

Exercise 5-3.

```
(literalize rock-climber
    age              ; young or old
    style            ; timid or bold
)

(p old-not-bold
   (rock-climber ↑age old ↑style <> bold)
-->
   (write (crlf) that is plausible))

(p bold-not-old
   (rock-climber ↑age <> old ↑style bold)
-->
   (write (crlf) that is plausible))

(p error::old-and-bold
   (rock-climber ↑age old ↑style bold)
-->
   (write (crlf) There are old rock climbers
                 and there are bold rock climbers
          (crlf) but there are no old, bold rock climbers))
```

Exercise 5-4.

```
a) (animal ↑type elephant ↑name <> Mnemosyne)

b) (animal ↑type <> elephant ↑name Mnemosyne)

c) - (animal ↑type elephant ↑name Mnemosyne)

d) - (animal ↑name Mnemosyne)

e) - (animal ↑type elephant)
```

Alternative (c), "There is no elephant whose name is Mnemosyne," is the logical negation of "There is an elephant whose name is Mnemosyne."

Exercise 5-5.

```
a) (pet ↑type dog ↑owner <dog-owner>)
   (pet ↑type cat ↑owner <dog-owner>)

b)  (pet ↑type dog ↑owner <dog-owner>)
  - (pet ↑type cat ↑owner <dog-owner>)
```

Condition (c) cannot be expressed in a single left-hand side using the present representation.

Exercise 5-6. Define a working memory element that serves as a switch — that is, it is allowed to assume one of only two states, say "odd" and "even." The switch will change state only when an incrementing phase is complete, so alternate incrementing calls will take place in alternate states.

```
(literalize switch
    status            ; "odd" or "even"
)
```

The working memory element class that carries the numbers to be incremented must also have an attribute that serves as a binary switch.

```
(literalize number
    value             ; a number
    status            ; "odd" or "even"
)
```

Finally, define an element whose presence in working memory indicates that incrementation is to take place.

```
(literalize incrementing)
```

At most one copy of this element may exist in working memory at any given time.

There is only one switch element. All status fields in the switch and in the numbers are initialized to the same value — say, "odd."

```
(make switch ↑status odd)
(make number ↑status odd ↑value 54)
(make number ↑status odd ↑value 40)
```

There is one rule to perform the incrementation if the switch has the value "even" and an analogous rule to perform the incrementation if the switch has the value "odd."

```
(p increment::even
   (incrementing)
   (switch ↑status even)
   {(number ↑status even ↑value <value>)              <number>}
-->
   (modify <number> ↑value (compute <value> + 1)
       ↑status odd))

(p increment::odd
   (incrementing)
   (switch ↑status odd)
   {(number ↑status odd ↑value <value>)               <number>}
-->
   (modify <number> ↑value (compute <value> + 1)
       ↑status even))
```

Notice that these rules complement the status field of the numbers but not of the switch.

There is one rule that changes the switch from "odd" to "even" and an analogous rule that performs the opposite action. Both rules remove the "incrementing" element.

```
(p complement::switch-even
   {(incrementing)                               <incrementing>}
   {(switch ↑status even)                         <even-switch>}
-->
   (modify <even-switch> ↑status odd)
   (remove <incrementing>))


(p complement::switch-odd
   {(incrementing)                               <incrementing>}
   {(switch ↑status odd)                           <odd-switch>}
-->
   (modify <odd-switch> ↑status even)
   (remove <incrementing>))
```

Because of specificity in conflict resolution, these rules can fire only after all numbers have been incremented.

The process of incrementing can be started by putting the "incrementing" element into working memory.

```
(make incrementing)
```

Exercise 5-7.

```
(literalize number
    value               ; an argument to the gcd function
    id)                 ; needed to distinguish arguments
```

```
(p get-arguments
   {(start)                                          <start>}
  -(number)
-->
   (write (crlf) Enter a non-negative integer)
   (make number ↑value (accept)
                ↑id (genatom))
   (write (crlf) Enter another non-negative integer)
   (make number ↑value (accept)
                ↑id (genatom))
)

(p gcd-step
   {(number ↑id <id-1>
            ↑value <larger-value>)          <larger-number>}
   (number ↑id <> <id-1>
           ↑value {<smaller-value>
                  > 0  <= <larger-value>})

-->
   (modify <larger-number>
       ↑value (compute <larger-value> \\ <smaller-value>))
)

(p gcd-result
   {(number ↑id <id-1>
            ↑value 0)                          <zero-number>}
   {(number ↑id <> <id-1>
            ↑value {<gcd> >= 0})                <gcd-number>}
-->
   (write (crlf) |The greatest common divisor is| <gcd>)
   (remove <zero-number>)
   (remove <gcd-number>)
)

(make start)
```

Exercise 5-8.

```
(literalize quadruple
    s                   ; state
    c                   ; character
    n                   ; next state
    a                   ; action
)

(literalize state
    s                   ; current state of finite state control
)
```

```
(literalize tape-head
    cell              ; current position of the tape head
)

(literalize tape
    cell              ; ordinal position
    c                 ; character
)

(p move-tape-left
   {(state
       ↑s <s>)                          <state>}
   {(tape-head
       ↑cell <cell>)                <tape-head>}
   (tape
       ↑cell <cell>
       ↑c <c>)
   (quadruple
       ↑s <s>
       ↑c <char>
       ↑n <next>
       ↑a LEFT)
-->
   (modify <state> ↑s <next>)
   (modify <tape-head> ↑cell (compute <cell> - 1)))

(p move-tape-right
   {(state
       ↑s <s>)                          <state>}
   {(tape-head
       ↑cell <cell>)                <tape-head>}
   (tape
       ↑cell <cell>
       ↑c <c>)
   (quadruple
       ↑s <s>
       ↑c <char>
       ↑n <next>
       ↑a RIGHT)
-->
   (modify <state> ↑s <next>)
   (modify <tape-head> ↑cell (compute <cell> + 1)))

(p write-to-tape
   {(state
       ↑s <s>)                          <state>}
   (tape-head
       ↑cell <cell>)
```

```
   {(tape
       ↑cell <cell>
       ↑c <c>)                              <tape>}
   (quadruple
       ↑s <s>
       ↑c <char>
       ↑n <next>
       ↑a { <a> <> LEFT <> RIGHT })
-->
   (modify <state> ↑s <next>)
   (modify <tape> ↑c <a>))

(p grow-new-cell
   (tape-head ↑cell <cell>)
 - (tape      ↑cell <cell>)
-->
   (make tape ↑cell <cell>))

(make tape-head ↑cell 0)

; make individual tape cells with initial data

; make individual quadruples with the program

; make initial state
```

ANSWERS FOR CHAPTER 6

Exercise 6-3. When working memory element 3 is removed, the token −(3) is passed to nodes 1 and 2, which update their left memories to ((5)). The token −(3 1) is then passed on to nodes 3 and 4, which update their left memories to ((5 1)). No rules had been satisfied by any combination involving element 3, so there is no change in the conflict set.

Exercise 6-4. Although the new element is of element class *context*, it does not match <context-1> and so is not propagated any further in the network.

Exercise 6-5. When working memory element 2 is removed, the token −2 is sent to nodes 3 and 4 when it is removed from the right memories. Since there are no consistent matches involving region-2, no further tokens are passed.

Exercise 6-6. Removing element 3 required deletions from four memories and therefore took the most work. Adding the new *context* element required only two one-input node tests to determine that it did not match and therefore took the least work.

Exercise 6-7. The alternative element class organization would make the rules much slower by creating large cross-products.

Exercise 6-8. Since <cnstnts> matches only one element that doesn't change, it doesn't matter where it goes as long as it is before <road-region>, which needs to have the value of <thresh> bound first. The <cntxt> condition should be placed before the <road-region> condition because there are many more matches to it and because the elements that match it change more frequently. Changing the order would cause unnecessary consistent-bindings checks whenever flags were changed. These changes would not affect the match to the context or the consistency of the match.

Exercise 6-10. Changing phases with rules is usually more efficient. Since the rule representation has specific rules for each phase change, there are no variables to consider and no large cross-products. The *phase-sequence* representation can be quite inefficient if there are many phases and therefore many elements in working memory representing adjacent pairs. The `switch-phase` rule has a large cross-product, namely the product of the number of finished phases in working memory, the number of phase-pairs, and the number of phases in any state. This observation suggests an improvement to the *phase-sequence* implementation—removing finished phase elements.

Exercise 6-11. A more efficient implementation is to have a *global-phase* working memory element. There will be only one instantiation of this element class in working memory. The *global-phase* element has a *phase* attribute that is initially set to "unchecked." When there are no more unchecked elements, the *phase* is set to "checked." This results in linear rather than quadratic matching time.

```
(literalize global-status
    phase              ; One of: checked, unchecked,
                       ;  region-to-fragment
    current-image      ; the image being processed
)

(p change-phase-2
   {(global-status ↑phase unchecked) <global-phase>}
 - (fragment ↑origin machine ↑flag unchecked)
-->
   (modify <global-phase> ↑phase checked))
```

ANSWERS FOR CHAPTER 7

Exercise 7-1. A stack would be the best data structure. Goals would be pushed on the stack when they are created and since the most recently created goal would be at the top of the stack, it would be the only goal that could be examined.

Exercise 7-2. There are two rules that conclude that organism-1 has the infection type bacteriodes.

```
GOAL: (organism-1 infection-type bacteriodes)
RULE1  0.7
       (organism-1 portal-of-entry gastrointestinal-tract) ?
       (organism-1 culture <CUL>) 1.0
       (organism-1 site throat) 1.0
       (throat isa sterile-site) 0.9
RULE2  0.4
       (organism-1 bacteria-type coccus) ?
       (organism-1 growth aerobic) 0.75
       (ChrisJohnson sex female) 1.0
       (ChrisJohnson age 55) 1.0

We set a goal to prove that the portal-of-entry was the
gastrointestinal tract:

GOAL: (organism-1 portal-of-entry gastrointestinal-tract)

RULE4: 0.7
       (organism-1 bacteria-type coccus) ?
and we set a disjunction of two goals and pursue the first:

GOAL: (organism-1 bacteria-type coccus)

RULE3: 0.5
       (organism-1 gram-stain gramnegative) 0.8
       (organism-1 growth aerobic) .75

This allows us to conclude:
-- PROVED: (organism-1 bacteria-type coccus)
-- CERTAINTY: 0.375
because [min(0.75, 0.8) = 0.75] * 0.5 = 0.375

This allows us to calculate the portal of entry:
-- PROVED: (organism-1 portal-of-entry gastrointestinal-tract)
-- CERTAINTY: .262

because 0.375 * 0.7 = .262
```

This allows us to conclude our top goal with certainty .262

Exercise 7-3.

a) This would not match because %things would match "walls floors ceilings" in the first condition and "walls ceilings floors" in the second condition. Since % denotes a string variable and not a set variable, the binding for the variable is not unordered and the two conditions would not simultaneously match.

b) This would not match because #x would have to match both "Arleen" and "Mark," but a variable can have only one binding at a time.

c) This would match since it is all right for variables to match values that happen to be the same. In this example #x and #z both bind to "Arleen."

Exercise 7-4.

```
(p house-high
   (house ↑cost { > 50000 < 150000 })
   (house ↑age { < 5 })
-->
   (house ↑quality high))
```

Exercise 7-5. Since the Rete algorithm is used, instantiations will be added to the conflict set when elements are added to working memory. Since the system has no negative matching and no **remove,** instantiations will never be removed from the conflict set because they don't match. Each instantiation will eventually become the most specific in the conflict set and will fire. The refraction principle will keep the instantiation from firing again.

The first two choices for a data structure do not order elements by their specificity, so a linear search would be the only way to find the most specific item in the conflict set. The tree data structure would reduce the time to find the most specific instantiation from O(*N*) to O(log *N*) and the time to add an instantiation would be O(log *N*) if the tree is balanced.

A priority queue is just as good as a tree for storing the conflict set. If a *heap* were used to implement the priority queue, then the time to add an instantiation to the conflict set would be O(log *N*), where *N* is the number of instantiations in the conflict set, the time to remove the best item is O(1), and the time to rearrange the priority queue is O(log *N*).

Exercise 7-6. Remember that filtering is just a simple form of matching. Filtering suggests certain elements that might match, but does not complete the match to reveal the conflict set. The rules that would be considered for matching in this example are `clear-before-moving`, `find-place`, `stable-movement`, `generic-goal`, and `table-movement`.

ANSWERS FOR CHAPTER 8

Exercise 8-1. We add a new context function to the database program. First, modify the definition of the function by removing the old definition of context "interact" and adding:

stop	terminate the database session
interact	determine what the user wants to do, stop, inform, or request an explanation; transfer to appropriate context

We add the rule **interact::enter-context:stop** to the **interact** rule cluster:

```
(p interact::enter-context:stop
   {(context ↑name interact) <interact-context>}
   {(response ↑text << STOP stop >>) <response>}
-->
   (modify <interact-context> ↑name stop)
   (remove <response>))
```

To implement the "stop" request, a design is needed. One could (1) simply execute a **halt** action; (2) remove the context and allow a halt because no rule is in the conflict set; or (3) ask the user if working memory is to be saved, get a file name, and have a user-defined function save working memory before halting as in (1) or (2).

Exercise 8.2. There are many different solutions possible for this problem. The solution we sketch here will (1) if the relation to be explained is primitive, print the same message as currently printed by **explain::primitive**; (2) if the relation to be explained is a deduced relation, print the same explanation as is currently printed by **explain-deduction** and the paraphrase-generating rules, and generate requests to explain the relations on which the deduction is based. To implement this solution strategy, all of the rules in the **explain** context need to be changed, except **explain::list-relations**.

The new **explain::specify-relation** rule is:

```
(p explain::specify-relation
   {(context ↑name explain ↑parameter nil)
       <explain-context>}
-->
   (write (crlf)
          Specify a relation to explain
          by giving its label)
   (make response ↑text (accept)
   (modify <explain-context> ↑parameter explaining))
```

The **explain::primitive** rule is adapted by (1) adding a condition for **↑ parameter explaining** to the **context** condition element; and (2) removing the **modify** action.

The **explain::deduction** rule is adapted by (1) changing the check for the value of **parameter** from "nil" to "explaining"; and (2) adding, at the beginning of the right-hand side of the rule, the actions:

```
(make response ↑text <condition-1>)
(make response ↑text <condition-2>)
```

Each paraphrase-generating rule is adapted by replacing the current **modify** action with

```
(modify <p-context> ↑parameter explaining)
```

Finally, a new rule to switch context back to "interact" is added.

```
(p explain::terminate
   {(context ↑name explain ↑parameter explaining)
       <explain-context>}
  - (response)
-->
   (modify <explain-context> ↑name interact
       ↑parameter nil))
```

Glossary

Action. In a **production system** with a **forward-chaining** architecture, the **right-hand side** of a **rule** consists of a sequence of actions, each of which performs some activity such as creating, deleting, or modifying **elements** in **data memory,** performing input/output, modifying **production memory,** and halting the **recognize-act cycle.** When a rule **fires,** the actions that constitute the right-hand side are performed in sequence, using the **bindings** that were created when the rule was instantiated.

Activation. For each **object** in an **activation network,** the activation level is an associated number representing the degree to which that object is to receive attention. Activations are propagated between related (connected) objects in the network. See also **directed activation** and **spreading activation.**

Activation cycle. In an **activation network,** the activation cycle is the period of time during which **activation** is propagated among adjacent **objects.** Typically, during each activation cycle activation is propagated one arc farther from the source of activation. One or more activation cycles take place during a single **recognize-act cycle.**

Activation network. An activation network is a graph, each node of which represents an **object,** with each arc representing a relationship between two objects. If the arc is labeled, the label is a number indicating the strength of the relationship. When a node is processed, its **activation** level may change, and the effects of this change are propagated along arcs to related nodes, resulting in changes to their activation level.

Agenda. A control mechanism that maintains a priority queue of **tasks** to be performed. The priority of any task may be altered dynamically.

Algorithm. A completely specified **procedure** for performing a computation in a finite amount of time. When contrasted with **heuristic problem-solving methods,** the term connotes a well-understood procedure that is guaranteed to find a solution if it exists, or to determine that no solution exists.

And/or tree. A **proof tree** in theorem proving and a **goal tree** in general problem solving are **trees** such that each node is labeled as either an *and* node or an *or* node. For *and* nodes, each of the child nodes specifies necessary subproofs or **subgoals** that must be achieved jointly if the parent node is to be achieved. For *or* nodes, each of the child nodes specifies a sufficient alternative subproof or subgoal, only one of which need be achieved if the parent node is to be achieved.

Antecedent. A statement of the conditions necessay for drawing a conclusion. In a **production system,** the **left-hand side** of the **rule** encodes the antecedent conditions for the rule to **fire,** while the **right-hand side** encodes the **consequent.**

Applicative language. A programming language in which computations are expressed as nested function calls rather than sequences of statements. Typically, applicative languages have no program counter and may not allow side effects. LISP is a well-known applicative language.

Architecture. The organization of a large system. In **production system** programming the term may be applied either to the application program or to the language which treats the set of **rules** as a program to be **executed.**

Attribute. A simple property attached to an **object.** In **production systems,** the **data memory** may be represented as a set of **attribute-value elements.**

Attribute-value element. A data structure for **elements** in **data memory** that encodes **knowledge** about **objects** in the form of a set of ordered pairs, the first element of which specifies the identity of an **attribute** and the second element of which specifies the value that the attribute assumes for that object.

Back chaining. See **backward chaining.**

Backtracking. A search technique that traverses a graph by choosing at each node one of several adjacent nodes to visit next. If the visited node returns failure, another node adjacent to the original one is visited. If all adjacent nodes return failure, the original node itself returns failure; otherwise it returns success.

Backus-Naur Form. A formal language for expressing **context-free grammars.** A grammar consists of a set of rewrite **rules,** each of which has a **left-hand side** and a **right-hand side,** separated by the metalanguage symbol ::=. The left-hand side of each rule is a nonterminal symbol of the grammar, and the right-hand side is a sequence of nonterminal symbols and terminal symbols. Nonterminal symbols are usually surrounded by the angle brackets < and >. Extended versions of Backus-Naur Form include additional metalanguage symbols to denote repetition and alternation. Formerly known as Backus Normal Form, the language is named for John Backus and Peter Naur, who introduced it in the original description of the ALGOL-60 programming language.

Backward chaining. A **problem-solving method** that starts with a **goal** to be achieved and recursively expands each unsolved goal into a set of simpler **subgoals** until either a solution is found or all goals have been expanded into their simplest components. When a subgoal is solved, it backs up its solution to its parent goal. In **production systems** with **backward-chaining** architecture, the applicability of a **rule** is determined by examining its conclusions (on the **right-hand side**) rather than its **antecedent** conditions (on the **left-hand side**).

Belief. (1) A statement that is not known or assumed to be true, as contrasted with a **fact.** (2) The confidence in the reliability of a statement that is not known or assumed to be true. The degree of confidence may be indexed by a **certainty** or **confidence factor.**

Binding. An association between a **variable** and a value for that variable that holds within some scope, such as the scope of a **rule**, function call, or procedure invocation.

Blackboard. A system architecture that employs a database or memory that is accessible to several processes, called **knowledge sources.** The memory that is common to all processes serves as a basis for communication of intermediate results among **rules** or knowledge sources. This architecture was introduced in the HEARSAY speech-understanding system.

BNF. An abbreviation for **Backus-Naur Form.**

Bottom-up. A strategy of proceeding from the simple and concrete to the complex and abstract. As applied to a problem-solving strategy, it refers to the method of starting with the accumulation of results from simple observations or facts and proceeding to more complex combinations or hypotheses. **Production systems** with **forward-chaining** architecture often engage in bottom-up problem solving. As applied to a programming methodology, the term refers to a style in which simple program components are written before the more complex ones. The opposite strategy is **top-down.**

Bound. A **variable** that has been assigned a value by the process of **binding** is said to be bound to that value.

Certainty. A number representing the subjective degree of **belief** attached to an assertion. The values that a certainty may assume lie within an interval, the upper endpoint of which denotes complete certainty that the assertion is true, and the lower endpoint of which denotes either complete certainty that the assertion is false, or complete ignorance about the reliability of the assertion. Certainties are also called **confidence factors.**

Cognitive modeling. The simulation of human cognition (i.e., perception, skilled action, memory, and thinking) in terms of information processing. Cognitive models often take the form of computer programs.

Compiled knowledge. **Knowledge** that encodes rules of inference in which implicit chains of reasoning are suppressed for the sake of efficiency.

Compiler. A program that translates a source program written in a high-level language into an object program in a lower-level language. When a program is compiled, it usually runs faster than when the same program is **interpreted.**

Composition. A **learning** mechanism that combines two or more **rules** that **fire** in sequence to produce a single rule that has the net effect of the component rules. The name is derived by analogy to the mathematical concept of function composition.

Condition. (1) An **antecedent.** (2) A **condition element.** (3) A proposition that summarizes the state of **execution** of a program; see **precondition** and **postcondition.**

Condition element. The **left-hand side** of a **rule** in a **production system** is sometimes expressed as a set of **patterns** (or templates) which are to be **matched** against the contents of **data memory;** each such pattern is called a condition element. When a rule is instantiated, each condition element has been found to match one element of data memory.

Confidence factor. Another term for **certainty.**

Conflict resolution. A search-control mechanism used to determine which of several **instantiations** in the **conflict set** to **fire** next. The process by which instantiations are chosen for firing is called conflict resolution.

Conflict-resolution strategy. A specific principle that can be applied to partially order the **instantiations** in the **conflict set.** Each instantiation that is found to be **dominated** by another instantiation according to this principle is discarded from the conflict set, precluding it from **firing** on that **cycle.**

Conflict set. The set of all **instantiations** generated by the **match** process during a **recognize-act cycle.** The process of **conflict resolution** selects one instantiation from the conflict set and **fires** it.

Consequent. The conclusion of a **rule** or logical proposition. In a **production system,** the **left-hand side** of the rule encodes the **antecedent** conditions for the rule to **fire,** while the **right-hand side** encodes the consequent.

Consistent bindings. A set of **bindings** of values to **variables** that satisfy the **conditions** of each **pattern** taken singly, and simultaneously satisfy all constraints that apply between all patterns in a set.

Context. A state in a problem-solving process. In a **production system,** the context may be represented by a special **working memory element,** which is often called a **context element, control element,** or **subgoal.** Often conceptually isolatable **tasks** that must be performed by production systems may be partitioned into subtasks that once initiated are expected to run to completion. The **rules** that constitute this task each have **condition elements** that must **match** the associated **context element.**

Context element. A **working memory element** that signals the state of the computation **(context)** and is used for purposes of control. This element is an instance of a **control element.**

Context-free grammar. A grammar for describing a **context-free language.** One metalanguage for expressing a context-free grammar is **Backus-Naur Form.**

Context-free language. A formal language in which each sentence can be generated by a grammar wherein the **left-hand side** of each rewrite **rule** consists of a single nonterminal symbol.

Control element. A **working memory element** the sole purpose of which is to store **control knowledge.** A **context element** is an example of a control element.

Control knowledge. **Knowledge** that bears on the selection of an appropriate **control strategy.**

Control strategy. A method for choosing the next action given many alternative problem-solving steps. In **production systems, backward chaining** is an example of a control strategy.

Controlled production system. A **production system** in which the control regime is specified by a finite-state machine for each rule set rather than by the production-system architecture.

Cross-product. In set theory, the cross-product, or Cartesian product, of a set **A** and a set **B** is the set of all ordered pairs **(a, b)** such that **a** is a member of **A** and **b** is a member of **B.** In a discussion of the **match** process, the term is used to designate the set of all potential combinations of matches for a sequence of **working memory elements.**

Cycle. A single iteration of a loop. In **production systems,** an **execution** consists of iterated **recognize-act cycles.** In the **Rete match algorithm,** a **match** cycle occurs every time a **working memory element** is added to or removed from **working memory.** In **spreading activation** systems, **activation** is propagated incrementally during a series of **activation cycles.**

Data directed. Controlled by changes in data rather than changes in goals. Used in contrast to **goal directed.** See also **demon** and **forward chaining.**

Data driven. Still another expression for **forward chaining.**

Data filtering. Restricting the portion of **data memory** that participates in the **match** process to a subset for the sake of efficiency.

Data memory. The global database of a **production system.** The contents may be partially or totally ordered on the basis of their time of creation or most recent modification. Data memory is typically the most volatile part of a **production system.**

Declarative knowledge. **Knowledge** that can be retrieved and stored but cannot be immediately executed; to be effective, it must be interpreted by **procedural knowledge.**

Declaration section. The section of a computer program in which constructs such as data types, **variables, procedures,** and functions are announced and sometimes defined. In OPS5 the declaration section defines **working memory elements,** indexes of **attributes, vector attributes,** and external functions.

Demon. A procedure that **executes** whenever a particular predicate about a database becomes true. In a **production system,** a **rule** that is not restricted to **firing** within any particular **context,** or as part of a **goal.** A demon rule is permitted to fire as soon as it is instantiated, regardless of the presence of any partially completed goals. The name comes from the unit of a perception program called *Pandemonium.*

Dependency. The relationship between a **consequent** and its **antecedents** that may need to be stored if the reasoning process is to be examined retrospectively. A graph in which the nodes represent assertions and the arcs or other nodes represent relationships is called a dependency network.

Directed activation. In an **activation network** directed activation is a method for propagating the **activation** from one **object** to another. The activation network is a directed graph, indicating that propagation is to proceed only in accordance with the directed arcs.

Discrimination. (1) A process of **learning** which distinguishes instances of a concept from noninstances. (2) The act of refining an overgeneralization of a concept to be learned so as to exclude noninstances that were once mistakenly classified as instances of the concept. (3) A particular learning mechanism that exploits feedback concerning erroneous classifications to refine an overgeneralization of a concept.

Domain. In mathematics, the set of values that the argument to a function may assume. In **expert systems,** a field of **knowledge** or class of **tasks.**

Domain expert. A human who is highly trained and proficient in performing the **task** for which an **expert system** is being built, and who serves to articulate this **knowledge** for the benefit of the **knowledge engineer,** who incorporates the expert's **domain knowledge** into the expert system.

Domain knowledge. **Knowledge** that is specific to a particular **domain.**

Dominate. When a **conflict-resolution strategy** leaves one **instantiation** in the **conflict set** but removes a second instantiation, the first instantiation is said to dominate the second.

Element. The most primitive unit into which a system can be decomposed. In OPS5, for example, the units of the **left-hand sides** of **rules** are called **condition elements,** and the units of **working memory** are called **working memory elements.**

Element class. The data type of a **working memory element.**

Element variable. A **variable** that is bound to an entire **working memory element** instead of to the values of that element's attributes.

Execute. Carry out the steps specified in a procedure or the **actions** in a **rule.**

Expectation-driven reasoning. A problem-solving strategy that generates hypotheses about events that are expected to happen, and focuses processing on **tasks** related to these events. The activity of this strategy is contrasted with the passivity of **data-driven** reasoning.

Expert system. A computer program, often written in a **production-system language,** that has **expertise** in a narrow **domain.**

Expertise. Proficiency in a specialized **domain.** An **expert system** is said to have expertise in its domain if its performance is comparable to that of a human with five to ten years of training and experience in the domain.

Explanation. The process of describing how an **expert system** reached its conclusions or why it asked particular questions of a user. Explanations may be used to justify decisions or problem-solving strategies, or to teach these strategies to the user.

Filtering. The exclusion of either data **(data filtering)** or **rules (rule filtering)** from the **match** process for the sake of efficiency.

Fire. **Execute** the set of **actions** specified in the **right-hand side** of an **instantiation** of a **rule.** The term is derived from neurophysiology: when a neuron generates an action potential (or spike), it is said to fire.

Forward chaining. A **problem-solving method** that starts with initial **knowledge** and applies inference **rules** to generate new knowledge until either one of the inferences satisfies a **goal** or no further inferences can be made. In forward-chaining **production systems,** the applicability of a rule is determined by **matching** the **conditions** specified on its **left-hand side** against the knowledge currently stored in **data memory.**

Frame. Another term for **schema.**

Generalization. (1) An abstract principle that captures commonalities among a set of specific instances. (2) The process of deriving an abstract principle, either deductively or inductively. (3) The **learning** mechanism by which an abstract principle is derived by making a specific principle more abstract. (4) In learning programs implemented as **production systems,** a learning mechanism that relaxes the constraints on a **rule** so that it can apply to a wider range of data.

Generative grammar. A formal grammar of a language expressed as a set of **rules** that can be applied to generate all the sentences of the language and no sentences that are not in that language. A generative grammar is not necessarily the best way to represent the grammar for purposes of classifying or parsing sentences in the language.

Goal. The end to which problem solving aims. In a **production system,** a goal may be represented in a separate memory or in a distinguished class of **working memory element.**

Goal directed. Another term for **backward chaining.** Used in contrast to **data directed.**

Goal tree. A **tree** data structure in which the root node represents a **goal** to be achieved, and the children of each goal represent **subgoals** that when achieved suffice to achieve the goal represented by their parent. A goal tree may be an **and/or** tree.

Heuristic. A principle (sometimes called a rule of thumb) that embodies some problem-solving **knowledge** and has some likelihood of yielding success more rapidly than an **algorithm** for solving the problem, but that is not guaranteed to work (either by increasing efficiency or in finding an existing solution) in all situations. The term was popularized by the mathematician George Polya.

Inference. The derivation of a proposition from other propositions. A complex series of inferences can be organized to proceed from **antecedent** propositions that are given to whatever **consequent** propositions are justified, in which case the **forward-chaining** process is called **data-directed** inference; or it can start from a specification of the desired consequents and proceed by trying to prove antecedents that will justify concluding the consequent, in which case the **backward-chaining** process is called **model-directed** or **goal-directed** inference.

Inference engine. (1) The portion of a **production-system language** that performs inferences by **executing** the **recognize-act cycle.** (2) The portion of an application program that performs **tasks** related to inferring new **knowledge** in the task **domain,** as opposed to those portions that perform tasks such as control, input-output, and optimization.

Instantiation. A **pattern** or formula in which the **variables** have been replaced by constants. In a **production system** an instantiation is the result of successfully **matching** a **rule** against the contents of **data memory.** It can be represented as an ordered pair of which the first member identifies the rule that has been satisfied, and the second member is a **list** of **working memory elements** that match the **condition elements** of the rule.

Interpreter. The part of a **production system** that **executes** the **rules.**

Knowledge. Any information that can be represented as either **declarative knowledge** or **procedural knowledge,** e.g., in the form of **rules,** entries in **data memory** or another database, or **control strategies.** Knowledge may be specific to a **task domain** or general enough to be independent of all domains.

Knowledge acquisition. (1) The process of extracting **domain knowledge** from **domain experts.** (2) The process of incorporating domain knowledge into an **expert system** by extracting it from domain experts and encoding the information into an internal representation such as **rules.** (3) An automated process by which a program accepts knowledge from domain experts and incorporates it into an existing **expert system.** (4) **Learning.**

Knowledge base. A collection of **knowledge** represented in the form of **rules, procedures, schemas,** or **working memory elements;** thus any highly structured and interconnected database.

Knowledge-based system. A computer program that applies specialized **knowledge** to the solution of problems. An **expert system** is a knowledge-based system that is intended to capture the expertise of human **domain experts.**

Knowledge engineer. A systems analyst who performs the **knowledge engineering** phase of building an **expert system.**

Knowledge engineering. The phase of building an **expert system** in which a **knowledge engineer** extracts **knowledge** specific to the **domain** from a **domain expert** and converts that knowledge into a form that is usable in a computer implementation.

Knowledge source. A collection of **rules,** procedures, and/or data that is used to solve problems of a very specific type. A knowledge source is larger than a rule but smaller than an **expert system.** In **blackboard** architectures, each process that has access to the shared memory is considered a knowledge source.

Learning. Any change in a system that alters its long-term performance. Learning in **production systems** may be effected by the automatic addition, deletion, or modification of **rules.**

Left-hand side. One of the two parts of a **rule,** the other being the **right-hand side.** The left-hand side specifies the **antecedents** that must be satisfied if the rule is to be applied. In **rules** of grammar, the left-hand side specifies a string of symbols that can be replaced by another string of symbols. In **production systems** that use a **backward-chaining** strategy, the left-hand side specifies the **subgoals** of the **goal** that is specified on the right-hand side. In **forward-chaining** production systems, the left-hand side is a set of **condition elements** that are to be **matched** against the contents of **data memory.**

Left memory. A data structure in the **Rete match algorithm** network that is associated with a node. It contains the combinations of **working memory elements** and variable bindings that constitute a consistent match for the **condition element** being tested at the node and all preceding condition elements.

LHS. An abbreviation for **left-hand side.**

Linear test and merge. An algorithm that employs a directed acyclic graph, performing sequences of tests along chains of directed arcs and merging results of tests at nodes where two or more chains intersect.

List. A sequence of recursively defined objects. In LISP, a sequence of zero or more atoms and lists surrounded by one set of matching parentheses.

Match. In a **production system** the match process compares a set of patterns from the **left-hand sides** of **rules** against the data in **data memory** to find all possible ways in which the **rules** can be satisfied with **consistent bindings** (i.e., **instantiations**).

Match cycle. The stage of processing that occurs in the **Rete match algorithm** whenever there is a change to working memory. It results in an updating of the Rete network and the **conflict set.**

Means-ends analysis. A **problem-solving method** that applies operators to states in a **problem space** to select a successor state that reduces the difference between the current state and some **goal** state.

Memory. A feature in the **architecture** of a computer system for storing information so that it can be read, written, executed, or some combination of the above. In **production system** architectures, there may be conceptually distinct memories for factual, problem-solving, and control knowledge.

Metaknowledge. Another term for **metalevel knowledge.**

Metalevel knowledge. The self-knowledge a system has about the extent and reliability of its **knowledge** about the **domain** and when and how to best use its **domain knowledge.**

Metarule. A **rule** that embodies **metalevel knowledge.** Metarules may be used to specify **conflict-resolution** strategies or to **filter** and order domain **rules.**

Model directed. Another term for **backward chaining.** Used in contrast to **data directed.**

Modus ponens. A **rule** of **inference** in logic: $(A)(B)((A\rightarrow B)\&A)\rightarrow B$

Monotonic. Unidirectional. In analysis a monotonic function is one that is either nonincreasing or nondecreasing. In inference a monotonic logic can only add propositions to a **knowledge base;** it can never remove them.

Natural language. A language used by human beings to communicate with one another and that is not the result of a design process; for example, English or Chinese. Very restricted forms of natural language can be used to communicate with some computer programs.

Nonmonotonic. Bidirectional. In analysis a nonmonotonic function is one that increases over part of its **domain** and decreases over another part of its domain. In inference a nonmonotonic logic can both add propositions to a **knowledge base** and remove them.

Object. An entity in a programming system that is used to represent **declarative**

knowledge and possibly **procedural knowledge** about a physical object, a concept, or a **problem-solving strategy.**

One-input node. A node in the **Rete match algorithm** network that is associated with a test of a single attribute of a **condition element.** It passes a **token** if and only if the attribute test is satisfied.

Ordering. A **conflict-resolution strategy** in which the dominance of one **instantiation** over another is determined by a static ordering that is imposed on the **rules.**

Parallelism. Performing more than one operation in a single unit of time. Parallel computer hardware **executes** more than one machine instruction during a single machine **cycle.** Parallel **production systems** fire more than one **instantiation** on each **recognize-act cycle.** Parallelism always can be simulated, albeit slowly, on serial machines.

Partial bindings. The set of **working memory elements** and **bindings** that constitutes a consistent binding for a prefix sequence of **condition elements** of a **rule.**

Partial match. A set of associations between **condition elements** and **working memory elements** that partially satisfy the **left-hand side** of the **rule.** Not all condition elements need be **matched;** sometimes a threshold specifies the minimum number that must be matched.

Pattern. An abstract description of a datum that places some constraints on the value(s) it may assume, but need not specify it in complete detail.

Pattern directed. Driven by configurations of data. **Production systems** are a special case of pattern-directed systems.

Post Production System. A mathematical model of computation devised by Emil Post and considered to be the origin of all other **production systems.**

Postcondition. A proposition that is true following the **execution** of a piece of code. If a **precondition** is satisfied preceding the execution of the code, then if the code executes correctly, the postcondition will be true following execution.

Precondition. A proposition that must be satisfied preceding the **execution** of a piece of code. If the precondition is satisfied and the code executes correctly, a **postcondition** will be true following execution of the code.

Problem-solving method. A procedure (either an **algorithm** or a **heuristic**) for finding a solution to a problem.

Problem space. A graph in which the nodes represent all possible states of partial or complete solution of a problem and arcs represent operators that transform one state to another. Finding a solution to the problem under consideration is represented by the isomorphic problem of finding a path from the node representing initial state to a node representing a **goal** state.

Procedural knowledge. **Knowledge** that can be immediately **executed** using **declarative knowledge** as data but that may not be examined.

Procedural language. A computer language (e.g., ALGOL, PASCAL, FORTRAN) in which language-level instructions mirror Von Neumann machine instructions and the state of an execution is defined by a program counter.

Procedure. (1) A set of instructions for performing a **task.** (2) A program that embodies an **algorithm** or a **heuristic.** (3) A **syntactic** unit of a program in a **procedural language** that can be parameterized so that the same segment of code can be invoked from different places in the program with different data. (4) Any representation for **procedural knowledge.**

Production. In **production systems,** another name for a **rule.**

Production memory. The set of all **rules** in a **production system.** The other components of a production system are **data memory** and the **inference engine.**

Production node. A special node in the **Rete match algorithm** network that associates a **rule** with the set of nodes that test whether the rule's conditions are satisfied.

Production rule. Another name for a **rule** in a **production system.**

Production section. The section of an OPS5 program that contains the definitions of **rules.** This section must follow the **declaration section.**

Production system. An **architecture** for **problem-solving** that employs a set of **rules** (stored in **production memory**), a global database (stored in **data memory**), and an **inference engine** that performs the **recognize-act cycle** of **match, conflict resolution,** and rule **firing.**

Production-system language. A computer language that employs as a prominent component an **architecture** that is a **production system.**

Production-system model. A style of problem-solving and programming characterized by a **production-system** architecture. Other models include procedural programming (e.g., PASCAL), applicative programming (e.g., LISP), logic programming (e.g., PROLOG), and object-oriented programming (e.g., SMALLTALK).

Production-system program. An application program that is written in a **production-system language** and in which a major part of the problem is accomplished by the **firing** of **rules.**

Proof tree. A **tree** data structure in which the root node represents a theorem to be proved, and the children of each node represent theorems that when proved suffice to prove the theorem represented by their parent. A proof tree may be an **and/or** tree.

Property. A characteristic of an **object.** Properties that have values are called **attributes.** The components of **frames** and **schemas**, which may be of arbitrary complexity, are sometimes called properties.

Reason maintenance. The process of keeping track of the **dependencies** between assertions in a **knowledge base** to assist in making and withdrawing deductions as new information becomes available.

Recency. A **conflict-resolution strategy** that favors **instantiations** whose **working memory elements** were most recently created or modified. This strategy lends sensitivity to a **production system**, since subgoals can be spawned as soon as new data arrive.

Recognize-act cycle. An iterative loop, each **cycle** of which consists of three successive phases: **match, conflict resolution**, and the **firing** of **rules.**

Refraction. A **conflict-resolution strategy** that prevents an **instantiation** from **firing** if it has fired on a previous occasion. Refraction derives its name from a property of neurons: During the refractory period, a short interval following the firing of a neuron, that neuron will not fire when stimulated.

Result element. A temporary structure used in OPS5 to build a description of a **working memory element** for the purpose of modifying **working memory.** The **modify** and **call** actions are implemented using result elements.

Rete match algorithm. An **algorithm** for efficiently determining which **rules** can be satisfied by the contents of **working memory** on each **recognize-act cycle** by computing **bindings** between patterns and data. This algorithm, devised by Charles L. Forgy, exploits redundancy in **production systems** by saving partial results of the **match** computation so that they need not be recomputed at a later time. The name comes from an English word meaning "network."

RHS. An abbreviation for **right-hand side.**

Right-hand side. One of the two parts of a **rule**, the other being the **left-hand side.** In **production systems** with **backward-chaining** architecture, the right-hand side specifies a goal to be solved, the subgoals of which are given on the left-hand side of the rule. In **forward-chaining** production systems, the right-hand side consists of a series of **actions** to be performed in the specified sequence when an **instantiation** of the rule is **fired,** using values that were **bound** to **variables** on the left-hand side.

Right memory. A data structure in the **Rete match algorithm** network that is associated with a **condition element.** It contains a list of **working memory elements** that **match** the condition.

Rule. A unit of representation that specifies a relationship between situation and action. Rules are ordered pairs that consist of a **left-hand side** and a **right-hand side.** In a formal grammar, rules specify the way in which sentences can be derived and parsed. In **production systems,** rules are the units of **production memory** and are used to encode **procedural knowledge.** A rule is also called a **production.**

Rule-based program. A program similar in spirit to a **production-system program** in that the **knowledge** is represented explicitly by means of **rules** rather than through procedures; but a rule-based program is not necessarily implemented in a general-purpose **production-system language** and need not make exclusive use of the **production-system** architecture.

Rule cluster. A set of **rules** that work together to achieve a **goal,** or the set of rules related to a **context element.**

Rule filtering. Restricting for the sake of efficiency the portion of **production memory** that participates in the **match** process to a subset.

Rule interpreter. In **production systems** another term for **interpreter.**

Rule memory. Another term for **production memory.**

Satisficing. A **problem-solving strategy** that terminates with success when a potential solution satisfies specified minimal criteria of acceptability. The solution is not necessarily optimal. In many problems, finding the optimal solution is unnecessary and prohibitively time-consuming.

Scalar. In programming languages, one of the primitive data types; typically an integer, floating-point number, character, logical value, or **symbolic atom,** but not a **list,** array (vector) or record (structure).

Schema. Any formalism for representing information about a single concept in terms of **properties** related to it. The properties are usually represented by a slot and can consist of attached **procedures** for computing properties that are not immediately available.

Segment variable. A **variable** in a **pattern** that can **match** a subpart of a **list.**

Semantic. Pertaining to meaning; by contrast the **syntactic** pertains to form.

Semantic network. A data structure for representing **declarative knowledge.** The structure is a graph in which the nodes represent concepts, and the arcs (which may be labeled) represent relationships among concepts.

Sensitivity. The responsivity of a system to the dynamically changing demands of its environment. The sensitivity of a **production system** is influenced by its **conflict-resolution strategy.**

Situation. A state of **data memory** corresponding to some set of properties in the **domain** being modeled by the **production system. Rules** are sometimes called situation-action pairs.

Specificity. A **conflict-resolution strategy** that prefers **instantiations** of more specific **rules,** typically measured in terms of numbers of **variables** and constants or numbers of **left-hand side** tests. This principle embodies the **heuristic** that rules with more detailed antecedents are more discriminating than those with fewer, and are likely to produce a better result.

Spreading activation. In an **activation network,** spreading activation is a method of changing the pattern of **activation** or attention in the network such that activation flows outward from active nodes, activating nodes that are connected directly or indirectly. Propagation occurs on one or more successive **activation cycles,** during which activation spreads to the next set of nodes not yet reactivated.

Stability. The continuity of behavior of a system. The stability of a **production system** is influenced by its **conflict-resolution strategy.**

Stepwise refinement. A programming methodology in which a program is first specified at a very high level of abstraction and then, in successive steps, abstractly specified parts of the program are replaced by slightly more concrete **instantiations** of the abstract description. The term is attributed to Niklaus Wirth and is almost synonymous with **top-down programming.**

State vector. An ordered **list** which fully describes the state of a system. The vector consists of a fixed number of items, each of which is a parameter of the current state.

Structural similarity. The syntactic commonalities among **rules** in a **production system.** Rules that have identical values for attributes, identical condition elements, or sequences of identical condition elements are structurally similar. The **Rete match algorithm** exploits structural similarity by sharing chains of **one-input nodes** in its network for rules with identical sequences of conditions.

Subgoal. One of a set of **goals** that when achieved suffices to assure that another goal is also achieved. In **backward-chaining** systems the unachieved goals are decomposed into simpler subgoals in the hope that the latter can be solved more readily. In **goal trees** the relationship of a goal to its subgoals is represented as the parent-child relationship.

Subproblem. Another term for **subgoal.**

Symbolic atom. A data type that permits only the primitive operations of assignment and testing for equality. Two symbolic atoms are considered to be equal if they have the same print name, which is a sequence of alphabetic and special characters used to specify the identity of the atom.

Syntactic. Pertaining to form or structure; by contrast, the **semantic** pertains to meaning.

Task. Another name for **context** or, in **backward-chaining** systems, for a **goal.**

Task domain. In **expert systems** this is another term for **domain.**

Temporal redundancy. The tendency of **production systems** to make relatively few changes to **data memory,** and hence to the **conflict set,** from one **recognize-act cycle** to the next. The **Rete match algorithm** exploits temporal redundancy so as to avoid recomputing all **matches** unnecessarily.

Time tag. A number attached to a **working memory element** that varies **monotonically** with time and is used for indexing the **recency** of the element.

Token. (1) An instance of a type. (2) A unique atom that can be used as a label. (3) A symbol used in the **Rete match algorithm** to represent a **working memory element.**

Top down. A strategy of proceeding from the complex and abstract to the simple and concrete. As applied to a problem-solving strategy, it refers to the method of starting with a complex problem and decomposing it into **subproblems** that are easier to solve. **Backward-chaining** systems often engage in top-down problem solving. As applied to a programming methodolgy, the term refers to a style in which the abstract program organization is determined in stages of increasing concreteness culminating with the writing of primitive components that can be directly **executed.** The opposite strategy is **bottom up.**

Tree. A graph in which there is exactly one path between any two distinct nodes.

Truth maintenance. Another term for **reason maintenance.**

Two-input node. Nodes in the **Rete match algorithm** network that merge the **matches** for a **condition element** with the matches for all preceding condition elements.

User-defined. Program units that extend an implementation language. Many programming languages permit the definition of complex program structures that can be referenced as a unit. Languages such as PASCAL, C, and OPS83 allow the programmer to define, name, and access nonprimitive data types. In almost all languages program segments (procedures, functions, subroutines) can be defined, named, and invoked with a syntax identical to that used for built-in functions. These nonprimitive units are called user-defined types and user-defined functions.

Variable. A term in a data or processing structure that can assume any value from a set of values. These values become the **domain** of the variable, which can be determined by **syntactic** or **semantic** properties. In mathematics, variables are used to allow propositions to apply to all values in the domain. In computer programming, variables may be assigned at most one value at a time from its type.

Vector attribute. In OPS5, an attribute that can assume a sequence of atomic values.

Working memory. Another name for **data memory** (e.g., in OPS5).

Working memory element. The unit of **working memory.** In OPS5, working memory elements are **attribute-value elements.**

Index